Edited by Heather Seymour
Cover art and design by Jason Lincoln Jeffers

ISBN: 978-0-615-68410-9

www.jasonlincolnjeffers.com

Printed in the United States of America
First Edition

THE NEXT HUMAN

A Guide to Personal and Collective Evolution

JASON LINCOLN JEFFERS

CHAPTER HEADING QUOTES

All chapter heading quotes are from the Matrix Trilogy: *The Matrix, The Matrix Reloaded,* and *The Matrix Revolutions.* Created, Produced and Directed by Andy and Larry Wachowski. © Warner Bros. Entertainment Inc. All rights reserved.

DISCLAIMER

I am not a physician. I cannot and do not prescribe medical treatment. Therefore, the information provided in this book is for educational purposes only. Any decision on your part on how you use this information is your personal choice and I am not liable or responsible in any way whatsoever for what you do with this material after reading it. The information in this book is not meant to diagnose, prescribe, or treat any disease. Please discuss any changes to your diet or to your health with a qualified, licensed health care provider.

CONTENTS

ACKNOWLEDGEMENTS

I am deeply thankful to my mother Connie for your selfless devotion to me from the day I was born. During my debilitating illnesses you were always there to help, to give, and to show compassion. You have sacrificed much for me and without your unconditional love, this book could not have come to be. I love you.

I extend my gratitude to my Aunt Sharon for your love and support throughout my life. During my darkest hours, you have been a glimmering light that has never failed to guide me through. And thank you for all the times you encouraged and inspired me to "get up" whenever I fell (which was a lot). You are both a teacher and a friend. I love you.

To my sister Connie Jo: Thank you for giving birth to two wonderful boys, my nephews Hudson and Aiden. You are a wise, loving, and caring mother to them and I am profoundly grateful to be able to share with you the boundless joy of watching them grow up. I love you.

To my cousin Heather: Thank you for your amazing editing skills and immense knowledge of the complex English language. Your help with this book has been invaluable and you have been an utter delight to work with. I love you.

To my friend David: Thank you for your loyal support of this book since I began writing the first words and thank you for showing me what a true friend is. I love you.

And finally, my eternal love and gratitude extend to my spiritual teachers, my beloved father and spiritual mother Helene, for their loving support and continued guidance. Thank you for urging me to put what I have learned into book form so that it can be a benefit to others.

Jason Lincoln Jeffers
Inside the King's Chamber sarcophagus,
Great Pyramid of Giza
December, 1976, Age 11

INTRODUCTION

How this book came to be.

A few weeks after my 24th birthday I began to notice my energy declining rapidly. I remember one day, after arriving at the gym and beginning my usual jog around the track, I barely had the endurance to complete one lap. In the months following, I began waking up feeling more tired than I did before I went to bed. Little did I know at the time, my life was being put on *hold*.

The prior two years had been mentally and emotionally tumultuous. My beloved father suffered his last year of cancer and had finally passed. Meanwhile I was enduring a "rollercoaster-ride" separation from my wife with whom I was married for two and half years. We had only lived together for eight months, and seven of them were miserable. I knew that I had to permanently end it with her and in the month following, circumstances became so much worse between us that I had finally summoned the strength to file for divorce, and so I painfully let her go.

A year later the fatigue escalated to the point where I had become nearly debilitated. To understand what it felt like, you'd have to imagine the fatigue you felt during your worst flu and then magnify it by ten. Then imagine feeling like that every day for years on end. Menial chores such as taking out the trash or going to the store to buy groceries became a heavy burden. At times, I could barely walk. Adding insult to injury, I appeared perfectly healthy on the outside so no one really believed me when I told them how I felt on the inside. Medical doctors couldn't find anything wrong with me. At the time, if someone told me I was going to have to feel that way most of the time for the following eleven years, I would have probably found some way to kill myself. Nevertheless, that's exactly what happened.

During those years of chronic fatigue I had come to hate the world around me. I hated my life so much that I wanted to just disappear, permanently. I didn't feel that I belonged here. The questions I frequently asked myself: "What's the point in living?" "Why is this happening to me?" "What did I do to deserve this?" People asked me all the time why I never smiled. And when they did, it only fueled a deep-seated anger toward them, at me, at my dreaded disease. I resented my very existence.

Looking back, those years of suffering were the most introspective of my life. Because I was forced deeply within, I became a seeker, a digger, and an *observer.* My keen sense of analysis combined with my innate intuition gradually honed over the years as I witnessed the behavior in others, and in myself. Eventually it culminated to a point where everything began to finally make sense. Nearly two decades of studying psychology, metaphysics, comparative religion, philosophy, alternative medicine, and anything else that would help me understand *why* I had been beat up by my classmates every year from third grade into high school, and *why* I had been suffering with anxiety and depression ever since I was a teenager, and *why* I had been debilitated by chronic fatigue syndrome for over a decade, and *why* I had continued to be emotionally and mentally abused by family, friends, co-workers, bosses, and just plain strangers, had finally begun to *pay off.*

I remember the day clearly in September of 2007—actually it was nighttime in midtown Manhattan. I was in my high-rise apartment over-looking one of the most breathtaking skylines on the planet. All the money I had made from my successful business in the seven years prior suddenly seemed trivial, meaningless. Because I was tormented, and literally in emotional pain *all the time,* I concluded that every ounce of luxury and freedom that my material success had afforded me was utterly *worthless.* I suddenly realized that I had imprisoned myself in a world of emptiness, of slippery surfaces that were ultimately preventing me from not only realizing who I truly am, but also from living life the way it was, well, *meant* to be lived. Status suddenly seemed absurd. Success in the material world around me became a foreign concept, some-thing of an abstraction. On that night that my first nephew was born, I decided that I wanted to reunite with a family that I hadn't seen nor spoken to in two and a half years. On that night, I made a choice to become a loving uncle. I began to cry, sob, travail uncontrollably and as the tears gushed down my cheeks, I found myself saying these words out loud: "I don't want to be angry anymore…I don't want to be *angry* anymore."

The *choice* I made on that night allowed a few rays of light to shine into my life, into my heart. In the months and years following I began to live every minute with the sincerest of gratitude. My priorities had changed, dramatically. Instead of getting another stressful job that would bring me another high income, I began to paint full time. Two years later, my second nephew was born and watching the two of them grow and mature became one of my reasons for living. I had suddenly become young again. A few years later I began to write down my thoughts, reflections, and observations. And subsequently that's how this book came to be.

Evolution is here.

Seemingly out of nowhere, words have appeared on paper, written through *me*. This book represents the sum total of a life of astute observation and insight. Even though I was raised by my loving father to be spiritual, I ostensibly had to venture out into the not-so-spiritual world to experience what it was like. And as it turned out, I wasn't too happy with what I found. Being naturally deeply sensitive, I absorbed the negative emotions—disrespect, apathy, greed, anger, jealousy, deceit, disgust, revenge—directly into my emotional body like a *sponge*. Eventually and over time, I had become a human reflection of the worst of humanity, projecting my contempt, judgment, and seething hatred outward onto the world. This, of course, only brought me more misery and *suffering*.

Winston Churchill once said, "If you are going through hell, keep going." I can honestly say now that, for the first time in my life, I am truly free. But I had to lose everything that I thought was real and important to get here. I had to shed a false sense of self. I had to surrender to what *is*. In the end I have learned one critical lesson: only love is real. So then, if only *love* is real, what does this ancient esoteric truth have to say about the current human plight? If you have any insight at all about what's going on in the world around you, then you have to come to the conclusion that something has to dramatically *shift* in our society if we're going to make it as a species.

As I write this, 17,500 nuclear warheads on Planet Earth are considered operational and at least 4,000 of them are on *hair-trigger alert*.[1] The nations of North Korea and Iran are scrambling to add their own warheads to the list. Pakistan's government is becoming more unstable every day from the threat of a radical extremist takeover. Its current nuclear arsenal consists of over 100 warheads, armed and ready.[2] Consider this: all it takes is the launch of *one* of them to cause a chain reaction that could annihilate hundreds of millions in a blink of an eye. Now consider the alternative: *evolution*. This thought remained in the back of my mind as I crafted the words you're about to read in the pages ahead.

We're all in this together. Whether we like it or not, we all live on the same terra firma, and even though many of us would if we could, no one can just pack their bags, hop on a spaceship and *leave*. And there's good reason for that, which is: we have to learn how to all get along, to live and let *live*, to love one another unconditionally. But transformation can only come from with*in*. It begins with one person and then two, then twenty, then two hundred, and then it can spread like wildfire. As Mahatma Gandhi said, "Become the change you want to see in the world." No words could be more pertinent for the human race today. This is it. We are not at *a* crossroads, dear reader, we are at *the* crossroads.

The time has come for us to begin acting like human *beings*, not human *doings*. Everyone is constantly doing this and doing that but during all of this *doing*, not enough is being *done* to solve the world's most serious problems. Sometimes we all get so caught up doing (such as habitually texting to no one in particular), we sometimes forget the really important stuff about life, about, you know, why we are all *here* in the first place.

People should not fear their governments. Governments should fear their people. We are living in an upside-down, topsy-turvy world where Big Government taxation, red tape bureaucracy, and corporate corruption runs amok. Unchecked and rampant, greed-motivated, apathetic corporate executives continue to spew deadly toxins into the environment, killing the wildlife, polluting the air, soil, water, atmosphere, and upsetting the delicate balance of Earth's ecosystem.

Non-conformity to the entrenched system of control through peaceful, spiritual *revolution*, both individually and collectively, is what is needed now if we are going to move beyond the social injustice, oppression, pollution, poverty, famine, conflicts, and incessant wars that pervade our planet. As we learn to honor the body's divine intelligence, an entirely new system of drug-free health care will emerge, as opposed to the ineffective Big Pharma "disease care" model that exists today. The time has come for us to look to solutions from higher levels of intelligence, higher levels of *consciousness*. Now is the time for us to draw a line in the sand and stand up for our divine Selves, to stop *playing the victim* as a species.

World peace is now no longer an option, a luxury, but has become a necessity for our survival. As we venture beyond the end of the Mayan Calendar at the end of 2012, a small percentage of humanity is evolving from an ego-identified, reactive, reality-ignoring, emotionally violent, self-destructive state of *suffering* into a heart-centered, egoless, Self-empowered, emotionally independent, creative state of *being*. Ethereally connected to Gaia Sophia, our Mother Earth, this burgeoning, Self-realized, spiritually enlightened, highly intuitive, compassionate new species of humanity will actualize the protective and balancing nature of the sacred feminine.

Ultimately, there is no way *out* of the problems that we currently face together as a species, only a way *through*. The *way* begins and ends with the personal evolution of the Self. In *The Next Human*, I will be your guide through this evolutionary journey of Self-mastery, through what I call the *transformation of the Seven Selves*.

Know that your personal evolution begins with exercising your divine birthright known as *free will*. This requires a total shift in your own perception of the world around you. When you are truly ready to transform, to make that leap of faith, then that's when your soul enters its *chrysalis* stage. You may remain in this stage for many months or many years. How long you remain here matters not. Eventually, you will emerge into a magnificent "butterfly soul" and begin flapping your wings, readying your newly evolved Self for takeoff. When this happens, other souls will want to be where you are. They'll want to fly with you. This is when you begin leading by example, by inspiration, and purely from the heart. And this is *true* leadership. Now multiply this metamorphosis times many millions of times through many millions of souls, and you'll have a planetary awakening the likes of which we have never seen in human history. This is where we are *now* as a species. So, you know, fasten your *seatbelt*.

EVOLUTION
101

THE PSEUDO SELF
TRANSCENDING THE EGO

Morpheus: *The Matrix...is the world that has been pulled over your eyes to blind you from the truth.*

Neo: *What truth?*

Morpheus: *That you are a slave, Neo. Like everyone else you were born into bondage, born into a prison that you cannot smell or taste or touch—a prison for your mind. Unfortunately, no one can be told what the Matrix is. You have to see it for yourself. This is your last chance. After this there is no turning back. You take the blue pill, the story ends, you wake up in your bed and believe whatever you want to believe. You take the red pill, you stay in wonderland and I show you how deep the rabbit hole goes. Remember, all I'm offering is the truth, nothing more.*

—*The Matrix*

Everything in nature evolves. This process is usually slow, taking millions of years. But every couple hundred millennia or so, an entire species takes a giant leap forward. For most of the past four billion years, life on Earth consisted of the microorganism and nothing more. After bacteria, algae, and fungi formed, evolution leaped forward around 230 million years BP (Before Present). In this Triassic period the dinosaur quickly became the dominant species on the planet. Its reign lasted for a staggering 135 million years. Today, the reptiles and birds are all that's left from this Dinosaur Age.

The brain development in the countless species of fish, amphibians, dinosaurs, and eventually mammals, provided the early vertebrates with a fear-based nervous system designed for one specific purpose: *survival*. It's this reactive survival mechanism that is designed to protect the animal from potential danger. The next major leap in evolution occurred around 4 million years BP when Ardipithecus ramidus, a.k.a. "Ardi," became the very first proto-human with an upright skeleton designed for standing and walking. His brain was about the same size as a chimpanzee's, and he possessed both hands and feet.[1] Two million years later, early hominids evolved into Homo habilis, meaning "handy man." This remarkable new species exhibited more advanced cognitive abilities and hand-eye coordination that allowed it to develop rudimentary tools.

Approximately 1.8 million years later, life mutated yet again and the brain formed a *neocortex* or "new bark" around 200,000 years BP when anatomically current humans (Homo sapiens) suddenly and inexplicably appeared on the scene—overnight and out of nowhere—from a Mitochondrial "Eve" in East Africa.[2] Eve was the human from whom all current humans descend on their mother's side, and through the mothers of those mothers and so on. Because it's generally passed from mother to offspring without skipping a beat, all mitochondrial DNA in every living person is directly descended from Eve.

It wasn't until the formation of the neocortex that humans had a *choice* whether to react to potential danger or not. This newly evolved brain conferred to humans its ability for highly developed planning and perception. Language began to be developed that led to higher forms of communication, both spoken and written. Providing food, shelter, and clothing for the family unit became a matter of personal pride, a heightened identification with the *self* that led to the development of more sophisticated models for living, as well as more effective means of protection from potential dangers looming on the horizon. Our tools suddenly became labeled as "possessions"—as did our *mates*. Our physical identities, instead of being perceived as *one with* nature, became viewed as distinctive and separate. For the first time in human history, the word *my* preceded the words *life* and *self*.

Today, the evolutionary stage of the brain's neocortex bestows us with the super intelligent ability to think, reason, and calculate mental operations at speeds that would rival a million desktop computers working at once. It's because of this modern new brain that we have, within the last century: split the tiny atom, rocketed ourselves to the Moon, cloned a wooly sheep, invented the personal computer/smartphone, created the Internet, mapped the human genome, produced life-like CGI and 3D motion pictures in high-definition surround sound, and developed space telescopes that allow us to see 47 billion light years away. And all of this has happened in a virtual *nanosecond* on the world-history time clock.

Recently, scientists announced to the world that they've constructed the world's smallest computer hard drive using only 96 atoms.[3] Conventional hard drives currently require 500 million atoms for each byte, but this revolutionary atomic drive can hold one byte of data all by its little self. This technological leap forward could one day soon mean that your computer screen will be displayed on the inside of an eyeglass lens, with the hard drive located in the frame.

When you observe the history of the human race, in every single case that our species has innovated its technology, it has consistently achieved a higher level of intelligence because the new technology (from

Paleolithic spears to Martian probes) has expanded our knowledge base exponentially. This, in turn, has allowed for a more efficient way of obtaining more information, which, of course, has allowed for a more efficient way of obtaining even *more* information. It has been a self-reinforcing, self-perpetuating, upwardly mobile spiral. In effect, our personal and collective evolution has been contingent upon us expanding our brain's capacity, pushing our creativity to the edge of the envelope, expanding our self-perception, and seeking out higher levels of intelligence. In the aforementioned evolutionary leaps, from microbes to modern humans, we have evolved in accordance with a biological and genetic predisposition. In other words, evolution has been a relatively autonomic process. Beginning with the Next Human, however, our evolutionary impulse will be a voluntary and, in fact, *conscious* process. Instead of transforming because we *have* to, we will learn to transform because we *choose* to. The Next Human will balance the exploration of the universe of form with an *inner* exploration of the Self that will facilitate a landmark awakening to an underlying, unified field of consciousness. This is the true nature of our next leap forward in physical, mental, and spiritual evolution.

The ancient shamans, yogis, mystics, monks, and gurus were well aware of a *pseudo self* that existed within the conceptual framework of the human mind. This illusory, falsely perceived identification, they believed, was the unknown *veil* that kept the light of the Source from reaching human awareness. Imprisoning us in fear, this clouded perception of the self was viewed as an evolutionary road block that had to be transcended before the soul could approach a state of non-suffering. Siddhārtha Gautama, also known as the Buddha or "the awakened one," referred to this transcended state as *nirvana*, an extinguishing of the fires of ignorance. Jesus was clearly referring to the transcendence of this pseudo self when he said, "the Kingdom of God is within you."[4]

Kabbalah, Gnosticism, Zen Buddhism, Sufism, and the Advaita Vedānta were ancient mystical and philosophical schools of thought inculcating this pseudo self as a psychic imprisonment, disinheriting humans from their birthright, a long overdue divine inheritance known as *free will*. Without it we cannot evolve and therefore remain powerless. With free will, on the other hand, We the People of Planet Earth can remake the world for the benefit of all.

In its nascent stage of development, the pseudo self permitted us to perceive the self as special and unique. This sudden shift in cognitive perception was a wonderful new way to see the self in relation to the world around us. But when you associate specialness with *separation,* you create a recipe for disaster of genocidal proportions. Albert Einstein referred to this sense of separation as an optical delusion of our own consciousness. It's as if the pseudo self says, "I am special only because I am *separate* from the other." This highly limited state of cognitive awareness can only be made manifest as feelings of inferiority or superiority. And it is this psychological dysfunction that always ends in some form of suffering.

From whence began with the dinosaur brain's response mechanism continues to be accessed today by the current human. This is because people are so completely identified with the fear-based reactions that are attached to their personal identity. From this pseudo self we have learned how to beat, maim, rape, behead, hang, stab, shoot, electrocute, torture, and blow up one another, again and again, countless times over, all in the name of separation. In the past century, humans have experienced more bloodshed due to war than in any other time in its history. But the pseudo self has had its time. The future belongs to the Next Human.

Breeding the worst evil.

The dictionary defines evil as a "force in nature that gives rise to wickedness or sin."[5] That's a rather vague definition if I've ever heard one. It just leaves you with another question: What is the underlying *cause* behind this mysterious "force in nature?"

Most people believe that the worst evil is exemplified by the likes of serial killers, child molesters, sociopaths, or with tyrants such as Adolf Hitler, Joseph Stalin, or Mao Tse-tung. But you may be surprised to learn that throughout history, it hasn't been the *sole* individual who's been responsible for the worst evil.

In the evil that sparked the genocide of the Jews by the orders of Hitler and his nazism, the genocide of the Russian kulaks by order of Stalin and his marxism, and the genocide of the Chinese counterrevolutionaries with Tse-tung and his communism, we always find a tribe, group, or nation of people who have completely identified themselves with an ideology who backed these leaders 100 percent with zeal and provocation. The worst evil therefore has not been committed by the lone serial killer who was inherently evil, but rather by large *groups* of individuals who aligned themselves with a common opinion or *belief*. You may observe that the majority of the humans within these groups were neither criminals nor psychopaths, but indeed models of normalcy, respectability, and rationality. They were nothing more than *average citizens*.

The breeding ground for the worst evil is a threefold process: It begins when a group of average citizens identify themselves with an idea or ideology, so much so that it is perceived to be inseparable from the absolute truth. Their entire sense of survival then becomes dependent upon this "truth." Consequently, they become so entangled with their belief system that protecting their ideology becomes inseparable from protecting their very existence.

Secondly, any person or group who expresses an opposing view to that particular ideology is unconsciously reduced from a human being to an inanimate object. And finally, breeding the worst evil requires that these average citizens *rise up* against their conceptualized enemy—all in an aggressive attempt to impose their belief system (sense of "I")—in the form of *physical violence.*

What is the cause behind the force in nature that gives rise to wickedness or sin? It is none other than the pseudo self, or what we also call the *ego.*

They know not what they do.

> *Jesus said, "Father, forgive them, for they know not what they do."*
>
> —Gospel of Luke 23:34

A three-year-old boy doesn't know what he's doing while he's knocking over your glass of red wine, breaking it, and staining the carpet. He simply doesn't know better. A baby girl doesn't know better when she screams so loudly that you think your eardrums will *pop.* And a puppy dog doesn't know better when it turns your brand new pair of dress shoes into a chew toy.

And so it is the same with people. Just because someone is considered an adult by his or her chronological age doesn't necessarily mean that he or she is an "adult" by soul criteria. In fact, a fair number of human souls on this planet are in their infancy stage. So whatever they do, no matter how heinous it may seem, their actions will always reflect *where they are* on the evolutionary ladder of consciousness. If people knew better, they would be behaving better. It's that simple.

An ant will have a higher level of consciousness than a fungus. A dog will have a higher level of consciousness than a squirrel. And a dolphin will have a more evolved consciousness than a tuna. And so it is with humans. Everyone will express their own individualistic opinion or belief based on where they are on this continuum. No One is separate from the divine, no matter how hard they try to be, or how many errors they make. What we call "mistakes" are a vital part of human evolution. The Next Human will look on human mistakes from a much higher perspective; therefore she will naturally practice non-judgment and compassion toward every One. Once the soul evolves to the point where it fully understands that it is not separate from the divine, it comes to realize that its true nature is eternal. In this chapter, I will show you how to recognize the ego in you, in the other, and in the collective. Once you can truthfully say, "*That* is the ego," you'll be taking your very first steps into a much larger world.

The egoic mind.

> *The height of a man's success is gauged by his self-mastery; the depth of his failure by his self-abandonment...He who cannot establish dominion over himself will have no dominion over others.*
>
> —Leonardo da Vinci

In ancient Greek mythology, the hunter Narcissus gazed down into a still pool of water and immediately fell in love with his own reflection. This surface reflection is a metaphor for your pseudo self, the ego. The ego is not your true, eternal Self, but is crudely constructed from an ephemeral mental concept you have come to identify with during your time here. The more you try to convince yourself that the ego is who you *are*, the more you will suffer because of it. Therefore, moving beyond human suffering requires moving *beyond* the ego. To the Next Human, the ego is seen as a cloak, a veil, a prison for the mind. It is the ultimate temptation, the unseen impetus that drives the soul away from the bosom of the Goddess.

Know that every ego requires an antagonist. No matter what happens in your life, the universe can never bring you drama, tragedy, disappointment, conflict, or heartbreak. Rather, it is your judgment, reaction, and resistance to what is happening that generates your suffering.

As long as you are identified with a "me against life" or "me against the other" perspective, things will continue to happen *to* you, rob you of your free will, and cause you to suffer. As a result, you will continue to be a victim to life. You can't control everything that happens in life, but one thing you can control once mastered: the *Self*.

Lost in the self-centeredness of the egoic mind, most current humans react to every challenge that comes their way, taking it all in at face value. Like automatons, their buttons are easily pushed because they only know what they feel on a very primitive level. Negative emotions such as disgust, anger, and repulsion easily surface and are projected onto others. Because these humans passionately cherish their own opinions, anyone with whom they don't see eye-to-eye is doomed to become the ego's antagonist, their enemy. This behavior is not intentional, of course, but they will act out this unconscious impetus nevertheless. The dangerously dysfunctional behavioral dynamic that I'm describing here exemplifies the current stage of human evolution.

The Next Human stage, on the other hand, will be one of *nonegoic* interaction. Instead of the mind, actions will be rooted in the *heart*. As your consciousness moves toward this higher state of being, the ego is removed from the equation. This is the only time that you can truthfully exercise free will. As long as you completely identify with your pseudo self, the choices that you make will always be reactionary to the challenges that arise in your life. In other words, your ego never truly takes action, only *reaction*. When this transcendental shift occurs, you'll find that the ego will be a concept that you've identified, not a concept that you've identified *with*. The latter means being *lost* in the ego. The former means being *freed* from the ego.

The word *ego* stems from the Latin "I myself." It's what the mind feels it possesses in this world as well as what it identifies the "my" with, such as "my God," "my life," "my body," "my car," "my house," "my job," "my race," "my nationality," and so on. I've been blessed to be the uncle of two wonderful nephews, Hudson (age three) and Aiden (age one). Hudson's ego is just beginning to develop and so his mommy sometimes has to correct him when he points to the Atlantic Ocean and says, "My ocean," or when he points to his little brother and says, "My Aiden." Thus, the ego is always acting in a possessive, first person tense that separates everyone and everything from the *self*.

The ego thrives on fear.

> *Fear is the path to the Dark Side. Fear leads to anger.*
> *Anger leads to hate. Hate leads to suffering.*
>
> —Yoda, *Star Wars Episode I: The Phantom Menace*

The ego is ultimately motivated by one thing: *power*. More specifically, power over the *other*. Because of this simple yet foreboding prime directive, the unconsciousness that is the ego is firmly rooted in the dark emotional frequency of *fear*. Imprisoning humanity deep within the catacombs of its collective psyche, the ego interacts directly with the emotionally reactive state that is intrinsic to the body's survival mechanism. This "fight or flight" response is rooted in the primal fear of death found in all animals. But fear is no longer necessary for our survival. Our species has already evolved past this point. You don't need to feel fear to know you shouldn't walk into oncoming traffic, just a little common sense.

So what prompts this incessant, fear-based reaction? Well, there are two sources of fear: *physio*logical and *psycho*logical. The physiological fear response is based on the *emotion* of fear which is rooted in the brain's fear center, the *amygdala*. In experiments over the last fifteen years, New York University neuroscientist Dr. Joseph LeDoux has traced fear inside the rat's brain, giving researchers the first authentic understanding of the neuroanatomy of emotion.

In a New York Times interview shortly after the release of his book, *The Emotional Brain*, LeDoux explained how cognitive scientists mistakenly confuse emotions with feelings.[6] Feelings, he says, are more like "red herrings," mere interpretations that could be either true or false surfacing from conscious or unconscious *emotions*. These more powerful underlying emotions are *hard-wired* to our central nervous system because they were necessary for the evolution of our species and every other species before us. LeDoux believes that this emotional network is centered around the amygdala where sensory information comes in and motor commands are sent out.

The amygdala is dormant most of the time, but when it receives a strong stimulus, hairs stand up on our necks, the heart races, adrenaline pumps, goose bumps spread, and our fight or flight hormones kick into high gear. The amygdala reacts to stimuli and then triggers a physiological response, a process that LeDoux would describe as the *emotion* of fear, which is separate from a conscious *feeling* of fear.

Feelings are always analyzed by the cerebral cortex (higher brain) in detail, utilizing information from various parts of the brain, and subsequently a message is sent back down to the amygdala.[7] These emotions of fear are falsely interpreted red herrings by the higher brain as "feelings" of fear, such as fear of inferiority, fear of inadequacy, fear of loss, fear of failure, fear of rejection, and just an all-around general fear of impending doom. But these are all *pseudo* feelings based on what may or may not happen to you in the future, not necessarily what is happening in the Now. Because you feel these fears first as emotions expressed in the body, they falsely appear as your ingrained fear of survival, even though they have nothing to *do* with your survival.

If the message is a false alarm, such as when you mistake a garden hose for a snake, the higher brain will try to abort the amygdala's alarm signals. But the person will have already felt a major jolt because of the initial arousal. This explains how emotion and cognition are separate but because neural connections from the cortex *down* to the amygdala are not as developed as connections from the amygdala back *up* to the cortex, the "dinosaur brain" amygdala exerts a greater influence on the neocortex than vice versa. It's like a shortcut mechanism for the brain. Once a primal emotion is activated, its deactivation is not an easy task.

When you don't utilize the neural connections from the cortex down to the amygdala, they become stagnant and ineffective. As the saying goes, "If you don't use it, you lose it." When you're ego-identified, you are so conditioned to *react* to situations—because of a fear of what might be happening to you at some point in the future—you never stop to use your higher brain's ability to *choose* whether to react or not. In other words, it doesn't have to be an "on" or "off" switch once you finally become aware that you have this power of *choice* already within your brain. So when you're controlled by the ego and therefore identify your entire existence with your own opinions, the fear of something as trivial as losing an argument to another is perceived as a fear of *death*. But this is merely a physiological reaction misinterpreted by your brain. Evolutionary speaking, fear-based emotions sent to the higher brain by the amygdala are designed to keep you alive and nothing more. But again, you're already *past* this stage in your evolution. In spite of this biological fact, however, most people spend a good portion of their lives running away from imaginary saber-toothed tigers, unaware that they're at the mercy of their own physiological reactions.

For the current human, the pervasive emotional and physical violence in society is the collective result of allowing your primal emotions to take you over. But there is a bright side. All animals are able to combine learned behavior with unlearned emotions. For example, all squirrels have an innate fear of foxes, but an individual squirrel may also recall a place at the creek where it was attacked by a fox. Subsequently, the squirrel learns to avoid that specific area of the creek. For modern humans, this rudimentary learned behavior is much more evolved. We can recall our past in detail and plan far into the future. So like the squirrel, you can also learn to avoid potentially fearful situations. You do this by becoming *conscious* of your ego, and realizing that when it's in control of your mind, it will interpret life's little challenges as threats to your very survival. Eventually you'll realize that all of your fearful and problematic situations are being created and blown out of proportion by the ego, and therefore can be avoided altogether.

Today, it is clear that inherited emotion-based reactions are no longer needed for survival, but are primarily serving to bolster the psychological hold that the ego has on the collective psyche. Because of this, the current human is not able to access his or her inherent free will.

The death of drama and the birth of free will.

Let's face it; we live in a drama-addicted society. In fact, most of our television programs today are reality shows centered around one thing: *drama*. Ironically, reality shows are shows about, well, *non*-reality. These shows reflect a perpetual state of stress-inducing drama that continues to be blindly accepted as a state of normalcy.

In recent years, there's been much speculation and discussion about whether we humans possess free will. The truth is that free will is available to everyone but very few exercise it. In the drama addiction cycle, when the body reacts to the fight or flight fear of death via the sympathetic nervous system, you are not exercising free will. You are at the mercy of physiological reactions going on inside your body, and nothing more. Now multiply this reactionary state with every experience in your life that has caused you to feel anxiety, worry, stress, depression, rejection, or anger. Is it in the hundreds? Thousands? Is it countless? Well then, where's the free will in *this* kind of life?

It is widely accepted today in the medical community that a large proportion of the visits to the doctor's office are not the result of physical problems but are instead attributed to psychological factors, many of which are the result of acute or chronic *stress*. The hypothalamus is the gland of the brain that links the nervous system to the endocrine system via the pituitary gland. It controls body temperature, hunger, sweat, thirst, fatigue, and circadian cycles. As a result, it's in charge of stress responses. It's part of the hypothalamic-pituitary-adrenal axis which are endocrine glands working together to switch your body's nervous system back and forth between two operating modes; parasympathetic and sympathetic.

When the parasympathetic mode dominates, you're in a "relax and renew" state. The sympathetic nervous system, on the other hand, is designed to put the body in a fight or flight mode. Let's say you get into an argument with someone at a party on the subject of abortion and her opinion clashes with yours, and as a result, your ego has declared her "the enemy" which, in turn, triggers the amygdala, resulting in the release of adrenaline, preparing you for any potential threat. But there is no threat. There is only a *difference of opinion*.

You have no free will when you're trying to control situations or other people. All you're doing is creating unnecessary stress in the body and contributing to the psychic disharmony of the planet. Here are a few brief examples:

A few weeks ago, I was at the dentist's office getting my teeth cleaned and while I was sitting peacefully in my chair, I heard an elderly lady in the cubicle next to me begin shouting at the top of her lungs, saying, "Let's get this show on the road! I haven't got all day! I've got work to do!" The dentist quickly returned and explained that he was simply waiting for the Novocain to take effect so that she wouldn't be in pain when he pulled her tooth.

Or...

The other day I observed a man yelling from his car at a teenage boy who was doing nothing more than walking across the street. The walk light was green and the man in the car was impatiently waiting for the boy in the cross walk to finish crossing so that he could make a right-hand turn. The impatient driver then began screaming at the boy, "Why don't you take your own sweet time, you idiot!" After the boy made his way about three-fourths of the way across the street, the driver then floored the car to turn right, screeching his tires, nearly hitting the boy.

In both examples, the angry display of impatience is a way in which the ego senselessly reacts to situations beyond its control. The ego actually feels threatened when things don't happen within its own timeframe. Like a little child, the ego must have what it wants *when it wants it.* This "life-threatening" fear is then projected onto the other in the form of blame. The other immediately becomes "the enemy" in the eyes of the ego just for making it wait. But in the first example, the dentist was not intentionally trying to make his patient wait; he simply wanted the painkiller to take effect. In the second example, the teenager crossing the street was not intentionally trying to delay the driver. He even had a green walk light. But to the ego, the other is always to blame. In both cases, neither individual exercised any free will because they both allowed a benign situation to control their behavior, increase their stress levels, and potentially bring harm to their physical bodies.

In reality, these unnecessary dramas of the ego play out in our society a million times a day, every day. Sometimes emotional violence escalates into physical violence. On Black Friday in 2011 it was reported on the news that a Christmas shopper pepper-sprayed twelve people waiting in line simply because she wanted to get to the check-out counter first. Because the ego has no control over itself, it projects its control *outwardly,* and in the process pollutes the planet with needless stress, drama, and violence.

All problems are ego-generated.

> *No problem can be solved from the same level of consciousness that created it.*
>
> —Albert Einstein

Life is meant to be enjoyed, not endured. If you're playing the victim to life, then you've already given up on life, and have declared that God, the devil, the universe, karma, or some mysterious "force" greater than yourself is somehow in control of your life, is the cause behind your suffering, and is for some unknown reason *punishing* you. In a way, you've succumbed to this force that, in reality, does not exist. Victimization is the ego's way of attracting the spotlight back onto itself. It is unconsciously played out for the sole purpose of extracting power guised as attention and sympathy from others.

If you're playing the victim, what you subconsciously fear the most is what you usually end up attracting *to* you. A dark cloud seems to follow you around wherever you go, and you'll constantly be running into obstacles around every turn. Life seems to be a desperate attempt at solving one annoying problem after another, and this never-ending onslaught eventually takes its toll on your health, causing you to become addicted to food, or alcohol, or drugs, or you just become chronically ill. And the more you fight this horrifying reality that the universe inflicts problems *on* you, the more tragic life becomes.

When you play the victim, you won't be exercising any free will at all. Zero. People take advantage of you. No, it's worse; they walk all over you. From the perspective of the Next Human, victimization is artificially constructed from the reactive, resistant, reality-ignoring, presence-dodging, drama-creating, life-battling, egoic mind. To the ego, life is nothing less than an ongoing pummel of problems that must be solved and counted. But all these problems are nothing more than an outer reflection of the chaos within. They're also energy for the ego to *feed* on. Over time, problems and conflicts become a necessity for the ego to sustain itself. Drama is drummed up so the ego can become the center of attention on the world stage.

If you're ready to stop playing the victim to life, then you must first learn to stop creating your own problems out of simple challenges. Don't put your challenges on the back burner and ignore them, hoping they'll just disappear on their own, because they won't. The challenges will dissolve, one by one, but you have to give them the attention they deserve. It's called *presence.* Otherwise they will keep coming back and situations will continue getting worse until you begin paying attention. The key is staying focused in the Now. If you're unable to do this right away, that's understandable. Begin by living in day-tight compartments. In other words, only believe what is happening during the day. When the ego begins fearing what may happen tomorrow, bring yourself back to the day, and address only what needs to be addressed in that time frame. In a month or two, strive to live in hour-tight compartments, and do the same. Then a few months later, focus on living in minute-tight compartments. Then second-tight compartments. Eventually you'll find yourself living in *now*-tight compartments. This is how you gradually invite presence into your life. Honoring the present moment and everything it brings, no matter what it is, is essential for ego transcendence and bringing an end to victimization. Practice observing the mind projecting itself into the past or into the future; then when you become aware of this, bring your attention back to the Now.

Once you become aware that you've been the initiator of your own problems all along, you'll no longer be asking, "Why do these things keep happening *to* me?" Instead you'll be asking, "What have I done to *create* this reality?" Here are a few examples:

Let's say that your company is cutting costs and as a result they've just laid a bunch of people off and even though you still have your job, you just got a pay cut, and because of this, you can no longer make the mortgage payment on your home, and that sporadic pain in your stomach that you've been hoping would eventually go away just got a little sharper.

If you're playing the victim, when challenges arise, instead of facing them head-on while they're still manageable, you will either...

A. Put them on hold and ignore them, hoping they'll magically take care of themselves and go away. Any and all messages that the universe has sent your way are left "unread." Weeks or months go by and no action is taken. Now you have a problem.

Or...

B. Attack the challenge with reaction-based fear and panic. Without taking any time to be still and ruminate on your challenge, a hasty and reactive decision is made. You become furious at your employer and end up quitting before you have time to find another job. Now you have no income at all and the weight of this reckless decision is bringing you more stress than you had before. Now you have a problem.

As the Next Human, however, a completely different behavior pattern emerges:

C. In this scenario, you understand that the universe takes its time. It's in no hurry and it's not going to *push* you, so there's no need to rush to decisions. During meditations and peaceful walks in the park you are able to enter into a place of deep presence. As you enter the peaceful Now, you automatically open yourself up to unforeseen opportunities and creative solutions.

When you realize that you can no longer afford your mortgage payment, instead of panicking and becoming stressed, you calmly and confidently begin looking for a better job, as well as considering that Internet business that you've been wanting to start. You know that somehow, someway, the universe is conspiring in your favor. You don't question or resist what is happening. You see it as an opportunity for something better to reveal itself. Then, from a place of inner peace and true Self-esteem, you take action. Because you've transcended your ego, you are now exercising the power of *free will.* You decide to quietly go job hunting. Fast-forward three months and not only have you found a better-paying job than you had previously, the benefits are better, and one of your new co-workers has expressed an interest in going into business with you because she shares your dream of owning an Internet company.

The lesson here is that by paying attention to your pay-cut situation from the get-go, you acknowledge and accept your challenge as the universe's way of saying, "Hey you, it's time to move on." The difference between this example and the victim scenarios is: because you transcended your ego, you didn't *react*. You said *yes* to your challenge, and then moved forward without any worry, stress, or anxiety. That's right; zero stress. Imagine that.

All problems are conceived by the egoic mind when challenges are seen as obstacles that must be either ignored or fought with all your might. Again and again, a simple situation is converted into a problem because the ego says, "I have to win against this situation or *beat* that challenge so that I can be victorious, and if I can't *win* then I'll be seen as inferior to others." This is how the ego twists a simple life event into something that is problematic. The entire challenge is seen as a matter of "life and death" and that's when stress and drama enter into the equation. Becoming consciously aware of your ego when facing each challenge in life is necessary for transcendence. Your only concern is what is happening in the Now.

Be grateful for your challenges because they are the impetus for your personal evolution. Becoming anxious, stressed, or obsessively worrying about each challenge that develops is the way the paranoid ego projects the mind into the future, and as a result, completely ignores the Now. "Problems" are simply the mind's way of mistranslating current events that could *at some imaginary time in the future* bring you humiliation, loss, and/or suffering. Therefore, nothing is intrinsically problematic. As you become more and more present to life, you automatically give life the attention it deserves. This is the only way to prevent problems from occurring in the first place. The Next Human will be grateful for his challenges and will calmly and effectively deal with them as soon as they arise. Subsequently, he won't be a victim to life.

The danger of cherished opinions.

The only true wisdom is knowing that you know nothing.

—Socrates

For the opinionated, the opinion and the self are *one*. The more ego-identified you are, the more you will identify with your own opinions. You will also tend to be emotionally entangled within your own situations, problems, experiences, and thoughts. If you are an opinionated person and someone threatens your belief system, your entire sense of survival will seemingly depend on your ability to defend those beliefs. This identification with your own opinions will only serve to cement your clouded state of unconsciousness, and create unnecessary suffering.

Polarity is sharpened by the ego because this aspect of the mind so closely identifies the self with a concept. The more closely you identify with an idea or ideology, the more polarized and difficult life becomes, and the more you will suffer. As long as you live in this polarized reality (hot/cold, up/down, good/evil), you cannot ignore or discard it altogether. You can, however, transcend it so that polarity is seen for what it is. Ergo, life becomes more favorable, benevolent, and cooperative.

I would like to be more specific about what an opinion is since most people are not aware just how dangerous their opinions can be. There are two types of opinions. The first type I refer to as an *egoic* opinion and constitutes about 90 percent of all opinions. The second type is *non-egoic* and is the opinion type of the Next Human. An egoic opinion is a group of thoughts about a thing or idea with which you are so closely identified, it is believed to be the absolute truth. And because of this emotional entanglement, that truth becomes who you see yourself to be: your identity. You and the opinion have become *inseparable*. So when someone else challenges your egoic opinion, that person is perceived as a physical threat to your survival. This is when the amygdala triggers the physiological response that a saber-toothed tiger is trying to eat you.

A *non*-egoic opinion, on the other hand, is a number of thoughts about a thing or idea that you are neither identified with nor emotionally tethered to. If someone challenges you, since you are not identified *with* your opinion, you remain a detached, non-judgmental observer of polarized views—even though one of those views is yours. You respect the other's opinion and clearly understand where he or she is coming from. As a result, no physiological response is triggered, and inner peace is maintained.

In the *Xinxin Ming* (Faith in Mind), a famous poem written by the third patriarch of Zen Buddhism, Master Chien-chih Seng-ts'an, says: "Do not seek the truth; only cease to cherish opinions." When you are ego-identified, however, all your opinions will be cherished. Why? Because the ego is all about polarity. It dissolves in a non-confrontational reality. Therefore, it separates itself from others so that it can feel superior to them *through* its cherished opinions. And *this* is how the polarity of the ego is played out between individuals, parties, groups, and nations.

So why is Seng-ts'an telling us not to seek the truth? How will we find wisdom if we don't pursue it? How will we find enlightenment if we do not *seek* it? The reason Seng-ts'an is instructing us not to seek the truth is because absolute truth, or the ultimate reality, is not something objective or conceptual, nor is it *separate* from you. It's not some "thing" you will discover in the way of opinion or belief, which is only a self-perception based on where you are on the ladder of evolutionary consciousness. Absolute truth is not something "out there" waiting to be found. Ultimately, there is no "out there." The entire universe is inside you. Opinions and beliefs, even words like "you" or "me," are nothing more than conceptual points of reference existing solely in the mind. They may have a practical value in daily life, but when assumed to be the absolute truth they distort perception.

Know that absolute truth cannot be found in a conceptual world. The world as we see it is manifested directly from our thoughts and beliefs. Therefore, our entire reality is conceptual. Everything we can create, from the words you are reading now to the language that you're reading it in, to the book that you're reading it *from*, was originally just a concept. Before any idea came to be, the mind had to dream it up first. In a sense, our entire society is an interactive construct that's manufactured primarily by the ideas stemming from a *hive mind*. An analogy for what I'm talking about here is perfectly illustrated in a scene from the movie *The Matrix* when Morpheus informs Neo that the "dream-walkers" are so much a part of the Matrix system of control, the "pseudo reality" that they will *fight* to defend it:

> *The Matrix is a system, Neo. That system is our enemy. But when you're inside, you look around, what do you see? Businessmen, teachers, lawyers, carpenters, the very minds of the people we are trying to save—but until we do, these people are still a part of that system and that makes them our enemy. You have to understand, most of these people are not ready to be unplugged and many of them are so inert, so hopelessly dependent on the system, they will fight to protect it.*

Zen Master Seng-ts'an viewed the world through an undistorted lens of enlightenment and was acutely aware how the "matrix of the mind" or system of our beliefs is capable of deluding us. He was well aware that seeking absolute truth is as absurd as a dog chasing after its own tail. Just as we understand that the dog already has its own tail from the very beginning, the Next Human will know that she need not search for ultimate truth beyond her Self. The very fact that you are conscious is proof enough that you don't need to actively seek out consciousness. It's simply the awareness that you already have "your tail." Know that you already *are* the embodiment of absolute truth in human form. Look no further.

Seng-ts'an says "only cease to cherish opinions," because opinions will always be rooted in the conceptual world of form. They are completely subjective and therefore *subject to* each individual's perception of their own reality as they *see* it. When you finally realize that none of your ideas about truth are real, it can be quite a shock to your mind. Note that Seng-ts'an is not saying you should never have opinions or beliefs. He's only saying not to *cherish* these opinions in your head. To cherish implies an emotional attachment, a distortion of reality, and a dangerously high value placed on it since the opinion is believed to be an intricate part of your very existence, and potentially a threat to your survival. This cherishing of opinions is what your pseudo self, the ego, *feeds* on.

Stop fighting and start allowing.

> *If we can really understand the problem, the answer will come out of it, because the answer is not separate from the problem.*
>
> —Jiddu Krishnamurti

On this planet, you have plenty of people who are currently living in an inner state of disharmony. Their lives are overflowing with drama, conflict, stress, and discord. They unknowingly perpetuate this chaotic existence because they so closely identify with their own polarized perspective of the universe. They've been conditioned to look upon the world with a "me vs. it" viewpoint. But this lens is seriously distorted.

The ego-identified current human can easily be compared to the aforementioned quote from *The Matrix* where the dream-walkers are always fighting to keep the system in place. Because most current humans are unknowingly controlled by their dinosaur brains, they are unconsciously programmed to believe that they must *fight* everything and everyone coming between them and their opinions, peace, health, survival, comfort, or security. As a result, our entire health care model is based on *fighting* disease, our entire business model is based on *fighting* the competition, and our entire political model is based on *fighting* another party. But *fighting* only yields our falsely perceived enemy *more power.*

The ego loves a fight because it motivates it into action. In many ways, the ego defines itself *through* the act of fighting. "We've got to keep up the fight!" says the ego, as if its very existence depends on it. And in many ways, it *does*. Next time you're listening to the news or reading an article about the current political scene, listen for the word "fight" and notice how many times it's mentioned. You'll be astounded. Similarly, whenever you hear about someone who's ill and trying to get well, listen for the word "fight" or "battle" when the media or the person with the illness describes the action she is taking against her falsely perceived enemy—the *disease*. It's always something like, "She fought as long as she could and her battle against cancer finally ended with her death." It's a rarity when you hear about someone actually winning a "fight" against a chronic and potentially fatal disease. It does happen, but most of the time they will lose the fight. Or, they will "defeat" the disease temporarily only to see the same or another disease crop back up a year or two afterwards. This is because the law of attraction dictates that whatever you resist, will ultimately *persist*. In other words, the frequency of *fighting* can only attract to it a like frequency of return *fighting*. If you doubt this, try entering a crowded room full of people and pushing your way through. Try shoving people to the side while you're screaming, "Get the hell out of my way!" and see what happens. You may soon realize that you'll have the entire crowd pushing you back—and out the *door*. On the flip side, if you whisper a gentle, "Excuse me, could you kindly allow me passage?" softly into the ears of the people in front of you, you'll probably find that the crowd will part like the Red Sea did for Moses. So stop fighting and start *allowing* the universe to do its job for you. When you do, you'll find life to be a lot less combative, and a lot more cooperative.

At the same time that there are many people living in a virtual hell on this planet, there are also those who are living in virtual *heaven*. This is the place where the Next Human resides: in a heaven on Earth. This is because he has learned how to surrender to the polarity of life. This acceptance of life, no matter what happens, manifests as a state of inner peace. And *inner* peace will eventually manifest as *outer* peace. It doesn't happen in the reverse. This is one reason why so many current humans are suffering. They keep waiting for the universe to bring them peaceful situations so they can, in turn, find peace within. Know that your outer reality is always a mirrored reflection of your *inner* reality. As this inner transformation occurs, life is no longer viewed as hostile because you'll realize that your reality begins and ends with *you*. Then you'll naturally project a more loving, grateful, and compassionate frequency onto the reflective universe, allowing for it to mirror these same qualities back to you. Instead of merely surviving, you'll be *thriving*. This is the shift in consciousness away from the egoic mind and into the *heart* that all the spiritual teachers are currently talking about. It all begins with a surrender to life. When you live in a place of constant surrender, you become a channel *for* a higher purpose from a *place* of higher purpose. Living purely from the heart is the way of the Next Human.

The heart has the true power.

He who is slow to anger is better than the mighty, and he who rules his spirit, than he who captures a city.

—King Solomon, *Proverbs 16:32*

When you align your will with a force that is infinitely greater than your ego, you align your Self with true power. Mahatma Gandhi, a humble little man from India who lived in the early 20th century, demonstrated to the world that the military might of an empire is insignificant compared to the power of the *heart*. Like King Solomon, Gandhi believed that the heart was mightier than the sword. And like Jesus, Gandhi expressed the importance of loving your enemy, saying, "If you express your love in such a manner that it impresses itself indelibly upon your so-called enemy, he must return that love…and that requires far greater courage than the delivering of blows."[8]

During the liberation of India between 1919 and 1946, Gandhi consistently demonstrated ego transcendence in lieu of a violent protest against the oppressive British Empire. His passive *satyāgraha* or "truth force" campaign consisted of non-cooperation with the British authority with nonviolent, non-resistant action, and became a hallmark example of this esoteric truth: It is the *heart* that holds the true power, not the mind. In so doing, Gandhi communicated a higher frequency "*no*" to British rule and oppression over the Indian people.

When you begin to realize the infinite power of your heart, you will naturally put the will of the heart ahead of the will of the mind. When you are ego-identified, however, your heart doesn't enter into the equation. Gandhi held no ill will toward the British Empire even though he had much reason to do so from an egoic perspective. He was thrown into jail four times and suffered immensely at the hands of British authority, but even when he was struck, he neither retaliated nor sought revenge. Gandhi exercised his free will through non-compliance instead of violence, and showed the world that a peaceful revolution is always possible. A personification of the Next Human, Mahatma Gandhi had exemplified that the greatest mastery of all begins and ends with the *Self*.

When you learn to transcend your ego, you are incapable of being violent in any way because your entire being is grounded in your heart. Thus, all your thoughts, words, and actions naturally become nonviolent. This passive, nonviolent approach to life is the essence of what is known in Jainism, Hinduism, and Buddhism as *ahimsā*. When you stop fighting and start allowing the heart to lead the mind, you become the embodiment of ahimsā.

Identifying with the world of form.

I want to be rich and I want lots of money
I don't care about clever I don't care about funny
I want loads of clothes and fuckloads of diamonds
I heard people die while they're trying to find them
—Lily Allen, *The Fear*

The ego identifies with the world of form early on. If you were a girl, you probably identified with your dolls, and if you were a boy, you most likely identified with your cars and trucks. This is the nascent stage of ego development. When you entered adolescence you made a transition from trucks or dolls into what brought you some kind of recognition, accomplishment or status. If you were a boy, when you began to drive, you probably identified with your car. If you were a pretty girl, you may have identified with your looks. If you were able to get straight As on all your exams and were a member of the Honor Society, you probably identified with how smart you were. Perhaps you excelled at sports and you identified with how well you played baseball, football, or hockey. If you were a musician, you identified with how well you played the saxophone or the violin. Maybe you loved to act and took a lot of theater classes. Well, then you identified yourself with that.

The pathology of the ego stems not from a temporal identification, but from the allowance of an emotional *clinging* to form because of a psychological lacking to feel "worthy of," "as good as," or "superior to" another. This feeling of *lack* is linked to the over-identification with the ego because a feeling of satiation can never be attained through it. You become psychologically *stuck to forms* and a mental handicap emerges. Dissatisfaction with life stems from relying on the world of form to bring happiness *to* you. But it can't because form isn't real. Everything perceived in the material world is based on electrical signals interpreted by your brain and nothing more.

I'm reminded here of a time many years ago, when a friend of mine had a girlfriend who was a jewelry salesperson. One time, I was on my way to the gym and ran into the two of them on their way out. She was crying, bawling, very distraught. I asked him what was wrong, and his reply was shocking. He said that she had lost her gold Cartier bracelet. She couldn't find it anywhere. By the looks of her torment I thought that someone in her family had died. Now, never mind the fact that she could have easily afforded to replace it and no doubt even had it insured. But the truth of it was that she had become so attached to her jewelry that the loss of the bracelet was emotionally akin to having a finger cut off.

The ego convinces the mind that you need to acquire a certain status, achieve recognition, or keep up with the other people in your life by accumulating lots and lots of "stuff" that's appealing to the senses. Or, for the biggest egos, keeping up with others is not enough. They have to show everyone who's "boss." Being seen as superior to others becomes their number one priority in life. Emotional intimacy takes a backseat to becoming financially successful. These individuals are driven by the whims of their egos and nothing more. They are selfish, inconsiderate, ruthless, and greedy. Money allows them to feel superior over others and the more they accumulate, the more powerful they feel about themselves. But in reality, they are lost in their own false image, consumed by their own narcissistic reflection. Whenever you pursue wealth for the sole purpose of inflating your ego, then you're in for a huge disappointment, not to mention on your way to a good deal of emptiness once it is acquired. Know that the ego is also reinforced through the *loss* of wealth, status, or success. Sabotaging your own material success in life creates energy too, albeit negative, but it's still energy for the ego to feed on.

The ego also likes to project your sense of self worth into the future by convincing you that you will be ultimately sustained by what could be. It's as if the ego says, "When you do this, then you'll be happy." But once you get there, you may realize that you're not so fulfilled after all, and then your ego says, "Oh, well I guess that's not it—I was wrong—there must be something that I missed...well, then um, let's see now, oh, I know; if I can only have this, achieve that, then I'll really and truly be happy." Then the cycle of codependency on the material world of form repeats itself all over again.

Frequently in the news we hear reports about famous celebrities or politicians who make public spectacles of themselves because of their egoic shenanigans. Their drama addiction cycles take them in and out of rehab, in and out of the courts, and in and out of the headlines. Many are found guilty of covering up their promiscuity or infidelity. Egomania is much more common in the celebrity or politician than it is in the average person because the identification with being in the spotlight, being adored by the public, or getting rich and famous, all buttress the delusion that he or she is someone *special* and therefore superior to others. When this feeling of superiority is combined with alcohol or drugs, it sometimes results in an engrained belief structure that becomes intractable. The ego may say, "I have proof that I am untouchable, unfathomable, and far superior to everyone around me." Grandiosity, deception, drug abuse, and hypomania are all symptoms of something rooted much deeper in the psyche: a complete identification with *form*.

Everyone's got one.

Be wary of the meek who mock the mighty. What may be interpreted by the naive observer as humility on the outside is not necessarily indicative of the size of the ego on the inside. Appearances can be deceiving, and as the acronym of EGO suggests: Everyone's Got One.

The feeling of power is intoxicating to the ego. This frequently occurs in the workplace when an employee is suddenly put into a position of authority, and as a result, a completely different personality emerges. The subordinate co-worker gets appointed to boss, and the ego, sensing *power*, comes out of hiding. The newfound power goes straight to his or her head. Sometimes these individuals can't control their egos and they abuse their power. Eventually, they may get fired or be forced to resign.

Tragically, it's not uncommon for people to commit suicide after a sudden loss of a job, money, home, power, or fame. In the past fifty years, countless celebrities, especially musical artists under the age of thirty, have died from drug or alcohol overdoses because they haven't been able to cope with their new-found fame or loss of it. Since all form is transitory, when you become ego-identified with status, recognition, or wealth, you will have wrapped your entire sense of "I" around dust in the wind.

Many times people will adopt a particular lifestyle or ideology so that the ego can fulfill its need to feel superior to others. In Christianity and Hinduism, the renunciate is someone who renounces all earthly pleasures while choosing to live an ascetic life devoid of material pleasures. But this doesn't necessarily mean that the renunciate has transcended the ego. To the contrary, he may have a bigger ego than a Wall Street banker. If this is the case, his entire impetus for becoming an ascetic in the first place is to feel superior to others. Similarly, this can also happen with people in the spiritual community. It's as if the ego says, "I am spiritual now, and therefore I am superior to those who are not." This is a danger that always looms in the labyrinth of the egoic mind. Another example is the spiritual teacher who has convinced himself that he is more enlightened than he actually is. These egoic gurus present themselves as having a unique niche on the truth. They may say something like, "I have finally defeated my ego, and if you follow me I can teach you to do the same." But you cannot defeat, suppress, resist, or *fight* the ego and win. And you can't make a truce with it either. It doesn't work that way.

Authentic power comes from your connectivity with the formless, nondual nature of the eternal Source, not the ego. The Next Human will be a living example of this. She will lightly tiptoe through the world as if she were walking on thin ice, and with a mind as hollow as a cave, she'll be intensely alert to the pseudo self in others. In this way, she will not *un*intentionally wound other egos and will not be fooled by those pretending to not *have* egos. She'll be able to instantly recognize the egoic guru because she will know that true gurus always point the way home, not to themselves.

A way through, not out.

If there isn't an emanation of love and joy, complete presence and openness toward all beings, then it is not enlightenment.

—Eckhart Tolle, *The Power of Now*

Instead of viewing ego transcendence as a way *out* of the current human condition, try seeing it as a way *through*. From this higher, Next Human perspective, you won't be deluding yourself into believing that you can actually avoid or escape the ego's clutches and the dysfunctional hold it has over your mind. If you think that it has to be a fight to the finish, that you have to see the ego as your enemy, or that you need to *escape* from its psychic imprisonment, well, you haven't transcended anything. This form of conditioning that perceives some other force or entity to be an adversary that must be *fought* is the very embodiment *of* ego. And so you're right back to square one.

Ego transcendence begins with *surrender* and ends with an acceptance of what is Now. When you look upon your fellow human and say, "You shouldn't be ego-identified," or "You shouldn't be unconscious," then you're still *stuck* in the egoic mind. Only the ego judges and wags its finger with condemnation. Instead, see the ego-identified as little children who simply don't know any better. They can also be viewed as individuals or groups who create a frame of reference representing where you *don't* want to be. See them as a "spiritual teachers" of sorts. Know that our society needs them because without them, there would be *no growth*. Once that frame of reference is established, either in a single person, group, or an entire nation, then it will be easier to see him, her, or them as an impetus for your personal evolution.

Dissolution of the ego.

> *Sever the chains of the ego. Set yourself free and witness the*
> *bright essence of your inner being. Discover within your*
> *heart the wisdom of a prophet without books, without teach-*
> *ers, and without prudence.*

—Rumi

The ego is no longer the ego when you recognize it. You cannot be both awake and asleep at the same time. If the ego is operating in you and *through* you, you won't know it. The very meaning of the word *ego* implies that you're not aware of it because you have completely identified your entire sense of self *with* it. Remember, ego is whatever you unconsciously identify *with*. So if you are ego-identified you will be completely oblivious to the truth that you and the ego are *one*. Those who have the biggest egos are usually unaware that they have an ego at all. I once had a friend who had a *gargantuan* ego. One time I mentioned to him that the ego was responsible for our suffering. His response was, "That can't be true because I don't have an ego and I suffer all the time." What you'll find is that people who are completely ego-identified won't even know what the ego is, much less be interested in learning anything about it. They simply cannot recognize the true meaning of it in themselves or in others.

So the moment you can truthfully say, "*That's* the ego," when observing it in yourself, will be when the ego loses its power *over* you and then it will no longer *be* the ego. It's dissolved! Instead, it becomes a mere thought pattern that you've identified. For example, let's say that you know someone "important" or famous in your community, maybe someone in a position of power or authority who is relatively well known among your peers. Egos love to associate themselves with "very important people" so that feelings of specialness—and *separation*—can be reinforced. Therefore name dropping is one of its favorite pastimes. So say you're out to dinner with friends and you say, "I have to call Angelina

Jolie." The moment you become aware that you've just "name-dropped" Angelina Jolie because you wanted others to be impressed with you is recognizing the ego in action. Upon reflection you may even admit to yourself that it was childish and pathetic. This recognition instantly dissolves the ego. This is the spark of enlightenment.

Or...

Let's say you're at a bar with friends and a beautiful woman walks in the room. Everyone's head turns and someone makes a comment on how beautiful she is. Then you say something like, "Yeah, but she's a whore." At that moment, you realize that your statement is a lie. You don't even know the woman, and you just made it up because your ego was either intimidated by her or perceived her as a *threat*. This recognition instantly dissolves the ego.

Or...

Let's say that in the past you've been giving a lot of free—and frequently *unwelcomed*—advice. This is one of the most common aspects of an over-identified ego. For example, let's say that a solopreneur friend of yours is showing you her brand new website that she has designed, written, and marketed all by herself. She's very excited to share with you her completed site, but about three minutes into the tour, you begin making some criticisms about what you would change about the copy of this page and the images on that page and the video and the marketing strategy so that the site would be "improved" and the whole time you're saying these things to her your mind is rationalizing that you're doing your friend a huge favor because, well, you just want to help her improve her site. However, your friend has not asked you for your advice—and this is the *case in point*. Your ego is asserting itself here when it doesn't need to be doing so, i.e. it feels the need to bring your friend's website up to *your* standards, not hers. Recognition of your ego's need to assert unsolicited advice to others so that it can feel superior to them dissolves the ego.

Or...

Let's say you try and make someone *wrong* in a discussion. The moment you recognize this intention to "wrong" the other, you'll find a glimmer of light there. This is the beginning of ego transcendence. If you can nurture that light and allow it to grow, you'll discover some freedom from the ego. There's no longer a complete identification with the egoic pattern. You'll find that there will be a transitional period of a gradual awakening to this pattern where you'll have one eye open, so to speak, and you'll become aware of the fact that you're still identifying with the ego from time to time because you've been conditioned to do so. That's fine, as long as you're able to eventually (even if it's a day or week afterward) see it for what it is. As you continue to do this, you will inevitably wake up to the egoic behavior in yourself and in others. This is the process of ego dissolution.

The key to dissolving the ego is in the consistent recognition of its dysfunctional behavioral patterns that can only be seen under the blinding spotlight of *presence*. If you do continue to be ego-identified, then instead of beating yourself up for that, be compassionate with yourself. Laugh at yourself with big Buddha belly laughs!

Eventually (even if it takes years), certain egoic urges will be caught *before* you express them. For example, let's say you're having dinner with some people with whom you normally don't associate with because of their staunch right-wing political views. They're discussing something about politics and everyone at the table is agreeing with one another on a particular topic. But from your experience, and from what you've learned, you are absolutely, positively sure that they are *wrong*. This is your ego wanting to come out of hiding, wanting to assert itself so that it can make others wrong, because when others are wronged, you are *righted*. And so at this point there will most likely be a conflict going on inside of you, between the ego and your conscious Self. But no one has asked for your opinion on the political matter and this isn't a board meeting where everyone gets to vote.

First, let's say that you eventually give in to the ego's urge to interject your opinion on the subject. This is fine because you're still learning, so if this is where you are, then be okay with that. You may say something like, "How dare you say that?! I've experienced that situation, and I've lived it. Therefore, I know you're completely wrong." Well, if that's the case, then you can only imagine where this is going to lead: an emotionally violent argument ending with a bruising of all the egos at the table.

Choosing not to make the other wrong, rather than doing so simply because you *can*, is a virtue of the Next Human. This is free will in action. There is no suppression of the urge, only a *choice* stemming from the light of your higher Self. Your challenge is only to recognize the ego, and then affirm to yourself: "I don't need to assert myself, and I don't need to be right. There's no life and death decision being made here, and no one has asked me for my opinion. Therefore, I choose to keep my divine mouth *shut*." The ego always needs to be righted in front of others so it can be seen as superior *to* them. *Rumi*nate on this for a moment. See the arrogance and haughtiness in this. Jesus understood this truth about the ego when he said, "So when you're invited, take the place of least honor. Then, when your host comes, he will tell you, 'Friend, move to a more honorable place.' Then all the other guests will see how you are honored."[9]

So, let's say that the outcome is the reverse and you decide to be still and say nothing. If you choose this higher road, then you will, at first, feel a diminishment, belittling, and a loss of self-esteem. But that loss of esteem stems from the *pseudo* self. Therefore it's not real self-esteem. It is a self-delusion. After all, how can that esteem be authentic when it's based on the absurd belief that you are superior to another human simply because you hold a different opinion than he or she?

The ego is neither your friend nor your enemy.

What I'm emphasizing here in this chapter (and indeed the entire book) is the importance that you refrain from masquerading your authentic Self as your pseudo self. Know that you are infinitely greater than a mere *concept* in your head. If you can learn to create a space *in between* your consciousness and the ego, move your awareness *beyond it* and practice living in your heart instead, then you will have transcended the ego. Some believe that we only need to control our ego, put it "in check," resist it, or retain its "good parts," so that we can have a distinctive personality, have fun in life, have self-esteem, or be motivated to put food on the table and keep ourselves safe from harm. **Not true to all of the above.**

Know that the ego is neither your friend nor your enemy. If you treat it as your enemy, you'll only be giving it more power. It will only sneak back up on you and come in through the mind's back door. If you treat the ego as your friend, believing that the ego is necessary for your personality, survival, enjoyment, or sense of self-worth, you'll still remain *trapped* in the egoic mind.

The ego's purpose is not to protect the physical body. To the contrary, because the ego is self-serving, it will only bring great harm to the body by way of codependency, stress, anxiety, depression, and physical disease so that it can protect itself and retain its hold over your mind. Know that the ego is responsible for turning your life upside down, and consequently keeping you asleep, unconscious. The physical body and sense of "security" as your mind defines it is actually undermined by the ego, not reinforced by it. How is an incessant state of drama-inducing stress protecting you from harm? Know this: excessive ego-identification is the underlying cause of all mental diseases and most physical diseases.

In regards to motivation for putting food on the table and taking care of your family, you'll be infinitely *more* motivated without the ego because you'll be firmly rooted in the selfless and nurturing nature of the *heart*. And regarding a personality, you don't need to be ego-identified to have a personality. Just as each and every snowflake is beautifully

unique, each individual soul will retain its uniqueness and divine specialness without any help from the ego. In fact, Next Humans will have
much *more* interesting, distinctive, and characteristic personalities than
the current human because the sentient program that each person falsely
identifies as their "self" will essentially be *unplugged*. In other words, the
ego is fundamentally *cloned* in everyone who has one. And so I ask you:
Where's the individuality in *that*?

Regarding the "no fun" objection to ego dissolution, I'm reminded
here of a time when I was at a coffee shop and I overheard a young
woman reveal some "juicy gossip" to her friend across the table. After
receiving the news, her friend laughingly and excitedly responded with:
"What would life be without *drama?*" And she said it in a way implying
that there would be no fun at all without drama, which is really the ego,
because you can't have drama without the ego. Well, if she had asked me,
I would have informed her that life would be a lot *more* fun, interesting,
and enjoyable because there would be a lot less suffering in the world, so
much so that war, oppression, and social injustice would be things of the
past. Then we could focus a lot more time and energy on healing the
wounds of the planet and on our creativity, such as manifesting a safer,
more interesting, enriching, and spiritual world where everyone prospers
according to their own *uniqueness*. You know, you don't have to give up
your specialness just because you give up your ego. It's simply a coming
to consciousness that everyone else is special too. Relationships would be
deeper, more passionate, and more meaningful. The outer human condition would reflect an inner state of peace, joy, compassion, and unconditional love. So, you know, *that's* what I would've told that young woman if
she had asked me what life would be without drama. Now as for the "self-
esteem" defense for keeping parts of the ego intact...

True Self-esteem vs. pseudo self-esteem.

Anorexia is absent among all tribal cultures. Ruminate on this for a moment. It's a disease that is germane to our "civilized" society. We are programmed to feel shame and guilt from early on when we don't measure up to others around us. This is because it is the ego that projects hurt onto others just as it is the ego that identifies with pain so deeply. Every negative emotion you've ever felt such as sadness, frustration, depression, rejection, anger, or humiliation has been a symptom of your wounded *ego*.

Egoic self-esteem forms when the child compares knowledge, abilities, talents, skills, strengths, looks, parental status, etc. to the same in other children. It begins when the child says to his schoolmate, "I can do this better than you can." This is a perfectly normal and healthy state of ego development in the child.

Low self-esteem is the result of the child saying, "I'm not good enough to do this," or "I could never do that." As the child matures into an adult, whether she develops high or low self-esteem, she remains trapped in the egoic mind and constantly compares the self—as either inferior or superior—to the abilities, talents, or success of others. This doesn't mean that you shouldn't strive to do great things. But it's a travesty to define who you *are* based on simply what you *do* or what you accomplish in the world of form. Remember, you are a human *being*, not a human *doing*. Instead of achieving great things to acquire great self-esteem, when you transcend the ego you will have automatically inherited true Self-esteem and therefore will naturally *be* great. Subsequently, you will effortlessly and happily achieve great things because the things—the *form*—will be a reflection, an outer *extension* of who you are *at your core*. When you already know and fully realize that you are divinely *great*, you begin achieving because you *choose* to, and are therefore implementing your previously untouched power of free will. Then you can achieve anything your heart desires without the immense pressure to show everyone "who you are." Ergo, all your achievements will manifest without anxiety, drama, or *stress*. On the other hand, when the underlying impetus for your achievements is to prove to yourself and others that by doing something you perceive to be "great," you will suddenly become worthy of greatness, then you will be achieving because you *need* to, because of an unconscious egoic compulsion, not because of a choice.

Know that nothing you ever *do* in the world of form can define who you *are*. No doubt, the ego has taken countless individuals all the way to the top of their fields, but with what consequences? Because the brain is polarized (two hemispheres, eight lobes), any success you achieve using brain-based manifestation may indeed get you what you want, but will also bring you a good deal of what you *don't* want right along with it. True Self-esteem is not derived from identification with accomplishments in the world of form. It is acquired from the Self-realization that you are a divine and eternal being.

In the media, I sometimes hear references to how important the ego is for the "success" of people in fields that require us to be competitive, such as in business or sports. Recently, I heard a commentator make a reference to Muhammad Ali, arguably the greatest boxer of all time. Ali's success was attributed directly to his giant ego, which, of course, had a lot to do with it. But I ask you: Where is his giant ego now?

Arrogance, haughtiness, and boasting about one's own accomplishments and/or abilities are dysfunctional behavioral characteristics indicative of pseudo self-esteem. Magnanimity and humility, on the other hand, characterize an individual with true Self-esteem. Pseudo self-esteem is an attempt to validate and compensate for something that is false, and therefore will always ends in suffering. But know that suffering at the hands of the ego has nothing to do with God or the universe punishing you for being arrogant, haughty, or self-absorbed. It has to do with your own inner transformation from your pseudo self into your authentic Self. This is indeed the purpose of *all* human suffering. This "self-destruct" mechanism encoded in every ego is so that the self ultimately has *no choice* but to go deeply with*in* and evolve into a being of higher consciousness—just as the caterpillar has no choice but to create its chrysalis so that it can evolve into the butterfly.

Because the current human is so identified with his own polarized ego, his understanding of basic human psychology is *upside down*. To wit: Muhammad Ali's esteem was false when he was a boxer, i.e. an over-compensation for something he feared on a deeper, unconscious level. Now his esteem is true. The time has come for Homo sapiens to achieve by *choice* rather than by a "pre-programmed software" called the ego. We simply don't need to go through the suffering process anymore. We have already evolved past this point. But you can only do this through ego transcendence. True Self-esteem is infinitely more powerful than pseudo self-esteem, because it is firmly rooted in the *heart*. Because the ego is the pseudo self, it can never bring you what you want without dire consequences. Dramas, conflicts, lawsuits, stress, depression, heartbreaks, physical diseases, and premature deaths are the heavy prices that countless individuals have paid throughout history for their ephemeral "successes." But this is not a very efficient way of achieving. There is a better way.

The Next Human will not strive to be better than the other for the sheer purpose of receiving a fleeting and *pseudo* sense of esteem. Instead, he will strive for personal achievement because of the enjoyment he receives by contributing to society and helping his fellow humans, not because he derives a sense of who he *is* out of it.

The ego is both offensive and offended.

The true value of a human being is determined primarily by how he has attained liberation from the self.

—Albert Einstein

At its worse, the ego's controlling, narcissistic, greedy nature is personified in the likes of corrupt politicians, dictators and despots, Wall Street bankers, corporate executives, and others who are motivated by one thing: *power*. It is this elitist minority who sparked the Occupy Wall Street protest movement of 2011. The Golden Rule interpreted by the ego is: "He who has the gold, rules." Consequently, it is these egoic power players who are currently running the world. But the balance of power is about to *shift*.

As mentioned, Einstein understood the importance of ego transcendence or what he called "liberation from the self." He observed the insanity that was perpetuated by the collective egoic mind during the aggressive expansion of the Nazi regime throughout Europe in the fourth and fifth decades of the 20th century. Hitler's incredibly dense ego demanded "breathing room" for Germany, an example of the ego's insatiable lust for power and dominion over the will of others. The need for power in an individual will always be contingent upon the density of his or her ego, which varies from person to person. Furthermore, the bigger the ego, the less it will enjoy being singled out because if there's one thing the ego doesn't like, it's hearing about its*elf*. If someone with a super dense ego has purchased this book (anything is possible), then he probably wouldn't have gotten this far. He may have either said, "This is just awful," or "What a load of crap," or "I can't stomach this." Or he would have put the book through a paper shredder by now.

For those with denser egos, any spiritually enlightening material will either not make any sense to them, or it will be perceived as a *threat*. But even that's fine because this book was not written for them. They would never glean anything from it anyway. It was written for those who are ready and *willing* to evolve. Readiness and willingness is vital for personal transformation. The egoic humans will awaken eventually, but it will happen according to their timeframe dictated by the free wills of their higher Selves. In the meantime, their egoic madness can serve as a catalyst for your own awakening. As long as you don't *react* to their insanity, you won't allow yourself to remain trapped on the wheel of karma.

The *law of karma* or "law of cause and effect" is a reciprocal relationship with the universe of duality. It's the way in which every action seamlessly reacts upon you, the initiator of that action, either reinforcing your current identity, or altering it. This karmic wheel will continue to spin indefinitely until you realize that you're the one perpetuating it because of your conditioned reactionary state. Most people think of karma as "what happens *to* them" but karma is really manifested by how you *react* to what happens to you. This perpetuates the egoic patterns, keeping you in the continuous flow of reincarnation or "re-incarceration."

Personal attachments and repeated personal offenses are both created and felt, initiated and received, by the ego. The ego feeds on the *hurt*. This is why most humans are so easily offended. The very word "offend" implies aggressiveness. It's nothing less than a personal intrusion or *attack* that the ego allows to trespass over an unprotected boundary. It's the sign of the victim rearing its ugly head. Thus, whenever you become offended, you are playing the victim by allowing the initiator of the offense, the other's ego, to offend/attack *your* ego. It's as if you say to the offensive individual, "I have received your attack...thank you very much, may I have another?" Unlike bullying, offenses are much more benign comments that usually aren't directed toward a sole individual, but typically come from public figures, movies, the media, or other sources that are addressed to a group.

For example, if you're gay and a political figure makes a controversial remark about gay people, you may say, "I am so offended by what he said!" Yes, you are. But only because you've allowed yourself to *receive* the offense. In martial arts, the first lesson you are taught is how to protect your body from an incoming blow. You are taught to *block* the punch or kick. If you don't, then you're allowing that blow to land on your body, causing pain and suffering. Similarly, when you observe your ego being offended by another's words, see through the veil of unconsciousness, transcend the ego, and understand that no one can hurt or offend the authentic Self, only the psuedo self. Then you'll be exercising free will and you won't be creating unnecessary suffering for yourself. Think of it this way: If someone says something either intentionally or unintentionally demeaning about you or anyone else, then it's only coming from the ego. You may recall this saying from childhood: "Don't stoop to their level." This is the level of the unconscious, overly aggressive egoic mind.

You are not separate from life.

Ultimately, there is no such thing as "my consciousness." There is only consciousness. As soon as you say "my," you separate yourself *from* consciousness, and therefore you delete yourself from existence. Know that you *are* consciousness. Similarly, there is no such thing as "my life." There is only *life*. When you precede the word "life" with a *my*, you suddenly are no longer a part of life, and therefore do not exist. This logic further substantiates that the ego, the "I," or "my" is a delusion. It is the pseudo self.

The goal of any authentic spiritual teaching is not to destroy the ego but to dissolve the experienced illusion of ego-identification, the concept that we are unchanging agents of awareness. We transcend this illusion by learning to experience the ego as a pseudo identity that's based on the fallacy that "my life" is something real. For the Next Human, all aspects of our identity emerge from within the awareness field of the inner Self, a Self which doesn't need to seek out awareness because it is already aware, a Self which doesn't need to *possess* because it is already *whole*.

Practice presence, not patience.

Instead of practicing patience, practice *presence*. Patience will come naturally with presence, but patience will always be something that the mind perceives as something more for it *to do*, and therefore is an *action* rather than a state of being. Presence, on the other hand, is non-action. It's allowing the universe to *present* itself to you as *it is*. This is your primary purpose in life. Everything else is secondary. When you can live every moment in the eternal Now, you won't need to be patient. You'll simply *be*.

Meditation transcends the ego.

You are neither your body nor your mind. Understanding this fully is the key to enlightenment and the gateway to the unmanifested nonduality of the Source. The Next Human will know that no number of opinions or achievements she can tack on to her brain will increase her sense of Self-worth. The primary aim of any useful spiritual practice is to deconstruct the attachment to thoughts, opinions, accomplishments, and beliefs with which your ego identifies. This will accelerate the transformation from your pseudo self to your authentic Self.

Know that the ego cannot exist in the Now. And this is the importance of daily meditation. It will also help you to relinquish your most engrained opinions. Through meditation you can come to see that the only thing that makes you suffer is your ego. Sitting quietly for a few minutes each day will help you to silently observe the egoic mind as it is. When you learn to allow the mind to calm and relinquish its thoughts, you will realize that everything you've wrapped your sense of "I" around will dissolve. Transcendence is moving beyond the mind into an eternal place of nonduality. When you cherish our own ideas and concepts, you believe them to be real and relevant, and then you process them into the pseudo self as feelings of inferiority or superiority. When you live in this egoic matrix of the mind, you are identifying with a polarized *non-reality*. To cherish your opinions, therefore, is to be imprisoned by your own mind.

Know that you don't have to be *of* this world to be *in* it. And you don't have to *mind* what happens in order to *care* what happens. This means having so much compassion for the world and every life form in it, that you won't contribute to a scintilla of the anxiety-ridden drama that plays out on the world stage. It's about loving the way things *are*, rather than holding back your love from the universe until it brings you what you want.

Cosmic consciousness is the deeper reality of who you are. It is the field of infinite love and intelligence that is whole. You can easily access it anytime you want by transcending the conditioned thought patterns of the mind. Presence is the key. You may have already discovered presence through extreme sports such as mountain climbing, skydiving, surfing, race car driving, gymnastics, or downhill skiing. Most people find presence through daily meditation. It's the place where thoughts dissolve like snowflakes in your palm. But however you choose to get there, here, when you finally discover the timeless presence of the One, you will also reunite your Self with the Source of the All.

Because we've all been conditioned to constantly think about this or that, assailed from birth by the stimuli of radio, television, the Internet, and most recently, smartphones, we've forgotten as a species what it's like to be in a place of peace or *non-thought*. If you've never meditated before, or have tried but failed to achieve non-thought, don't worry. With daily practice, you can find a place of peace and stillness from within.

The reason why so many people find it difficult to enter the realm of nonduality is because they're simply trying too hard to get there. The first rule about meditation is that there *are no rules* about meditation. In Zen Buddhism, *zazen* is a meditation that is simply called "sitting." The very word *meditating* implies that you are doing something and this, of course, defeats the entire purpose of meditation. So, don't try to meditate with the intention of doing it properly or improperly. The important thing is that you practice *sitting*, preferably at the same time and in the same space, every day.

You may choose to light some candles and incense. Turn off all external stimuli such as the television, computer, and your cell phone. Close your eyes and focus your attention on a mantra, your breath, or your body. Breathe deeply through your nose and out through your mouth three times. Returning to a peaceful state of non-doing, non-thought, non-action, and non-static is achieved only by *allowing* it to happen. Do not resist your thoughts. Simply allow them to play out and silently observe them as if they were clouds floating by. Do this until your thoughts naturally, on their own volition, begin to subside. Be still, be quiet, and slowly enter the realm of non-form. You may want to repeat the mantra, "I am," or you may choose to repeat the sacred mantra "Aum." You may also merge the two together, such as with "I am. I ammm. I auummmmm. I auuhhmmmmm. Auuhhhhmmm. Auuuhhhhhhmmmmmmm." In ancient Sanskrit, the three phonemes, *a, u,* and *m,* represent the beginning, duration, and dissolution of the universe. The sound "Aum" or "Om" is the reflection of the absolute reality, the nondual, eternal One. Do this every day and watch your anxiety, stress, and nervous tension dissolve.

If you enter into a meditation with thoughts such as "I have to meditate," or "I have to remove my thoughts," then automatically you've created something more for your mind to *do*. If you try and suppress the mind, it will naturally push back because if it didn't, that would mean the end of the mind. Understand that the mind is only a *tool*, like the body. You are already complete without your mind because before the mind came into being, you already *are*.

Transcendence practices.

⊛   When you observe your mind craving superficial and material things, ask yourself, "Do I really *need* this? Do I want this because it makes me feel superior to others?" If the answer is the latter, then choose to let the desire go.

⊛   Whenever you observe yourself being offended by something someone says, stop. Know that the only reason they are verbally "attacking" you is so they can feel superior to you. See through the veil that is the ego and you won't allow yourself to suffer.

⊛   The next time you find yourself using the words "my life," stop. Be aware that you've just allowed your ego to "possess life" and therefore created a false separation between life and *you*.

⊛   When you find your inner dialogue comparing or contrasting another to your status in life, *stop*. Be still. Watch what your ego is doing. Become a silent observer. Don't resist, just watch. Understand that this is your ego's need to feel either superior or inferior to others and nothing more. Know that everyone is equal. No one is intrinsically better or worse than you.

⊛   When your inner dialogue says things such as, "Why do these things keep happening *to* me?" or "It's the story of my life," or, "It's always something," *stop*. Be still and observe the ego silently from a detached, higher perspective. Understand that this negative reinforcement is creating and substantiating your reality, and the reason the problems keep happening *to* you is because of this inner dialogue, and nothing more.

⊛ When you observe your thoughts obsessing over a negative perception of yourself such as your intelligence, competence, skills, talents, or looks, *stop*. Be still. Observe these thoughts from a place of presence. Know that these obsessive thoughts are keeping you perpetually *stuck* in a state of dissatisfaction that stems from a false self-perception. Your reality is constantly being created by this negative reinforcement.

⊛ When you become dissatisfied or frustrated about the way life is "treating" you, *stop*. Be still. Meditate. Go within and know that you're only playing the victim to a mysterious "force" that is falsely perceived as a punisher. There is no punishing God and no punishing universe. There is only your egoic perception based on pre-conditioned thought patterns. Transcend these negative mental patterns and you will have freed your mind.

THE PHANTOM SELF
REVEALING YOUR UNKNOWN FACE

Neo: *Smith?*

Oracle: {nods affirmably} *Very soon he's going to have the power to destroy this world, but I believe he won't stop there. He can't. He won't stop until there's nothing left at all.*

Neo: *What is he?*

Oracle: *He's you, your opposite, your negative, the result of the equation trying to balance itself out.*

Neo: *And if I can't stop him?*

Oracle: *One way or another, Neo, this war is going to end. Tonight the future of both worlds will be in your hands or in his.*

—*The Matrix Revolutions*

There is an esoteric truth that the universe will repeat the same exact situations, same exact conflicts, and same exact problems over and over again until we wake up to the reality that we are the cause *of* them. As the esteemed Spanish philosopher George Santayan warned, "Those who cannot remember the past are condemned to repeat it."[1] As a species, we seem to have collective amnesia.

In 1889, peace activists William Randal Cremer and Frederic Passy formed the Inter-Parliamentary Union (IPU) that, at its peak in 1914, included twenty-four nations. Arbitration, negotiations, and diplomacy were its primary aims in the resolving of international disputes that could lead to war. Despite its best efforts, however, two power blocs emerged because of opposing alliances between the European Great Powers. It was the polarization of these two alliances that led to the first industrialized warfare in history, resulting in the **deaths of 15 million troops and 7 million civilians.**[2]

By the time World War I ended in 1918, the physical, sociological, economic, and psychological carnage it had left in its wake was paralyzing to Europe. As anti-war cries came from all around the world, the First World War was declared to be the "war to end all wars." And the underlying causes leading up to it would not go without a thorough investigation. One of the primary causes identified was the *race to build arms.*

The League of Nations was founded in 1920 as the result of the Treaty of Versailles for the purpose of establishing collective security, disarmament and settling international disputes through negotiation and arbitration. Its membership peaked in 1935 with a total of 58 nations on board. One of the goals of the League was to protect the rights of minority citizens. The League lacked its own army and so it depended on the military might of the Great Powers to enforce its resolutions. This didn't work out so well. Tough sanctions that forced Germany to defer enforcement of the anti-Jewish laws only served to fuel anger and resentment toward the League and ultimately sparked the emergence of the

Nazi Regime led by Adolf Hitler beginning on January 30, 1933. It ended with the horrific **deaths of 66 million people**.[3]

In 1945, after the end of World War II, the United Nations (UN) was founded to replace the failed League of Nations. Like the IPU and the League before it, its purpose was to prevent wars between countries by providing a platform for dialogue. The UN Charter specifically prohibits any war unless it is out of self-defense or when it is sanctioned by the UN Security Council. If these requirements are not met, international law describes it as a "war of aggression."

In January 2003, a CBS poll reported that 63 percent wanted President George W. Bush to find a diplomatic solution rather than go to war with Iraq.[4] Only four nations—the U.S., U.K., Australia, and Poland—participated in the Iraq invasion on March 20, 2003, due to the opposition to it by traditional U.S. allies such as France, Germany, New Zealand, and Canada. On February 13, 2003, a month before the invasion, there were staunch anti-war outcries from around the world and in Rome, a record-breaking three million people assembled in protest. Between January 3 and April 12, 2003, thirty-six million people across the planet took part in nearly 3,000 protests against the Iraq war. The secretary-general of the United Nations, Kofi Annan, said that the war in Iraq was an "illegal act that contravened the UN charter."[5]

After World War II and the Holocaust, the International Military Tribunal at Nuremberg referred to "a war of aggression" as a "supreme international crime."[6] Perhaps no person on the planet is better qualified to identify and describe our crimes in Iraq than Benjamin Ferencz, a former chief prosecutor of the Nuremberg Trials who convicted twenty-two Nazi officers for the deaths of more than one million people in the famous Einsatzgruppen Case. He had this to say about the Iraq war:

> *The United Nations charter has a provision which was agreed to by the United States, formulated by the United States, in fact, after World War II. It says that from now*

*on, no nation can use armed force without the permis-
sion of the UN Security Council. They can use force in
connection with self-defense, but a country can't use
force in anticipation of self-defense. Regarding Iraq, the
last Security Council resolution essentially said, 'Look,
send the weapons inspectors out to Iraq, have them come
back and tell us what they've found—then we'll figure
out what we're going to do. The U.S. was impatient, and
decided to invade Iraq—which was all pre-arranged of
course. So, the United States went to war, in violation of
the charter.*[7]

The purpose for the U.S. invasion of Iraq on March 20, 2003, was to
confiscate weapons of mass destruction (WMDs). Eight years, nine
months, and over $845 billion later, **4,802 coalition troops have vio-
lently perished along with over 100,000 innocent civilians**.[8] The U.K.
and U.S. contended that Iraq possessed WMDs, which we now know was
either an intentional deception on their part, or because of false information reported by the intelligence agencies. Either way, the entire purpose
of the Iraq War was based on a fallacy. It never needed to happen.

When the U.S. violated the United Nations Security Council decision
and declared war without the UN's approval, it undermined and refuted
everything the UN stood for, and because of this left the UN powerless
and ineffectual to carry out its prime directive to ensure peace. The
Inter-Parliamentary Union, League of Nations, and the United Nations
were all formed with the intention of preventing war and maintaining
peace through means of communication, diplomacy, and mediation. And
yet this is where they have all *failed*.

The Iraq War was also called the "war on terror," an oxymoron. War
is terror. You could just as easily call it "war on war" or "terror on terror."
The mere declaration of war against terror implies that it will be never-
ending. How can you win a war when your enemy is a *concept*? Only the
egoic mind is so deluded. Moreover, violent resistance to war/terror will

inevitably feed into the exact same frequency of war/terror and will only serve to perpetuate it. In physics, Newton's *third law of motion* says that "for every action, there is an equal and opposite reaction." In ancient Chinese philosophy it is called the *law of polarity* or "yin yang." In Sanskrit it's called the *law of karma*. "What resists persists" says the *law of attraction*. As we continue to ignore the natural laws of the universe we will continue to reap the consequences. To wit: In the 20th century alone, 219 wars caused the violent *deaths of over 160 million people*.[9,10] And so I ask you: When does the madness *end?*

The war on terror has failed. The war on poverty has failed. The war on drugs has failed. The perpetual "war on this" and "war on that" only expands government bureaucracy, increases our taxes, and empowers the military industrial complex. Ignorance to the natural laws of the universe prolongs the peace that humanity so desperately needs *now*. The incessant war machine that currently plagues our planet underscores the failure of the twelve-decade-long peace movement that began with the Inter-Parliamentary Union in 1989. Retaliation and revenge for one attack after another only feeds into the same volatile, destructive energy. Know that the balancing universe *does not take sides*. From its unbiased perspective, fighting is fighting, resistance is resistance, and reaction is reaction—no matter *whose* side you're on. This means that fighting war with more war, or fighting terror with more terror, will *never* bring peace. The Next Human will intuitively know that when you *push* against a force in this realm of polarity, it tends to push *back*.

Nothing satiates the ego's lust for control more than removing the rights of citizens. If you take a brief look at history, you'll find that dictators have often used fear as a *tactic* to dissolve the personal liberties of the masses. Just before World War II, Adolf Hitler used the fear of communism to drive the German people into the hands of fascism. Benito Mussolini did the same with the Italian people. Similarly today, because of the primal emotions of fear, anger, and revenge toward Islamic extremists for what they did on September 11, 2001, the American people are being driven like herds of sheep into the "securing" arms of Big Gov. bureaucracy. To carry out their agenda of *control*, the constitutional rights of the American people are gradually being reformed through proposed bills and legislative laws. In this way, our rights as citizens are dissolving right in front of our eyes.

The perpetual war against terror is ostensibly being used as a *pretext* for government agencies such as the Transportation Security Administration (TSA) to trample on our liberties—all in the name of "protection." "It totally voids the concept of the Fourth Amendment, searches and prodding and poking…with no permission," said U.S. Congressman Ron Paul in a recent interview on CNN after his son, Senator Rand Paul, was not allowed to board his flight unless he agreed to a pat-down search.[11] Paul stressed that the searches are not voluntary, as the government argues, because Americans are not allowed to take commercial air flights without doing precisely what the government demands. "They trap us into it," Paul said.

Not only does the TSA, as if by rote, treat U.S. senators as potential terrorists, but its agents are also permitted to intimately probe and molest a person's private areas, from six-year-old boys and girls to elderly men and women. And this is all looked upon with complacency because the mind rationalizes, "They are doing this to keep us *safe*, and therefore it's worth the humiliation and violation of our Bill of Rights." But there is no evidence that any of these demeaning molestations are making us any safer. What we do know, however, is that it communicates the message to Big Government that it won't matter how many rights they take away from the people, as long as they do it all in the name of "safety," they'll be able to get away with it.

Today, there is no communication tool more tailor-made to the freedom of speech than the Internet. But recently even this liberty is being threatened by Big Gov. lobbyists who, in the name of "protecting copyrights and the counterfeit of goods," introduced two bills: Protect IP (PIPA) and Stop Online Piracy Act (SOPA) which were crafted to allow

Big Gov. to get court orders requiring Internet service providers to block access to the sites, potentially censoring any and all information published. Fortunately, due to the protest blackouts by Google, Wikipedia, and other Internet giants, these anti-piracy bills did not get passed. There's nothing wrong with protecting copyrights, but when it's done in a blanket-like law that allows Big Government to dictate to you what you can or cannot say on the Internet, that's infringement on your freedom of speech.

But clearly the most damaging of all the recent attempts by Big Government to remove the liberties and civil rights of the American people has come by way of the National Defense Authorization Act for Fiscal Year 2012 (NDAA). In the act, "Section 1021 provides for the possibility of the U.S. military acting as a kind of police force on U.S. soil, apprehending terror suspects—including Americans—and whisking them off to an undisclosed location indefinitely," noted Congressman Paul.[12] Furthermore, any American suspected of "terrorism" will have no right to an attorney, no right to trial, and no day in court—all clear violations of our U.S. Bill of Rights.

In 1789 the American government was fashioned with the intention to secure our rights as citizens, not take them away in the guises of "federal emergencies" or "wars on terror" or "personal safeties" or "copyright infringements." There should be no *loopholes* to our Bill of Rights. Period. Otherwise, it undermines the validity and effectiveness of the entire U.S. Constitution. This is nothing but asinine, egoic-minded deception. If we Americans want the rest of the world to enjoy our democratic way of life, then let's stop occupying their nations and rebuilding them as we see fit, and begin leading by *example*. The first thing we can do is start protecting our *own* rights, without the help of government bureaucracy and power-hungry politicians. We do this peacefully by electing ***all new*** government leaders who are not bought and paid for by the Big Gov. lobbyists and Super PACS for their own greedy self-serving agendas. There is never a reason that government should be allowed—at any time, for any condition, under any pretext—to sidestep, violate, or remove *any* of our rights as citizens. And if it does, then the American people have the duty and the *right to abolish* such an encroaching government and lay the foundation for a *new one*. As founding father Thomas Jefferson so eloquently stated in the American Declaration of Independence:

> *We hold these truths to be self-evident, that all men are created equal, that they are endowed by their Creator with certain unalienable rights, that among these are life, liberty and the pursuit of happiness. That to secure these rights, governments are instituted among men, deriving their just powers from the consent of the governed. That whenever any form of government becomes destructive to these ends, it is the right of the people to alter or to abolish it, and to institute new government, laying its foundation on such principles and organizing its powers in such form, as to them shall seem most likely to effect their safety and happiness.*[13]

And as Jefferson later said, "A government big enough to give you everything you want is big enough to take away everything you have."

A mad, mad world.

In 1999 I was struggling through my ninth straight year of chronic fatigue syndrome. It was also my third year working as an intern at the St. Louis Psychiatric Rehabilitation Center, recording the behavior of patients diagnosed with advanced delusionary schizophrenia. My job as a behavioral technician entailed silently observing the patients and recording their abnormal behaviors for clinical research. I really felt for the patients, some of whom I grew rather close to, even though they were barely aware of my existence. The state was doing its best to rehabilitate them so they could successfully reintegrate with society. I can't recall any that did. I used to wonder how they got there and what had caused this dreadful mental disease known as schizophrenia. I didn't understand how the human mind could get so far removed from what most of us define as reality that it ended up serving as its own hellish prison.

In hindsight, I am grateful for those years I spent working in the psychiatric hospital because they prepared me for the ubiquitous insanity that I would later be observing in society in the years ahead. These mentally dysfunctional behaviors include narcissism, greed, deceit, bullying, judgment, intolerance, bigotry, oppression, hatred, revenge, sadomasochism, and emotional and physical violence. With the exception of narcissism and sadomasochism, these serious dysfunctions of the human psyche are not currently labeled as "mental disorders" by the American Psychological Association (APA) because they are, for the most part, deemed *normal*. And in 2013, even narcissism will no longer be recognized by insurance companies, hospitals, treatment facilities and protocols as a mental disease. According to a recent article in The New York Times,[14] the upcoming revision of the *Diagnostic and Statistical Manual of Mental Disorders*, the DSM-5, does not include "narcissistic personality disorder." Ostensibly, narcissism has become so pervasive in our society that it too is being viewed by our psychological community as perfectly acceptable behavior.

In the film *The Matrix*, Trinity informs Neo that "the Matrix cannot tell you who you are."[15] And so it is the same with the matrix of the mind: the *ego*. In spite of this esoteric truth, however, the current human is so identified with his ego that he simply doesn't know where his pseudo self ends and his true Self begins. A super dense ego, the likes of which can be found in those diagnosed as narcissistic, won't see anything abnormal with the fact that nearly half the human population currently lives below the poverty level, that 2.6 billion are left without access to clean water, and that 80 percent of our species currently lives on less than $10 a day.[16] Moreover, they won't see anything wrong with the fact that millions more of our fellow humans continue to be violently slaughtered and maimed in needless wars. Instead, they will continue to live out their materialistic lives, apathetic to the suffering masses around them.

When we finally reach the end of our tireless search for truth, we find ourselves face to face with the pervasiveness of society's madness and collective dysfunction. It is here where we finally discover that the enemy was never elusive, and never who we imagined him or her to be. At the moment of our Self-realization, we understand unequivocally that the enemy was always *us*.

The phantom self.

Just below the threshold of consciousness lies an opposite, a negative, a hidden self. The eminent psychologist Carl Gustav Jung believed that this negative self or *shadow* was created during ego development in childhood, when we are at some point deemed worthless, inferior, unacceptable, or inadequate. Subsequently, the pain from our wounded ego manifests as a cover-up process to prove to others that we are not these terrifying things. When we don't want to face these feelings about ourselves, we *project* them onto others by way of moral deficiency. In his book, *Aion*, Jung sums up the shadow by writing, "Projections change the world into the replica of one's own unknown face."[17]

This shadow of the ego also manifests in every human as an emotional body, energy field, and no doubt DNA encoding. Because every thought you have is a simple form of energy, when toxic, negative thoughts are allowed to accumulate, they fester, ferment, and become emotional in nature. If ignored or denied over time, these darker emotions tend to cling to your psyche and become tar-like and parasitical. The more your ego represses these primitive thoughts and feelings, the darker and denser they become. Left unresolved, they inevitably manifest as anxiety, depression, disgust, hatred, anger, and *rage*. In the dungeons of the subconscious, these shadowy, repugnant aspects of the ego actually *feed* on emotional pain. Alternately masochistic and sadistic, this pain parasite preys on human hosts.

Jung viewed his collective unconscious as a secondary psyche, consisting of archetypes and imagery that were impersonal in nature and concurrent in all individuals. Conversely, a primary psyche was defined by Jung's *personal* unconscious which stored our individual memories, repressed fears, and the dark shadows of unresolved pain. Contemporary spiritual teacher Eckhart Tolle also believes in this "dark shadow cast by the ego," which he refers to as the *pain-body*.[18] In his book, *The Power of Now*, he describes it in detail:

> As long as you are unable to access the power of Now,
> every emotional pain that you experience leaves behind
> a residue of pain that lives on in you. It merges with the
> pain from the past, which was already there, and be-
> comes lodged in your mind and body. This, of course,
> includes the pain you suffered as a child, caused by the
> unconsciousness of the world into which you were
> born."[19]

Tolle further elaborates that the pain-body is a "negative energy field," and that some "can drive their hosts to suicide."[20,21] Like Tolle, I see the pain-body as a synthesis of personal pain that we unknowingly conceal from others based on our individualized repressions *and* a collective pain that resides within the energy field of a hive mind. I also view the pain-body as a psychic parasite and as a *physical* manifestation of the *mental* ego.

The more you are identified with your emotions, the more they become a prominent part of the physical body. The Austrian psychiatrist Wilhelm Reich extended the consequences of psychoanalysis to the body, especially to the muscles and visceral functions. He believed suppressed emotion can be stored in the body as bioenergetic tension that leads to the formation of neuro-muscular "armor."[22] William James, the father of American psychology, believed that emotions were the body's reaction to stimuli. Like Reich and James, I believe that fear does not precede a bodily reaction, fear *is* the bodily reaction. Therefore, the more you identify with your emotions, the more they become an intricate part of the physical body, and the more your body and your emotions merge into *one*. Consequently, a prolonged identification *with* or attachment *to* fear-based emotions such as intolerance, judgment, hatred, contempt, and anger, will inevitably manifest in the body as physical pain and disease.

Furthermore, I see both the ego and the pain-body as a DNA encoding or "program" that has been passed on in every human born into this world since the dawn of our species. And just as the software program on your computer performs its functions identically in every other copy of the same version, the basic programming of the ego and its shadow, the pain-body, will essentially be *cloned* in all humans. This "unknown face" that resides in the current human is what I call the *phantom self.*

You create your own judgment day.

> *Do not judge others, and you will not be judged. Do not*
> *condemn others, or it will all come back against you.*
> *Forgive others, and you will be forgiven.*
>
> —Gospel of Luke 6:37

None of us likes to admit that we are flawed in some way. When we are made to feel inferior, we tend to do everything in our power to keep these weaknesses out of sight. Accentuating the opposite of what we secretly despise in ourselves is what the ego's shadow, the phantom self, is all about. It frequently projects its own inferiority onto others by judging them. "He's a moron," or "She's hideous," the phantom says. Whatever the ego projects onto others via its shadow it will always, *always* secretly despise in it*self.*

For example, if you ask someone for their honest opinion about you and you don't like their answer, your ego is projecting its shadow, the phantom. Any time you have an emotional opinion about someone you don't know, you're projecting your phantom self. If you feel misunderstood all the time, you're projecting your phantom self. When you finish sentences for another, you're projecting your phantom self. Whenever you stereotype, condemn, blame, judge, or hate others for whatever reason, you will be projecting your phantom self.

The above scripture in the Gospel of Luke makes an astute observation in the psychology of human behavior. When you judge another person, your phantom self will be projecting your own unconscious issues *outwardly*. These unaddressed issues are themselves a judgment of one's own self, or more accurately put, a false perception of the self stemming from repressed trauma.

Judgment Day is not a time in the future when a judgmental, egoic God will look over your records of a previously lived life and lay down an appropriate punishment for you because of your mistakes or sins. Properly inferred, this scripture defines the natural law of judgment that can only come from the phantom self. When you fully understand the phantom, you will realize that it's simply impossible to judge another without first judging your*self*. The judgment doesn't come after the fact, and especially not after your life.

So judging yourself is a prerequisite for judging another. Because this self-judgment gets projected onto others automatically, the soul will continue to attract the same trauma to itself either in this life or the next, until it awakens to the truth that it alone is responsible for creating its own reality, and ending the cycle of karma. Continuing to *judg*e others only insures that you will reincarnate your soul into another lifetime of suffering. But, again, this is not punishment. It's only necessary to draw you *in*ward, toward the spiritual dimension. Just as you're more likely to wake up from a nightmare than a pleasant dream, you'll be more likely to awaken to your true Self through suffering than you would without it.

In essence, the phantom acts as a *mask*, a false persona that's created by the wounded ego to hide whatever it fears as too painful to accept. When an inner conflict is not made conscious, it's destined to manifest as your reality. The phantom keeps the past alive with its pain projections, and thus the cycle of pain is perpetuated, over and over, until it's made fully conscious. Only then can the pain be faced and dissolved.

When you finally learn to exercise compassion for your Self and forgive your Self rather than judge your Self, the other will automatically be forgiven. Because *the other* is always a mirror reflection of *you*, forgiving your Self means that you've already shown compassion, non-judgment, and forgiveness for the other. Furthermore, know that no priest, no pastor, no rabbi, no imam, no dogma, no religion, and no deity has the power to grant you forgiveness. Only *you* have that power.

Walking the straight and narrow path.

The golden mean is the desirable middle between two extremes, one of excess and the other of deficiency.

—Aristotle

When you point a finger at the other, the remaining three will be pointing at *you*. The next time you rush to judgment about someone, stop and ask yourself, "When is the last time I was guilty of that exact same thing?" If you're completely honest with yourself, you may be surprised to learn of your hypocrisy.

Judgment cloaks itself in many forms. Blame, intolerance, self-righteousness, condemning, criticizing, and complaining are all forms of judgment. They are projected by the phantom so that it can feel a little better about itself by mercilessly deriding others. It's a subtle attempt by the ego to take power away from the other by verbalizing distorted and repressed beliefs that are unconsciously rooted in your unknown face, the phantom self. The type of criticism I'm referring to here is not of the constructive type but rather has to do with contemptuous derision that ultimately serves no purpose other than to mentally bully the other person. Simply put, it's a personal *attack*.

Like destructive criticism, complaining serves the ego's purpose to feel superior to others, to justify its existence, and little else. When you complain, you are blaming someone else or life in general for your problems. Chronic complainers complain about life all the time as if they are superior *to* it. When you complain, what you're really doing is vocalizing your own suppressed feelings of inferiority in relationship to the world in which you live. You're playing the role of *victim* to life, rather than honoring or respecting what *is*. Chronic complaining is the mind's way of venting all the negative thoughts that it thinks on a daily basis. Psychologists have estimated that we think about 60,000 thoughts in a given day. Well, you can probably guess what percentage of these thoughts is negative if you're a chronic complainer. Garbage in means garbage out.

Chronic condemners run roughshod over everyone in their path because they've convinced themselves that they're superior life forms, and will frequently remind you that they have a better idea, a better solution, a better way of doing things than what is currently in place. Nothing that already *is* ever meets with their approval. They simply know better than everyone else, always.

We have observed the result of the projection of blame, destructive criticism, and condemnation consistently in the U.S. government where a rigid party polarity has consistently manifested as gridlock between the Democrats and the Republicans in both the House and Senate for the last decade. Blame always comes from both sides. We have seen congressmen and senators placing their allegiance to party principles before what's truly in the best interest of the country. With the exception of only a few, our government leaders have become political automatons, walking and talking robots that can't seem to get past their party's ideology, and as a result, the entire nation suffers.

While "Rome burns to the ground," the members of the two-party system continue to argue, ranting on incessantly, and refusing to compromise or respect the other party's point of view. Lost in the static of their egoic minds, most politicians today don't give a bean about doing what is right, they're only concerned about *being* right. After President Obama's health care plan initially passed in 2010, several angry Republicans actually sent death threats to their Democratic counterparts. Yes, *death threats* to those in favor of providing free *health care* to the masses. And the Democrat, just like the Republican, continuously dismisses whatever the other party says simply because the other party has said it. As a result of this maddening polarization, little gets accomplished and few *real* problems are being solved.

There is currently a passionate divide in American politics today that is so emotionally charged, both sides seem to be living in two different sets of reality. But as long as the legislators remain emotionally entangled in their own opinions, continue to speak *past* one another rather than *to* one another, they will only widen the rift. Presence, respect, understanding, and non-emotional detachment rather than egoic entanglement is required for government leaders in *all* nations to reach compromise, cooperation, and mediation in the political arena. Entrenched opinions will only constrain the nation in divisiveness and polarity extremism. The Next Human will abolish the behemoth two-party system in the U.S.A. because she will want to vote for a *person* rather than a "party puppet" who's bought-and-paid-for by special interest groups and lobbyists with their own self-serving, egoic agendas.

We can also observe the phantom blame game going on between atheistic science and conservative religion. In recent years, a fair number of atheists—some being prominent scientists—have written books attacking religion and God. They've declared war on religion, war on God, declaring it all to be delusional, the reason behind our countless wars, and the cause for most of society's problems. In the process of their zealous recklessness, however, they've ignored the spiritual teachings that lie in the heart of all religions. Perhaps it's not the belief in God that's been the cause of war but the over-zealousness in *defense* of one's own God. This utterly insane "my God is greater than your God" mentality must be transcended if we're to bring an end to radical extremism on all sides.

Psychologically, there is no difference between this finger-pointing behavior coming from the extreme left of science and the finger-pointing coming from the creationists on the extreme right of Judeo-Christian theology. These creationists believe in the book of Genesis literally. They believe that the earth was created in six days and that it has been in existence for only 6,000 years. They don't believe in evolution at all. They attack the validity of science and ignore all the evidence it has brought to the table on the subject of creation. This extremist point of view from the creationists is a direct antithesis to the atheistic "God is the cause of all our problems" point of view. It is the exact same projection of phantom blame but polarized to other extreme. The creationist, like the atheist, dismisses whatever the other says simply because the other has said it. One polarity's theory blindly ridicules and diminishes the other polarity's theory. But it's still only *theory*. Neither side is consciously seeking the truth because their egoic agendas cloud their sensibilities. Their aim is only to cram their opinions down the throats of their adversaries. They seek to *wrong* their "enemy" so that they can, in turn, be *righted*.

At this point you may be asking, "What if one side *is* right and the other *is* wrong in a debate? Doesn't the mere fact that one side is *right* justify its zeal?" Try not to think of disputes as one side being right and the other being wrong. To the Next Human, both sides are right based on their individual perspectives. Everyone clings to their own truth based on their own uniquely conditioned understanding of reality. Just because you have a different *view* of the world than your neighbors doesn't mean that they are wrong. This is why people argue, fight, create conflicts, and cause **wars**, because the ego says, "You are wrong and I am right, and therefore you are my enemy." To the Next Human, this is utter madness.

When we become egoically *wrapped up* in our opinions, we are no longer in control of them, our opinions control *us*. Consequently, rational thinking and sensible reasoning is abandoned in exchange for zeal and provocation. Extremism, no matter which side is taken, is the path to *evil*. You never see a terrorist with a moderate political stance, do you?

The Next Human will always chose the *middle way*, the straight and narrow path in between the two extremes. This is how you transcend polarity, and this is the way, the *tao*, to lasting peace.

Intolerance is insanity.

When they kept on questioning him, he straightened up and said to them, 'If any one of you is without sin, let him be the first to throw a stone at her.'

—Gospel of John 6:37

The Next Human will never be intolerant of another human. She will know instinctively that we are all One, that we are all in this together, and that we need each other alive to thrive. When you view the other as a "foreign entity," as the ego does, you are stunting your growth and preventing your awakening. For the Next Human, the entire population of the planet will be viewed as a "human family," where every single One is treated with equal respect, equal rights, and unconditional love.

Intolerance from racism, homophobia, and bigotry are forms of deep-seated hatred for another human being. This hatred toward the other is an egoic suppression of the boundless compassion of the *heart.* When the ego projects the phantom, either individually or collectively, it will judge another human based on religion, race, creed, culture, ethnicity, gender, sexuality, looks, status, and past mistakes. In so doing, it desensitizes and diminishes a soul into a mental concept that has nothing to do with reality. It does this because of a suppressed fear that one is *inferior* to the person being judged.

The phantom self doesn't tend to delve too far beneath the surface of things. It sizes up another human from a very limited and narrow-minded perspective. Just as Narcissus was infatuated with his own surface reflection, the very embodiment of the phantom gleans just enough from surfaces alone to reinforce its superficial judgment. Intolerance is the way it compensates for what it unconsciously feels it personally lacks on an inner level, thus it is ultimately a form of *self-hatred*. Thus before you can hate the other you must first hate yourself. In every way that the ego projects itself via the phantom, an unknown hatred of the *self* will be lurking behind the veil.

A prime example of human intolerance was displayed in a 2010 debate over a Muslim mosque being constructed near Ground Zero. The debate was extremely polarized, reflecting the collective Islamophobia that has run rampant in the U.S. since 9/11. On September 8, 2010, the leader of the Islamic community center, Imam Feisal Abdul Rauf, was interviewed on CNN and had this to say about the debate:

> *The battlefront is not between Muslims and non-Muslims. The real battlefront is between moderates on all sides of all the faith traditions and the radicals on all sides...the radicals actually feed off each other and in some kind of existential way need each other, and the more that the radicals are able to control the discourse on one side, it strengthens the radicals on the other side and vice versa.*[23]

There is a profundity of insight in this statement. I couldn't describe the polarity of the ego any more succinctly. What Imam Rauf is saying here is that the Muslim or non-Muslim moderates are not the cause of terrorism, but rather the extremists on *both* sides. The mosque protestors exemplified the ego's pre-programmed directive to feel *superior* to the other by actively seeking divisiveness and separation between *it* and its "nemesis." This "feeding frenzy" described by the Imam is rooted in a fear-based reaction that is currently prevalent within America's Tea Party and conservative *right*. This very same right-winged outcry fueled the support for America to declare war in Iraq, Afghanistan, and now potentially in Iran. Remember, the ego can only empower itself through an *adversary*.

The mosque controversy became even more polarized when prominent politicians chimed in. Rick Lazio, a Republican candidate for New York governor, questioned whether Imam Rauf might have links to "radical organizations." And former House Speaker Newt Gingrich depicted the Cordoba Initiative, the organization behind the mosque, as "deliberately insulting" in their attempt to build a monument to Muslim victory near the site of the twin towers.[24]

But all this finger-pointing was for naught. Instead of rushing to judgment, if these paranoid politicians would have taken the time to do their homework, they would have learned that Imam Rauf is a *Sufi*, and the Cordoba Initiative is a multi-national, multi-faith effort to dramatically improve relations between people of *all* cultures and religions. Hence their mission is not to foster hatred and tensions between Muslims and Christians but, contrarily, to create a "prosperous center of intellectual, spiritual, cultural and commercial life."[25]

Furthermore, Sufism contrasts sharply with the extremist beliefs of jihadists and conservative Muslims. It is a pluralistic incarnation of Islam, accessible to the learned and the ignorant, the faithful, and *nonbelievers*. Sufism is a much more progressive version of Islam that allows far more freedom to women. It is clear to me that we should be supporting and encouraging Imam Rauf and his Sufi followers, not *alienating* them.

On July 22, 2011, there were two sequential terrorist attacks in the cities of Oslo and Utoya, Norway. They were planned and executed by Anders Behring Breivik, an Internet blogger with right-wing extremist views who participated for years in online forum debates over Muslim immigration into Europe. Breivik expressed his Islamophobic ideas by taking the role of "knight in shining armor" to preserve a Christian Europe and restore the historic Middle Age crusades against Islam. He also espoused extremist and xenophobic views stemming from numerous other militant ideologies such as right-wing populism, ultra-nationalism, cultural conservatism, far-right Zionism, and Serbian paramilitarism.[26,27] This is an example of the potential dangers of *all* extremist views, no matter what ideology they stem from. Extremism is ultimately the cause of terrorism, whether it comes from a Muslim extremist or a Christian extremist.

After his arrest, Breivik was diagnosed with paranoid schizophrenia, concluding that he had been psychotic at the time of the attacks and was therefore criminally insane. But perhaps insanity should not be limited to those who go the full length to carry out their terrorist plans. The insanity that is terrorism always begins with a single thought. That *thought* is of intolerance for another person—which, of course, is the phantom's projection of a seething hatred of one*self*. Intolerance for another human or group of humans simply because they share a differing belief or opinion is, in and of itself, *insane*. It is an obliviousness to the reality that you are twisted, deceived, deluded, and motivated by the dark emotions of your phantom self.

"The devil made me do it," is a defense that frequently comes from those who perform egregious acts and then don't fully understand *why* they did it. Taken over by the "phantom devil," they unconsciously bring harm and suffering to others around them. Because they *know not what they do* they are ultimately not responsible for their acts. However, they are also subject to the laws of karma. Therefore, society will determine an appropriate punishment in accordance with its laws.

In a sense, *all* criminals such as thieves, murderers, rapists, terrorists, and the like—in this context—are insane when they commit their heinous acts, not only the "Anders Breiviks" of the world who are diagnosed with delusionary schizophrenia. Violating the rights of other humans by robbing them of their life savings, sexually abusing them, or murdering them, is reducing the human being to the same conceptual level as an inanimate object. And that's as delusional as it gets. If we truly want to bring an end to terrorism—and all violent criminal acts—we must begin by *evolving past* the phantom self veiled within each and every one of us, one soul at a time. There is no other way.

A shadow of deception.

It is discouraging how many people are shocked by honesty and how few by deceit.

—Sir Noël Peirce Coward

Alcoholics, drug addicts, sex addicts, thieves, hackers, grifters, adulterers, con artists, and others who keep their compulsions out of sight are examples of the deceitful side of the phantom self. These individuals have convinced themselves that they are keeping the truth safely concealed from the world, which may be true for a while, but the truth is also being concealed from them*selves*. When it comes to secrets, it's as if the phantom says, "Take it to the grave."

Once the phantom self has established a track record of successfully deceiving the other—such as with the cheating husband who consistently gets away with his infidelity behind his wife's back—it's a very difficult behavior to alter. The adulterer's phantom will get a euphoric *high* out of pulling the wool over his wife's eyes. Thus the deception cycle will continue. Remember, the ego's prime directive is power *over* the other and its darkest nature is expressed through its need to deceive. Thus, tricking others becomes an addiction, a neurosis, and in some cases even a psychosis, hence the term *pathological liar*.

Some phantom-controlled individuals become so proficient at lying that their entire existence transforms into a living lie. These people couldn't tell the truth if their life depended on it. Contemporary author and psychiatrist M. Scott Peck documents clinical cases of individuals who are narcissistic, apathetic, and deceitful in his book *People of the Lie*. Dr. Peck believes that evil is something we *become* in a desperate attempt to hide from ourselves. He says that "evil is not committed directly, but indirectly as part of a cover-up process," originating "not in the absence of guilt but in the attempt to escape it."[28]

Deception in all its forms is one of the many ways in which the phantom is projected onto the world. If you are keeping secrets from others, then you are denying something much deeper and painful in yourself. Avoidance, or denial of *authentic* suffering, is what the phantom is all about. The deeper the state of denial, the more your unknown face will be projected onto others. Freedom from the phantom self is only possible through an *acceptance* of your dark side, of your shamed secrets.

Memoir 10.20.05.

Shuffling up the street—as if guided by radar—and moving silently toward me is the homeless figure of a man, emerging from a dark alleyway. As he makes his way into moonlight, I can see that he's clearly a vagrant, his stained tuque crumpled on the top of his head, barely concealing a mat of densely packed unwashed hair underneath. I'm in no generous mood tonight but he spots me anyway and as he passes beneath one streetlamp, then another, I've composed myself to sufficiently avoid him. I'm standing in the middle of the thin strip of sidewalk next to a walk light post waiting for it to turn green and the bum, draped in dirty, shredded clothing, is now within feet of me and I get a good look at him: late fifties, lanky, absurdly healthy-looking pink skin, wrinkle-free, and piercing, bright green eyes that seem to *twinkle.*

"Hey, mister, mister, can you help me?" He asks earnestly.

"Nope, sorry, *can't.*" I say, shunning him away with my right hand as if he were a gnat.

"I'm homeless and hungry, sir. Can you help me?" He asks again, desperately.

"Listen, I said *no.*" I moan impatiently while tapping my right foot on concrete and staring at the neon red "don't walk" sign on the opposite side of the street—where I'd rather be.

"Just a few dollars please, sir?" The twinkling hobo presses.

"Can't help you. Don't have any cash on me," I lie.

"Please sir, I'm really hungry, just five dollars so I can get a hot meal."

"I...SAID...NOOOOO!!!!!" I find myself suddenly screaming at the top of my lungs, turning directly into his face, losing my temper completely.

The walk light turns green and I proceed to cross the street away from him. I then turn my head to make sure he's not following me and he's just standing there, staring at me with a calm and compassionate smile. To my amazement, I sense no hostility, no disappointment, and no objection to my emotionally violent behavior. It was as if, well, as if he somehow *expected* it. I continue to walk away from him but before I can successfully escape his eyeshot, he speaks one more time.

"Why are you so *hateful*, sir?" He asks meekly.

I stop and look down at the sidewalk for what seems like a very long time. After pondering what this poor homeless man has just asked me, I respond hesitantly,

"I'm not hateful...I'm just...just being *firm*."

A parasite of pain.

The body's nervous system is designed to be a guide toward evolutionary awareness. This guide, while acting as a means of learning and conditioning, can either escort us toward a perpetuation of our behavior by generating *pleasure*, or it can signal us to halt our behavior by generating *pain*. Thus, we are psychologically and physiologically geared to feel both pain and pleasure. Feedback about what is helpful and what is not appears to be prevalent among all living organisms. This pleasure/pain guidance system helps to keep us within a narrow bandwidth of homeostasis—the internal state of equilibrium within our bodies. We become imbalanced when we deviate from this straight and narrow path. This imbalance sometimes manifests as chronic anxiety or depression, bipolar disorder, obsessive compulsive disorder, panic attacks, and other forms of neuropathy, sociopathy, or psychopathy. Whatever form of imbalance arises, it's designed to prompt us to go deeper within and acknowledge our suffering until we "wake up" asking, "What have I done to *create* this reality?" The pain/pleasure guidance mechanism is what, in the end, serves as an alarm clock for our evolutionary awakening.

Know that pain is not the same as suffering. Pain is temporal, normal, and a necessary impetus for growth. Suffering, on the other hand, is chronic, and seemingly never-ending. Suffering is created when we believe that pain is necessary, pain is good, and pain is our friend. We don't consciously intend to be in pain; we unconsciously *will* it. Chronic pain, whether physical, mental, or emotional, is like an idiot light in your car that flashes "low in oil." It means that something critical to your growth is seriously being ignored in your life and there are psychological issues that need to be addressed before you can move toward healing the mental and physical bodies. Suffering is an incessant state of pain that exists among people who are unconsciously mistaking their pain for pleasure. This is the true nature of the pain-body, and this is why its host doesn't healthily retreat from pain, but instead is drawn to the falsely perceived pleasure of pain, over and over again. When active, the host of the masochistic pain-body will thrive on ridicule, diminishment, abuse, and in some extreme cases, emotional torture.

Until you recognize how the pain-body manifests through you, you will be fooled by it and may easily backslide into unconsciousness whenever it resurfaces. The first step is to realize that you have identified yourself with the pain entity. Think of it as a field of energy that thrives on your self-deprecation, guilt, shame, dejection, anger, hatred, heaviness, anxiety, depression, stress, and fears of impending doom. However it manifests, it will cause you to periodically relive your first trauma at the time when you began your identification with it.

Try to see the pain-body as heavy baggage that you carry around with you. The heavier or denser the pain-body, the more baggage you are carrying, and the easier it is to set it off and bring on an attack. If this is your case, you're like a walking time bomb, hypersensitive and raw to the point where the slightest little tease results in a burning tension that consumes every muscle and bone in your body. Anger swells and adrenaline pumps. The emotional violence is then projected outward onto the other in an inner dialogue that says something like: How dare she say that about me? Does she not know who I *am?* The ego becomes inflamed and feelings of self-diminishment and inferiority are immediately compensated by deeper feelings of hatred and contempt toward the other.

If you are hosting the pain parasite, most of the time it will be dormant. It becomes active when you suddenly feel it very strongly. As in the above example, the pain-body will actually *attract* derisive comments from a friend, co-worker, or partner because it needs to be verbally abused so that it can feed on yet another experience of pain. Know that the pain-body needs food just like you and me. It actually receives a sick pleasure from provoking others so that it can create instant reactions from them. It instinctively knows what works and it knows what buttons to *push*. And if you're the host, you usually won't be aware that the pain-body will be doing any of this at the time. It will make snide and thoughtless comments toward others that they will find terribly offensive but at the time that you're saying these hurtful things, you won't *know* that you're hurting them. And when the pain-body does finally get a reaction from them, it will love it. The whole drama, as long as it can continue, becomes a feeding frenzy. The madness that your pain-body musters up is necessary for its ability to sustain its control over your mind as well as its grip over the minds of others.

As with all egoic projections, complaining about others and blaming them for your own problems will often go hand-in-hand with a dense pain-body. It instinctively knows that it can be successful at keeping the pain alive simply by verbalizing all of its "problems." When you are carrying a heavy pain-body, your pain will always be projected onto another person such as a partner, friend, boss, co-worker, or family member. Many times pain-bodies will project their pain onto public figures, such as government leaders or others in authority. Ex-partners also receive the brunt. "It's her fault that I'm broke and living with my mother," cries the bitter pain-body. So for those carrying around with them all this heavy baggage, their pain is always the fault of the *other* and never the self.

Obsessive thinking also plays a role in reinforcing your addiction to pain and suffering. The mind obsesses on a particular mode of suffering such as when a bulimic vomits up her meals or when a drug addict goes through withdrawals after a weekend binge. This hellish suffering, as bad as it is for the host, prompts the unknown phantom to prompt the host into even *more* binge eating or drug abuse. Or it could be an addiction to drama in relationships and the constant bickering and fighting that manifests with couples who are frequently accusing each other of behavior that could easily be observed by an innocent bystander as *nuts*. When immature behavior doesn't get transcended, you remain psychologically frozen, emotionally arrested at the age of three.

Pain will frequently get replaced with pleasure when it becomes too unbearable and you don't want to address the truth of the matter, which is: *you are addicted to pain.* Unfortunately, most pain-addicts are unaware of the fact that they are suffering at all. I suffered severely for nearly a decade before I acknowledged my emotional pain. And then when it became so unbearable that I could no longer ignore it, I did everything in my power to control it, *suppress* it. But the more resistance I gave my pain-body, the stronger it became, and the more suffering I continued to endure.

The phantom predator.

I classify the pain-body into two categories; the *aggressive* type, and the *passive* type. When I refer to the *aggressive* type, I'm referring to the pain-body type that typically expresses itself onto others in an assertive, *outwardly* way. I call this type the **phantom predator.** The *passive* type, on the other hand, will typically suppress the pain-body *inwardly*, internalizing the suffering. I call this type the **phantom prey.** Although some hosts will alternate between the behavioral patterns defined in both types, usually the individual host will exemplify either one type or the other. It's also important to note here that most phantom predators won't know that they're bullies. Contrarily, all phantom prey hosts won't know that they're victims. I know this may be hard to believe because it's sometimes so obvious to the casual observer, but it's true nevertheless. This is why I also call the pain-body the *phantom self.*

A phantom predator will prefer a violent argument over a civil discussion any day of the week, and will frequently become opinionated during a peaceful conversation just so it can stir up a heated debate. The emotional *charge* that it reaps from the ensuing drama is pure energy for this pain parasite to feed on. In a discussion, it's not the truth it seeks, but rather the energy harvested from *wronging* others while pushing all of their buttons. Bullies or super dense phantom predators who thrive on hurting people both emotionally and physically are unconscious carriers of this psychic parasite. Both types of pain-bodies are attracted to emotional and physical violence displayed in TV shows and movies.

You can recognize a phantom predator simply by looking deeply into the eyes of its host. His or her voice may have a condescending tone to it and he or she will usually be deriding someone or some*thing.* These hosts are impatiently waiting for an excuse, *any* excuse, to provoke an emotional argument so they can sap your energy and feed on your anger. The conversation may begin with them probing for information about you, hoping they can find some "ammunition" with which to diminish you later on. Because the pain-body is deeply rooted in polarity, its host will frequently bring up a topic such as religion or politics so it can create an argument out of it and then take up the opposite side.

When the phantom predator becomes active in you, it will quickly consume your mind until you are one with it. Your entire thought process and sense of self will be completely aligned with its agenda. The phantom will have taken over you, your speech, your sight, your perception, and most vital for it, your dark emotions. This is when you become your phantom self. The true you has "left the building." This is what I refer to as a "phantom attack." And at that very moment, at the time of consumption, the last thing in the world you want is to be at peace. You want war. So what do you do? You go looking for trouble.

If you came upon a wise old sage when you were consumed by an aggressive pain-body and he said to you, "There is such a thing as life without pain," you'd probably kick his teeth out. This is because the sage would not be talking to you, he would be talking to the phantom. Remember, you're long gone. People possessed by phantom predators *want* you to be angry with them; they *want* to provoke an attack from you. Their motto is "Bring it on!" They are the rabble rousers, always looking for a fight, and they'll enjoy making fun of you in front of others, the more public the better. If they can somehow humiliate you, they know there's a good chance your pain will *swell*. And if your pain swells, they can feed on it. You won't even have to utter a single word—the energy from your emotional reaction alone will be enough to sustain it.

In relationships, the phantom may remain hidden for many weeks, even months, where both partners are living in a state of peaceful bliss and everything seems as right as rain. And then one day, when you least expect it, your partner's phantom will suddenly arrive and say, "Nice to meet you." Let's say that something you do, or don't do, triggers an attack and your partner makes a snide, condescending, and cutting remark (seemingly out of nowhere), and as he makes the hurtful remark his face will be distorted and sick-like. That's when you'll be left wondering, "Who *is* this stranger?" And that will be your introduction to his phantom self.

The amount of time an aggressive pain-body remains active will greatly depend on how dense it is and, of course, how much of a reaction it can provoke from others. The more people it can upset and get a *rise* out of, the better it feels about itself. And the more intensely suppressed the childhood trauma in the host, the heavier the pain-body will be. This primal trauma gets continually re-triggered every single time the pain-body becomes active. It's as if the phantom says, "Because I've been hurt in the past, I deserve to be angry and take out my revenge on others." In this way, the phantom predator secretly justifies its sadism.

Attack of the phantom.

When viewing the pain-body as a parasitical, unknown entity, it's easier to practice non-judgment and compassion for the individual who's hosting it. In this way, we can make a distinction between the self and the emotionally violent phantom that has *consumed* the self. For the aggressive pain-body, phantom predator type, there are usually five stages through which a **phantom attack** escalates. There is a potential sixth stage which is physical violence, but that occurs only in a small percentage of the cases. I will describe each stage as if you are the person on the receiving end of the attack.

Stage one. The first stage of a phantom attack is when the host of the pain-body becomes assertive and turns a pleasant discussion into a heated debate. Much of the time the argument will be over something completely inconsequential or superficial. The pain-body host will be so vehement about asserting his or her own opinion that the topic's importance is irrelevant.

Stage two. The second stage is when the phantom begins pushing your buttons. It will instinctively know your weaknesses and what annoys or hurts you the most. It will then *zero in* on your wounded "pressure points" until it provokes a reaction out of you. The phantom seeks a reaction from you because this is energy for it to *feed* on.

Stage three. The third stage is when the face of the host becomes twisted and repulsively contorted. The eyes will change dramatically, become sick-like, frightened yet fierce, and will express a look of hatred, disgust, or contempt. The host's auric field will become denser and darker, and the light in the eyes will dim. You may even notice a slight chill or heaviness in the room. The person that you thought you knew will be gone and the host will no longer be listening to you. From this point forward you'll be talking directly to the phantom.

Stage four. The fourth stage is when the host raises his or her voice in an attempt to drown out yours. It may also keep interrupting you in the middle of a sentence so that you're unable to finish your point. This is the phantom's desperate attempt to violently force its opinion upon you. Its aim is to weaken you in any way it can, and also to convince you that it is *right* and therefore you are *wrong* so it can feel superior to you, effectively diminishing your power. As your power wanes, the phantom's power *rises*.

Stage five. The fifth stage is when the phantom adds foul language to the mix because curse words are more hurtful and therefore more effective at pushing your buttons so that it can extract more "tasty" pain out of you. If this fails, it may resort to pouring a drink on you or picking up a physical object (such as a cell phone) and throwing *it* at you. And you can't win against the phantom. It's futile to try and every attempt to fight it will only add fuel to the fire. It will desperately keep coming up with rationalizations for its anger so that it can justify its violent behavior.

Stage six. In the worst case scenario, the phantom alienates and desensitizes the human being into an inanimate object. It is at this level of consciousness where physical violence is rationalized. This is the sixth stage of a phantom attack. Although this stage represents a relatively small percentage of total attacks, it still generates a significant problem for our species. We can observe this stage in the physical bullying, domestic violence, rapes, murders, terrorism, and wars that plague our planet. This stage represents the extreme shadow opposite of the divine Self—the darkest side of human experience.

The phantom prey.

For every number of phantom predators there is a phantom who does not attack others overtly. Instead, they suppress their pain and keep it hidden. I call these *passive pain-bodies* or *phantom prey*. Because they seldom release their pain outwardly like phantom predators, a good number of these individuals are in pain most, if not all, the time.

Hosts of phantom prey cannot say no. They simply don't know when to draw a line in the sand and create healthy boundaries around the Self. They are the "do-gooders," the "doormats," and the types who allow others to walk all over them. Phantom prey will typically have a history of others "doing them in" or taking advantage of them in some way or another. They will thrive on playing the victim in life and it seems as if they'll always have a "dark cloud" floating over their heads because no matter how hard they try to get ahead, "it's always something" that happens to them that brings them more suffering. If this sounds like you in *any* way, then know that what your mind is rationalizing as "selflessness" is not *true* generosity or unconditional love. In other words, when you give so much of yourself to others that you have little or nothing left *of* yourself or *for* yourself, then that's self-abuse, not love. Abundance can only be given from abundance. Furthermore, when you chronically allow others to take advantage of you, bully you, or abuse you in any way, what message do you think you're sending to those people? It's as if you're subconsciously saying, "Your abusive behavior is perfectly acceptable, so keep it coming."

After many years of being abused by others, the passive pain-body will fester, suppressing the host body's immune system, and chronic anxiety or depression will eventually manifest as a physical disease such as: cancer, chronic fatigue syndrome, Crohn's disease, recurring migraines, chronic muscle and joint pain, colitis, irritable bowel syndrome, rheumatoid arthritis, fibromyalgia, systemic candida, and other chronic pain diseases. Often it forces the host into substance abuse, addiction to food or prescription drugs to escape their chronic emotional pain.

One of the most common reasons people begin a path toward spiritual transformation is to cope with their emotional and/or physical suffering. It may be from an acute or chronic physical illness, an ongoing addiction to drugs or alcohol, or chronic emotional anxiety brought on from stress at work or a failing relationship. Most likely they come to the end of the same road over and over again until they have an epiphany that affirms, "What I've been doing is simply not working. The time has come for me to change my ways."

If you possess the courage to heal, pain-body counseling works if you have the patience, desire, and dedication to stay on the path. Many times, people will make great strides but then fall back onto their old self-destructive patterns. The key is not giving up. If you fall, pick yourself up and get back into counseling. Faith, persistence, and a belief that you don't deserve to suffer can get you over the hump and past your chronic pain.

Since we as a species are preconditioned to believe that life is supposed to be a constant state of suffering, that we all have our "crosses to bear," and that we must "pay our dues," then that will be the inevitable outcome. Whatever you identify with and believe with emotion will manifest as your reality. If you didn't define yourself through *misery* and *suffering*, it simply wouldn't happen. Yes, you are that powerful. To transcend suffering, what is required is a coming to consciousness that you don't need to play the martyr anymore. It's simply not your job to carry the weight of the world on your shoulders.

The pain-body is an energy field that forces us inward so we can awaken to the stark reality that we are conditioned to an inner mantra that continually says, "Pain cannot be abandoned. I seem to be made to suffer; it's my lot in life." But this masochistic attitude only tightens the grip that the phantom has on you and reinforces the non-reality that suffering is acceptable, even enjoyable.

Phantom prey are typically introverted or anti-social, though the severity of their introversion will vary depending on their density from host to host. The eyes will usually appear to be distorted, glassy, or aloof. The face will be expressed as supine or docile. When these types have to be in the public eye, they act as if they want to meld into the background. Nervousness, anxiety, depression, and a feeling of being misunderstood by the world are common characteristics.

Some people who have super dense passive pain-bodies won't be able to be around others for long periods of time simply because everyone will be constantly pushing their buttons, and the pain will simply be too unbearable for the host to endure. Of course, the phantom loves the pain, but the host is only human. The phantom is not. Therefore phantom prey may desperately try to steer clear of phantom predators because they have the power to bring them a great deal of suffering. But until they become *aware* that they're carrying a heavy pain-body, they won't be able to dissolve it, and therefore they'll continue to attract the predator type into their energy field.

Phantom prey will frequently exemplify what I refer to as "poor me syndrome" which is simply a negative mental construct that these hosts have slowly and steadily acquired since childhood. By the time they reach adulthood, the negative programming will be firmly engrained into the psyche. When the pain-body becomes active, this mental pattern will become amplified and an unknown inner affirmation will go something like this:

> *The world is a hostile place. Something bad is always happening to me. I can never get ahead. I can't seem to get rid of my disease, no matter how many doctors I see. I just wish people would leave me alone.*

Because this ongoing dialogue comes from the unknown face of the phantom, the host will be oblivious to it until he or she awakens and dissolves the parasite. But until then, words similar to this will repeat in the head, day after day, week after week, month after month, year after year. Enter the law of attraction and then you can understand why becoming *aware* of your phantom self is so important.

People with poor me syndrome will let you know in subtle, and sometimes not so subtle ways that they have this disease by what they frequently or periodically repeat out loud. "It's always something," or "Shit happens," or "Life sucks and then you die," or "Just my luck," are the most common phrases I hear repeatedly verbalized from this type of host. They will frequently put themselves down in one way or another, and, of course, this is all fuel for the pain parasite to sustain itself indefinitely. Many will go through their entire lives playing the role of the victim because it brings to them what their phantom desires most: *more pain*. Some will act it out through chronic illnesses which they will talk about to others, *a lot*. As soon as you meet these people, and they know they've got your attention, they will begin dumping all of their problems on you. They are nothing less than "psychic vampires" who are hoping to siphon as much of your sympathetic energy as they can in the process. They want you to feel sorry for them, and they want you to *share* their pain.

Phantom prey are frequently attached to people who slowly self-destruct or spiral downward into a depressive state of self-pity, self-loathing, and self-hatred, accompanied by an addiction to food, alcohol, and/or drugs. In addition, they will usually surround themselves with phantom predators who will be contributing to their self-destruction over time. Subsequently, the aggressive type will consistently be reinforcing the passive type's "I am a failure at life" mantra that repeats incessantly. Remember, the pain-body expresses itself as an *addiction* to pain. Therefore both prey and predator pain-bodies will be doing everything in their power to ensure that the pain, in some way, no matter how slight or severe, continues. Only through phantom self-transcendence can they end the negative inner dialogue, separate themselves from the mental bullies, and be freed from their chronic suffering.

Putting an end to bullying.

Whatever words we utter should be chosen with care for people will hear them and be influenced by them for good or ill.

—the Buddha

The phantom predator's modus operandi cannot be defined more completely than in the dysfunctional behavior of the dreaded *bully*. Bullies exemplify the phantom's sadistic side in the way they receive pleasure out of hurting and hating others. Between the ages of six and ten, my stepfather would use a willow tree switch or a two-by-four to "discipline" me. I never became a bully myself, but I did become a victim of bullying. My stepfather's harsh discipline—what would today be considered child abuse—facilitated a conditioned, internal belief structure that said: "It's normal to be on the receiving end of violence. I deserve to suffer. Inflicting pain onto others is a perfectly natural and acceptable behavior in this world." Consequently, every school year, from the third grade until my sophomore year in high school, I was verbally harassed, picked on, and physically beaten by other boys in school. It also didn't help that I was an average of two years younger than my fellow classmates and therefore always smaller.

The phantom pain parasite will keep the mind of its host in a state of rationalization, convincing the bully that his or her bullying is justified. Phantom bullies thrive on the excitement of abusing those with whom they view as inferior and weak. The phantom predator always requires a phantom prey to feed on. The predator and prey phantoms, therefore, become a seamless hand-in-glove *fit* for one another in the polarity energy exchange of each bully attack. Because the pain from my primal trauma remained firmly ingrained inside my pain-body, I unknowingly projected my anger and fear outwardly onto my classmates. That psychic energy *imprint* is what attracted the bullies to me, like a fox to a rabbit. Not only was my repressed anger unconsciously perceived as a threat to their egos, my small size amplified me as easy prey. The resonance of fear in me attracted a *like* resonance of fear in them. The only difference is that they were the predators and I, the prey. Both serve as unconscious hosts of the pain-body parasite.

Bullies also enjoy deriding others behind their backs. After all, as long as they're pointing their fingers at others, all attention will be diverted away from their own unaddressed, unattended, and completely repressed fears of inferiority. They will incessantly criticize, condemn, and verbally abuse everyone around them while their cowardly phantom selves remain safely concealed. Bullies foster tension and hatred, and never learn to give it a rest. Their phantoms are so in control of their thoughts that the only thing that matters to them is to succeed at offending and embarrassing others in some way, over and over again. It's all about diminishing the other so they can feel superior to them, feed on their pain, and take away their *power*. This need is so embedded and unconscious that it's inseparable from their very sense of survival.

In childhood, we learn the saying: "Sticks and stones may break my bones but names can never hurt me." But nothing can be further from the truth. Names can be just as hurtful, and in many cases, *more* so. In the same way that a physical punch is energy released and received, a verbal punch is energy released and received. The verbal attacks from pain-body bullies can be just as violent as a physical attack because the victim will mentally repeat that verbal message a million times, over and over again, for months on end. This negative programming is what bolsters the pain-body and strengthens it. Over time, it may become too unbearable for the victim to live inside of their own body, because they're in pain all of the time. This chronic pain is why so many pain-bodies drive their hosts to *suicide*.

If you're hosting a passive pain-body, you will probably be attracting bullies to you like moths to a flame. They will seek you out, come up to you out of nowhere, yell at you from across the street, send hate-mail to you, and this will all happen despite the fact that you do everything in your power to keep out of sight and "fly underneath their radar."

The more abusive strangers you attract, the more you'll wish that no one will notice you. You simply want the world to leave you *alone*. If you've noticed a pattern like this in your life, where people you don't really know consistently make negative, derisive comments that hurt you deeply, then congratulations, you are truly ready to dissolve the pain-body and heal. By this point, your pain-body has no doubt been enduring chronic abuse over a very long period of time, dating back to your primal wound in early childhood. Becoming *aware* of this negative pattern of attraction is the first step toward dissolving it.

In the U.S., suicide is the third leading cause of death among young people, resulting in a staggering 4,400 deaths per year.[29] Bully victims are between two to nine times more likely to consider suicide than non-victims, and a study in Britain found that at least half of suicides among young people are related to bullying.[30] According to recent statistics reported by ABC News, nearly 30 percent of students are either bullies or victims of bullying, and in the U.S., 160,000 kids stay home from school every day because of the fear of bullying.[31] These alarming statistics underline the severity of the bullying epidemic and the importance of why the pain-body should be dissolved *before* you have children. If not, the karmic cycle will only be perpetuated.

The only way to put an end to bullying is through education and enlightenment. If you have a child who is either a bully or a victim of bullying, the answer is the same in both cases: *heal the trauma*. Get the child into therapy or counseling and educate them about the harm that bullying brings. Show them the numbers of suicides and explain to them that it's not worth taking your life because of something someone else says or does. Bullies simply don't know any better. The truth is that bullies are deeply unaware of the pain they inflict and are only reacting from a firmly entrenched *fear of inferiority*.

If you are currently a victim to physical bullying, by all means find someone with authority who can help. Call the police if you must. You can also ask someone to protect you who is bigger than the bully. Or learn how to defend yourself. I began taking karate classes in my junior year of high school and made sure that the word got around. Shortly after, the bullying stopped. All bullies are cowards and sometimes all it takes is for you to stand up for your Self to bring the bullying to an end.

Again, the specific frequency of the phantom energy can only attract to it the same *like* frequency. This is a very important lesson to learn. If you are attracting these abusive people into your life then it's certainly not by accident. The reason is your own frequency of *fear*. And so you may be asking by now, "How do I change this negative frequency in myself?" The solution is simple but not easy. It involves acknowledging the negative patterns of your own mind and the negative thoughts that repeat in your mind that are both silently and verbally directed toward other people. Once you can identify these thoughts as they surface, you'll begin to become conscious of your own judgment toward others at its *source*. It is this consistent regurgitating of angry thoughts toward others that is the *root cause* of your abuse and the reason why you continue to attract pain predators into your life.

During my twenties and thirties, I had two male friends who frequently bullied me. It was more than playful teasing, and many times led to public humiliation. Before I could truly heal, I had to terminate the friendships because, no matter how much I tried to communicate how abusive they were, they just didn't *get* it. It's sad when you have to let friends go that you've known for many years. But when your soul grows a little faster than your friends', it may be necessary for your healing process. I simply decided one day that I was no longer going to be a victim to verbal abuse. And so, for the sake of my Self-protection, Self-respect, Self-love, and inner peace, I drew a line in the sand, and calmly but firmly said, "No more."

Addressing childhood trauma.

When chronic pain becomes too unbearable, we turn to blotting it out through pleasure-seeking activities such as gambling, bar-hopping, drug abuse, spending sprees, sex addiction, food addiction, secret love affairs, and other escapes. But pleasure-seeking is only an escape and doesn't really do much to address the underlying problem. It simply prolongs it and in many cases will bring on even more intense bouts of suffering by sabotaging your relationships, jobs, or career. The pleasure-seeking addictions often screw up your life by alienating you from people you love and by draining your bank account. In the end, the only way you can free yourself from your chronic pain addiction is by going deeply within and becoming aware of your primal trauma. You begin by asking yourself, "Where did this pain begin? At what point did I start to believe that I deserve to go through life in a chronic state of pain?"

I'm very familiar with the pain-body as I carried a very heavy one for most of my life. The physical abuse that I endured by the "disciplinarian" hands of my stepfather contributed to its development. The more pain you have to endure as a child, the denser the pain-body becomes *in* you. To better understand the pain-body, visualize yourself in a dentist's chair with the dentist probing around in your mouth with a sharp instrument. Even though he may not be poking you 100 percent of the time, your body will be in a constant state of high anxiety, anticipating the pain that may or may not be coming. This is how I lived my life every single day for over three decades. And this is what it's like to be hosting a heavy pain-body.

Needless to say, it doesn't take much to unnerve you when you're living every moment of life on pins and needles. The primal wound I endured when I was a child recreated itself over and over through abusive friendships and relationships until I finally became conscious of the truth that I was somehow *attracting* the abuse to me. When that awareness finally fermented, I became empowered to stop identifying with the pain-body and began creating a *space* in between my authentic Self and the phantom self. Subsequently, I was no longer creating painful scenarios, and no longer attracting abusive people into my life. My pain-body had begun to dissolve.

Dissolution of the pain-body.

The Next Human will have already learned how to forgive others for all past wounds or "crimes" committed toward her, no matter how heinous, because she will know that this is what it means to express compassion and unconditional love *outwardly.* Conversely, he will also have learned how to forgive the Self for any and all hurts or "crimes" that he has committed toward others because this is exercising compassion and unconditional love *inwardly.* Know that if you're not ready to emanate unconditional love, compassion, and forgiveness toward *both* the Self *and* the other, then you're not yet ready to dissolve your pain-body.

Your pain-body is a shadow that is cast by the ego to cope with the pain that it endured during its first trauma. This shadow of pain is then projected onto others by way of moral deficiency. Remember, the pain-body is a distinctive and *separate* energy field that is part of the collective hive mind. It's not *your* pain-body per se because it was already here when you arrived on earth. However, it is no doubt a DNA encoding which also activates any negative karma that you've carried over from past lives. In so doing, it reinstates the pain that your soul has not yet been able to relinquish. Consequently, inadequacy, victimization, self-pity, self-abuse, self-hatred, martyrdom, shame, and *guilt* continue to imprison the soul. The pain-body is fueled from physical illness, mental illness, anger, drama, conflict, and daily stress. It works in tandem with the ego as a means to carry out its agenda, which is the perpetuation of pain and suffering in the physical body.

In my experience working with clients with heavy pain-bodies, I've found that there are typically four stages in which the pain-body dissolves. They are as follows:

Recognition stage. Recognizing the pain-body for what it is when it becomes active is important. With some, the pain-body will become *aggressive*, hence the pain will be projected more sadistically, and with others it will be *passive*, resulting in chronic masochism. Over time, the body learns that pain is normal and it will develop pain in various ways. There may be a tenseness or constriction of the muscles, migraine headaches, chronic back pain, or there may be a burning or tightness in the abdomen. Some may develop a chronic debilitating disease.

At one point, my pain-body became so incredibly *dense* that I had to remove myself from my family, friends, or anyone that I knew intimately for two and a half years. During that time, there were frequent periods where the pain became so unbearable that I simply wanted to *die*. I also became frequently consumed with rage, so much so that it felt as if my entire body was doused with gasoline and set on fire. The more you love someone the more it hurts when he or she pushes your buttons, and when you're carrying a heavy pain-body, you are hypersensitive to everything that is said to you. The slightest little tease or derisive remark will feel as if you're being pricked by a thousand needles. The most innocuous words are twisted around and perceived as a hostile attack. That's when every day of your life becomes a walk through *hell*.

You begin transcending your phantom self by acknowledging the fact that you have a pain-body of which you've been completely unaware. Its inability to thrive within you will be directly related to your rising awareness *of* it. As you begin to recognize the pain-body in yourself and in others, you'll begin the process of dissolution. Know that the pain-body is not something to be feared, rejected, resisted, or hated. It was, in fact, necessary for your personal evolution, and so in this way it has served its purpose. Recognition, acceptance, and gratitude for its role in your Self-realization is required now to initiate and facilitate pain-body transcendence. Over time, the light of your consciousness will diminish your phantom self and will preserve you in a gradually increasing state of non-drama, non-conflict, non-reaction, and non-projection.

The first step is to simply ask yourself, "What do I find distasteful, disgusting, or despicable in others?" Whatever comes to your mind, write it down. Keep a log of these negative emotions. Perhaps you'll begin to observe yourself periodically judging others or calling them derogatory names. Public figures may also be the target of pain projections. For example, you may hate a particular politician simply because you disagree with his or her political views. Realize that your emotion-based judgments are only psychic projections and are therefore rooted in your unknown face.

Think of a person with whom you secretly or openly despise for one reason or another. It could be a famous person or it could be someone close to you, like a friend, boss, co-worker, or family member. Write the name of this person down. Now write down the qualities that *unnerve* you the most about this person. What makes you angry about him or her? After doing this, you may ask yourself, "What do I do to prove to myself that I am not these same dreadful things?" Close your eyes and think hard. Perhaps you're judging this person of being over-critical or rude. Write down a time when you were over-critical or rude toward another person. Perhaps you're judging him or her of being selfish or greedy. Now ask yourself, "How and when have I also shown signs of selfishness or greediness?" Maybe you're judging this person for cheating on a partner. Try to recall a time in your distant past when you cheated on a partner. You may have to go back to childhood to do it, but if you're truly *angry* at someone for being disloyal, there's most likely going to be a repression of guilt about your *own* disloyalty lurking somewhere in your relationship history. If you're being completely honest with yourself, you may be surprised to learn of your hypocrisy. This is the stage of phantom recognition.

Liberation stage. The next step after you recognize the phantom in yours*elf* is to work toward your liberation *from* it. As you bring in the power of presence into your daily life, the phantom will gradually loosen its grip over your mind since you'll no longer be completely identifying *with* it. When you reach the point where you can observe the pain-body surfacing, you'll want to practice seeing it as a separate energy field. See it for what it is. Be mindful of it, but offer it no resistance. This will mark the beginning of your liberation from it.

In the weeks and months ahead, as you awaken to your unknown face, anxiety or depression may surface. Feelings of disgust, hatred, and repulsion toward yourself or others will bubble up and need to be addressed. If this occurs, then allow these feelings to come. It's perfectly okay to re-experience them. This is a crucial part of the healing process. Burying your emotions down deep again will only make them stronger. And then they will only resurface when you least expect it, causing you more suffering.

As you discover that you've been guilty of the exact same negative qualities that you've been secretly or openly hating in others, you'll begin to consciously hate these same qualities in yourself, as opposed to *unconsciously* hating them in yourself. That's good. This is part of the awakening process. The deeper the repulsion, the better. In a sense, it will be like vomiting up something that doesn't agree with your stomach. This is the psyche's natural way of getting rid of what's toxic. Eventually, these feelings of self-disgust will dissipate as you project less and less of your phantom onto others.

If you do incur stress, anxiety, or depression during your pain-body dissolution, there are a variety of drug-free methods that I recommend to remedy this. For me, daily meditation was helpful. Take just a few minutes a day, usually at the same time, to sit quietly and go within. Another way to release stress and toxic emotions is to go on nature walks. Or if you live in the city, go on city walks. Try not to read signs because this activates the mind. My long walks became a sacred time which afforded me a spaciousness that was instrumental in the releasing of my negative, repressed emotions. If you can find a park nearby, then I suggest focusing your attention on birdsong, the wind, the squirrels, the flowers, the trees, and the butterflies. Stop thinking and start paying attention to your surroundings. This is excellent practice for allowing the state of presence into your daily life. The important thing is to get out of your head and allow your mind to become still. When you can do this, you'll find that your stress will be relieved.

You may also enjoy something more vigorous than walking, like running, biking, swimming, or hiking. Or it could be a brief but intense workout at the gym. Any physical exercise is a healthy way to relieve stress. Practicing tai chi, yoga, or Pilates is also excellent, and so is getting pampered from a hot stone massage or from a detoxifying, relaxing sweat in a Sunlighten infrared sauna. These are healthy ways to release pent-up toxic emotions that may surface during your liberation process. Whatever you do, don't watch the news. It will only reactivate your pain-body. And stay away from negative people at all costs. Purchase some deep relaxation meditation music such as nature sounds or flute music. Light some candles and incense. Run a hot bath. Schedule a time now in your calendar to release your dark emotions. You'll be glad that you did.

Acceptance stage. Know that your secrets will keep you sick. Until you can accept what your phantom self is secretly hiding from the world, you cannot transcend it. In this exercise you'll take a few minutes to write down what your phantom is concealing from others. Your secret could be an extramarital affair, or a hidden addiction to food, sex, drugs, or alcohol. It could be something that you secretly hate or despise in yourself, such as cheating on your spouse, gambling, or a part of your past that you feel is too painful to "let out of the bag." The mere act of keeping it cloaked and repressed will also keep you in an arrested state of suffering.

If you want to truly be free, you must dissolve your secret life. Admitting that you keep a secret to yourself is the first step. Asking for support from another is the second. Find a compassionate confidant such as a friend, life coach, counselor, guru, priest, pastor, imam, or rabbi in your life who will listen to you without judgment. Once the secret is out, there will be no need to defend it or project it. And it will no longer be a secret.

The truth will be revealed, and the very act of communicating your secret with a confidant will diffuse its power to control you.

As you become cognizant of your own pain projections, you'll begin to accept them in others, and in turn, accept them in yourself. This acceptance stage is the precursor to transcending the phantom self. At this stage it's important to realize that it's perfectly okay and normal to have projected negative feelings onto others because it has served as an impetus for your awakening. It was, in fact, a necessary *step* on the ladder of your evolutionary consciousness.

Transcendence Stage. Know that whenever you judge others, you won't be *aware* that you're judging them. You and the judgment are *one*. The enlightening moment when you finally observe yourself judging others will signify the time when you have awakened to your phantom self and ergo, *you will no longer be judging them*. Again, you can't be both asleep and awake at the same time. At that point, you will only be identifying a negative behavior pattern that has existed within your egoic mind. Awareness to judgment *dissolves* judgment and the process of phantom transcendence will have begun. You may stay at this stage for many months or even years. It won't matter how long you remain here, as long as you consistently practice presence and vigilance whenever you fall back into your old patterns, either verbally or silently. This will also mark the beginning of learning how to love others unconditionally and to forgive them, no matter how deeply they've hurt you or how severely they disgust you. This unconditional love toward every One is the way of the Next Human.

When you can consciously observe your own negative thoughts toward others when they arise, you will no longer be judging others, and therefore won't be sending out the negative energy into the ethers. Instead, you'll be observing your phantom self in action. This will mark a breakthrough in your spiritual awakening. As the thoughts come and you observe them, realize that the ego is projecting negative thoughts onto others because it doesn't want to *face* its repressed fears. Seeing this for what it is will facilitate the letting go of repeating negative thought patterns in your mind. This is the key to transcendence. Forgiveness toward those who have brought you pain is your challenge now.

Transcendence takes time because the patterns of negativity have simply replayed themselves over and over in your head throughout your life. You haven't noticed the thoughts before because you haven't learned to stop identifying *with* them. As you separate your Self from the negative conditioning, you will observe the thoughts of self-diminishment surfacing less and less. Eventually you'll begin to notice that you'll no longer be bothered by bullies. Instead, you'll find your divine Self attracting loving, caring, and compassionate people to you.

The pain-body re-experiences itself through the masochistic conditions such as victimization to bullying, oppression, and a deep-seated, subconscious fear of impending doom. These feelings get reinforced by the situations that reoccur as a result of the pain-body's ability to attract its own *like* energy. Emotionally stuck in the distant past, a typical pain-body host will consistently relive the very same emotions that became blocked during the forming of his or her *primal wound*, and every other negative emotion that it has accumulated along the way.

Just as with *ego* dissolution, we are neither suppressing the pain-body nor trying to get rid of it. This will only empower it. I tried fighting my suffering for many years with a variety of different diets, medical treatments, therapies, and undergoing a series of physiological and psychological examinations in a desperate battle to *defeat* my diseases. But my pain-body didn't begin to heal until I completely surrendered *to* it. I eventually said, "Well, this is the way it is, and therefore I honor and respect that." When this shift in consciousness occurred, I began listening to my body and paying attention to what it was trying to tell me. Only by repeatedly practicing *presence* and an unconditional love to what *is* will you be able to initiate and complete pain-body dissolution.

The underlying cause for chronic suffering stems from an identification *with* it, a resistance *to* it, and the belief in the non-reality *of* it. In other words, chronic suffering stems from you adopting a false and negative perception of your true Self. At some time in a distant former life, your mind has learned to subconsciously affirm, "I deserve to suffer." Subsequently, the pain-body will keep recreating suffering scenarios in lifetime after lifetime until you wake up to the truth that you're the one creating it all. Through your phantom self you have also learned to pronounce judgment on yourself after each life. The truth is that no one is punishing you but *you*. And if you have the power to perpetuate your suffering, then that also means that you have the power to *end* it. This begins with forgiveness *of* and compassion *for* the Self. And that's not an easy thing for people to do. The reason why people aren't loving their fellow humans unconditionally is because they haven't yet learned to love their *Selves* unconditionally. Don't be fooled. Most current humans secretly hate themselves in spite of their jovial facades. And it's this underlying, unconscious *shame* that gets projected outwardly onto others.

Why do you think the majority of people rush to judgment toward others? Why do you think so many people are eager to punish and take revenge against others for anything and everything they do wrong? Why do you think so many people harbor animosity and hatred toward others just because they make mistakes? All you have to do is take a visit to your local newsstand and take a look at the cover of all the "gossip" magazines. It's truly appalling how we treat one another. Unconditional compassion and forgiveness rarely enter into the human equation. This is why most current humans are projecting their pain onto others in the form of blame, bullying, condemnation, violence, and intolerance. True forgiveness envelops both the Self *and* the other. Suffering perpetuates because this negative self-concept called the *ego* gets carried over from one life to the next as your true identity while your higher Self is, for the most part, *shunned*.

Suffering often begins with the refusal to accept reality as it *is*. Our higher Selves try to communicate to us this reality all the time and yet we continue to ignore the message. It's as if the higher Self says, "You are creating this conflict and that problem because you are addicted to pain, and if you continue to stir up drama, it will inevitably result in more *trauma*." Here's the equation:

ADDICTION TO DRAMA = TRAUMA + REACTION = KARMA

Since karma is not what happens to you, but instead a *reaction* to what happens to you, it only plays out when you haven't yet learned how to become present and love your Self and others *unconditionally*. When you reach the point where you're able to forgive your Self and others for any and all "mistakes" committed—going back countless lifetimes—then that very moment will mark the end of the karmic cycle. From that point forward you'll no longer be perpetuating the *wheel*.

Even though you may not be aware of the past life trauma that initiated your emotional pain-body (unless you've had a past-life regression), you can still dissolve it completely in the current life. To do this, you must re-experience the time in your distant past when your pain-body replayed the "echo" of your primal wounding from a past lifetime. Also note that many are completely unaware that they were abused at all as children, when in fact they were, severely. If this is you, then I urge you to go deeper within, through meditation, and search for that primal wound. If you are suffering now, I guarantee you it's rooted in a trauma somewhere from your childhood.

The following exercise will help you to forge a transformational path of peace, joy, and tranquility by initiating the dissolution of your pain-body, your phantom self. It is a guided meditation for those who seek to heal their primal wound and past life trauma.

1. Become seated in a meditative position and close your eyes.

2. Place your tongue on the roof of your mouth just behind your teeth. Keep it there throughout the entire meditation. Inhale slowly through your nose

from your diaphragm (not your chest), allowing the air to push your lower belly out. Exhale through your mouth. Repeat this seven times, focusing your attention on your *breath*.

3. Now visualize the time in your life when you experienced your first emotional trauma, no matter how slight or severe. This time may have been in early childhood between the ages of four and ten. Or it may have occurred when you were older.

4. Focus on that event for a few moments. See the person who inflicted the trauma, whether it was a parent, sibling, classmate, friend, whoever. Focus on this time in your life until you have a clear picture of it in your mind.

5. All of the pain in your life initiated from your identification with this early trauma, which was an echo of a primal wounding from a past life. It is time now to heal this pain, and retrieve your soul, your true Self. Know that there is a hidden treasure that lies at the heart of this trauma.

6. Visualize the eyes of the person who initiated this emotional wounding. See the repressed pain in his eyes. As you're observing this, know in your heart of hearts he simply didn't know any better. Realize that if she knew better, she would never have hurt you. She was simply reacting from her own trauma, caused by someone else during her childhood.

7. Now visualize a portal of soft pink light in the exact center of your chest—in between your ribcage just above the sternum. Keep visualizing it until you can

actually feel a sensation there, such as warmth, tingling, pulsing, or heaviness.

8. Imagine this portal of pink light in the middle of your chest is spinning, like a vortex. Focus your mind's eye on it spinning in the middle of your chest for several minutes or as long as you desire in complete stillness.

9. Now send this person who caused your childhood trauma this soft pink light emanating from your chest. Consciously send him love, compassion, and forgiveness *via the light*. Send him the thought wave, "I forgive you and understand that you were hurt, too." Stay here in this place, for as long as you need, pulsing the soft pink light from your chest toward her and then visualize the light engulfing her entire body until you see her *smile*. Keep visualizing the pulsating, healing pink light until her body is completely consumed in it. Stay here for as long as you can, then release this person with love, compassion, and forgiveness.

THE PHYSICAL SELF
HONORING THE INTELLIGENT BODY

Morpheus: *We've done it Trinity. We found him.*

Trinity: *I hope you're right.*

Morpheus: *You don't have to hope. I know it.*

Neo: *Am I dead?*

Morpheus: *Far from it.*

Dozer: *He still needs a lot of work.*

Neo: *What are you doing?*

Morpheus: *Your muscles have atrophied and we're rebuilding them.*

Neo: *Why do my eyes hurt?*

Morpheus: *You've never used them before. Rest, Neo, the answers are coming.*

—*The Matrix*

The accumulated wisdom of conventional medicine has proved insufficient to cure the vastly growing number of chronic diseases and have any impact whatsoever on the epidemic numbers of people who are dying from them every day. Perhaps this is due to the fact that conventional medicine does not approach healing from the same level of intelligence of the body itself. Ergo, it keeps missing the *mark*.

The Next Human will understand that the mind controls the body, not the reverse. Therefore, no disease will be believed to be incurable because the very *belief* that it *is* will only undermine the body's natural healing ability to cure itself of the disease. As the world renowned spiritual healer Bruno Groening presciently said over sixty years ago, "When the time is right, everybody will be able to obtain help and healing from within."[1]

When you learn to trust in your own divinity, you will quickly discover that you already possess the power to heal the physical Self from with*in*. When you learn to be still, surrender, and begin paying attention to your body during meditation, you may start to feel strange sensations that you haven't felt before. You may even notice that everything in your body feels somehow different. Perhaps you'll sense a subtle, powerful, tingling energy, and an inner knowing that your body is alive and free from all restraints. Trust in this feeling and nurture it.

If you're currently chronically ill, as I have been in the past, know that the intelligent body is sending you a message right now that it's not receiving what it needs to make the necessary repairs. Think of your body as a battery. When you pay attention to it, acknowledge its wisdom, and feed it what it needs, it will be permanently charged and not only will you maintain perfect health as a result, but you'll also become a "battery charger," a natural *healer* for others. The Next Human will realize that the intelligent body responds to thoughts and emotions just as a computer responds to its keyboard and mouse commands. The more stressed, anxious, and drama-addicted you are, the faster physical diseases will develop, and the longer they will linger.

Because the nervous system controls all body functions, if you cut off the nerve supply to the heart, your heart will stop beating. Without the nervous system, your body cannot function and you will die. Therefore, it's vitally important that you do everything in your power to ensure that your brain stem is free from all nerve interference. Later in the chapter, we will delve into a remarkable specialization of alternative medicine known as *upper cervical care.*

If you are continually taxing the body through stress, neglect, lack of cellular oxygen, and a diet devoid of sufficient nutrients, then over time, your physical Self will become drained of *life force* energy. When this happens, the body's defenses are lowered, the immune system becomes suppressed, and the cells stop their natural process of detoxification and rejuvenation. Instead of a healthy respiration of oxygen, the cells become bogged down by the fermentation of sugar. Consequently, toxins accumulate, preventing the cells from carrying out their crucial functions. Chlorine, heavy metals, pesticides, fungicides, antibiotics, air pollutants, sugar, fluoride, trans fats, genetically modified organisms (GMOs), and other carcinogens that you take in daily from your water and food create the proper environment for disease to flourish over time. This can eventually result in a serious toxic accumulation in your cellular body.

In the United States, we are programmed from infancy to accept that physical disease is normal. But I can assure you that it is not. Being sick is not normal. Being in perfect health *is.* All disease is either avoidable or curable. Yes, even genetic disease. All disease stems from a toxic emotional body which further springs from an imbalanced ethereal body. Disease does not begin and end with the physical Self. By the time it finally manifests in the body, it's simply a "red flag," a surface-based *symptom* of a much deeper, underlying cause that is rooted in both the psyche and the emotional pain-body. For those who are learning metaphysics for the first time through this book, the first lesson to learn about your body is that it is simply a covering, a *sheath,* and indeed the outermost layer of your eternal Self. In simpler words, you are not your body. And you are also not your mind. Therefore, before the physical Self can be allowed to heal, a focus on the healing of the mental *and* emotional bodies is a necessary prerequisite. It simply will not work in the reverse. This is why this is the *third* chapter in the book.

The time has come for the West to embrace the Eastern approach to medicine such as Ayurveda and yoga from India, acupuncture, chigong, and tai chi from China, and Reiki from Japan. Other holistic healing modalities include nutritional therapy, massage therapy, infrared therapy, and upper cervical care. These alternative approaches to medicine are indeed the *health care system* of the Next Human. No doubt, the West has been excellent in its scientific and technological advances to medicine. Reconstructive surgery for physical trauma, heart surgery, and organ transplants has made significant strides and advances within the last century. So has our understanding of DNA. And this is a wonderful thing. However, when it comes to curing chronic illnesses, Western medicine has seriously failed. Its "disease treatment" approach will never be able to permanently correct chronic imbalance in the body because this is not the way the intelligent body *works.*

The human body is a perfectly calibrated machine when it's given what it needs and then allowed to do its *job.* All you have to do is keep it "charged." This begins with a single thought. If your body is currently imbalanced and you are suffering from a chronic disease, then the primary cause of this is your thoughts, your belief structure, and your lack of faith in your body's innate ability to heal itself. The typical current human expects her body to perform without malfunction or loss of energy no matter how much *junk* she feeds it. Believe it or not, most people treat their cars with much greater care and respect than they do their bodies. If people treated their cars with the same contempt, they simply wouldn't run. It's only due to the intelligent body's divinely engineered resilience that we are as "healthy" as we are as a species. When you consume a nutrient-void, sugar-dense, starch-based, genetically modified diet that's inordinately high in food additives, toxic chemicals, artificial flavorings and colorings, pesticides, and preservatives, it's a wonder of science that more of us aren't being naturally *embalmed* after we die.

The philosophy of wellness, according to the Next Human, is to put the physical Self *first* on the list of priorities, not last. What can you do without your health? Nothing. You can't work. You can't take care of your family. And depending on the disease, you may not be able to take care of yourself. So pamper your body. Invest in it. Feed it what it needs before you feed it what you want. The body you have now is the only one you'll have in this life so I suggest you do whatever it takes to keep it in perfect health.

The failure of conventional medicine.

> *The writer is fully aware that his message is not ortho-*
> *dox; but since our orthodox theories have not saved us,*
> *we may have to readjust them to bring them into har-*
> *mony with Nature's laws. Nature must be obeyed, not*
> *orthodoxy.*
>
> —Weston A. Price, Nutrition and Physical Degeneration (1939)

Today, I am immensely grateful for being in perfect physical health. But this was not always so. In fact, for more than two decades of my life, I was riddled with many chronic diseases at once, some of them debilitating. In 1996, after a decade of spending upwards of $40,000 on a variety of treatments for chronic fatigue syndrome, chronic dizziness from an inner ear disorder, anxiety and panic attacks, depression, mercury toxicity, TMJ syndrome, acid reflux disease, systemic candida, irritable bowel syndrome, hypoglycemia, and borderline type 2 diabetes, I finally realized that conventional medicine wasn't going to cure me of anything.

After many years of going inward and meditating for answers, eventually my inner voice spoke to me clearly, saying, "Stop *fighting* your diseases and treating them as *the enemy*. Instead, see them as the way in which your intelligent body is trying to communicate to you." The solution to my chronic suffering suddenly became apparent. I had to start *listening* to my body and paying attention to it.

The intelligent body requires more than **100 nutrients each day** if it's to function according to its genetic and cellular programming. In fact, your body's total health is ultimately determined by the state of the somewhat simple yet highly intelligent biological *cell*. Varying combinations of cells make up every organ and tissue, and approximately 75 trillion cells are constantly being replaced by new ones. Around 24 billion cells are renewed every day. Typically, the surface of the small intestine is replaced every five days and your body will re-grow an entirely new skin every seven weeks or so. Most body cells are replaced within eight to ten months, with bones taking several years. The intelligent body innately knows exactly how, why, where, and *when* to red-flag every cell and tissue, break it down, repair and rebuild it, and it does all of this without you having to give it a single thought. Why not empower it to replace its damaged cells with perfectly healthy ones?

According to the American Cancer Society, over 1,638,000 new cancer cases will be diagnosed in the U.S. this year, and more than three out of four Americans have a diagnosable chronic disease.[2] But don't believe anyone who tells you that your body's disease cannot be cured. In this dimension, every toxin has its tailor-made antidote, and every disease has its own cure. The law of polarity guarantees it. But the cures aren't going to come from the drug industry. After all, how many chronic diseases can you think of that modern medicine has actually *cured?* You better think hard.

Marketing executives working for pharmaceutical companies dream up names for "new" diseases every day of the year. And then they'll make acronyms for them in an attempt to make them sound more authentic. This is followed by a patent so that a chemical can be marketed as a panacea or "cure" for a targeted disease—that is, until enough people are harmed or killed by the drug and it's taken off the market. Billions of dollars have been invested in research for a myriad of chronic diseases such as cancer, AIDS, Alzheimer's, Parkinson's, diabetes, and muscular dystrophy. After twenty-seven years and billions of dollars spent on research, we still don't have a cure for HIV, and in the United States we spend over $5 billion every year on cancer research and treatment development with absolutely *zero* to show for it.[3] This is because cures can only come from the intelligent body itself when it's empowered with the right tools to do so. Ever hear of spontaneous remission? There have been 489 documented cases of spontaneous remission for cancer alone from 1900 to 1987.[4]

Know that there is really only *one* disease of the physical Self. It's called *imbalance*. In my more than two-decade-long personal journey toward extraordinary wellness, I have become aware of only four factors that blocked my body's self-healing powers:

1. *Stress, anxiety, depression*
2. *Malnutrition from improper diet*
3. *Upper cervical imbalance*
4. *Accumulation of toxins in the cells*

In the prior two chapters, I have revealed my life-long education regarding what I've found to be the most significant causes of disease in the body: self-imposed *mental abuse* from the pain-body manifesting as chronic *stress, anxiety, and depression*. In this chapter, I will focus on the appropriate diet for your genetic physiology, and the nutritional requirements for your body. I will also reveal how to safely and efficiently eliminate carcinogens and harmful environmental toxins, as well as the optimal way to keep the brain stem free of nerve interference. When you learn how to effectively eliminate these remaining three self-healing blockers, your body will be *free* to maintain a continuous anabolic state of renewal.

Listen to your body. It's more intelligent than you are. It was designed to take care of itself, on its own, without you having to worry about it. Unfortunately, in America we've been given false information about what the physical Self needs to be in perfect health, and consequently, our "health care" industry is not doing its job properly. In fact, as you'll learn from the clinical studies I've referenced in this chapter, most of what you are being told by government agencies and mainstream nutritionists is actually the *opposite* of what you should be doing to stay healthy. The Next Human will reform the defective system that is currently in place so that a more holistic, natural, nutrition-based, preventive, and *drug-free* paradigm of health care can become readily available to the masses.

A disease care system.

> *Besides real diseases we are subject to many that are*
> *only imaginary, for which the physicians have invented*
> *imaginary cures; these have then several names, and so*
> *have the drugs that are proper for them.*
>
> —Jonathan Swift, *Gulliver's Travels*

In America and most of the Western World, we don't have a health care system. We have a *disease care* system. This cockeyed, drug-based, dangerously *upside-down* approach to healing the intelligent body, exists primarily because our medical doctors are not taught the appropriate amount of holistic healing modalities, preventive or alternative medicine, proper nutrition, detoxification, and stress-reduction techniques necessary for the rejuvenation and healing of the physical Self. Primarily, medical professionals are educated on how to treat disease using drugs and/or surgery, and that's *it*. Subsequently, these are the two options that insurance companies cover.

Here in America we are conditioned from birth to believe that disease is a perfectly natural and "normal occurrence" in the physical Self. In other words, we are made to believe that the intelligent body, which performs all of its trillions of diverse, intricate, and concurrent functions every second on its own—without any help from us—is just *too stupid* to keep itself free of disease. We don't stop to think that maybe it's not the body's fault that it becomes sick in the first place. Perhaps it's something that *we* are consistently and unknowingly doing to it that's *so* harmful, *so* sabotaging, and *so* overwhelming to its immune system that it breaks down, allowing viruses, bacteria, parasites, and carcinogens to damage it on a cellular level. After all, if you pumped a mixture of gasoline and seawater into your car's engine, how long do you think it would run?

The U.S. Department of Health estimates that more than 50 percent of Americans take at least one prescribed pill a day. As a result of this pill-popping insanity, one American *dies* every nineteen minutes from prescription drug abuse, and in 2007 there were a shocking 27,000 unintentional deaths caused by drug overdoses.[5] Since 2008, the world has watched the remarkably creative talents of Heath Ledger, Amy Winehouse, Michael Jackson, Whitney Houston, and countless others added to this sad and alarming statistic. Overdose deaths involving prescription drugs, in particular opiates, sedatives and tranquilizers, increased more than *200 percent* from 2001 to 2007.[6] In fact, by 2006, overdoses of prescription painkillers alone were already causing more deaths than overdoses of cocaine and heroin combined.[7]

According to a 2003 medical report, nearly 784,000 people in the United States die every year from conventional medicine mistakes.[8] Of these, at least 106,000 are from adverse reactions to prescription drugs. Some estimate that these numbers are closer to 200,000 because of underreported cases. The United States spends $282 billion annually on deaths due to medical mistakes, which is a conservative estimate because most medical errors are not reported.[9]

On the tube, we are constantly inundated by prescription drug commercials targeting the disease-ridden consumer for everything from acid reflux to erectile dysfunction. This highly flawed system of disease care is fueled, of course, by the pharmaceutical companies, a.k.a. "Big Pharma," so they can continue to brainwash the masses into believing that prescription drugs are a completely safe, natural, and a *necessary* way of treating disease—all the while raking in hundreds of billions of dollars a year in the process. In fact, the global prescription drug sales market is expected to reach a staggering $1.1 trillion (1,100 billion) by 2014.[10] Adding insult to injury, the World Health Organization (WHO) reported that the United States spent more than any other country on health care, yet ranked **39th** in the world for infant mortality, **43rd** for adult female mortality, and **42nd** for adult male mortality.[11] A 2010 report from the Commonwealth Fund reported that "among the seven nations studied—Australia, Canada, Germany, the Netherlands, New Zealand, the United Kingdom, and the United States—the U.S. ranks last overall," as it did in the 2007, 2006, and 2004 editions."[12] This report also showed that the U.S. came in **dead last** on dimensions of access, patient safety, coordination, efficiency, and equity.[13] The 2007 report showed that the U.S. spent $7,290 per person on health care, more than *double* that of any other country in the survey.[14] In 2011, life expectancy from birth in the U.S. is 78.49, which is ranked **50th** in the world, below most developed nations and some developing nations.[15] And so I ask you: What good is *all the money* we're spending on health care *doing* us anyway? This utterly asinine, completely backwards pharmaceutical-based model of *disease care* equates to the following typical scenario:

1. An individual becomes sick with a "disease."
2. This person goes to the doctor and becomes a "patient."
3. The body's disease must be treated so the doctor prescribes toxic, cellular-damaging drugs.
4. The patient then goes to the pharmacist to buy the drugs and becomes a Big Pharma customer, usually for life.

After this autonomic process is complete, it then falls on the poor patient to deal with a profusion of drug side effects, many of which are either confused *with* or experienced *as* significantly worse than the symptoms of the disease itself. Some of the most common prescription drug side effects are: drowsiness, skin rashes or hives, abdominal pain, blurred vision, nausea, vomiting, constipation, diarrhea, ulcer formation, dizziness, headaches, loss of appetite, memory loss, palpitations, dry mouth, loss of coordination, ringing in the ears, swelling of hands and feet, intestinal bleeding, and fainting. Yes, believe it or not, *unconsciousness* is a common side effect of prescription drugs. And as if all of this weren't egregious enough, add to it the aforementioned dangers from adverse reactions and accidental overdose. To the Next Human, this current disease care system is nothing less than *criminal*.

The cellular body requires oxygen.

The truth is that the intelligent body cures itself of disease all the time. From birth, cancer cells are killed by the body's natural immune system until one day, it's simply not capable of doing it anymore and cancer remains unchecked and develops into tumors. And then the medical community calls this "getting cancer," which is inaccurate because we all get cancer all the time, and your body, if *allowed*, keeps the anomalous cells at bay.

In 2005, cancer surpassed heart disease as the number one cause of death in America.[16] Despite the *hundreds of billions* of dollars spent on cancer research in recent decades, a cure for cancer continues to elude the medical industry. In every case of cancer development, a cellular shift occurs from oxygen respiration to sugar fermentation. These cancer cells then transform into anaerobes that lose their initial programming: sustain the life of the body. The cancer cells then proceed to take on a new and more sinister function: replicate until the living host dies.

Approximately 4 billion years ago, before the earth contained an oxygen-based atmosphere, the very first forms of life fed on just two nutrients: sugar and protein. Stored within the DNA of every living organism today lies the memory of this biological fact. The very first living cells lacked a nucleus (prokaryotic cells) and fed anaerobically on proteins and sugar. Later, after the development of an oxygen-based atmosphere, higher organisms developed from cells containing a nucleus (eukaryotic cells) and the use of *fat* became a nutrient source for the first time. These *oxygen*-feeding cells use *fatty acids* and *ketones* for fuel, just as most mammalian cells do to this day. Because fat is an aerobic nutrient, it forms the basis of oxygen metabolism in the human body. In simpler words, anaerobic cells feed on *sugar* and aerobic cells feed on *oxygen*.

In 1924, scientific researcher, Otto H. Warburg, M.D., wrote about oxygen's relationship to the pH of cancer cells internal environment. He firmly believed that there was a direct relationship between cancer and oxygen. In his work, "The Metabolism of Tumours," Warburg demonstrated that all forms of cancer are characterized by two basic conditions: acidosis and hypoxia or *lack of oxygen*.[17] He found that cancer and oxygen deficiency go hand in hand because he proved that cancer cells are *anaerobic* and therefore cannot survive in the presence of oxygen. So if they can't feed on oxygen, what do you think cancer cells feed on? Yep, that's right: *sugar.*

Cancer loves sugar because, just like with prokaryotic cells and the fungi candida yeast, it's *anaerobic.* Dr. Warburg proved that the primary cause of cancer is the replacement of the respiration of oxygen in normal body cells by the fermentation of *sugar.* When grapes ferment into wine, the yeast interacts with sugars in the juice to create ethyl alcohol, causing an anaerobic reaction and the release of carbon dioxide. Like cancer, the candida yeast thrives because of sugar fermentation inside the cells. Therefore, for cancer *and* candida (yeast overgrowth) prevention, the body *has* to maintain a steady, healthy respiration of *oxygen* in the cells, rather than an ongoing *sugar* fermentation in the cells.

I believe that the primary cause of oxygen deficiency in the cells is a chronic deficiency of essential nutrients, vitamins, amino acids, minerals and trace elements. If the cellular body's nutritional needs are constantly met then each cell will consistently be replaced by a *healthy new cell* which will sustain a strong immune system, resulting in the body's natural ability to keep both candida and cancer cells at bay. The multitude of biochemical reactions and other cellular functions that the intelligent body seamlessly performs every second of every day require these essential nutrients in every single cell. Therefore, chronic nutrient deficiencies and excessive sugar intake result in cellular oxygen deficiencies, and eventually to disease.

Your unknown sugar addiction.

Obesity is threatening the world's future food security, according to a 2012 study that calculated the United States accounts for almost a third of the world's weight due to obesity, despite the fact that it only makes up 5 percent of the world's population.[18] Using the WHO data from 2005, scientists calculated the average global body weight at 137 pounds, but North America weighed in at a whopping *178 pounds.*[19]

In 1850, the average American consumed about thirty pounds of sugar annually, and obesity was unheard of. Today, the average American consumes *156 pounds* of sugar (an entire wheelbarrow full) annually, contributing to an obesity statistic of 26 percent, with a staggering 63 percent considered overweight.[20,21] In 2011, the USDA estimated the average American consumes nearly *two tons* of sugar in a lifetime. Yes, that's *per person.*

Most of this sugar comes from high fructose corn syrup (HFCS), which is the main ingredient in processed foods, from sandwich meats to pretzels to ketchup. When you read your nutrition labels, you'll quickly notice that sugar, in one form or another, is added to over 80 percent of the products in the supermarket. And unless you live on a Stairmaster, all that sugar will get converted into fat by your body. Carrying excess weight around will increase your risk for deadly conditions such as heart disease, kidney disease, and diabetes. In 1893, there were fewer than three cases of diabetes per 100,000 people in the United States. Today, that ratio is nearly 2,700 times higher, reaching 8.5 percent of the current population.[22] New figures from Diabetes Health Intelligence suggest that more than one million people in the U.K. are thought to have undiagnosed type 2 diabetes.[23] In the U.S., this figure is at least seven million.[24]

So, what's causing this type 2 diabetes epidemic? I believe it begins and ends with an unknown sugar addiction. Molecularly speaking, your body can't tell the difference between fructose from peaches or honey, lactose from milk or yogurt, galactose from navy beans, or sucrose from maple syrup. Furthermore, all high glycemic index (GI) carbohydrates such as grains, legumes, corn, rice, and white potatoes, will immediately get converted into glucose in the bloodstream, causing your blood sugar levels to soar. For example, two slices of whole wheat bread can raise your blood glucose levels more than two tablespoons of pure sugar.[25]

Insulin is a pancreatic hormone that helps the body metabolize blood glucose by binding with receptors on cells, much like a key fits snugly into a lock. Once the insulin has "unlocked the door" into the cell and glucose is inserted, it is then either burned for fuel or stored as fat in the form of glycogen. Every time you consume excessive sugar alone or from starch, the pancreas has to produce an unnaturally high amount of insulin which eventually becomes toxic to the cells. Eventually your cells require downtime from the abnormal and unhealthy barrage of insulin. So what does the intelligent body do to counterbalance this onslaught? Well, it downgrades the number of receptors so that the cells don't have to receive the insulin as often. When these cells fail to respond adequately to circulating insulin in the blood, glucose levels go through the roof. When the body is healthy, the liver helps regulate glucose levels by lowering its secretion of glucose in the presence of insulin. However, over time, *insulin resistance* is created by the intelligent body to protect itself from the incessant barrage of insulin caused by a diet excessive in high GI carbohydrates. And there's your *cause* for the new epidemic: type 2 diabetes.

It was previously thought that fructose didn't have much of an impact on insulin, but a recent study at the University of California Davis has found that fructose (found naturally in honey, corn, and fruit) is actually *more* dangerous than glucose when it comes to developing diabetes or heart disease.[26] Liver abnormalities and fat deposits showed up only in the study group that consumed fructose-sweetened drinks with their meals. Moreover, in this group, the liver converted the sugar into a higher amount of fat while the subjects consuming similar amounts of sugar from glucose showed no such change. The fructose-drinking volunteers were also more resistant to insulin.

Most of the sugar you encounter in food products isn't pure glucose, but rather HFCS, which on average comes in a 55/45 percent fructose/glucose ratio. The reason for this is because of the *sweetness* of fructose compared with glucose. One of the huge problems with fructose lies in the conditioning of our children from birth to the excessive sweetness of HFCS, which is the main ingredient in soft drinks, pastries, cookies, candy, and other processed foods. When children are given the option of an apple over a piece of candy, they will opt for the candy because of the sweetness level. Once the taste palate becomes conditioned to all this HFCS, the mild sweetness of a much healthier sweet pepper may taste bitter in comparison.

In response to this study's findings, Dr. Walter Willett, chair of the department of nutrition at the Harvard School of Public Health, noted that consumption of sugary drinks containing fructose can *double* the risk of diabetes, with half of that risk due to the excess weight, and the other half due to the high fructose intake.[27] The bottom line is this: Both glucose and fructose are bad for the body. Fructose is worse. Just remember this next time you reach for a glass of orange juice. An 8 oz. glass will contain about 20 grams of sugar from fructose. So if you like natural juice, you may want to adhere to the green sugarless kind. Even carrot juice contains a fair amount of sugar. Of course, fruit contains nutrients that your body needs such as vitamins C and antioxidants, but these essential nutrients can easily be supplanted by the sugarless veggies.

Other contributors to insulin resistance include lack of sleep, long-term prescription drug use, lack of exercise, steroids, and excessive alcohol or tobacco consumption. But the cause of insulin resistance is not due to an overabundance of sugar *only*. It is due to a combination of this factor plus a lack of sufficient protein and *fats*.[28]

Another recent study at the University of Illinois corroborated the above study, confirming that the metabolism of fructose is much more complex than previous data had indicated, and that we may be paying a high price for it. The study also suggests that a carbohydrate response element binding protein is responsible for the fructose effect on certain genes that trigger the production of fat.[29]

The following are just a few of the numerous negative effects of excessive sugar consumption:

- *Decreases oxygen in the cells (creating an anaerobic environment ideal for cancer).*
- *Creates an imbalance of bacteria in the gut, prompting candida overgrowth which can lead to IBS, colitis, Crohn's disease, and other digestive tract disorders.*
- *Increases fluid retention, fat storage, and weight gain.*
- *Interferes with calcium, magnesium, and trace mineral absorption.*
- *Leads to insulin and leptin resistance (hormonal imbalance).*
- *Increases risk for hypoglycemia, type 2 diabetes, and metabolic syndrome.*
- *Leads to ADD in men and depression in women.*
- *Is as addictive as nicotine, caffeine, cocaine, or heroin.*

In the last fifty years, during the same period of this ever-increasing sugar addiction trend in the U.S., we have simultaneously watched the rates of obesity (especially in children), type 2 diabetes, cancer, cardiovascular disease, stroke, ADHD, systemic candida, irritable bowel syndrome, yeast infections, chronic fatigue syndrome, colitis, Crohn's disease, osteoporosis, and Alzheimer's all skyrocket to epidemic proportions. Coincidence? Unlikely.

Besides sugar, it's wise to stay away from all artificial sweeteners like aspartame, saccharin, and sucralose. Recent studies showed that people who use artificial sweeteners (despite their zero-calorie claims) are heavier, more likely to have diabetes, and are more prone to be insulin-resistant compared with nonusers.[30] Sucralose, or its marketing name Splenda, was initially created to be an *insecticide* but when it was realized to be sweet (believe it or not an assistant who was told to *test* the ingredient actually thought he was being told to *taste* it), they decided to develop it as an artificial sweetener.[31]

The only sweetener I've found to be safe for human consumption is Stevia, which is available in its pure state from the brand Stevita. Their website is www.stevitastevia.com. Be wary of commercial Stevia products that add maltodextrin or other additives to it. Stevia is a natural herb that is derived from the South American rebaudiana plant and has been used by the indigenous tribes without any side effects for centuries. It's about thirty times sweeter than sucrose (table sugar), so a little goes a long way.

Honoring your body's primal physiology.

99.99% of our genes were formed before the development of agriculture.[32]

—S. Boyd Eaton, M.D.

Homo sapiens is a term used to describe a number of varieties of the genus *Homo* dating back to about around 2 million BP when Australopiths evolved into *Homo habilis*, meaning "handy man." This new species displayed more advanced mental abilities and hand-eye coordination which allowed it to develop sophisticated tools for its survival. As a result, it was able to access a wider variety of fat and protein sources, such as seafood, reptiles, amphibians, birds, insects, and grass-fed wild game that were rich in omega-3 fatty acids. Because of Handy Man's higher degree of intelligence, the more brain food he was able to get his hands on allowed for further refinement in tools, which, in turn, allowed for even more fat and protein consumption. It was a self-perpetuating feedback loop that proved itself effective for our ongoing physiological evolution.

For the next two million years or so up until the advent of modern agriculture around 13,000 BP, climatologists have determined that we humans have spent most of our genetic history on Earth during an ice age. In the late 1980s, a group of scientists called the Greenland Ice Core Project (GRIP) drilled cores nearly two miles deep into the ice, reaching ice layers that had formed around 250,000 BP. After analyzing the data, they found that each and every ice age during the last 250,000 years actually began rather abruptly, typically following spikes in global temperature. Each time this abrupt change occurred, the climate descended into a full-blown ice age, sometimes within less than ten years.[33] During an ice age, the entire planet endures extreme ranges of high and low temperatures, from droughts to floods, glaciers to wildfires. Paleo humans had to adapt to these extreme conditions or perish. Consequently, fossils of human feces dating from 300,000 to 50,000 BP have revealed a serious lack of plant material in the diets of the subjects studied.[34] Because of this climatological history, it's highly likely that our Homo sapiens ancestors thrived for nearly all of our genetic evolution primarily on fat and protein sources from animals, birds, and fish.

This paleo diet is still maintained today by the remote and tribal Inuits (Eskimos), fishers and hunters in the arctic who have had to adapt to the harsh winter temperatures. Relying on the hunting of whales, walrus, caribou, seal, polar bears, muskoxen, birds, fish, and Arctic Fox, the Inuit diet is high in protein and extremely high in fat. For the average Inuit, about 75 percent of the daily energy intake is derived from fat.[35] Since it's not possible to cultivate plants for food in the Arctic, the Inuit gather those that are naturally available.

In the 1920s, anthropologist Vilhjalmur Stefansson lived with and observed a tribe of Inuit. The study showed conclusively that the Inuit's extremely low-carbohydrate diet revealed no adverse effects on their health, nor his own. Stefansson found no signs of heart disease in spite of their extremely high saturated fat intake. He also observed that the Inuit were able to get the necessary nutrients, such as vitamin C, from their traditional diet of raw meat such as ringed seal liver and whale skin.[36]

Physiologically, the current human species hasn't changed at all since the advent of our hunter gatherer ancestors. Today, the modern human is both genetically and biologically identical to our paleo forbearers. Before the advent of agriculture, grains and fruits were very scarce and therefore consumed rarely. Primarily, the hunter-gatherer diet consisted of naturally organic, grass-fed wild game, organ meats, eggs, insects, reptiles, amphibians, seafood, birds, wild plants and vegetables, and on occasion, some nuts, seeds, and seasonal wild fruits such as berries. And that was *it*. Compared to our modern diet, this paleo diet had little if no fiber and was roughly *ten times higher in fat*.

So this is our genetic history whether we like it or not. This is the way it is. Our paleo ancestors wouldn't be able to fathom what has become of our species on a dietary level. It is truly astounding how much the resilient body can take before it breaks down and allows for disease to set in. The body of Homo sapiens is simply not genetically evolved or physiologically engineered to be a carbivore, i.e. to rely mainly on carbohydrates for its fuel. If it were, the body would require lots and lots of carbs to maintain perfect health, but according to evolution, it clearly does not. If our species was truly meant to live on a carb/glucose-based, low-fat diet, then the body would certainly be able to handle drinking a 20 oz. Coke (the liquid equivalent of 16 sugar cubes) on a regular basis without any ill effects. But it clearly can*not*. This is why America is rated so low compared to every other country in the world for its physical health. This is why so many Americans are riddled with some form of disease. Wake up America!

Surely, if the intelligent body was designed for a high-GI (glycemic index) carbohydrate, starch-based, low-fat diet—as the Academy of Nutrition and Dietetics recommends—it would not be resisting the absurd amounts of insulin that the poor pancreas has to incessantly churn out into the bloodstream every time you wolf down a plate of pasta. But in fact, not one granule of sugar, not one crumb of bread, not one bean, not one kernel of corn, not even one grain of *rice* is required by the body to be in optimum health. Not *one*. The intelligent body produces its own glucose in the liver for red blood cells. The body does, however, require a sufficient amount of oxygen, water, nutrients, vitamins, minerals, protein, as well as both saturated and unsaturated *fat*.

The key to switching off your body's hunger.

In 1995, a magic bullet for obesity seemed within reach. Big Pharma raced to fashion a newly discovered hormone called *leptin* into an anti-obesity pill. Sixty million obese Americans eagerly awaited a drug that would keep their appetite in check for life. But seventeen years later, obesity still remains as perplexing as ever to scientists and there's nothing remotely resembling a magic bullet. Leptin, the *king* of the hormonal chain of command, secreted by fat cells (yes, *fat* cells) to turn off hunger, has turned out to be a little more complex than initially thought.

There is not a single endocrinologist in the world who can duplicate the intricate and delicate balance of the intelligent body's endocrine system. Anything you do to micromanage a single hormone in the body will, like dominos, affect them all. Hormones are the chemical messengers that tell your cells what to do. There are over 75 trillion cells communicating in our body at any given time. Hormones make sure that each individual cell receives the correct information and subsequently performs the right functions. There are over 100 different hormones playing their unique roles in determining when you should feel sleepy at night and when you should feel rested in the morning. Hormones govern everything in your body, including blood pressure regulation, emotions, digestion, sex drive, stress control, infections, and the burning and storage of fat. Any attempt to *lose fat* without first activating the fat burning hormones will be in vain.

Have you ever gone on a diet only to end up rebounding, ending up heavier than you were before you started? The reason why fad diets don't work is because they create a hormonal imbalance in the body. They communicate to the body, "Famine is here." So what does the intelligent body do to counterbalance this? It stops burning fat, because *fat* is designed to keep it alive during famine emergencies. All of this is controlled by leptin.

In 1994, Jeffrey M. Friedman, M.D., Ph.D, and his colleagues published a landmark paper in which they identified a gene in mice and humans called *obese* (ob) that codes for a hormone later named *leptin*, after the Greek word "leptos," for *thin*.[37] Leptin is the body's mechanism for signaling satiety. Fat cells secrete leptin, which travel through the bloodstream to the brain's hypothalamus, the control center for hunger, thirst, sex drive and other primal functions. When the body has stored enough fat, the hypothalamus is inundated with leptin, prompting it to suppress appetite and make us feel *full*.

Prior to Friedman's groundbreaking research, little was known about the components of the homeostatic system that controls weight, with many scientists questioning the very existence of such a system. Due to Friedman's work, body fat is now understood to be a complex endocrine organ, and leptin is now understood to coordinate our metabolic responses to thirst and starvation, which is the body's number one priority: *survival*. It was previously believed that the thyroid gland controlled mammalian metabolism. But the thyroid answers to leptin (like a corporal answers to a general) which oversees all the energy reserves, inflammatory response, and even controls the arousal mechanism between the sympathetic and parasympathetic nervous systems.[38]

Peculiarly, researchers found that the majority of obese people typically had very high levels of leptin circulating in their blood. Friedman's lab went on to discover that high leptin levels are associated with leptin *resistance,* in the same way that people with type 2 diabetes are insulin resistant. Friedman believes that 90 percent of the 60 million obese people in America suffer from leptin resistance.[39] But *why?*

A recent study at the University of Florida showed conclusively that the consumption of high amounts of *fructose* causes leptin resistance and elevated triglycerides in rats. The rats consuming the high-fructose diet subsequently ate more and gained more weight than the rats fed a fructose-free diet. Researchers hypothesized that a high-fructose diet in humans could lead to leptin resistance, which in turn could lead to exacerbated weight gain, especially in people living in industrialized countries that consume a diet high in high fructose corn syrup.[40]

There is also a direct correlation between *insulin* and leptin. Insulin increase in response to the caloric load provokes a simultaneous dose-dependent rise in leptin, an effect potentiated by high cortisol levels.[41] There is now considerable consensus among the scientific community that the adipocyte hormone *leptin* and the pancreatic hormone *insulin* work hand-in-hand in the regulation of food intake and energy balance. Leptin and insulin levels are positively correlated with both body weight and body fat.

In addition, insulin and leptin concurrently provide important negative feedback signals to the central nervous system, proportional to the energy stores of the body.[42] In conclusion, a diet high in sugar/carbs may eventually lead to leptin *and* insulin resistance. Therefore *diet* is the only way to maintain a proper hormonal balance, and subsequently switch off the body's hunger.

The intelligent body prefers ketones for fuel.

So by now you're probably wondering what your body is supposed to be running on if you eliminate glucose/starch from the diet. After all, we're taught that our bodies require a regular consumption of complex carbs to burn for fuel, right? Even Olympic athletes have to consume an inordinate amount of carbohydrates before they practice and compete, because, well, the body needs lots and lots of glucose for energy, right? Well, in a word, *no*.

If you are a carbivore who is adhering to a carb-based diet, you'll probably start to get tired and hungry about two to three hours after you eat. So what do you do to compensate for this hunger and lack of energy? You reach for a cafe latte from Starbucks, of course. But from an evolutionary standpoint, that's *nuts*. Nature is simply not that inefficient, or stupid. Frequently going days at a time without a meal, our paleo ancestors would have starved to death long ago if they had to depend on complex carbs for fuel. *Homo sapiens* never evolved to have a long-term dependency on the sugar glucose for fuel. If it had, we would have had a very different digestive system with more protruding jaws, more ideal for the consumption of raw plant food, and most likely more than one stomach. But as it turns out, the human body cannot digest the cellulose in plant foods, and in spite of this fact, many holistic nutritionists today are recommending a high fiber, all raw food diet. But raw plant foods are not easy for anyone to digest, particularly anyone with digestive problems like candida or IBS. The cellulose cell walls of all plant foods must be broken down before they can be easily digested, and in order for the nutrients in them to be bioavailable. There are only two ways to do this: cooking and fermentation. By steaming, cooking, or fermenting your plant foods, you'll be allowing your body to have a far higher *yield* of essential vitamins and minerals than you would from eating them raw. Furthermore, you'll be much kinder to your colon because you won't be assaulting it with ridiculously unnecessary amounts of bloating, gas-causing fiber. As previously mentioned, ice age humans consumed practically *no fiber at all* for hundreds of thousands of years. And in spite of what you hear from the media, the facts cannot be refuted. To wit: a 16-year long study of 89,000 women "found no association between the intake of dietary fiber and the risk of colorectal cancer" as reported in the 1999 *New England Journal of Medicine.*[43]

Again, the only tissue in the body that requires glucose is red blood cells and the body manufactures glucose on its own without any help from our diet. So if the body doesn't require glucose for energy, then what exactly is it supposed to be running on? We again look to the *fat* cells. Handy Man became the first human species to construct tools for survival because he ate more brain food, i.e. *fat* and *protein* found from animals. Food became a lot less available for Handy Man, who lived concurrently with a hominid called *Paranthropus boisei* in East Africa. *Boisei* developed an enormous lantern jaw with powerful chewing muscles and huge back teeth to help him grind down and digest the tough plant foods. But because Handy Man's jaw and teeth were too small, he couldn't eat the tough plant foods that *boisei* did. So Handy Man became a scavenger, living off of gazelle, water buffalo, and other game animal carcasses left by lions, leopards, and tigers.

Because meat is relatively easy to digest, calorie-rich, and nutrient-dense, Handy Man lost the need for the large intestines of apes and earlier hominids. This freed up a surplus of energy for use by one organ in particular: the *brain*. At this stage in our evolution, a bigger brain meant greater intellect.[44] But big brains require much more fuel to operate, to wit: the human brain actually utilizes 20 percent of the body's total energy production. Handy Man's ability to utilize a larger percentage of his brain's capacity marked this earlier version of Homo sapiens as an evolutionary leap forward because he was able to safely and effectively extract the energy-producing by-products of fat metabolism known as *ketones*. Ketones are important organic compounds that are vital for your brain's chemistry, and are, in fact, the *preferred source of fuel* for the intelligent body.

The good news is that allowing your body to run on ketones, rather than glucose sugar, comes with lots of perks. Fifteen million people are expected to have Alzheimer's disease by the year 2050 in the U.S. alone. It turns out that ketones are not only potential treatment for Alzheimer's disease, they are also potential treatment for: Parkinson's disease, Huntington's disease, multiple sclerosis, amyotrophic lateral sclerosis (ALS or Lou Gehrig's disease), drug resistant epilepsy, brittle type I diabetes, and type 2 diabetes.[45] Ketones may also help patients recover after a heart attack, and *shrink* cancerous tumors.[46]

In 2008, a randomized controlled study showed a clear benefit for treating refractory epilepsy in children with the ketogenic diet.[47] Because of the resulting low-GI carbohydrate intake, a ketogenic diet allows the liver to convert fat into fatty acids and ketones. The ketones then pass into the brain and subsequently *replace glucose* as an energy source. This diet was actually the main form of treatment for children with epilepsy until the anticonvulsant drug Dilantin was developed in 1938. In addition to its epileptic benefits, clinical studies have shown that ketogenic diets provide protection for the brain as well as disease-modifying benefits for a broad range of degenerative brain disorders and may also be protective in traumatic brain injury and stroke.[48] These observations are supported by other studies that show that ketones protect the brain against diverse types of cellular injury.[49] A woman with bipolar disorder who also had high insulin levels recovered so quickly with a ketogenic diet that she was allowed to come off her medication within six months.[50]

In a recent German study on cancer patients, a ketogenic diet resulted in a complete regression of cancer in one patient within two and a half months, and then, interestingly, after the diet was discontinued, the tumor reoccurred.[51]

According to the Anxiety Disorder Association of America (ADAA), anxiety disorders are the most common mental illness in the U.S., affecting 18 percent of the population.[52] And about half of those with anxiety disorders also experience depression.[53] Both diseases are closely associated to hormonal and chemical imbalance. Obesity is the number one medical cause for hormonal imbalance. Chemical imbalance in the brain is the most widely accepted hypothesis behind the cause of depression. Other causes include psychological trauma and social issues. The typical psychiatric remedy is to treat this chemical imbalance with drugs such as tricyclic antidepressants and monoamine inhibitors. The monoamine hypothesis is a biological theory stating that depression is caused by the under-activity in the brain of monoamines, such as dopamine, serotonin, and norepinephrine. In 1999, anxiety disorders cost the U.S. more than $42 billion a year, almost one-third of the country's $148 billion total mental health bill.[54]

Like our physical health model, our current mental health model is based on linking causes of diseases directly to symptoms. I believe that the underlying cause of depression runs much deeper than a mere chemical imbalance. That only leaves us with the question, "What caused the chemical imbalance?" Treating symptoms of the disease—which is merely the outlying surface—is what the current medical paradigm is all about, and this is why it's so seriously *flawed*. In the case of depression, this treatment modality is falsely based on the precept that it is perfectly normal for the brain to be—in one-tenth of the population—utterly deficient in the chemicals that are absolutely critical for its health. And this precept is ludicrous. Instead of, again, blaming the *body* for its own deficiencies and anomalies, perhaps we should be looking at what the patient's diet and lifestyle is doing to his or her body to be causing the underlying imbalance in the first place. And I believe it all begins with our dependency on *sugar* for fuel.

As it turns out, a ketogenic diet may also be extremely beneficial for both anxiety *and* depression. In 2003, researchers found a positive correlation between type 1 and type 2 diabetes, and severity of depression in patients.[55] Some scientists are theorizing that the ketogenic diet could add stabilization to brain regions associated with anxiety disorders. As mentioned in Evolution 101, the amygdala is responsible for fear processing and anxiety in the brain. When the neurons in the amygdala switch from glucose metabolism to *ketone* metabolism, this insures stability to the brain tissue which, in turn, quells chaotic activity in the neurons. In theory, this stabilization should restrict excessive neuron firing in this region and, subsequently, decrease symptoms of anxiety.[56] Besides the brain, all other vital organs prefer ketones over glucose for fuel, especially the heart. A 12-week study at Kuwait University study showed conclusively a ketogenic diet is not only safe but it "favorably modified the risk factors of heart disease in obese patients," and that a "ketogenic diet is a natural therapy for obesity."[57]

It's important not to confuse the words "ketoacidosis" with "ketosis." Ketoacidosis can be dangerous, but is rare, and typically only happens in those who have untreated type 1 diabetes, once the level of sugar in their bloodstream goes out of control. Ketosis, on the other hand, is simply the state in which the body burns fat for fuel in lieu of sugar. Humans and hominids have been successfully and safely living in a state of ketosis since Handy Man roamed the earth, around 2.3 million BP.

Humans have only been consuming complex carbohydrates for food since the onset of agriculture around 13,000 BP, and have hence been dependent on sugar for fuel. The industrialization of agriculture, which has only occurred within the last century, has dramatically altered the way we eat as a global culture, mainly in the urban cities around the world. Food that is fast, processed, genetically modified, and pre-packaged has contributed to a dramatic increase in high-GI carbohydrate consumption in the modern diet. Consequently, we've seen the death rate from a broad variety of chronic degenerative diseases rise exponentially. According to the World Health Organization, approximately 220 million people worldwide now have type 2 diabetes. Patients with type 2 diabetes not only have a serious chronic disease to cope with, they're also at higher risk for coronary heart disease.[58]

Nearly a century ago, Otto H. Warburg showed conclusively that cancer cells rely on the fermentation of sugar for energy. Therefore for cancer prevention, the intelligent body *must* maintain a steady, healthy respiration of oxygen in the cells, rather than an unhealthy sugar fermentation in the cells.

For me, a ketogenic diet not only completely healed my systemic candida, but restored a hormonal imbalance, and eliminated my hypoglycemia and borderline type 2 diabetes. It also greatly contributed to the dissolution of my anxiety, depression, and chronic fatigue syndrome—all of which my body endured for nearly twenty years, with eleven years of it debilitating. I know firsthand that a low-GI carb, sufficient fat and protein, nutrient-dense, ketogenic diet is *far* more beneficial for the body than the high-GI carb, low fat diet currently recommended by the United States Department of Agriculture (USDA) "food plate."

The most nutrient-dense foods on the planet.

Now that you know that you don't have to consume *any* carbohydrates to be healthy, you can make some clear headed choices on the ones you *will* eat. Obviously vegetables are carbohydrates, but they're also low-GI carbs for the most part. The GI or *glycemic index* is simply a measurement of how carbohydrates in foods impact our blood sugar levels. High-GI carbohydrates, like bread, are *rapidly* digested and absorbed, thus resulting in sharp spikes in blood sugar levels. In contrast, *low*-GI foods, like broccoli, are *slowly* digested and absorbed, thus producing smaller rises in blood sugar.

When you were a kid and your mom said, "You better eat your spinach so you can grow big and tall," she knew what she was talking about. It's the starchy, high-GI carbs, such as cereals, breads, pasta, white rice, and white potatoes that should be consumed sparingly, if at all. If you can focus your diet on low-GI carbs, then you'll be allowing your intelligent body to run on *ketones* and therefore maintain a much healthier and more efficient metabolism.

I'm going to present to you now some nutrient-dense, low-GI vegetables, herbs, and spices that I have found to be *superfoods* and very beneficial for the body:

Sweet Potato. Sweet potatoes are not related to the species known as "white potatoes," comparably having much lower starch content and therefore are considered a low-GI carbohydrate. They will actually raise your blood sugar 30 percent *less* than a white potato. According to the USDA, the sugar content in the sweet potato is about the same as a sweet pepper (but with half the fructose), and has a lower sugar content than a sweet onion, red beet, or carrot.[59] But what's *truly* amazing about this wonderful plant vegetable is that it actually *lowers* insulin resistance, so much so, that a particular white-skinned variety called *caiapo* is sold commercially in Japan without medical prescription as a nutraceutical for the prevention and care of type 2 diabetes. Studies of extracts from the peel of caiapo have revealed that it has the ability to lower blood glucose by increasing insulin sensitivity without affecting insulin secretion.[60]

The orange variety, found prominently in North America, is rich in the natural plant compound chlorogenic acid, as well as carotenoids, both of which also help reduce insulin resistance. Center for Science in the Public Interest (CSPI) ranked the sweet potato number *one* in nutrition of *all* vegetables. In fact, just one sweet potato contains about 14,000 IU of vitamin A, nearly three times the recommended daily intake (RDI).[61] And they have more potassium—known for lowering high blood pressure—than bananas, with a fraction of the sugar.

A recent American study showed that a marked decrease in insulin resistance was indicated in human subjects when sweet potatoes were added to the diet.[62] Another recent study found that among 2,000 men, those whose diets were richest in beta-carotene (a carotenoid found in sweet potatoes) were more likely to survive prostate cancer than those whose diets contained little of the nutrient.[63] The Nurses' Health Study at Harvard Medical School found that women who ate lots of foods rich in beta-carotene, such as sweet potatoes, reduced their risk of breast cancer by as much as 25 percent.[64] And besides beta-carotene, they contain another carotenoid known as lycopene (also found in tomatoes), a powerful antioxidant that neutralizes free radicals, thereby conferring protection against prostate cancer, breast cancer, atherosclerosis, and associated coronary artery disease.[65]

But the good news about sweet potatoes doesn't end here. There's also a unique, purple-fleshed variety which happens to be my personal favorite. Because it has a lighter texture than the orange variety, it cooks a little faster, and if you add a little Stevia to it, a sweet but sugarless dessert pudding can be made out of it. Differing from the carotenoid-based orange-fleshed variety, this purple-fleshed potato is colored by richly concentrated flavonoid pigments called *anthocyanins*. Fruits and flowers with anthocyanins come in the pigments of red, purple, or blue (such as blueberries), and have been the topic of extensive recent research. A growing body of laboratory-based evidence suggests that they may have health effects against: cancer, aging and neurological diseases, inflammation, diabetes, bacterial infections, and fibrocystic disease.[66] Anthocyanins exhibited memory enhancing effects, and have also been shown in clinical studies to reduce cardiovascular disease and improve visual functions.[67, 68]

And, believe it or not, it gets even better. It just so happens that this purple variety of sweet potato is a *staple* in the diet of the healthiest people living on the planet. A 25-year-long study of more than 600 centenarians proved that the Okinawans (from the island of Okinawa of

Japan) enjoy the longest life-expectancy in the world. But not only are they the longest living, they're also the healthiest while they're alive. Their rates of cancer, heart disease, and stroke are the lowest in the world. The Okinawan purple version of the sweet potato is called the *imo*, and its name is synonymous with good health, to wit: *Nmu kamatooin* is a common saying there, meaning, "Are you getting enough imo?"[69] The sweet potato (and its cousin, the yam) truly qualifies as a superfood and an excellent way to get vitamins, minerals, and powerful antioxidants into your body while also keeping your hormones in perfect balance.

Green Tea. All tea contains powerful antioxidants whether its white, green, black, or oolong. However, recent research suggests that *green* tea is best for the body because of its high amount of polyphenols. The major polyphenols in green tea are called *flavonoids*. *Epigallocatechin gallate* (EGCG) is viewed as the most important active component. Research at the University of Kansas has suggested that EGCG is at least *100 times* more effective than vitamin C and 25 times better than vitamin E at protecting cells and their genetic material, DNA, from damage believed to be linked to cancer, heart disease and other life-threatening illnesses.[70]

Greens. Vegetable greens and wild greens come in hundreds of different varieties which include spinach, all varieties of chard, and kale. The Cretans (from the Mediterranean isle of Crete) come in a close second to the Okinawans when it comes to longevity and overall good health and one of the reasons for this is because greens are consumed with nearly every meal. Greens are a superfood because they are rich in chlorophyll, protein, niacin and phosphorus, vitamin A, vitamin C, vitamin E, vitamin K, thiamin, riboflavin, vitamin B6, folate, calcium, iron, magnesium, potassium, copper, and manganese.

Sea greens come in over 2,500 varieties, and among the most beneficial for the body are chlorella and spirulina, both of which provide an ample supply of essential nutrients, trace minerals, iodine, and are an easy-to-digest *complete protein*. Iodine is known for its function in the thyroid gland which makes hormones that help to regulate metabolism. Cancer-fighting phytoestrogens called *lignans* have been found in large amounts in kelp and other seaweed. Several studies of female mice showed a protective effect of kelp against chemically induced cancers.[71]

Chlorella contains more than 20 vitamins and minerals including B complex, beta-carotene, vitamins C and E, iron and calcium. It also has one of the highest sources of chlorophyll of any food on the planet, which is a liver detoxifier, a bowel cleanser, and a catalyst for the absorption of other elements, including iron. Because of its unique ability to bind with mercury, lead, and cadmium, chlorella has become increasing popular in recent years as a chelating agent for heavy metals. Studies have demonstrated a superior ability to safely draw these toxic metals from the gut and intestinal tract, where they accumulate.[72] Clinical studies on chlorella also have shown to reduce high blood pressure, lower serum cholesterol levels, accelerate wound healing, and enhance immune functions in patients suffering from the chronic illnesses of fibromyalgia, hypertension, and ulcerative colitis.[73] Chlorella contains large quantities of folate, vitamin B-12 and iron, and therefore helps to improve anemia and hypertensive disorder in pregnant women.[74]

Spirulina was a food source for the Aztecs and other Mesoamericans until the 16th century. It's an excellent source of potassium, calcium, copper, iron, magnesium, manganese, phosphorus, selenium, sodium, and zinc. It is bio-available in chlorophyll and beta-carotene, as well as sufficient in all B vitamins with the exception of B-12. A recent study showed that it's effective in the treatment of allergic rhinitis.[75] Another study in Korea found that spirulina has favorable effects on lipid profiles, immune variables, and antioxidant capacity in elderly male and female subjects.[76]

Garlic. The ancient Romans used garlic poultices to prevent wound infections, and this practice continued up until World War I. Studies have found garlic to be effective at inhibiting bacterial growth as well as for the treatment of asthma, candida, colds, diabetes, high cholesterol, and high blood pressure.[77] Modern science has shown that garlic is a broad-spectrum natural antibiotic, and that the bacteria in the body do not appear to evolve resistance to the garlic as they do to many modern pharmaceutical antibiotics. This means that its positive health benefits can continue over time rather than helping to breed antibiotic resistant bacteria. Studies have also shown that aged garlic can have a powerful antioxidant effect.

Hot peppers. Habañero, serrano, cayenne, chipotle, ancho chili peppers, jalapeño peppers, and the dozens of other varieties of hot peppers are super-dense sources of nutrients—three tablespoons chopped are equivalent to the U.S. RDI of the antioxidant vitamins A and C. Because they are a thermogenic food, the capsaicin found in hot peppers helps burn fat.[78] Capsaicin and vitamins A and C in hot peppers also aid in the dissolution of fibrin, a necessary component for blood clots. These vitamins also support the health of blood vessels, which helps them normalize blood pressure. The capsaicin in hot peppers may also have an unexpected health benefit as an anti-inflammatory, specifically for headache, migraine relief, and in addition, the anti-inflammatory effects of hot peppers may also be able to help reduce swelling associated with arthritis and asthma.[79] These little tongue burners are jam-packed with essential nutrients and are used all over the world to spice up dishes. They also taste great in salads!

Cucumber. The mighty cucumber doesn't receive its due for the amount of nutrition it has condensed within its light, crisp, hydrating flesh and skin. Cucumbers are a valuable source of conventional antioxidants including vitamin C, beta-carotene, and manganese. Additionally, cucumbers are loaded with a variety of flavonoid antioxidants. Extracts from cucumber have been shown to provide specific antioxidant benefits, including increased scavenging of free radicals.[80] Fresh cucumber extracts have also been shown to reduce unwanted inflammation in animal studies.[81] Interestingly, Big Pharma is actively studying cucurbitacins, a group of compounds found in cucumbers in a hope to develop new anti-cancer drugs.[82] Cucumbers contain most of the vitamins needed to meet standard recommended daily nutritional needs. They are nutrient-dense in vitamins B1, B2, B3, B4, B5, B6, and B9, as well as rich in vitamin C, calcium, iron, magnesium, phosphorus, potassium, and zinc.

Cinnamon. Cinnamon may be more than a simple spice. It may also be an insulin substitute for type 2 diabetes, according to cellular and molecular studies at the University of California, Santa Barbara, Iowa State University, and the U.S. Department of Agriculture. According to Don Graves, an adjunct professor of molecular, cellular and developmental biology, cinnamon has a bio-active component that can potentiate the activity of insulin which can treat and prevent type 2 diabetes.[83]

Coenzyme Q_{10} is an oil-soluble, vitamin-like substance that is found in most eukaryotic cells, primarily in the mitochondria. It is *the* essential nutrient for heart health. Recent research has shown that CoQ_{10} has the ability to lower blood pressure without significant side effects.[84] It is also being investigated as a potential treatment for cancer as well as a relief from the side effects of cancer.[85] Topical application onto gum tissues has shown to improve periodontitis and gingivitis.[86] One study indicated that low dosages of coenzyme Q_{10} has anti-oxidant benefits, and a combination of a diet rich in polyunsaturated fatty acids and coenzyme Q_{10} supplementation leads to a longer lifespan in rats.[87] It has also been shown to provide effective relief for migraine headaches.[88] The best sources of CoQ_{10} are organic extra firm tofu, grass-fed organic meats and poultry, and wild caught fish.

Turmeric. A culinary spice and healing remedy, turmeric is a major ingredient in Indian curries, and this relative of ginger has been used for centuries in Chinese and Indian medicine as an anti-inflammatory agent to treat a wide variety of conditions, including flatulence, jaundice, menstrual difficulties, bloody urine, hemorrhages, toothaches, bruises, chest pain, and colic.[89] Even more potent than its volatile oil is the orange pigment of turmeric, which is called *curcumin*. In numerous studies, curcumin's anti-inflammatory effects have been shown to be comparable to the commonly used pharmaceutical drugs, as well as over-the-counter anti-inflammatory agents such as Motrin. Unlike drugs, curcumin produces no toxicity and no side effects.[90] Recent research has demonstrated that curcumin may provide a well-tolerated and effective treatment for inflammatory bowel syndrome (IBS) such as Crohn's and ulcerative colitis.[91] In another study of patients with rheumatoid arthritis, curcumin produced comparable improvements in shortened duration of morning stiffness, lengthened walking time, and reduced joint swelling.[92]

Cystic fibrosis is a fatal disease that attacks the lungs with thick mucus, causing life-threatening infections, and afflicts about 30,000 American children and young adults who rarely survive beyond 30 years of age.[93] The mucus also damages the pancreas which interferes with the body's ability to digest and absorb nutrients. A recent study in mice showed that low doses of curcumin can make most of the symptoms disappear. According to researcher Michael Caplan at Yale University, curcumin "can almost completely correct the measurable defects of the disease."[94] Other studies have shown turmeric to be effective in the treatment of inflammatory bowel disease, cancer, alcohol-related liver disease and, most recently, Alzheimer's disease.[95]

New tests by a team at the Cork Cancer Research Centre in the U.K. show that curcumin can destroy gullet cancer cells in the lab within 24 hours. Director of cancer information at Cancer Research U.K., Dr. Lesley Walker noted that this research "opens up the possibility that natural chemicals found in turmeric could be developed into new treatments for esophageal cancer."[96] Recent studies have linked the frequent use of turmeric to lower rates of breast, prostate, lung, and colon cancer. Laboratory experiments with mice have shown that curcumin can prevent tumors from forming, and research conducted at the University of Texas suggests that even when breast cancer is already present, curcumin can help slow the spreading of cancer cells to the lungs in mice.[97]

This is just a snippet of the actual health benefits from research studies around the world on turmeric. It is truly a superfood worth having in your cupboard. So pour on the turmeric, from your sweet potatoes at breakfast time to your fish at dinner time. Your intelligent body will thank you!

Squash. Zucchini, all squash varieties, pumpkin, and hechima (an Okinawan favorite) are related gourd or cucurbitaceae vegetables that have amazing health benefits. These superfoods may contain one or more of eight distinct but related proteins that have anticancer, antiviral, anti-AIDS, and immune-enhancing compounds.[98] They're also excellent sources of vitamins B1 and C, folic acid, pantothenic acid, and potassium. Winter squash is an excellent source of vitamin B6 and niacin. Recent studies have shown that their carotenoids exert a protective effect against cancer, heart disease, and type 2 diabetes.[99]

Brassica. The cruciferous or brassica genus of plants includes over 30 wild species and hybrids, including: broccoli, cabbage, cauliflower, Brussels sprouts, kohlrabi, rutabaga, turnips, bok choy, kale, collard greens, mustard, horseradish, wasabi, and rutabaga. They can all give the body what it needs to do its job of staying disease-free. When it comes to nutrients, broccoli is the *mother lode.* It is a source of essential vitamins and minerals, including calcium, magnesium, potassium, iron, zinc, selenium, as well as carotene, thiamine, riboflavin, niacin, folate, and vitamins C and K. In fact, only 3.5 oz. of broccoli contains the recommended daily intake of vitamin C. It has a powerful ability to chelate heavy metals, carcinogens, and other toxins out of the body. Researchers have recently identified one of the key reasons for this detoxification benefit, which is that specific phytonutrients are found in a special combination in broccoli that are effective in supporting all the steps in the body's detoxification process, including activation, neutralization, and elimination of harmful contaminants.[100]

According to the USDA, ounce for ounce, boiled broccoli has more vitamin C than an orange and as much calcium as a glass of milk, without the sugar. Moreover, all the nutrients in broccoli are highly bioavailable. For example, the body can absorb about 50 percent of the calcium in broccoli compared to only 5 percent of the calcium in spinach.[101] Broccoli also has one of the highest supplies of vitamin A in the produce section. But the real benefits are its cancer-protective components. Food chemist Dr. Paul Talalay and his research team at the Johns Hopkins University School of Medicine in Baltimore, Maryland, have discovered that broccoli (as well as other brassica vegetables) is rich in chemicals shown to stimulate the body's production of its own cancer-protecting substances, called *phase two enzymes*. Talalay says that these enzymes are able to neutralize potential cancer-causing substances before they have a chance to damage the DNA of healthy cells.[102]

Nutrients are essential for the intelligent body.

Next to air and water, nothing is more important to the body than nutrition. The body simply can*not* perform its trillions of cellular functions without them. The essential nutrients include: Vitamins A, B-complex, C, D, E, K, phosphorus, iodine, calcium, magnesium, selenium, copper, zinc, manganese, chromium, and molybdenum. Your body requires all of them for cellular turnover and to maintain its healthy anabolic state of repairing and rebuilding organs, muscle, tissue, and bones. A diet that includes the aforementioned superfoods is the optimal way for the body to assimilate these nutrients.

I believe that the cause of so many chronic disease epidemics in America is directly related to the malnutrition that comes from an improper diet. Consuming mostly high-GI processed foods has dangerously supplanted a vitamin-dense, mineral-dense, antioxidant-rich diet that would potentially consist of vegetables, herbs, spices, and superfoods that the body needs to do its job properly. Every time you ingest a hamburger, fries, and Coke, you are essentially programming your body to carry out specific functions, most of them detrimental. Contrarily, when you eat a healthy kale salad with wild caught salmon and nutrient-dense veggies, you'll be programming your body to do specific functions, all of them beneficial.

When you feed your body nutrient-void, highly processed, high-GI carb, sugar-rich food on a regular basis, what do you think you are communicating to it over time? It's probably going to sound something like this: "I do not care enough about you to give you the appropriate nutrients to do your job properly." So what's your body going to do in return? It's going to communicate back to you in the only way that you will listen: *disease*. In other words, it will be saying to you, "Stop beating me up all the time by subjecting me to so much stress and that nutrient-void food you've been dumping into me because if you continue to do so, I'll break down and will be in need of some serious repair." On the other hand, if you give your body the proper vitamins and minerals it requires from a nutrient-dense *diet*—just as our paleo ancestors did—*then* what will you be communicating to it? You'll probably be saying something like this: "I'm grateful for you. I respect you. And I trust that you will use the information that I'm giving to you to stay completely healthy and disease-free." Perfect health is all about paying attention to your intelligent body, honoring its divine wisdom, and acknowledging whatever it's communicating *to* you. Foods that are loaded with carcinogenic additives, embalming preservatives, toxic chemicals, pesticides, fungicides, antibiotics, trans fats from hydrogenated vegetable oils, starchy carbs, as well as all sugar-rich foods and drinks are **killing us**.

More and more people now are consulting nutritional therapists in lieu of medical doctors for expert advice on their diet and rightfully so. Believe it or not, only somewhere between 30-40 percent of U.S. medical schools have a required nutrition course.[103] So at most, 40 percent of

U.S.-educated physicians have taken only one course in nutrition, most often in their first year. That's right, *one course*.

The intelligent body needs complete protein.

As I thoroughly explained earlier, your body is genetically engineered through evolution to require a specific amount of protein on a daily basis, preferably equally distributed with each meal, and I cannot stress the importance of it being *complete*. As a rule of thumb, I measure out an amount the size of my palm (about one-fourth of my plate), whether it be tofu, fish, poultry, or meat. A complete protein is one that contains significant amounts of all the essential amino acids since your body is unable to synthesize them on its own. Just like chlorella and spirulina, *soy* is also a plant food that is a complete protein. Meat, poultry, seafood, dairy, and eggs are all complete protein foods.

Soybeans originated in Southeast Asia and were first domesticated by Chinese farmers around 3100 BP. They've been safely consumed ever since by billions of Asians throughout the centuries. If you're a "soy skeptic," I suggest you investigate what the Okinawans do with soy and take a leaf from their cookbook. Non-GMO (genetically modified) and organic, their tofu has less water than their Japanese neighbors, making their tofu firmer, and higher in fat and protein. Not only does this increase the flavor of the tofu but it also increases the isoflavone (a flavonoid) content. In recent studies of populations that consume fair amounts of soy isoflavones, such as the Okinawans, there is a marked lower incidence of breast cancer and other common cancers. The Okinawans consume soy mainly in the forms of tofu and miso soup, averaging about three ounces per day.[104] The isoflavone-rich soy in their diet may be another important factor in their health and longevity. Like the sweet potato, soy is a nutrient-dense, low-GI carb. The flavonoids in soy result in antioxidant-like, cancer-preventative benefits, and unlike flavonoid-rich fruits, soy is sugar-free. If Okinawan tofu is not available from an Asian food market where you live, organic extra firm tofu is an excellent substitute.

One major component of soy skepticism is that it's high in phytic acid, or *phytates*, which are antioxidant compounds found in relatively high amounts in whole grains, legumes, nuts and seeds. The chief concern about phytates is that they can bind to dietary minerals such as iron, zinc, manganese, and calcium, and slow their absorption. Phytate-associated deficiencies of iron and zinc do occur in some third-world countries where people mostly eat grains, not soy.

According to world-renowned wellness author and alternative medicine guru Andrew Weil, M.D., the presence of phytates in soy should not be a concern. He wrote in a recent article that there is no scientific data suggesting that eating whole soy foods leads to mineral deficiencies, and there's no reason to worry about phytates "as long as you're eating a balanced diet."[105] Contrarily, new research from animal and test tube experiments have shown that phytates are also a phytonutrient—just like beta-carotene, lycopene, lignans, flavonoids, and anthocyanins—that demonstrate powerful antioxidant benefits. Some of these include: anti-inflammatory effects, normalization of cell growth, cardiovascular and diabetes benefits, as well as reducing the proliferation of cancer cells.[106] Another component in the soy debate is that it's produced as a GMO food more than any other. This is true; however, in America, most soy brands now offer USDA organic soy products. And the plus is that many organic soy products are now the same price as non-organic. The following is what the manufacturer must do before the product can receive the label *USDA Organic*:

- *95-100 percent of the ingredients must be certified organic.*
- *Food products cannot be exposed to chemical fertilizers, various synthetic substances, irradiation, sewage sludge, or genetically modified organisms (GMOs) in organic production.*

- *No antibiotic or synthetic hormone can be used in organic meat and poultry.*
- *100 percent organic feed is required for organic livestock.*

A three-ounce piece of meat contains about 21 grams of protein. The U.S. protein RDA is 46 grams for the average adult female and 56 grams for the average adult male. For each 100-calorie serving, tofu contains 11 grams of complete protein. By comparison, 100 calories of ground beef provides 8.9 grams of protein, and a 100 calorie serving of cheese contains 6.2 grams. So when choosing your complete protein, whether it be soy or animal-based products, I highly suggest you buy organic, no matter what country you live in. Animal foods in America that are not organic are ridden with steroids and antibiotics, not to mention the fact that the animals and fowl are kept in abominable conditions, allowing for stress-induced toxins to accumulate in the meat. I also recommend buying free range, *grass-fed* organic meats instead of grain-fed meats, because they are rich in omega-3 fatty acids, a vital part of a longevity-promoting, heart-healthy, ketogenic diet. If you aren't able to find them locally where you live, you can purchase grass-fed meats directly online at: www.grasslandbeef.com.

The cholesterol fallacy.

> *Going in with statin drugs to stamp out cholesterol is the equivalent of preventing the firemen who arrive to put out a fire from doing their job—and blaming them for the fire.*
>
> —Nora Gedgaudas, *Primal Body, Primal Mind*

Cholesterol has gotten a pretty bad rap in recent decades. You've probably been reminded by the media many times, over and over, that cholesterol and saturated fat are very bad for your body. But as it turns out, nothing could be further from the truth. If dietary cholesterol were bad for the body, then human breast milk wouldn't contain a significant amount of it. Breast milk provides a higher proportion of cholesterol than almost any other food, and over 50 percent of its calories come from *saturated fat.* Both cholesterol and saturated fat are *essential* for the normal growth of babies and children, especially the development of the brain.[107] In spite of this biological *fact*, the American Heart Association is now recommending a low-cholesterol, low-fat diet for children. As a result, commercial formulas are now dangerously low in saturated fats and soy formulas are devoid of much needed cholesterol. This is insane!

Not only is dietary cholesterol *not* bad for your health, it's also *not* the cause of heart disease as you've been made to believe. The truth is the intelligent body *needs* dietary cholesterol. The brain, for example, consists of about 2 percent of your body weight, but contains *20 percent* of your body's cholesterol. Professor of pediatrics and of cell biology and physiology at the Washington University School of Medicine, Guojun Bu, Ph.D., says that cholesterol plays a *critical role* in the permeability of the brain's cell membranes and synaptic functions, and any defects in its metabolic regulation are likely to be contributing factors for Alzheimer's disease.[108] It also plays a vital role for the body's immune system. None of the steroidal hormones, such as vitamin D, adrenaline, cortisol, estrogen, or testosterone can be produced in the body without it. Cholesterol also helps in the formation of your memories and is a vital component for neurological function. In fact, it is *so* important on *so* many levels that the liver is actually capable of—in a famine emergency—manufacturing cholesterol without dietary intake.

Biologically speaking, the body is not really geared to consistently shoulder the burden of cholesterol manufacturing. It is a taxing and onerous process that's supposed to occur *only* in an emergency. Providing the body with sufficient cholesterol is *your* job through *diet.* If you don't consume sufficient dietary cholesterol, then the consequences can be catastrophic to your health, especially your heart health. In humans, *triglycerides* are a mechanism for storing unused calories, and their high concentrations in blood are always associated with the consumption of high-GI carbs. For example, when your diet consists of high-GI foods such as rice, beans, bread, cereal, corn, pasta, and white potatoes, the high levels of insulin that is released by the pancreas prompts the liver to do the following: (1) If your body is in need of energy, it will burn that sugar for fuel. (2) If you don't need energy at the moment or glycogen stores are full, then the sugar from the carbs will then be converted into cholesterol and/or triglycerides, which gets stored as *fat*.[109] Since most people don't get sufficient daily exercise, the latter is the most common scenario.

As wellness author and lecturer Diane Schwarbein, M.D., says, "Weight gain is not about calories. It's about hormones."[110] So, every time your insulin levels go up because of high-GI carb intake, your body will store fat. Because sugar is so harmful to the body on so many levels, the body springs into action to do everything it can to *restrict* the amount of sugar that gets released into the bloodstream and the brain. This is where the pancreas comes in with its insulin production, and where the liver comes in with its cholesterol and triglyceride production—but *only* if you're *depriving your body of dietary cholesterol* while also consuming most of your calories from hi-GI carbs. This is when you're communicating to your body: "Famine is here." To address this famine emergency, the body sends in insulin to activate a critical enzyme in your liver called "HMG Co-A reductase" that results in an *over*production of cholesterol directly from high-GI carbs.[111] This *internally* excessive manufacturing of cholesterol greatly contributes to the damaging arterial plaque that causes heart attacks.[112] This means that a low-fat, low-cholesterol, high-GI carbohydrate diet will *ensure* a high insulin production accompanied by a burdensome internal production of cholesterol by the liver, potentially leading to **heart disease and stroke**.

So eating *non-fat* or *low-fat* foods with insufficient dietary cholesterol while at the same time maintaining a high-GI carb intake pretty much *guarantees* a consistent overproduction of cholesterol within the body. Because cholesterol is so crucial for the body's survival, it does this to save itself from certain death. Contrarily, ***dietary cholesterol does not play any role whatsoever in this pernicious cycle.*** In fact, the only way to *lower* your body's internal cholesterol production is to *increase* your dietary intake, meaning the only way to switch *off* the HMG Co-A reductase enzyme is by backing off the carbs and eating a sufficient amount of dietary cholesterol, effectively communicating to the body, "Famine is over."[113]

When HMG Co-A reductase is effectively blocked, cholesterol cannot be converted from sugar. Big Pharma is well aware of this fact, which is, of course, why their *statin drugs* artificially do this same exact thing, but only at the high cost of overtaxing the liver and depleting the body's own reserves of the coenzyme CoQ_{10}, a vital nutrient for heart health.[114] And then there's the toxic side effects of statins such as headaches, insomnia, flushing of the skin, muscle aches, drowsiness, dizziness, nausea and/or vomiting, abdominal cramping and/or pain, bloating and/or gas, diarrhea, constipation, skin rash, and liver damage.

But again, cholesterol is not bad for the body and increasing evidence has shown that "blocking" its production has *zero* effect on heart disease. To wit: Vytorin and Lipitor, the two biggest cholesterol-lowering statin drugs, rake in *billions* of profit for Big Pharma, yet recent studies have shown that these drugs have *no effect* on heart disease. A five-year study found that Vytorin did not reduce strokes or heart attacks compared to placebo.[115] "There's a conspiracy of false hope," says Harvard Medical School's John Abramson, M.D., adding that statins are not preventing anything and may actually be doing more harm than good.[116]

If you're taking statins for your high cholesterol, not only are they completely worthless but they may actually be dangerous to your health. A new study in the *Archives of Internal Medicine* found that statins increase the risk of diabetes by 71 percent in post-menopausal women.[117] And since diabetes is one of the primary causes of heart disease, this study calls into serious question current guidelines from physicians and medical associations who regularly prescribe statins to women for the prevention of heart attacks. But in spite of these alarming new findings, the 2004 National Cholesterol Education Program guidelines expanded the previous guidelines to recommend that even *more* people without heart disease take statins (from 13 million to 40 million).[118] How upside down is *this?*

In a recent interview, Dr. Abramson said that "there is not a single randomized control trial that shows that cholesterol-lowering statin drugs are beneficial for women of any age or men over 65 who do not already have heart disease or diabetes."[119] In spite of this, however, 22 percent of adults 45 or older take a statin drug, making it the most commonly prescribed class of medications in America, and probably the world. To wit: in 2009, U.S. patients filled 201.4 million prescriptions for statins, nearly *double* the prescriptions written in 2001, just four years after they were introduced.[120]

In a recent article, health educator and wellness advocate Mark Hyman, M.D., noted that 99 out of 100 men who take statin drugs receive no benefit, adding that over $20 billion a year is spent on statin prescriptions where 75 percent of the patients receive no proven benefit.[121] And yet the statin trend continues to climb even though 50 to 75 percent of people who have heart attacks also have *normal* cholesterol levels.[122] Another study at the Honolulu Heart Program showed older patients with lower cholesterol have *higher* risks of death than those with higher cholesterol.[123] The ENHANCE trial study showed that aggressive cholesterol treatment with the medications Zocor and Zetia lowered cholesterol much more than one drug alone, but led to *more* arterial plaque and no fewer heart attacks.[124]

There are literally hundreds of clinical studies validating that statin drugs are not only useless, but may actually be *increasing* the rates of heart disease. In 2008, political commentator Tim Russert was taking statin drugs at the time of his death despite the fact that his cholesterol levels were completely normal. This was yet another tragic case of doctors prescribing it for "preventive measures." And if all of this weren't egregious enough, in 2011, Pfizer introduced a "kid-friendly" version of Lipitor, adding innocent children to their target demographics!

Saturated fat is vital for good health.

...no relation between saturated fat intake and risk of coronary heart disease was observed in the most informative prospective study to date.

—Walter Willett, M.D., *American Journal of Public Health*

The failure of the medical establishment to have any positive *impact at all* on the ongoing surge of chronic, degenerative diseases is exemplified in their hubris stance that the miraculous and sacred human body is just *too dim-witted* to know what's best for it. As I have clearly pointed out in this chapter, dietary fat is not only part of your evolutionary physiology, it is a necessary component for optimum wellness. You simply *can't have* good health and longevity without it. This inane, incessant programming that "fat is bad for the body" and "low-fat diets are best" has nothing to do with *science* and everything to do with making hundreds of billions of dollars a year for Big Agriculture and Big Pharma. And tragically, this misinformation is making us *sicker*, not healthier.

The medical community has been conveniently pointing its finger at the so-called "bad cholesterol" called LDL (low density lipoprotein) for the primary cause of arterial plaque that leads to coronary heart disease. But, again, this is pseudo-science. HDL and LDL are not even cholesterols, but rather lipoprotein transport mechanisms *for* cholesterol. Since cholesterol is insoluble in blood, it must be transported in the circulatory system inside of lipoproteins, such as HDL and LDL, serving as "molecular addresses" that determine the start- and endpoints for cholesterol transport. So by making LDL the sole cause for heart disease, Big Pharma continues to rake in billions with its utterly useless statin drugs while the *true* cause behind heart disease remains suppressed.

The brain, heart, liver, and muscles consume most of the energy used by the body and prefer *ketones* from fat as their source of fuel, not sugar. Unsaturated fatty acids are defined as having one or more double bonds while saturated fatty acids only have single bonds. As a result, saturated fats are much more stable than their unsaturated counterparts. This is why the saturated fats of butter, lard, ghee, and coconut oil are denser and therefore solid at room temperature.

Because fat contains more than twice as many calories per gram as carbohydrates and protein, it's the most efficient source of energy. And *efficiency* just so happens to be what biological evolution is all about. When you eat fat, it can be burned for fuel right away or stored away for later use. Saturated fat, the misconceived "bad fat," makes up nearly *half* of your body fat. Without a high intake of it, our paleo ancestors would never have been able to survive long winters and avoid starvation.

The polyunsaturated vegetable oils, pushed by the USDA as "heart healthy," such as corn oil, safflower oil, soybean oil, and canola oil, are anything but, especially for cooking. The high temperatures of cooking can readily damage unsaturated fats and oils because of their shared bonds. Polyunsaturated fats are the most unstable, and when exposed to the high temperatures of cooking, they easily become oxidized, forming free radicals that can lead to cellular damage. Free radical damage from vegetable oils are a major contributor to atherosclerosis and heart disease. ***These are the bad fats***—*not* the saturated fats—and these are also the oils that are mainly used in restaurants and in the manufacturing of processed foods. Moreover, not only are these vegetable oils the *worst* for cooking but they are also GMOs, which act as "foreign intruders" to the intelligent body's immune system. To learn more about the hazards of genetically modified foods, go to www.geneticroulette.com.

Fats that contain a higher percentage of saturated fatty acids, such as the highly nutritious coconut oil, palm oil, and grass-fed butter are perfect for cooking at higher temperatures because they're very stable. Coconut oil is one of the best sources for saturated fat because it improves digestion and absorption of other nutrients including vitamins, minerals, and amino acids. It also significantly improves the utilization of blood glucose and insulin secretion, relieving stress on the pancreas. Because coconut oil improves calcium and magnesium absorption, it supports the development of strong bones and teeth, helping to protect the body against osteoporosis and inflammation. It's lower in calories than most other fats, helps to regulate thyroid function, and, unlike some other oils, does not deplete the body's antioxidant reserves.

The unique physiological and nutritional benefits from consuming coconut oil have been recognized in a wide variety of countries around the world for centuries. Unfortunately, in America, it has been denigrated by the USDA and every other Big Gov. food agency because it's considered a saturated fat. But a review of coronary heart disease literature relevant to coconut oil clearly indicates that at its worst, coconut oil is completely *neutral* with respect to arterial plaque formation, and, in fact, is much more likely to be *beneficial* for the prevention and treatment of heart disease.[125] Lauric acid from coconut oil is converted to monolaurin in the body, a key component in human breast milk, and is therefore used in infant formula.[126] Because much of the saturated fat of coconut oil is in the form of lauric acid, a recent study found that it may be a better alternative to partially hydrogenated vegetable oil.[127] Furthermore, coconut oil may not carry the same risks as other saturated fats because it consists mainly of medium chain fatty acids.[128] It's also great for your skin!

The American Cancer Society, the National Cancer Institute, and the Senate Committee on Nutrition and Human Needs all have made claims that animal fat is linked not only with heart disease but also with various cancers. But strangely, when researchers from the University of Maryland examined the data they used to make such claims, they found that animal fat was *not* linked to cancer, and vegetable fat *was*.[129] A comparison of human populations between northern and southern India revealed a similar pattern. People in northern India consume 17 times more animal fat yet have shown a seven times *lower* incidence of heart disease from people in southern India.[130] The diet of the Maasai and kindred tribes of Africa has for centuries been based primarily based on milk and beef from grass-fed cattle. They are free from coronary heart disease and have excellent blood cholesterol levels.[131] Inuits in the Arctic eat excessive amounts of fat from fish and marine animals, yet they are free of disease and exceptionally healthy. A study of Puerto Ricans revealed that they have very low incidences of colon and breast cancer in spite of the fact that they consume high amounts of animal fat.[132]

A survey of 1,700 patients with hardening of the arteries, conducted by the famous heart surgeon Michael DeBakey, found *no* correlation between the level of cholesterol in the blood and the incidence of atherosclerosis.[133] A Medical Research Council survey showed that men eating butter had *half* the risk of developing coronary heart disease than those using margarine from vegetable oil.[134] A survey of South Carolina adults found no relationship of blood cholesterol levels with the intake of red meat, animal fats, fried foods, butter, eggs, whole milk, bacon, sausage and cheese.[135] An extensive study of diet and disease patterns in China revealed that the region in which the populace consumes large amounts of whole milk had *half* the rate of heart disease as districts in which only small amounts of animal products were consumed.[136] Many Mediterranean cultures have very low rates of heart disease even though fat—including highly saturated fat from organic, grass-fed meats such as lamb, sausage and goat cheese—comprises a large percent of their caloric intake.

The good health of the Japanese, who have the longest lifespan of any nation on Earth, is generally attributed to a low-fat diet. But this is simply not true. Although the Japanese eat few *dairy* fats, they consume moderate amounts of saturated fats from eggs, pork, chicken, beef, seafood, and organ meats. Moreover, because they eat shellfish and fish broth on a daily basis, the Japanese likely have a *higher* intake of dietary cholesterol than most Americans. What they *don't* consume in fair amounts: sugar, vegetable oil or margarine (trans fats), bread, cereals, and processed foods. The lifespan of the Japanese has increased since World War II along with an increase in animal fat and protein in the diet.[137] The Okinawans have the lowest death rates of coronary heart disease than any other people in the world yet their diet consists of generous amounts of pork and seafood and they do all their cooking in lard.[138] Next to the Okinawans, the Cretans, Swiss, Austrians, and Greeks are the world's longest living peoples, yet their diets are moderately high in saturated fat.

And as a final example, let's take a look at the French. Anyone who has eaten anywhere in France has probably observed that the French diet is *loaded* with saturated fats in the form of butter, eggs, cheese, cream, liver, meats and rich patés. Yet the French have a *lower* rate of heart disease than many other Western countries. The mortality rate of heart attacks in France is an astounding *50 percent less* compared to the United States, and in the Gascony region, where goose and duck liver are a staple in the diet, this rate drops to 75 percent less.[139] This phenomenon has gained international attention as the "French Paradox." In the book *Cholesterol and The French Paradox*, clinical nutritionist and naturopathic physician Frank Cooper argues that this paradox is due to the **lack of hydrogenated oils and trans fats** in the French diet.[140] Harmful trans fats are actually *banned* in many European countries but not in the United States.

Omega-3 fatty acids are essential for metabolism.

One of the reasons the Cretans lead the world in health and longevity is due to their significant intake of essential omega-3 fatty acids from fresh-caught fish such as salmon, mackerel, and sardines. Cretans had the lowest rates of heart disease of all populations observed in the Seven Countries Study despite the fact that they had one of the highest-fat diets (37 percent of calories from fats).[141] Because animals in Crete consume omega-3-rich grass instead of omega-3-void grains, their pesticide-free, antibiotic-free, naturally organic meats, milk, cheese, and eggs are excellent sources of omega-3 fatty acids.[142]

Omega-3 fatty acids, which include ALA, EPA, and DHA, are fats commonly found in marine and plant oils. Inside the cellular structure of plankton, grass, and some seeds and nuts lie the sources for ALA, a parent class of omega-3 essential fatty acids. Omega-3 fatty acids are considered *essential* fatty acids because they cannot be synthesized by the body yet are *vital* for a healthy metabolism. Meat from grass-fed animals accumulate significantly more omega-3 than grain-fed animals, which accumulate more omega-6 fatty acids.

Even if omega-6 fatty acids are not present, a mere 6 percent of the omega-3 short chain form, ALA, will be converted by the body into long-chain forms of EPA and DHA, a rather inefficient process. But typically (especially in an American diet) when ALA is consumed, omega-6 (found mainly in vegetable oils) *will* be present, and if so, it *competes* with omega-3, allowing only *2.7 percent* to be converted.[143] Therefore flaxseed oil and hemp oil—a major source of ALA—are not the best omega-3 food or supplementation sources, which are regular fish oil and Antarctic krill oil that is purified and mercury-free. The best food sources for omega-3 foods (in already converted DHA and EPA) are all organic, grass-fed meats and dairy, as well as wild-caught fish such as salmon, sardines, halibut, cod, herring, mackerel, and bluefish. Instead of frying at high temperatures, make sure you bake (or slow cook on a grill) your fish so that the omega-3 fatty acids are not destroyed.

The modern American and global urban diet is in dire need of balancing omega-3 with omega-6 since the latter is in overabundance due to the high-GI carb intake, as well as high consumption of processed foods made with vegetable oils. Because of modern agriculture, *grass*-fed sources for meat and dairy have diminished significantly, allowing *grain*-fed meats—a major source of omega-6—to become the mainstay. This is potentially very dangerous to our immune and metabolism health. In the body, a competition plays out between man-made *trans fats* and precious enzymes known as delta-5 and delta-6. These unhealthy trans fats are found in margarine, vegetable shortening, commercial baked goods, fast foods, processed foods, commercial salad dressings, and vegetable oils. They may appear on products labeled as "hydrogenated" or "partially hydrogenated" oils or other such substances. Trans fats are *major* contributors to heart disease. Some of the most common food sources of trans fats are: tortillas, potato chips, boxed cookies, microwave popcorn, commercial pastries and breads, fast foods such as French fries, as well as all hydrogenated oils. Anything that doesn't exist in nature is probably not going to be compatible with the intelligent body. So, you know, avoid them like the plague.

Because of the prominence of omega-6 and trans fats intake in the modern industrial diet, a healthy ratio between omega-3 and omega-6 must be established from food and supplementation to ensure that sufficient omega-3 is allowed to be metabolized by the body. Furthermore, metabolites from omega-6 are more inflammatory than those of omega-3, another reason why they should be consumed in a balanced proportion; healthy ratios of omega-3/omega-6 range from 1:1 to 1:4. Clinical studies suggest the evolutionary paleo diet, rich in grass-fed game animals, seafood, and other sources of omega-3, may have provided such a ratio.[144]

Omega-3 fatty acids reduce triglyceride levels, and regular intake may reduce the risk of secondary and primary heart attack.[145, 146] Some potential benefits have been reported in cardiac arrhythmias.[147] There is preliminary evidence that omega-3 EPA supplementation, either with DHA or medication, is helpful in cases of depression.[148] There is also evidence that supplementation with omega-3 fatty acids may reduce anxiety.[149] Several studies report possible anti-cancer effects for breast, colon, and prostate cancer from the dietary intake of omega–3 fatty acids.[150,151]

In a study regarding fish oil published in the *Journal of Nutrition* in 2007, sixty-four healthy Danish infants from nine to twelve months of age received either cow's milk or infant formula alone or with omega-3-rich fish oil. Infants supplemented with fish oil showed improvement in immune system function.[152] Current research also suggests that the long-chain omega–3 fatty acids may be beneficial in inflammatory diseases. A large body of evidence supports a protective effect of omega-3 fatty acids for Crohn's disease, ulcerative colitis, and rheumatoid arthritis compared to those receiving standard anti-inflammatory drugs.[153]

Acupuncture for infertility.

Acupuncture is a drug-free alternative medicine modality practiced in traditional Chinese medicine that's been used successfully to treat patients for a variety of diseases (with little or no side effects) for thousands of years. It is implemented by manipulating thin, solid needles inserted into "acupuncture points" in the skin. Stimulating these points can correct imbalances in the flow of *chi* or "life force energy" through channels known as *meridians*. Current scientific research supports acupuncture's efficacy in the relief of certain types of pain and post-operative nausea.[154] My sister, Connie Zack, received some remarkable benefits from acupuncture in her search for an alternative treatment that would help her become pregnant. Here's her story in her own words:

> *I was struggling with infertility for several years and tried many different methods. Then one day a friend of mine recommended an acupuncturist who had been known in the community as an excellent healer. Her grandfather was a Chinese acupuncturist and she was well-versed in his techniques.*
>
> *When I explained to her what I was trying to accomplish, she expressed with confidence she would definitely be able to help me. The first time I went she ex-*

plained it would be a long shot to have success during my current cycle, but she would give it her best. She then explained if I didn't get pregnant, she would definitely help me the next cycle.

The acupuncture was not successful the first cycle as she anticipated; however, I followed her instructions to the letter going two days a week for a month the next time, and to my delight found out I was pregnant on Christmas Day.

I followed the same procedures after my first child was born, and was able to have a second child less than two years later. I will always be grateful for the recommendation from a girlfriend to go see Mary, the acupuncturist, as I am confident she is part of the reason I have two beautiful boys today. As a result, I would highly recommend acupuncture treatments to anyone.

The importance of pure H_2O.

Unfortunately, in the United States—a country that spends *twice* as much on health care than any other in the world—water from the tap is not fit for human consumption. Because it has been allowed by the U.S. Environmental Protection Agency (EPA) to contain certain levels of fluoride, chlorine, arsenic, cyanide (yes, *cyanide*), mercury, lead, and dozens of other toxic chemicals and compounds, we have been, in the last several decades, forced to drink bottled water.[155] But as of 2006, bottled water suppliers in the U.S. have been legally allowed by the FDA to add fluoride to their water to "assist in the prevention of dental cavities," prompting praise from the American Dental Association.[156]

Unlike drinking water utility companies, which have to publish their lab results in a public record, water bottlers don't have to notify anyone of their findings, including consumers who inquire. According to the EPA,

"Some bottled water is treated more than tap water, while some is treated less or not at all."[157] The Kansas Department of Health and Environment tested eighty samples of bottled water and found that *all eighty* of the samples contained detectable levels of chlorine and fluoride.[158] Seventy-eight of the eighty contained nitrates, fifty-three contained chloroform, twenty-five contained arsenic, and fifteen tested positive for lead.[159] And this is *bottled* water!

Industry and government have long had a powerful motive for claiming that fluoride is safe. But maintaining this position has not been easy since fluoride is one of the most toxic substances known. During the 1940s, ionic fluoride was a chemical that was used in the Manhattan Project to produce the atomic bomb. For most of the 20th century it's been a toxic waste byproduct expelled from the large paper, aluminum, and phosphate fertilizer manufacturing plants in the United States. After realizing that it was causing genetic damage to the wildlife, the Environmental Protection Agency intervened and forced the manufacturers to dilute the fluoride with water, put them into tanker cars, and dispose them in a toxic waste dump. But, of course, this was costly. In the 1930s, scientists employed by the *exact same* industrial manufacturers suddenly decided that it could be beneficial for the teeth and would prevent tooth decay, and as a result, the industries saved millions of dollars a year by not having to dispose of it safely and properly. Instead they conveniently transferred it over to the municipal water companies where it was put into the drinking water.

Okay. First of all, why in the world would you ever want to *drink* fluoride for cavity-prevention? I mean, you wouldn't think of drinking sunscreen lotion for sunburn-prevention would you? Secondly, fluoride is more toxic than *lead*. Thirdly, it depletes the body of iodine which is essential for thyroid function. Fourthly, ninety-seven percent of Western Europe has either eliminated or *banned* fluoridation of drinking water. These countries include: Austria, Belgium, Denmark, Finland, France, Germany, Iceland, Italy, Luxembourg, Netherlands, Northern Ireland,

Norway, Scotland, Sweden, and Switzerland.[160] Fluoridation of the water in the countries of India, China, and Japan is also banned. But like toxic *trans fats*, the U.S. Food and Drug Administration (FDA) says it's perfectly safe for human consumption!

While water fluoridation is often credited with causing the reduction in tooth decay that has occurred in the U.S. over the past 50 years, the same reductions in tooth decay have occurred in all western countries, most of which have *never* added fluoride to their water. Yet according to comprehensive data from the World Health Organization, their tooth decay rates are just as low, if not *lower* than the tooth decay rates in the United States.[161]

The side effects of fluoride include mottled teeth, osteoporosis, calcification of tendons and ligaments, skin rashes, mouth lesions, headaches, joint pain, gastric distress, chronic fatigue, and vision problems.[162] Fluoride ingestion has also been associated with IQ deficits in children, depression, heart disease, thyroid disease, bone cancer, neurological disorders, and kidney disease.[163]

Nothing is more important and nourishing for the intelligent body than pure, clean water. Your body needs both the hydrogen and oxygen from water not only to survive but also to be in perfect health. Unfortunately, due to over-processed foods, mineral-deficient soil, pesticides, chemical fertilizers, chemical preservatives, and drinking over-chlorinated and over-fluoridated water, most people don't get enough hydrogen ions daily. Consequently, the cellular body becomes damaged, hydration levels decrease, and cells age.

When your body is dehydrated, cells cannot assimilate essential nutrients, remove waste and relieve pain from conditions like arthritis or fibromyalgia. Dehydration also occurs as a side effect of caffeine, which is the most widely consumed drug on the planet. Caffeine effects include anxiety, dizziness, headaches, sleep disorders, and many common ailments. So if you're drinking caffeinated beverages all day long, all you're doing is depleting your cells of hydrogen and oxygen, which means you need to consume greater amounts of pure clean water to rehydrate.

The bottom line is this: Unless the bottled water is labeled as de-ionized, purified, or distilled, you may be taking a risk that it contains excessive amounts of chlorine, fluoride, and other harmful toxins.

The healing power of upper cervical care.

In 1995, I was introduced to a highly specialized modality of chiropractic care known as *upper cervical care*. At that time, X-rays were taken by a chiropractic physician of my skull and upper spine and it was revealed that I had developed an abnormal curvature of my top vertebrae known as an *upper cervical subluxation*. I was then shown an X-ray of a normal, healthy upper cervical spine and the difference was *astounding*.

My doctor explained that my inner ear disorder and subsequent chronic dizziness, as well as the TMJ syndrome that I had been enduring for so many years, were no doubt caused by the two car accidents I had when I was a teenager. He informed me that auto accidents are one of the major causes of vertebral subluxations, but even a fall or slight trauma to the head or back could be enough to contribute to a misalignment of the upper curvature of the spine.

Because the nervous system controls all body functions, if you cut off the nerve supply to the heart, your heart will stop beating. If you cut off the nerve supply to your lungs, your lungs will stop breathing. Without the nervous system, your body cannot function and you will die. Upper cervical care chiropractors focus on locating the underlying *cause* of the disease from the nerve center *source*, then removing the interference on the level of the nerves themselves so that the intelligent body is "freed up" to do its job more efficiently and effectively, thus restoring itself back to perfect health.

The brain facilitates communication via trillions of nerve fibers to every part of the body by way of the spinal cord. In between the spinal cord and the brain is a bundle of nerves called the *brain stem*. Nerve supply to every organ, muscle, joint, tissue and *cell* in the body begins from the brain stem, the "command center" of the intelligent body. The brain stem directs and delegates all the functions of the body such as breathing, heartbeat, motor function, equilibrium, and the regulation of the sympathetic and parasympathetic systems. Because of the important neural structures concentrated in this small portion of the nervous system, the slightest of damage to this area may have *profound* degenerative effects.

The brain stem is sheathed by the atlas (C1) and axis (C2) vertebrae and when completely aligned and freed of nerve interference (from upper cervical care adjustments), the rest of the spine and skeleton will automatically realign itself (like a domino effect), thus restoring the nervous system to its optimally healthy state. As a result of this vertebral realignment, the body is allowed to regenerate tissue, repair cellular damage and heal itself naturally without drugs or surgery. An upper cervical correction is painless, non-invasive, very controlled, and gentle; there is no pulling, tugging, or jerking of the head. The adjustment allows the head, neck, and spine to return to the proper position, thus removing the interference and restoring *balance* to the body.

It is this inter-relationship between the upper cervical spine, the central nervous system, and the brain stem, that affects every aspect of human function, including touch, hearing, vision, mental processing, regulation of hormones, motor control, and immune system regulation. But perhaps most importantly, when properly aligned, upper cervical care helps the body maintain an *anabolic state* of repair and renewal.

Unlike conventional chiropractors, upper cervical care chiropractors only focus on maintaining the alignment of the C1 and C2 vertebrae, thus keeping the brain stem *freed* from nerve interference. And it is this unique, specialized, and revolutionary approach to chiropractic care that allows for a much *broader range* of healing throughout the body. Not only has chronic back, muscle, and joint pain been shown to be relieved or eliminated completely with upper cervical care, but there have been thousands of case studies conclusively showing its effectiveness for: recurring ear infections, asthma, sinus infections, migraines, chronic fatigue, depression, epilepsy, carpal tunnel, multiple sclerosis, fibromyalgia, diabetes, digestive disorders, trigeminal neuralgia, high blood pressure, TMJ syndrome, Meniere's disease, inner ear disorder (vertigo, dizziness, tinnitus), and many other diseases.

In a 2011 case report, a nine-year-old girl with uncontrollable blinking of the left eye and fainting spells, previously diagnosed by a neurologist as occipital lobe epilepsy, demonstrated resolution of signs and symptoms following the reduction of an upper cervical subluxation.[164] In a 2003 case, upper cervical care was used for a nine-year-old male who had been suffering with Tourette syndrome (TS), attention deficit hyperactivity disorder (ADHD), depression, asthma, insomnia, and headaches since the age of six. Upper cervical care corrected and stabilized the patient's subluxation. After only six weeks of care, all six conditions were no longer present and all medications were discontinued with the exception of a half dose of Wellbutrin. At the conclusion of his case at five months, all symptoms remained absent. The response to upper cervical care suggests a correlation between the patient's traumatic birth, the upper vertebral subluxation, and his neurological conditions.[165]

An 87-year-old female suffered frequent episodes of vertigo, tinnitus and nausea for 45 years. She was in a car accident a few years before the onset of her episodes. Immediately following an upper cervical adjustment, she reported complete alleviation of vertigo and dizziness. When she awoke the next morning, the tinnitus had also been alleviated.[166] In a case report of a 47-year-old female diagnosed with multiple sclerosis (MS) at age 44, she had cognitive problems, loss of bladder control, leg weakness and paresthesias in her arms and legs. After only four months of upper cervical chiropractic care, all of her MS symptoms were gone, and even after two years all symptoms remained absent.[167]

Otitis media with effusion (OME), most commonly known as an "inner ear infection," is one of the most common diagnoses of children by pediatricians in the United States. There are thousands of case studies that show upper cervical care has helped clear the infections up without antibiotics. One case study of a three-year-old girl with chronic recurrent inner ear infections and a resulting hearing loss showed rapid improvement and complete reversal of OME with upper cervical care after three unsuccessful implantations of tympanostomy tubes and multiple medications. The patient reported an increase in hearing and the child's mother reported the child had less ear pain, was less irritable, and had better speech after just one upper cervical care adjustment.[168] In another OME case report, a two-year-old girl suffered for over a year from chronic sinus and ear infections every other month, each time requiring two to three courses of antibiotics. She also experienced chronic, green sinus discharge and her nose was completely blocked. During her initial evaluation, an upper neck injury was discovered. Her mother recalled that during her daughter's birth, vacuum suction was used to extract her and it had fractured her collar bone. After upper cervical chiropractic care was administered, her nose drained until all of the green discharge was absent and no additional sinus or ear infections occurred.[169]

A 23-year-old professional female ice skater sustained a concussion by hitting her head against the ice. Following the concussion, tension and migraine headaches persisted over the next twelve years, during which she utilized daily pain medications. Upon discovering an upper cervical subluxation, an upper cervical care chiropractor administered treatment for her. Shortly afterward, she showed an immediate reduction in symptoms; the complete absence of all symptoms occurred within three months.[170] Another case reported a 45-year-old female who experienced two major physical traumas and ten car accidents leading to complaints of an eleven-year history of fibromyalgia. Symptoms included migraine headaches, chronic neck pain, upper and lower back pain, numbness in fingers, sciatica, right knee pain, depression, and duodenal ulcers. Upon examination, an upper cervical subluxation was determined by x-ray and pattern analysis. Upon correction of the upper cervical subluxation, the patient had complete resolution of fibromyalgia as well as most of the symptoms.[171]

Like straightening teeth, an upper cervical subluxation takes the body a little time to correct, especially if it's a long-term chronic condition like inner ear disorder, joint pain, or MS. In some cases, the results are immediate, while others take a few months, and still others years. For me, since I had my car accidents when I was a teen, my upper cervical spine had already been subluxating for over fifteen years before I began my first upper cervical treatments. And so it required a few years of treatment before my inner ear could completely heal and all of the dizziness was gone. So you have to be committed to getting well. I made sure I made every single one of my appointments because just like any chronic illness that develops over time, the body *reverses* the chronic condition *over time*. Upper cervical care has also greatly contributed to relieving my chronic fatigue syndrome and overall health and well-being. It has literally been a "life saver" for me. I cannot recommend it enough for *everyone* because even if you are disease-free, upper cervical care is one of the best ways to stay that way, which can only help to improve your longevity. You can find an upper cervical care practitioner near you at: www.upcspine.com.

Empowering wellness with infrared therapy.

Infrared or radiant heat comes from the sun naturally, and is in fact a beneficial form of light that all living things require for health and well-being. Unlike conventional saunas, the infrared sauna heats the body directly without having to heat the air in between. This results in its much lower power-consumption and shorter warm-up time.

In 1999, I purchased an infrared sauna because my holistic dentist recommended it for detoxifying mercury out of my body. At the time, I was undergoing chelation therapy for mercury toxicity which was not giving me much relief and was taking a very long time to get the mercury out of my system. The mercury toxicity was caused from my amalgam dental fillings, half of which contained mercury, the most toxic element on earth, second only to plutonium. Every time I chewed my food, microscopic amounts of the mercury was released into my digestive tract and subsequently absorbed into my tissues and cells. Even though I had replaced the mercury-laden amalgams with non-toxic composite fillings, the mercury still remained inside my body, contributing to my chronic fatigue syndrome. And so I decided to take my dentist's advice.

An infrared sauna emits three wavelengths of infrared light: near, mid, and far. Different parts of the infrared spectrum are more effective than others at targeting various health benefits. For example, the far-infrared (FIR) output is important for optimal detoxification of heavy metals such as mercury, cadmium, lead, and aluminum, toxic chemicals and compounds such as chlorine, arsenic, formaldehyde, and fluoride, and other harmful carcinogens. As toxins are released, the body's anabolic state of renewal is reactivated, resulting in a boost to your immune system.

I'll never forget when I purchased my first infrared sauna. It was so relaxing and tranquil. I felt calm, passive, at peace. After I showered the sweat off my body, I felt cleansed, purified. I knew immediately that I had received a revolutionary healing product that could be used in the privacy of my own home on a daily basis. I called it my "rejuvenation chamber." Within two days after using it for the first time, I was so excited that I became a dealer for the product. Eight months later, I founded Sunlight Saunas (now Sunlighten) to spread news to the world about the wonderful benefits of an infrared sauna.

Infrared therapy has shown to be a beneficial treatment for a broad variety of conditions including chronic fatigue syndrome, heavy metal toxicity, fibromyalgia, high blood pressure, muscle and joint pain, obesity, skin disorders, poor circulation, and many others. In one study, seventeen patients with rheumatoid arthritis (RA) and seventeen patients with ankylosing spondylitis (AS) were treated for a four-week period with a series of eight infrared (IR) treatments. Pain and stiffness decreased clinically, and improvements were statistically significant during an IR session. Fatigue also decreased. In the RA and AS patients, pain, stiffness, and fatigue also showed clinical improvements. The study concluded that infrared therapy has statistically significant beneficial effects during treatment in RA and AS patients.[172]

Infrared therapy stimulates the circulatory system, causing the heart to beat more vigorously and blood vessels to dilate, which help cleanse the circulatory system and more fully oxygenate the body's cells. Better blood circulation means more toxins flow from the cellular level to the skin's surface to improve cell health, aiding in muscle recovery and strengthening the immune system.

Several studies have shown that LEDs (like those found in a Sunlighten mPulse sauna) stimulate white blood cell production and collagen growth by increasing energy at the cellular level. A study done at the Medical College of Wisconsin demonstrated that LED-produced near infrared (NIR) helps promote cell health and regeneration.[173] A study from The American Society for Biochemistry and Molecular Biology concluded that LED near infrared (NIR) restores enzyme activity and reduces cell death by 50 percent.[174]

Results from a 2009 study showed Sunlighten saunas to be beneficial for lowering weight and waist circumference in just a three-month period. And for those who are sedentary due to medical conditions such as osteoarthritis, cardiovascular or respiratory problems, results were even more profound.[175] Another study showed that thirty-minute infrared sauna weight loss sessions can burn upwards of 600 calories. During a sauna weight loss session, your core temperature increases and the body works hard to cool itself. While using an infrared sauna, there is a substantial increase in heart rate, cardiac output and metabolic rate, causing the body to burn more calories. Blood flow is reported to rise from a normal five to seven quarts per minute to as much as thirteen quarts per minute.[176]

Studies conducted by NASA concluded that NIR LED light significantly promotes faster cell regeneration, wound healing and human tissue growth. Human cell growth increased by 155 percent to 171 percent in some cases and wound size decreased by 36 percent.[177] A study published in *The Journal of Cosmetic and Laser Therapy* showed significant improvements in skin appearance after just twelve weeks of sauna skin therapy using NIR technology. Participants experienced a reduction in wrinkles and crow's feet, as well as improved overall skin tone, including softness, smoothness, elasticity, clarity and firmness.[178]

According to Dr. Jeffrey Spencer, a sports medicine expert from the University of Southern California, "infrared wavelengths penetrate the body to create heat, which creates profound therapeutic benefits. They increase blood flow to the muscles, delivering more concentrated oxygen, which creates more energy to heal." A recent Japanese study published in the journal *Internal Medicine* showed that chronic pain patients experienced a 70 percent reduction in pain levels after the first session of infrared sauna therapy. Pain scores also decreased significantly and remained low throughout the observation period. Researchers concluded that infrared heat therapy is effective for chronic pain treatment.[179] A 2003 study conducted by the Department of Dermatology and Institute of Medical Research showed that use of NIR heat therapy helped the production of white blood cells to alleviate inflammation and reduce swelling, two key factors in easing bodily pain.[180]

The far-infrared heat generated by a Sunlighten sauna produces sweat that carries nearly 20 percent of toxins, compared to a traditional "hot stove" sauna where the toxin yield is only 3 percent. As a result, a sauna detoxification in a Sunlighten sauna is up to seven times more effective than in a traditional sauna.[181] Dr. Mark Hyman, New York Times bestselling author and editor-in-chief of the peer-reviewed medical journal *Alternative Therapies in Health & Medicine*, says, "Sunlighten saunas improve circulation, help with weight loss, balance blood sugar and improve detoxification."

Because infrared saunas heat your muscles with infrared rays, they produce an increase in blood flow similar to regular exercise which also results in the relaxation of sore and aching muscles and joints. Furthermore, because of the drug-free pain relief and efficient detoxification benefits, you'll find that your overall health, metabolism, and energy will improve, allowing the body to maintain cellular turnover, resulting in a boost to your immune system. To purchase your personal Sunlighten sauna, go to www.sunlighten.com.

The sun is vital for your health and well-being.

Vitamin D is a steroid hormone that influences virtually every cell in the body, and is easily one of the most potent cancer protectors. A recent review article published by Loyola University Chicago Marcella Niehoff School of Nursing concluded that adequate intake of vitamin D may prevent or delay the onset of diabetes and reduce complications for those who have already been diagnosed. The study co-author and professor, Sue Penckofer, Ph.D., R.N., said that "Vitamin D has widespread benefits for our health and certain chronic diseases in particular," and that this article "further substantiates the role of this nutrient in the prevention and management of glucose intolerance and diabetes."[182]

There are two factors for vitamin D deficiency: one, malnutrition; and two, lack of exposure to the sun. If you live in a region that gets very little sun in the winter, and you consequently suffer from seasonal affective disorder, then you most likely have a vitamin D deficiency. The sun is the principle source for vitamin D which the body needs to support healthy immune function. Without it, your body will die. Moreover, if you *overprotect* your body from the beneficial rays of light from the sun, you'll be depriving it from the most abundant source of vitamin D.

Nowadays everyone pours on the SPF sunscreen lotion all over their body which, of course, prevents the natural vitamin D from entering into the skin. But the recent ill-purported recommendation by the U.S. FDA for SPF sunscreen protection may be doing us all much more harm than good. Recent research published by the British Journal of Dermatology concluded that the sun is nothing more than a scapegoat in the development of melanoma, and the sharp increase may actually be due to the fact that people are being diagnosed with melanoma skin cancer even when they have only a minimal, non-cancerous lesion, and these diagnoses appear to be skewing disease rates significantly. The research also found that *lack* of sunlight, not too much, is a more likely culprit for the rising trend in melanoma cases.

As it turns out, people who work near windows only get the harmful UVA light from the sun and don't receive the healthy, vitamin D-rich, UVB light since only the former can pass through glass. The researchers' hypothesis was "one factor involves indoor exposures to UVA passing through windows, which can cause mutations, and the other factor involves insufficient levels of vitamin D3 received from the sun."[183]

If you're out in the sun so long where you have to be wearing SPF 50 to protect your skin, then, well, you're probably out in the sun too long. Put on a shirt and a hat, or get under a tree. When I'm out in the summer sun, I apply coconut oil to my skin and then *slowly* and gradually increase my sun exposure over a period of days and weeks, naturally. As nutritionist Nora Gedgaudas says in her book, *Primal Body, Primal Mind*, "The only people genuinely benefiting from sunscreens in this world are the ones who sell them."[184] She also says that most SPF sunscreens are formulated with potentially rancid omega-6 oil, as well as toxic and carcinogenic chemicals that not only block the vitamin D-containing sunlight, but also impede the production of vitamin D in the body.[185] Rule of thumb: if it's made by man with synthetic chemicals and marketed in a bottle, then it's probably not appropriate for the intelligent body. Taking care of your body means adhering to all natural and *organic* substances. And throw away all your moisturizing lotions that are riddled with chemicals and trans fat-laden hydrogenated oils. Pure coconut oil is far more beneficial to your skin anyway, and it smells great naturally without chemical perfumes. Remember that your skin is the largest organ, so whatever you apply to it gets absorbed and assimilated directly into the bloodstream.

Exercise smarter, not longer.

Exercise is extremely important for metabolism, weight management, and overall health and well-being. It improves insulin and leptin regulation. But exercise cannot make up for a nutrient-deficient, starch-based diet. I exercise every day and recommend my clients do the same. However, long-distance, time-consuming, endurance exercising over time will actually contribute to weight gain rather than weight loss.

When you spend an hour a day on the treadmill or in an aerobics class or jogging, sure, you'll burn fat, but in the long run, what you are actually doing is training your body to become as efficient as possible at making fat more *available* for burning. The intelligent body does this to counteract this onslaught of ridiculously unnecessary endurance exercising, day after day, week after week, month after month. It will ramp up its ability to convert every single calorie of food that you consume directly into fat. Why? Because from an evolutionary standpoint, you are communicating to the body that you're going to continue to burn as many calories as you can for as long as you can, and so your body responds by doing everything in its power to compensate for this "famine emergency." And contrary to popular opinion, running for an hour or more a day does not improve your cardiovascular health. The human body is simply not designed to be pushed over the edge and taken to its extreme limits on a continual basis. Not only are you conditioning your body to store fat more efficiently, you'll be more susceptible to soft-tissue injuries and stress fractures to your knee, hip, and ankle joints.

When you look at nature, guess how many animals spend more than an hour at a time, every single day, exerting *all* of their energy? That's right. None. This is because evolution selects the species that are the most efficient at energy *conservation*, not energy consumption. The cheetah, for example, can only sprint to its maximum speed of 70 miles per hour in very brief bouts.

So, when it comes to exercising, remember that less is always more. Instead of jogging for an hour, switch to sprinting as fast as you can for only twenty minutes. Instead of spending an hour in a spinning class, get on the Stairmaster and push your body to its limit for twenty minutes. If you feel that you need to burn more calories, then try working out for twenty minutes twice daily—once in the morning and once in the evening. These brief, higher intensity bouts of exertion and maximization of heart rate will serve to dramatically boost your oxygen intake, expand the capacity of your heart and lungs, and rapidly burn blood sugar and glycogen stores. And one more thing: If you adhere to a *ketogenic diet*, your body will be storing less fat because it won't be constantly bombarded by soaring glucose levels from high-GI carbs, and therefore you won't need to exercise as much to maintain the same body weight. Subsequently, as your insulin levels normalize, your body's ability to burn fat increases—without alarming the body that a famine is coming. This is how you turn your body into an efficient fat *burning* machine, rather than an efficient fat *storing* machine.

In summary.

There is really nothing more important than your health. When you are ready to put the physical Self first, honor your body and everything it's communicating to you in the Now, then you will naturally attract to you the appropriate healers, therapies, and foods to you that will allow it to go to work, do its job, and make the necessary repairs. Doctors don't heal. Only the body's divine intelligence can do that.

As we learn to take care of the physical Self first, respect it, trust it, and most importantly, *listen* to it, an entirely new system of health care will emerge on the planet. In the New Earth, preventive medicine will be the primary model of health care, as opposed to the drug-based, symptom treatment model that exists today.

Big Pharma spends *hundreds of millions* of dollars each year on government lobbying to ensure that their dominion over our disease care system remains firmly entrenched. But their system is highly corrupt because it is motivated by one word: *greed.* And this is why it has to go. The Next Human's job as the new species of the planet will be to abolish this egoic system that has nothing to do with helping people become healthy and stay healthy. It's time for a new health care model that will put the sacred human body first, not the stock of giant corporations.

For the first time in human history, information is readily accessible to anyone and everyone who wants to know the *facts* about what is making us healthier and what is making us sicker. Because of the power of the Internet, all clinical studies are now literally seconds away from your fingertips. Understand that this current corrupt system exists only as a reflection of our collective *ignorance.* So the information given here in this chapter and indeed this entire book is only meant to whet your appetite for more. There are more facts available to the public now than ever before, and all at the speed of, well, *light.* So, you know, *use it.*

EVOLUTION
401

THE MIRROR SELF
TRANSFORMING RELATIONSHIPS

Trinity: *Neo, I'm not afraid anymore. The Oracle told me*
that I would fall in love and that that man, the
man that I loved would be the One. So you see,
you can't be dead. You can't be. Because I love you.
You hear me? I love you.

—*The Matrix*

For most current humans there will be an underlying, subconscious fear of entering into a deeply intimate relationship—a fear based on repressed, unaddressed *trauma*. This fear, however, is made real by the egoic mind and subsequently experienced as negative emotions in the physical body. In the ancient world, the heart always came first and the mind followed. Like just about everything else, the current human has this process *reversed*. It is the heart that holds the true power, and only *it* can heal the wounds created by the mind, the ego. For those who love from the heart, their joy is immeasurable. Ego love, on the other hand, is not only limited, but always ends in suffering for both partners. The Next Human will resurrect the balanced power of the heart, that which our ancestors referred to as the *divine love* of gods and goddesses.

In this chapter I've written some short stories. Even though I've changed the names of the people and places in them, all of them are true. Sometimes I've revealed the story exactly as it played out, and sometimes I've combined several stories into one. All of the stories are about the hardships we endure in relationships, and the universe's way of *unveiling* ourselves through them.

In this, the third dimension of hardcore duality, everything "out there" will always be a *reflection* of what each and every One of us believes to be true on a deeper, inner, and more profound level. Imagine each person here as a movie projector and the film that feeds through the projector's narrow beam of light as the brain's perception of this global reality that we call "the world."

Just as your partner *mirrors* your personal frequency of energy on a very subtle, vibratory level, the world as a whole is none other than a mirrored reflection of the *collective* frequency—including its collective pain-body—that is summed up by its seven billion inhabitants. Our entire modern society—its governments, institutions, structures, organizations, industries, and systems—is all a *reflection* of the current level of collective intelligence and evolutionary awareness. I call this projected global reality the *collective mirror*.

There has been much written lately on the subject of a cabal or "hidden government" whose elite power players operate solely from behind the scenes, owning the major banks, running the military industrial complex, and secretly pulling the strings of world governments, all motivated by a one-word agenda: *control.* Certainly, egoic-minded men who wield extraordinary power have but one thing left to strive for: *more power.* Thus, if such a clandestine government does indeed exist, it would not surprise me in the least. But the validity to this or other theories should neither occupy your valuable time nor be your primary concern. Even if there is any truth to it, before you can do anything about it, you must first *master the Self* and awaken to your own divinity. Once the divine Self is finally actualized and you've evolved into the Next Human, then *no* person and *no* elusive government can enslave you. Enslavement exists only within the matrix of the *mind,* which is perfectly capable of manifesting fears into reality. Therefore, doom and gloom *beliefs* can only manifest as doom and gloom *realities.* This is the way the reflective universe works. So if you truly want to change the current reality for the better, then I suggest practicing detachment from the collective mirror when you meditate and refrain from identifying with your fear-based emotions. Instead, start believing in your own intuition, creativity, and immortality. Start believing in your *Self.* A path of panic and paranoia about what may or may not happen in the world is a dead-end street. Next Humans *own* their divinity, and are therefore *fearless.*

Know that the people in power are all part of a system. And so, of course, it's in their best interest to keep that system in place. That's their *purpose.* Because most current humans are ashamed of themselves and indifferent to their divine potential, they primitively react to events instead of going within and becoming heart-centered before taking action. This ego-based, dysfunctional behavior allows the same predatory people to keep their seats of power. Subsequently, Big Government bailed out the Big Banks after their corruption resulted in the Global Financial Crisis that left 10 percent of the U.S. working class unemployed.

The Next Human's purpose, on the other hand, is to be still, present, cautious, and *vigilant* so that she can successfully transcend the chaos that plays out in the collective mirror. Just because you *care* what happens doesn't mean that you have to *mind* what happens. When you're minding, you are mentally and emotionally entangled in the mirror. Minding is doing and *doing* is not being, and that will only amplify your reaction to what you see and hear, what already *is*. Know that detachment and transcendence are necessary for your peace of mind. And for the Next Human, peace of mind always comes *first*.

Receiving and giving have become completely imbalanced in our society for too long. As a species, we've been *giving* a great deal more to those in power than we've been receiving. If there *is* a hidden agenda that resides behind the veil of our current power structures, then it's only there because of *us*, reflecting a predator/prey dynamic onto the world stage. Like a weakened immune system that allows a virus to invade, the current condition of the human psyche has allowed the oppressive powers of the Big Five oil companies, Big Pharma, Big Agriculture, Big Government, Big Corporations, Big Banks, corrupt politicians, despots, and terrorists to shape the world as they see *fit*. Simply put, as a species, we've been playing the role of the *victim*. Because this collective pain-body is the condition of the current human, then it's only natural that oppression, manipulation, and deception will be seen and felt. Like a movie screen that can only display the imagery projected upon it, the collective mirror that we interpret as our "reality" can only show us what *we* project upon *it*.

The good news is that all of this is changing, and rapidly. The current financial and political system is metaphorically being held together with tin foil and chewing gum. The "house of cards" is about to collapse. And this is ultimately a *good thing* because, like all endings, it paves the way for a new beginning, a New Earth. It means the ending of a society that allows for billions of its own people to go on living below the poverty level, without adequate shelter, clean water, or nutritious food. It also indicates the rising of a brand *new* global economy where every One benefits, not just a select few.

There are two streams of consciousness flowing through the collective mirror today. At the same time that a certain percentage of our population is becoming more and more narcissistic, an equal percentage is exponentially increasing in spiritual awareness, and acquiring a higher understanding of the natural laws of the universe. The Next Human's job as the new species for the planet will be to dissolve the current system of control. In the United States, about 10 percent currently own 70 percent of all the assets. This toxic imbalance can only change from within. It all begins with Self-mastery.

In 2011, the world witnessed an Egyptian revolution and the over-throwing of its thirty-year oppressive president, Hosni Mubarak. It also watched the deaths of tyrants and key terrorist leaders, including Muammar Gaddafi, Osama bin Laden, Anwar al-Awlaki, and Kim Jong-il. Occupy Wall Street began in New York City on September 17, 2011, and within a few short weeks had spread to hundreds of cities around the world. Subsequently, Time Magazine chose "The Protester" as its "2011 Person of the Year." I believe that this is only a sneak preview of what's coming in the decade ahead.

The Next Human will instinctively know that all of humanity is ultimately connected at its core, where our spirits join with the One. Recognizing this divinity within each and every One of us is the only path to freedom from all oppression, seen or unseen. In the Next Human society, there will be no tolerance for abusive dictators, corrupt politicians, banking conglomerates, oil magnates, or government officials who *thrive* while the majority of the population merely *survives*.

You are who you attract. It's the law.

Do your thoughts center around animosity, regret, bitterness, or anger toward an ex-partner? When you think of a past partner, do you look down upon him or her in a shameful, inferior manner? Do you see any of your ex-partners as being "beneath you" or "not good enough for you" or "undeserving" of your love? If you have answered *yes* to any of the aforementioned questions, then I can promise you that you will eventually have the same negative feelings about your next partner. Guaranteed. Why? You *are* who you attract. It's the law. Until you transcend your negative shadow emotions, the next relationship will be doomed to become your *mirror self.*

Many people spend months, years, and even a lifetime festering anger and hatred toward past partners, replaying in the head all their mishaps, foibles, and acts of insanity. And of course, all of this drama is shared with everyone around them because, well, that rationalizes and reinforces just how "horrible" their ex-partners were. After all, it's always your partner's fault that the relationship failed in the first place, right? Well, if you've identified with any of this then you'll benefit greatly from the information in this chapter. I will show you how every relationship you've ever had has been nothing less than a reflection of your*self.*

The key to happiness in relationships is becoming happy with yourself *first.* Only the emotionally independent are free. And these are few. Until you can learn to open your heart and love your partner unconditionally—without expectations, requirements, or a list of qualifications—you will be loving from your mind, not your *heart.* And this is not true love.

On the flip side, when you evolve into the person you want to attract, embody the principles that you admire in others, and become a living example of an affectionate, giving, and compassionate soul, you will naturally attract the same in a partner. If you want to be with someone who is spiritual, self-aware, emotionally intelligent, present, caring, attentive, and non-judgmental, then you'll want to begin working *now* to transform yourself so that you exhibit these very same qualities. Then, instead of attracting your mirror self, you'll be attracting your mirror *Self.*

Codependency, the crutch.

> *I don't need anyone to rectify my existence. The most profound relationship we will ever have is the one with ourselves.*
>
> —Shirley MacLaine

You were born into this world by yourself and you will leave this world by yourself. Codependency, also known as *neediness,* is an inherent compulsion to be with another because you are not happy with what you see within. When the view of one's self becomes so repulsive, the mind will naturally seek a replacement for it elsewhere; specifically, in another.

Codependency is always rooted in the strings attached to the love given. It's as if the ego says, "I will love you if you make me breakfast," or "I will love you if you support me," or "I will love you if you convert to my religion," or "I will love you if you are faithful to me or treat me this way or that, and if you fail to do any of these things, then I will not love you back." Anger, resentment, conflict, and bitterness are common feelings stemming from a codependent relationship. And so the "love" given from the *needy* will always be tethered with preconditions.

For the codependent, what is initially perceived as true love frequently turns into hatred. This is because codependency is, by its very nature, an *unnatural* state of being. It's an inner compulsion to be with a partner, rather than a *choice* to be. When you feel as if you *have* to be with another human because of a lacking to be complete, then the universe can only send you the same resonance of *lacking* in a mate. It's as if the universe says, "Here you are. This is a mirror of your needy self."

A codependent relationship is all about "what you can do for *moi,*" and so the relationship is formed with specific expectations; if the other doesn't measure up, then it's off to greener pastures. This is why relationships that are based mostly on sex, status, fame, or money are short-lived. Codependent relationships are also, to varying degrees, quite abusive. But the people who are in them are not consciously aware that they're being abused. And that's one of the reasons why they remain *in them* for so long. Because their own pain-body needs to receive abuse as energy for it to *feed* on, they typically remain in denial of their own suffering until it reaches a point where they become chronically ill and the abuse simply can't be ignored any longer.

When you understand that the person that you're with intimately is none other than your mirror self, you'll begin to see relationships from a much higher perspective. If you are currently in a happy relationship that's free of abuse, discord, or apathy, then your partner has already become a reflection of your own *divinity*. However, if you're reading this, you're probably not in this type of relationship. Like most current humans, you're probably involved in a relationship that, at least from time to time, brings some form of suffering to both partners. If this is the case with you, then you'll want to pay close attention to the words in this chapter.

Most codependent relationships involve a tennis match of the two partners projecting diminishment onto one another from the shadows of their phantom selves—ranging from sarcastic, belittling "teases" to outright derisive *attacks*—on a daily or weekly basis. This emotional abuse is usually ongoing, and it won't matter if other people are around to observe the madness or not, the verbal abuse will typically continue uninterrupted while the couple remains unembarrassed of their absurdly childish and mutually degrading behavior. In fact, when there *is* an audience, the derisive comments may actually escalate because that's when it becomes a *show*. The ego always knows when it's "on stage." The conflicts in a codependent relationship will not only erupt over asinine matters but will also be based on egoic needs or expectations that one person has for the other, such as what they should or shouldn't wear, how they should or shouldn't act, what they should or shouldn't say. "I *need* you to do this and you *have* to do that," says the assertive ego.

By the way, when expressing personal wants in a relationship dynamic, the vocabulary of the Next Human will exclude the words "need," "should," "must," and "have." Instead she will use the words: "perhaps" or "maybe" or "I suggest" because these are words that form a request, not a command. Next time you turn on the tube and watch the news or a reality show, listen closely to how many times egoic phrases such as, "He *should* comply," or "She *needs* to stop that," or "You *have* to listen to me," is uttered. You'll be surprised. In a relationship, it is neither necessary nor advisable to be delegating commands like an army sergeant. That's only asking for trouble and begging for resistance. Being gentle, suggestive, and non-intrusive with your partner is the way of the Next Human.

Favor shares the abused mind.

All abuse is accompanied by favors and acts of kindness. These "loving" acts of kindness solidify the state of codependency because it perpetuates the utter indifference that most people have to their own diminishing, humiliating, ongoing abuse. If you are currently in a relationship and you are suffering (to any degree) because of it, then you *are being abused*—no matter how caring that person may sometimes appear to you on the surface. This is symptomatic of the phantom prey, which is an addiction to the abuse you receive from a codependent relationship without any realization of it. *Fear* prevents the host of a phantom prey from standing up for their Selves in any abusive relationship, whether it's from a boss, co-worker, friend, family member, or partner. It's as if the ego justifies the abuse by saying: "That's just the way he is but I love him anyway," or "She's under a lot of pressure right now so I completely understand," or "I've already made my bed. Now I have to lie in it." If you observe your mind participating in these rationalizations, then *stop*. Listen to what your mind is doing. You're not helping abusive people transform and dissolve their pain-bodies by permitting them to go on abusing you. And trust me, if you set the precedent by allowing them to continue to abuse you, then I can assure you, they will receive the signal that their bullying behavior is perfectly appropriate for others to endure as well. So you're not doing *any*one any good by being "afraid of hurting them" or by being "Mr. or Ms. Nice" or by "killing them with kindness." That's *devolution*, not evolution.

Know that loving the other unconditionally does *not* include loving them even though they are abusing you. Why? Because that's not love at all. That's self-abuse. And this act of "selfless love" is how the mind rationalizes the abuse in the first place. But this is a self-deluding fantasy and only contributes to the phantom prey's addiction to more pain, misery, and suffering. Next Humans will always put the Self *first* and therefore will never, *ever* allow a partner to abuse them in any way.

There are many subtle forms of abuse that occur frequently by pain-body predators toward unassuming victims. Consequently, the pain-body prey absorb this pernicious energy into their bodies like a *sponge*. This is a major contributing factor to the anxiety and depression epidemics that we have today. One of the most common forms of abuse that gets overlooked is what I refer to as pin-pricking or *needling*. This is when the abuser makes very subtle comments on a daily or weekly basis to a fellow co-worker, friend, family member, or partner that, to the casual observer, may appear as "playful teases." At the time the needle is administered, it feels kind of like a mosquito bite, but over long periods of time, these pin-pricks accumulate, fester, and intensify the pain in the host's pain-body to the point where a chronic, degenerative disease develops. There's nothing wrong with playful teases, as long as they come infrequently and are sincerely playful. However, when the source is a pain-body predator, you can rest assured that the teases will be neither infrequent nor playful. Needles are delivered by the pain-body parasite to inflict pain so *inconspicuously* that it goes totally unnoticed by its prey. It becomes the expected "normal and acceptable" behavior from the predator. This way, the vampiric entity can *siphon the pain* from unsuspecting victims on a continual basis without scaring them off.

In the more subtle form of abuse I'm referring to here, the pain-body predator will be giving an inordinate amount of free, unwelcomed, disrespectful, and assertive advice that is usually accompanied or followed by back-handed compliments, and will typically be a friend, co-worker, family member, or partner who's alternately *kind* and *mean* to you on a continual basis. In other words, they compliment you frequently, but they also *deride* you just as often, if not more so. They may say things such as: "You are *so* talented and you do such wonderful work," but then later they'll say, "That's your character flaw," or "You need to listen to me because you don't know what you're doing," or they'll destructively criticize you over insignificant things. Most of the time these predators will exercise their needling in the form of *control*. For some odd reason, they feel the need to intrude on your business, whether it be personal or professional. They may say things such as: "You are so creative *but* you need to do this if you want to be a success," or "You are the smartest person I know *but* if you had followed my advice, that would never have happened to you," or "I'm your greatest fan *but* if you don't stop painting and get a real job then you'll never amount to anything."

The pain-body predator has learned to *adapt* to the pain-body prey's rationalizing mind so that it's able to get away with a continuous, abusive feeding frenzy that sometimes continues for decades. I have witnessed countless relationships endure this "Dr. Jekyll/Mr. Hyde," passive/aggressive, loving/bullying, nurturing/needling behavioral dynamic on a regular basis where the victim simply shrugs as if the abuse never occurred. They simply take it. But over time, all that pin-pricking adds up. And, of course, the physical body can only endure so much. Then people wonder why they come down with cancer, IBS, chronic fatigue syndrome, fibromyalgia, Crohn's disease, colitis, systemic candida, and other chronic, lingering, painful illnesses. In many cases, it's nothing more than the ongoing emotional abuse from someone close to them materializing itself as disease in the body. The prey are simply being "needled to death" by a partner, friend, or family member, and, because the abuse is always layered in the fog of ambiguity, they remain totally oblivious to it. And if you're attracting abusive people to you then I would take a serious look at your own mind and observe how many times a day you're allowing *it* to abuse you.

Because abuse in a codependent relationship is frequently accompanied by a soothing layer of salve, it's easy for the phantom prey to justify it. Seemingly "kind and loving" behavior from the abuser typically comes in a variety of ways, such as: financial support, job security, gifts, good deeds, praises and compliments, and other forms of help or assistance that cements the codependent's rationalization process, ensuring that the abuser's presence remains in the victim's life. An extreme form of this is what I call the *sadomasochistic* relationship. More subtle forms of abuse include: coldness, apathy, selfishness, inconsideration, neglect, derisiveness, condemnation, and harsh, destructive criticism.

If you are being abused on a continual basis by anyone, no matter how "nice" or "helpful" or "cool" they may appear to you then *wake up* and listen to your mind's ability to rationalize their insanely destructive behavior. Get yourself away from these parasites as fast as you can and *stay* away from them, no matter *who they are*. Then allow your Self the time to heal, completely. A Next Human's love will not be ambiguous. It will be clear and honest, and he will always treat everyone with equal respect, compassion, and loving kindness. He won't pin-prick, deride, demean, degrade, harshly criticize, condemn, or degrade anyone for *any* reason at *any* time. And he won't dish out compliments with strings attached because his sincere praise will always come from the *heart*.

The abusive boss.

It is a man's own mind, not his enemy or foe,
that lures him to evil ways.

—the Buddha

In the workplace, many people with passive pain-bodies may become vulnerable to superiors with aggressive pain-bodies who verbally abuse them. Sometimes the boss feels that he or she has earned a "free pass" to verbally *pound* on subordinates. The abusive boss will act as a psychic vampire who feeds on the pain he creates by beating up everyone "beneath" him. But no matter how much the abused try to conceal their wounds, the predatory boss will instinctively know when he's hit his mark, and this is why his bloodthirsty pain-body keeps coming back for more. This is usually a situation that must be confronted head-on in order to prevent further abuse.

Remember that you're dealing with an energy field that becomes volatile and explosive if triggered. So you have to be very careful when dealing with the pain-body-possessed superior who vents her pain by abusing subordinates in the workplace. Sometimes it may be possible to go over her head to *her* superior and report the abuse.

I know it's hard to do, but know that underneath the abuser's hardened exterior is a sensitive, suffering soul that is unconsciously acting out his or her own pain. And I can assure you: their suffering will become more and more apparent as time goes by. They may become chronically ill or lose everything. I've seen that happen many times. Their negative karma is not your concern, though. If you're in this situation, then your primary concern is to learn how to protect your Self.

Typically, it won't matter what you say in your defense once your boss's pain-body has reached a full-blown *stage four* and he's yelling at you because he won't be listening to you at that point. If you generate any resistance, no matter how slight, you'll only be adding "fuel to the fire." Instead, if you can become completely present while practicing non-judgment toward your abusing boss *while* he's verbally assaulting you, you will elevate your awareness to the level of Zen master. Know that presence is not only passive, it can also be *forceful.* The more present you become, the greater the possibility that *spontaneous right action* will emerge from it. In ancient Sanskrit, this is the state of *kriya shakti.* Kriya is spontaneous action that does not generate *re*action, as opposed to karma, which manifests compensation proportionately. In this scenario, you can *shield* yourself from the abuser just by being still and saying nothing. This requires emptying your mind completely of all thoughts of judgment toward your aggressor. If you can do this successfully, you may find that the bullying boss will no longer find you a target because he or she won't be able to detect your "prey frequency." You'll be safely flying underneath the radar. So, the key here is to *empty your mind of all judgment.*

If you remain a victim then you'll be bottling up your anger and letting it fester, which can only lead to severe stress, anxiety, and depression. Sometimes, spontaneous right action allows you to verbalize what you feel in a way that won't generate resistance from the bullying boss. As words come to you spontaneously (without pre-thinking them), express what you feel in a calm, clear, and concise manner. You may say something like, "Beating me up is no longer acceptable. I deserve to be treated with *respect.*" And then end it. You're in and you're out. Don't linger in a discussion because that creates opportunity for an argument which you'll never win. Speak cogently. These words will be manifesting a "high-frequency *no.*" Then if he or she still continues to scream at you, peacefully walk away.

As you learn to see your Self as divine, your true sense of Self-worth will begin to emerge. Next Humans will not allow others to beat them up or treat them with disrespect because they will have drawn powerful and healthy *boundaries* around their Selves where no one is allowed to *cross.* No one. If you ever find yourself in this type of situation, instead of allowing your boss to go on abusing you, perhaps you can communicate to her just how abusive she is in a non-confrontational manner. Just make sure you do it after her pain-body has become dormant. You could either approach her calmly in a soft tone of voice or send her an email with a cordial yet firm message that conveys how much you've been hurt and that you would appreciate it if she could be kinder to you in the future. If she becomes defensive, however, and/or if her behavior still doesn't change after you've stood up for your Self completely, then be prepared to walk away. And I mean *out the door*. But don't do so in a huff or a rage, giving her the finger on the way out. Leave the workplace peacefully and by all means after you've secured employment elsewhere. Otherwise, you'll only attract another bullying boss at your next employer.

The sadomasochistic relationship.

In the partner-abusive sadomasochistic relationship, the egoic need to feel *superior* in one partner is counterbalanced with the egoic need to feel *inferior* in the other. This behavioral dynamic will surface frequently in most codependent relationships—to varying degrees—with the roles sometimes shifting back and forth between partners. Typically, the male plays the role of sadist and the female the role of the masochist but I've seen plenty of relationships with these roles reversed.

The underlying thought patterns that serve to control the victim's behavior will reflect the crucifixion or "martyr" archetype. Those who believe that suffering is necessary before sins can be atoned will be represented here, such as the battered wife who keeps returning to her husband for more punishment. Guilt, shame, and deep humiliation become prerequisites for a personal salvation and a sick masochistic pleasure is harvested from being emotionally tortured. It's as if the victim's mind says, "There must be something very wrong with me. I am essentially worthless. And for me to redeem my worthiness, I must continue to suffer more pain and humiliation." These messages will lie just beneath the threshold of consciousness, and thus the native remains trapped in a rationalized, repetitive cycle of masochistic behavior that is allowed to continue without interruption for years on end.

Conversely, in the sadistic pathology, the underlying messages that control the abuser's behavior will reflect the patriarchal or "warrior" archetype of a judgmental God who puts forth commandments that one most obey him before his love or protection is given. For the sadist to feel secure, he must wield a power that emulates the thunderbolts of Zeus. Therefore, he only attracts to his lair a partner who fits the subservient, masochistic personality type.

Usually, the masochist awakens to the nightmare of this relationship dynamic before the sadist because the masochist tends to be slightly more aware of her suffering. Just as it has been the female gender that's been oppressed for millennia, today it is the women who are evolving ahead of their male counterparts. This is no doubt because the male is more apt to identify with the ego than the female. In the male, the ego dominates primarily because of his genetic and hormonal propensity to protect and provide for the family unit. This requires an extra boost of bravery so that he can effectively hunt, kill, and be victorious in battle. Moreover, in clinical psychology, it is broadly accepted that the male gender is unable to recover from emotional trauma as readily as the female. This is due to the fact that the feminine gender is generally not as ego-identified as the masculine gender, and since all emotional wounds stem directly from the ego, this allows for greater resiliency in women.

In the sadomasochistic relationship, the masochist's pain-body will always become more and more sensitive over time. It's much like a wound that's never allowed to heal because it's constantly being pierced or stabbed until eventually the pain of the wound reaches a level that is so deep and gaping, it can no longer be ignored. The sadist/abuser and masochist/victim are, metaphorically speaking, two sides of the same coin. It is indeed a *symbiosis*, and the more time spent in the relationship, the harder it is for this pair to part ways. If children enter into the equation, then this will only complicate matters further and keep the couple together longer. But children will subconsciously pick up on the abuse, no matter how slight it may be, and this will contribute to the formation of *their* pain-bodies.

Know that all abusive relationships are ultimately about one thing: *power*. When one person has power *over* the other, and exercises that power freely, then the relationship is always abusive and highly dysfunctional. Power shifts do happen, but this doesn't make it any less dysfunctional. Wielding power over another human being is what the ego is all about. This toxic imbalance prevents true love to flow from the heart. Usually the only hope in this scenario is for the victim to summon enough strength to finally stand up for the Self, draw boundaries, and *leave*.

If this is your situation, then I suggest becoming completely present during abusive situations, such as when your partner is cursing, demeaning, or yelling at you. If you shout or curse back, it will only antagonize and amplify his or her pain-body attack. Instead, begin practicing spontaneous right action. You could also suggest that the two of you enter couple's counseling. During your partner's phantom predator attacks, be prepared to walk out the door until he or she cools off. Repeat this over time and observe if the abuser's behavior subsides or wanes. If it doesn't, and if counseling doesn't help, you may consider leaving the relationship all together. If, however, you leave the relationship angrily and don't take the time needed (usually years) to deal with your own repressed anger and dissolve your passive pain-body, you are destined to attract yet another phantom predator into your life, perpetuating the cycle. Also, if you at any time fear for your safety, then by all means call the police or get away as fast as you can. It's not wise to remain in a relationship with anyone whom you fear on any level.

When I was very young I married someone whose heavy pain-body was a perfect match to my own. As you can imagine, it was a destructive, highly volatile, emotionally draining, power-seeking relationship where the sadist/masochist roles reversed periodically between her and me. Needless to say, it brought much pain and suffering to both of us. Later in life, I was involved in a business partnership that mirrored my early marriage with similar power plays and conflicts. So I know firsthand what it's like to be in a tumultuous, traumatic, sadomasochistic partnership. It is nothing less than a living *hell*.

Drake and Jasper.

> *An insincere and evil friend is more to be feared than a wild beast; a wild beast may wound your body, but an evil friend will wound your mind.*
>
> —The Buddha

Drake was a personal injury attorney who loved nothing more than to run roughshod over people, verbally deriding, demeaning, debasing, and insulting everyone in his aggressive path, including all of his friends— and he did not discriminate between them when it came to expressing his brutally foul mouth. Now, let me premise this by saying that in his twisted mind, Drake probably saw his frequent derision as harmless teases. And that's precisely how his friends were able to mask his abuse. That and the fact that Drake was handsome, Harvard educated, and very intelligent. Because he took his college SATs straight out of 8th grade, he skipped high school altogether, allowing him a four-year head start against everyone else his age—all of whom he saw as the "competition." For Drake, life had but one ultimate purpose: making a fortune, and he was, by the age of twenty-five, more than halfway there.

Jasper met Drake through a mutual friend while playing pool one night at a Cambridge bar. A doctoral student at Harvard, working toward his Ph.D. in clinical psychology, Jasper found Drake fascinating—a Jungian study of sorts—and was in total awe of his dramatic flair and "self-confidence." The two became the best of friends within days after they met and began hanging out together often. But it wasn't long before Drake began belittling Jasper, poking and deriding him both privately and publicly. To Jasper, the derisive jabs were hurtful, and many times humiliating. But Jasper just ignored them because, well, being friends with Drake came with lots of *perks*. To wit: Drake drove a Ferrari, and so as long as Drake looked cool, well, Jasper looked and felt cool, too. The truth is that when you are a slave to your own ego, there's only one thing that impresses you: *a bigger ego*. But bathing in the light of Drake's inflated ego always carried with it a heavy price, and Jasper paid that price every time he took his abuse. Because Drake enjoyed the fruits of his success comparatively early in life, he probably felt that it gave him free reign to verbally plow over others whom he saw as being inferior. Unfortunately, most current humans define success based on material accomplishment alone. But nothing could be further from the truth.

Drake also enjoyed bragging about his early-in-life accomplishments to others, a lot. One spring eve many years ago, Jasper and Drake met for dinner on the patio of one of Boston's most popular French bistros...

JASPER   Dressed to the nines and Cheshire-grinning, Drake makes his entrance as the maître d' escorts him to the patio table where I am sitting, awaiting his majesty. Two stylish young women at an adjacent table, noticing Drake's handsome looks, turn their heads in admiration.

"How's Rain?" Drake asks as he unlocks his $2,500 Louis Vuitton briefcase, producing what appears to be a paycheck, then handing it to me for inspection.

"She's, uh, she's well, I think she's moving to New York... which is probably a good thing because, frankly, I'm getting a little tired of her standing me up all the time," I say as I retrieve the check that's made payable to "Drake Carrington" as a result of a personal injury law case settlement that he and his partner just won. The amount: $197,356.33.

"Yeah, well, remember what I've been trying to teach you, my young Padawan: chicks are the *enemy*," Drake reminds me after ordering himself a dry martini.

"I suppose a congratulations is in order," I say while handing the check back to him, seriously impressed with the amount, pretending not to be.

"Thanks Jaz. And when the Griffon case settles next week, I'll be getting paid at least *triple* that," Drake says delightfully while retrieving the check from my hand, then adding, "Sometimes *I'm* even astounded at just how awesome I am."

"You know, Drake, this is not the *real world*," I say straight to his smug, self-satisfied face before taking a sip of a twelve-year-old scotch, then sinking back into a well-cushioned, wrought-iron chair. After a conspicuously long pause, there's a dramatic alteration in Drake's facial expression which, after he takes a few sips of Belvedere, turns from self-glorifying pride to self-diminishing *disgust*. He becomes quiet, pensive, as if he were pondering every word and analyzing the daunting implications each syllable had for him.

"Dude, you're *wrong*. You simply don't know what you're talking about. I can assure you that you're completely mistaken," Drake finally says while reaching for his drink. He takes a large gulp of fine vodka, steadying himself. I feign a smile and say nothing. A few moments later, he continues with his ridiculous rant.

"This *is* the real world, are you fucking kidding? Of course it's real. What else is there? You're simply deluding yourself with that pseudo-psychology you read in your spare time. Stick to what you're being taught in school, buddy. That's what we *know* is real. My god, how many people are endowed with a formal education, much less a Ph.D. from Harvard? Be grateful for Christ sakes of what you're being taught by your erudite professors and stop reading all that New Age nonsense on the side," Drake says before he downs the rest of his drink, then continues his barrage.

"This is *it* my friend, so you'd better, you know, get *used* to it. There *is* nothing else. Nothing. Nada. Zip. And when you die, that's *it*. It's all over. You're going to be flushed down the drain of death never to be heard of or *seen again*. It all ends with no one remembering your name. So, you know, *deal*."

Drake was visibly shaken at this point over my retort to his "I am infinitely more successful than you are" face-rubbing.

"I don't know why you're getting so upset over this. I mean, it was merely a philosophical observation, you know, a personal epiphany, that I, well, had recently; one that I thought I could share with you in a light-hearted conversation over dinner. But apparently I've been overly optimistic." I say to him sincerely.

Drake is now grimacing with a scary, sick-like distorted countenance that I would later come to know all too well. He then motions the server over to our wobbly table for two and orders another martini, double this time. I order another scotch, then ask myself: Why does dinner with Drake always have to be so goddamn *stressful?*

"You're wrong dude, dead on wrong. How does it feel to be so fucking *wrong?*" A few minute-like seconds pass. The air thickens and the temperature drops.

"You know, you shouldn't believe everything you read in those bullshit-laden books you collect and display like trophies in your condo. You're starting to sound, uh, well, a little *wack*."

"Maybe, but it's just my opinion, nothing more. You seem to be getting a little defensive over nothing," I'm offering to him as the server presents me with a freshly poured tumbler of Glenlivet.

"Hah! Defensive? Who's getting defensive!? I'm just not buying any of that metaphysical, pseudo-science crap that you're selling so why don't you just keep your nut job, crazy ass philosophical opinions to your fucking *self*."

After a "friendship" that lasted nearly ten years, eventually Jasper's pain-body had become so raw that he simply couldn't bear to be around Drake any longer. True friendship is something to be treasured, not endured. The Next Human will treat his friends with the utmost respect and will never deride nor diminish them in any way. This is because he will know that a friend is nothing less than his mirror Self.

Jasper and Cara.

> A lot of what I've been learning in the last two years is due to therapy—about my sexuality, why things go wrong, why relationships haven't worked. It isn't anything to do with anybody else; it's to do with me.
>
> —Boy George

One night out on the town, Jasper and Drake met Cara, a bubbly and vibrant young woman with piercing green eyes and pixie-styled locks who hit it off with the both of them instantly. After the two dashing young men chatted with her for a short while, Jasper asked Cara if she wanted to join Drake and him for a late night meal at Nell's, a popular restaurant down the street. She did.

At dinner, the three indulged in an intellectual discussion about the music world since Drake played the guitar and Cara loved to sing. "We should start a band!" Drake enthusiastically suggested. After about an hour of exuberant conversation, it seemed clear that Drake and Cara would end up together. After dinner, Jasper excused himself, informed them that he was going home, and that the two of them should "enjoy themselves." They did.

As the months passed by and winter morphed into spring, Cara and Drake would see each other about three or four times a week, or whenever she could secure a babysitter for her three-year-old girl, Clair. And as it turned out, Clair was a major reason why Drake kept himself emotionally distant from Cara. At the age of twenty-six, he was not exactly ready to become a father. Jasper began to suspect that Drake was just using Cara for sex. And as it turned out, he was right.

Cara wanted to marry Drake and give Clair a sibling. An intensely passionate and nurturing woman, she was very serious about Drake, and this worried Jasper. He really liked Cara and the two had become close friends over the many months. The last thing Jasper wanted to see was Cara hurt by Drake. During the long, hot, and humid summer months, Drake would get into fights with Cara, sporadically break up with her, and leave her stranded at bars and restaurants around town. Jasper would frequently get a late night call from her asking to be picked up. Many nights, she ended up sleeping on Jasper's sofa.

By the end of October, Drake and Cara had broken up and re-mended their relationship a total of *eight times*. It was emotional torment, and Cara was starting to have panic attacks as a result. Her doctor prescribed Valium for her anxiety. She confided her deepest feelings with Jasper, who was sympathetic, always offering a consoling ear. But for Drake, this was the norm. He thrived on chaos. Jasper also knew that Drake felt superior to Cara on many levels. After all, she didn't possess the same Ivy League education, nor did she have the upper class breeding. She was raised on a farm, and even though she was intelligent, Drake saw Cara—like he did everyone else—as being *beneath* him. He was also well aware that she wanted to get married, and the fact that she had a daughter only cinched his reluctance to propose.

One cool and breezy autumn night, during one of their "relationship breaks," Cara showed up at Jasper's condo and asked if she could spend the night. Jasper, as usual, invited her in and offered her a glass of wine. Afterward, she curled up on his Italian leather sofa while Jasper ignited a fire…

CARA   After half a glass of Jasper's oak Chardonnay, the Valium and Percodan I popped on my way here are starting to kick in and combined with the soothing light of Jasper's fire, my nerves are finally starting to calm.

"I had another fight with Drake tonight." I begin.

"Really? I wouldn't have been able to tell," Jasper says to me facetiously in his sexy voice.

"Oh, god, Jasper, what the hell is *wrong* with me?" I ask, giggling like an idiot.

"There's nothing *wrong* with you darling. Your only crime is that, like *moi*, you're simply too trusting," Jaz says while elegantly waving his right hand in the air. Sparks fly out of the fire and are immediately extinguished by a slate-covered hearth.

"I can't help it. I love him. Am I delusional to think that he's going to marry me? I mean, it's been nearly a year, hasn't it? I'm trying to remember; when was it that we all met?"

"It'll be a year the week after Thanksgiving. Yes, you are delusional if you think Drake's going to propose. You know how he feels about becoming a father. It's simply out of the question. He's too self-absorbed. You know that. How many times have we had this conversation, Cara?" Jasper becomes comfortable in his Barcelona chair, reaches for his glass of wine and then sinks back, crossing his legs. He gives me a deep, long, penetrating glare, as if he's trying to send me a subliminal message.

"I know, I know. I'm such a *mess*." I say, turning my gaze back to the firelight.

"Well, at least you're a *beautiful* mess," he says, smiling seductively.

"*Thanks* Jasper. You're always so kind to me. Why couldn't it have been the two of *us* who ended up together instead of me and that self-absorbed man?" I ask honestly.

"I don't know, sweetheart. That's a question I ask myself all the time. Karma, I *guess*. After all, it's not like we're not *compatible*."

Jasper's smiling at me with a look that makes me want him *now*. But I can't. I would never be able to face Drake again. And what if he decides that he wants to marry me? And then he finds out about Jasper and me? I can't do it. I smile a seductive smile right back at him followed by another sip of his Bargetto.

"Why can't I meet someone as kind and caring as you, Jaz?"

"You did my love. You met *me.*"

"Why is he the way he is? I mean, why isn't he sweet like *you?* And for Christ sakes, why doesn't he want to be a father to Clair? Is she not worthy of his love and attention?"

"Of course she is, and so are *you.* That's what I've been trying to tell you for nearly a year. You are more than worthy—*too* worthy in fact. Drake doesn't deserve the two of you because he's not appreciative of the love and attention you give him. I mean, really, Cara, he treats you like *shit.* You deserve to have your love returned to you, don't you think?" Jasper refills my wine glass as the poplar wood in the fire crackles.

"I...suppose...so." I manage to muster underneath my voice while I lose myself in Jasper's golden brown eyes.

"I mean, you have to learn to stand *up* for yourself, love, and not let him abuse you like this. It's as if you're a fish living in a catch and release stream, and he's the fisherman who keeps reeling you in and tossing you back. How much longer are you going to put up with his psychotic behavior? You look frail, darling. It's obvious to me that you've lost weight—weight that you didn't need to lose."

Jasper gets up and walks to the entryway closet where he retrieves a cashmere blanket and a pillow. He then comes over to the sofa, sits down next to me, then leans over me as if he's going to kiss me on my lips but when I remind him that he's Drake's best friend, he kisses me gently on my forehead instead. He smiles a handsome smile, tells me goodnight, and then he's off to his bedroom, leaving me here, without him.

In a fetal position, I lie awake for as long as I can fight the sedatives, staring into the fire as it dwindles. I want to join Jaz in his bed, so badly I can barely contain myself. But I don't. I just lie here, wondering what could be…

Cara and Jasper never consummated their love for one another. Fear of true intimacy kept them apart. Cara allowed Drake to torture her for another six months while her health declined and her drug habit worsened, and she eventually ended up in the hospital after a severe car accident broke both her arms, several ribs, and took out most of her front teeth. Cara's passive pain-body had her convinced that she totally deserved the alternatively hot/cold, passive/aggressive abuse from a man like Drake rather than the sincere, gentle, loving affection from a man like Jasper.

Jacob and Percy.

A friend to all is a friend to none.
—Aristotle

Jacob had been friends with Percy since junior high, for about twenty-three years. Jacob's passive pain-body absorbed *all* of the abuse that Percy's aggressive pain-body could possibly dish out. During their two-decade-long friendship, whenever they would see each other, Percy would often compliment Jacob on his accomplishments in the business world, but at the same time, would subtly deride him about anything and everything, putting him down and making him feel, well, subservient. Being highly analytical and logical, Percy's personality greatly clashed with Jacob's, who was much more sensitive and creative. Since childhood, Percy always felt that he needed to dominate and control Jacob.

About ten years ago, Jacob terminated his friendship with Percy because, at the time, he was going through a very traumatic divorce, and although Percy was very supportive to Jacob regarding the divorce, Percy began harshly criticizing Jacob's father (for no apparent reason) because of his spiritual beliefs. You see, Percy was agnostic, and Jacob, like his father before him, was very spiritual, which seemed to offend Percy, a lot. Jacob's father had written several books on metaphysical subjects that Percy knew about but never read. Percy had never met Jacob's father because he and Jacob's mother had divorced before the two became friends. Jacob's father also died when the friends were still in college. Percy was well aware that Jacob was quite close to his father, and that the two shared their spiritual beliefs.

Even though spirituality was rarely brought up, for some reason Percy seemed determined to make it an issue in the middle of Jacob's divorce, when he was at his weakest, and thus his pain-body was the heaviest. Suddenly and inexplicably, Percy began sending Jacob emails harshly deriding Jacob's deceased father as if he was intentionally trying to kick him while he was down. The effect that the divorce was having on Jacob's nerves was so devastating on so many levels that he simply couldn't take any more harsh criticism from anyone. Email exchanges became heated and increasingly more derisive from Percy who kept on saying how "silly" Jacob's father was and that he had "wasted his entire life teaching New Age bunk" and on and on and on until finally, Jacob had had enough. He terminated his twenty-three-year friendship with Percy and never looked back. But one day, seven years later, Jacob was doing some work on his laptop at a Starbucks cafe down the street from his apartment when he suddenly hears a familiar voice call his name…

JACOB   When I look up, I see Percy standing across the room next to the barista, waiting for his coffee. Ecstatic to see my childhood friend, I smilingly motion him over, and ask him to join me. We excitedly catch up on the past seven years and become the best of pals again within minutes. Percy informs me that he's visiting his father who is recovering from back surgery and will be in town only for a few days.

We decide to meet for dinner the following evening and

catch up a little more. During the conversation I notice that Percy is slyly projecting blame and guilt onto me for "dumping him" and sending him "hate mails" and ending a friendship that had begun when we were twelve. The reality of the situation was the opposite. It was he who initiated the conflict by attacking my father. But I say nothing and, because I don't want to create another conflict, I don't stand up for myself. It seems apparent to me that Percy is bitter that I haven't spoken to him for so long.

A few weeks later, Percy comes back to town to visit his recovering father and texts me to meet again for dinner so we decide to meet at our favorite sushi bar in downtown Chicago. Within minutes into the conversation I notice that the needling is becoming a lot more frequent and a lot less subtle. He keeps badgering me about my "hate mails" *I* sent to *him* seven years prior. He also keeps bringing up that *I* turned my back on *him*. Guilt keeps being dumped on me. In spite of this horrifying energy I'm receiving from him, I still say nothing and try to convince myself that he'll get over his bitterness. As it turned out, I couldn't have been more mistaken.

A month later, Percy comes back to town to visit his father again and texts me to meet for dinner and I reluctantly accept. Not surprisingly, nearly the same exact scenario plays out with Percy dumping guilt on me during the entire conversation. Afterward I feel completely drained.

Another three weeks go by and Percy calls me.

"Hello?"

"You need to come over to Trent's first thing in the morning. We're helping him move." Percy firmly informs me.

"O...*kay*..." I say before I can think of a clever excuse to avoid the situation because I really don't want to be around Percy anymore but before I can say anything else, he hangs up.

Trent is a mutual friend from childhood whom I still see on occasion.

After loading and unloading a large U-Haul into Trent's new apartment with most of his belongings, there are just a few remaining "odds and ends" that need to go into storage. Percy suggests that I go with him in Trent's pickup truck to haul the rest of Trent's stuff into storage while Trent stays and cleans up his apartment. Trent agrees with Percy, and so after loading the pickup, Percy and I are off to Trent's storage unit downtown. On the way, we stop at a sandwich shop and pick up some lunch which we'll eat after we unload the truck.

After we arrive at the storage unit, I begin unloading the truck's contents into the storage room while Percy, oddly enough, leans against the side of the truck and starts *glaring* at me as if I'm doing something wrong. I ask him why he's not helping but he just crosses his arms. Unsure as to why he's just standing there giving me the "evil eye," I continue to unload the truck since I'm starving and just want to get the job done so that I can eat my lunch. By the time I have over half the truck unloaded, I watch Percy walk back into the cab, grab the bag containing my sandwich and walk away with it.

"Percy, what are you doing? That's my lunch!" I cry out to deaf ears while Percy continues walking all the way to the end of the storage facility alleyway where a garbage dumpster awaits him. Watching, perplexed, Percy tosses my uneaten turkey sub (along with my iced tea) into the dumpster. Since I'm minutes away from completing the job, I continue unloading the remaining contents of the truck into the storage room until I get to the last two boxes and can clearly see that they aren't going to fit. I suddenly realize that a slight adjustment to the stacking is going to have to be implemented.

"Now you see just what a fucking moron you are? Look at

yourself. Just look at your ineptitude! If you had waited for me to direct you, since you are obviously incompetent, then I would have told you that you can't put that lamp there, that chair there, and all those boxes of books over there. They simply won't *fit* that way." Percy says as he's walking back up the alleyway to the storage unit after disposing of my uneaten lunch.

I'm taken aback. The incident that had occurred seven years prior seems to be repeating itself right before my very eyes, except this time, inside of via email, it's happening in person.

"I'm sorry. I guess I misestimated. I'm simply doing the best I can, Percy. You don't have to yell at me and call me names. I'm just trying to help Trent out." I'm in such a state of shock that I can barely muster the words audibly.

"Well you're not helping very much now are you? Now we're going to have to *redo* everything because of your idiocy," Percy instructs, waving his right arm as if he were a general in command of a battalion. He then commences to take everything out that I had put in, one item at a time.

"Percy, you don't have to do that. All we have to do is make room for these two boxes. This is a complete waste of time," I say in a desperate attempt to prevent Percy from blowing things out of proportion.

"No! You *idiot!* We have to rearrange *everything* because of your stupidity. You don't know what you're doing and now I'm going to have to clean up the mess you made." Percy continues to carry out every box, chair, stereo component, painting, and lamp that I have already placed carefully into storage.

"But Percy, we're not interior designers and this is not a home. It is a *storage* unit…" Percy suddenly drops the box of books he's holding onto the ground from a standing position and makes a move toward me. Reacting to his lunge, I take a few steps back.

"Get the fuck away from me!" Percy screams at the top of his lungs. I take another five steps backward, turn around and proceed to walk down the alleyway away from Percy. Reaching into my pocket, I retrieve my iPhone and text Trent the words: "Percy has lost it." Ten seconds later, Percy's Blackberry rings. It's Trent and he wants to know what the hell is going on.

"Oh my fucking God! You mean that little crybaby had to call his big brother to whine and complain. He completely screwed everything up here, Trent. This room is a disaster zone. You might as well hang a 'condemned' sign on the door. I'm having to put everything back together the right way for you now. Jacob is nothing but a waste of space. He doesn't know how to do anything right. Never did. He's a fucking *moron* impersonating a human being. So just let me get this job done *right* for you and we'll be back in a few." Percy hangs up and then recommences with his angry rant at me, saying, "You *had* to text Trent, didn't you? You had to do it. You had to be a little crybaby."

I'm just standing here, observing Percy's expression of sheer hatred and contempt toward me in stunned silence. I'm realizing that at this point, anything I say or do will only antagonize him and make him angrier. So while Percy redoes everything I just did—*his* way—I pace up and down the alleyway in a vain attempt to vent my frustration and quell my hunger. About twenty minutes later, after watching him rearrange the entire storage unit and reorganize everything as if it were going to be photographed for the cover of Decor Magazine, Percy closes and locks the door. My childhood buddy then gets back into the driver's seat while I join him silently on the passenger side. Not one word is uttered on the thirty-five minute drive back to Trent's apartment. Afterward, I glance at my iPhone and there's a text from a sympathetic Trent that reads: "You're good to go. Thanks for your help."

Now, the first thing that I began wondering was why in the world would Jacob attract Percy back into his life in the first place? It seemed plausible to me that the reason for Percy's anomalous appearance at Starbucks after all those years was because of a "victim frequency" in Jacob that had somehow resurfaced after seven long years of healing. And since Percy no longer lived in the same city as Jacob, the odds of them running into one another were nothing less than astronomical. Moreover, Jacob rarely went to Starbucks to work, preferring the solitude of his apartment. After ruminating on this "chance meeting" for a few days, the answer finally came to me.

Jacob admitted that during their first dinner conversation, Percy began making his bitterness apparent. He began accusing Jacob of sending him angry and hateful emails. Not only was Percy *not* apologetic for his personal attacks on Jacob's father seven years prior, he was intent on blaming Jacob for the entire break-up. He was not willing to take responsibility for any of it. But because Jacob had not seen Percy in seven years, he missed their friendship. That nostalgia superseded Jacob's inner voice which was trying to communicate to him that Percy had not grown, was still toxic, and thus a replay of the same scenario of emotional violence that occurred seven years prior was inevitable if he continued to ignore the "red flags."

But Jacob did ignore them—over three consecutive, highly stressful, dinner encounters. Consequently, the abuse became progressively worse until eventually he found himself cornered—the universe's way of forcing him to *wake up* to the reality that Percy was still possessed by his own aggressive pain-body, and therefore would only continue to abuse Jacob if allowed. Fortunately, Percy's stage five pain-body attack did the trick. Immediately afterward, Jacob woke up to the reality of the situation and decided to terminate the friendship again, this time for good.

It's sad when one has to say goodbye to a childhood friend. But when one friend awakens and the other does not, the relationship can become lethal for both. Jacob had dissolved nearly all of his pain-body during those years. Note that Jacob never retaliated in anger against Percy. He could barely even speak out loud. Afterward he realized that anything he said would only infuriate Percy further, so he kept his mouth *shut*. On the long ride back to Trent's, he uttered not one word.

So even though what may have been left of Jacob's passive pain-body attracted Percy to him at the Starbucks encounter, it was still left up to Jacob to protect his sacred Self. After the initial dinner conversation where the red flags were blatantly waving in his face, Jacob could have ended it again with Percy. But he didn't. What I also found interesting was that it was Percy, not Trent, who informed (instead of asking) Jacob to help Trent move. It was almost as if he wanted him there so he could siphon more pain out of him.

The lesson here is: *always be present*. The sentient universe has a clever way of waking us up whenever we tend to "snooze off." If Jacob had already evolved into a Next Human, he probably wouldn't have even made the first dinner date because he would have automatically *known* from feeling Percy's energy that he had not grown at all and was therefore still toxic. There would have been no need for the subsequent meetings and *beatings* in order for Jacob to realize that Percy's predator pain-body was still on the hunt for prey.

Alex and Ema.

The mother-child relationship is paradoxical and, in a sense, tragic. It requires the most intense love on the mother's side, yet this very love must help the child grow away from the mother, and to become fully independent.

—Eric Fromm

One night while smoking a Macanudo Gold cigar at Harry's Bar, where Alex liked to hang out, he noticed a new server who—when she wasn't waiting on tables, was admiring him in the mirror behind the bar. She was naturally very pretty but for some reason made an effort to conceal her beauty by not wearing mascara. Her Caribbean blue eyes were almond-shaped, Asian-like, and her skin was porcelain white. Alex immediately asked the bartender about her and it was revealed to him that she was in graduate school, studying to be an accountant. Alex, an already successful entrepreneur, was going through a messy legal battle with a business partner. As a result, he was experiencing a lot of anxiety and wanted desperately to have some fun. But Alex, now forty, never had much luck with women. He had never been able to maintain a relationship longer than two months.

Handsome and charming, women were always attracted to Alex and he never had problems getting dates. But he went on very few because he was very particular. Being an "all or nothing" passionate lover, the problem for him was his habit of going through the entire relationship by the end of the second date. After about the third time of seeing Ema at Harry's, Alex finally decided to approach her and fire up a conversation. When he did, he instantly noticed a similar jade pendant that she had around her neck, mirroring the one he had hanging around his. It was a Chinese dragon. The only difference was that hers was of pink jade from China and his was of green jade from Taiwan. And so the romantic encounter began with them discussing how they had acquired their jade dragon pendants.

In between her attention to her customers, Ema would hover around Alex while he sat at the bar, smoking cigars, flirting, smiling, and chatting with him. By the end of the night, Alex decided to ask her out, and Ema graciously accepted...

ALEX   Lovely Ema and I agree to meet at a popular Italian bistro just down the street from Harry's in the trendy, urban, riverfront neighborhood where I live. When I arrive, she's already seated at the ice bar, her long, straight, silky, sand-colored hair draped heavily along her back, like an Arabian mare's mane. She's wearing a Rachel Zoe white linen sundress and Ferragamo sandal flats that show off her perfectly formed, nicely manicured feet. I walk up to her and place my right hand gently on her left shoulder. She turns and smiles, but that's when I notice—to my disappointment—that she's *still* not wearing mascara. After chatting for a few minutes, the hostess informs us that our table is ready so we follow her to a cozy table for two in the corner. A small jazz band at the front of the room plays *Love Calls* by Kem.

After a few minutes into the conversation, I begin to notice a sporadic, slightly distorted expression on Ema's face whenever she talks. She keeps furling her brow and her mouth seems to contort, especially when she's stressing a point. While I'm wondering how I could've possibly missed this before, Ema is rambling on about her depressed teenage years when she was frequently abused by her alcoholic mother with whom she is now estranged. For a reason unknown to me I decide not to share with her the fact that I *too* am estranged from my mother.

After dinner, I invite Ema to my apartment to view my artwork. Being an art-lover, she eagerly accepts. Other than her distorted facial expressions, everything seems to be going quite smoothly on our first date. I'm actually having a good time.

She's beautiful and I'm *very* attracted to her.

When we get back to my loft, she explores my oil paintings, one wall-sized piece at a time, and peruses my books, hundreds of them, stacked on backlit teak cases all arranged alphabetically by author. I light some candles and pour some expensive Pinot Noir. She's very complimentary of my work, especially the abstract portraits, and seems to be well educated in art history, which I appreciate. After we chat about her recent hiking trip through Europe, her visit to Paris, her love for the Louvre, we relax in each other's arms on my Corbusier sofa.

The longer I'm with Ema, the more my desire for her deepens. I want to kiss her badly. But when I finally make my move, she pulls away. Perplexed by this rejection, I ask her why she won't let me kiss her. She explains that she prefers to move "slowly." I respect her wish and after about another half hour or so, she thanks me for a nice evening and leaves.

The next date with Ema didn't end so well. A week later, I pick her up at her apartment and drive her to a trendy seafood restaurant not too far from where she lives. During the dinner conversation, I notice that she is criticizing just about everything I say. And it doesn't appear to matter what the topic of the conversation is; she's vehemently *opposed* to my views on the subject. Ostensibly, all of my observations on philosophy, politics, the economy, and modern culture are, for now, inexplicably and for some odd reason *clashing* with hers. During her derisive commentaries, I'm also observing her face contort to the point where it's beginning to repulse me. But as horrifying as this is, it's her *harsh criticism* toward my opinions about things—the fact that she's disagreeing with and deriding nearly everything I'm saying—that's beginning to boil my blood.

After dinner, I make a second attempt to kiss Ema while opening the car door for her. And again, inexplicably, she pulls back.

"Just out of curiosity, when were you planning on allowing me to kiss you?" I ask, sincerely frustrated.

"I told you, I like to take things *slowly,*" she says, smiling like a cretin, repeating the exact same words from our first date, but this time she draws out the word *s-l-o-w-l-y*.

My anger swells. I'm now thinking about the $350 I've spent on her so far and all I've gotten in return is a hard dose of verbal diminishment. How could she change from being so sweet and affectionate on the first date to being so derisive and cold on the second? In an effort to punish Ema for not letting me kiss her, I don't speak to her at all the whole ride back to her place. Not even a grunt. This doesn't go over so well. By the time we arrive at her apartment, she's screaming, "This has happened to me a hundred times before! I don't understand why we can't just go out and have a good time!" When I pull up to her apartment, she gets out and slams the door with both hands as hard as she can. My ears pop. I inspect the glass in all the windows to make sure none of it is cracked.

Upon returning to my loft, I review her email from three days prior when she told me at dinner that she had called but left no message. So I decide to check my cell phone to validate if she had, in fact, *called*. There was no record of it. She had obviously lied to me. Hungry for revenge, I frantically craft a return email, confronting her with her lie and that the consequence of this was I was no longer going to see her. I press "send" and my email war with Ema commences.

No more than four minutes later, I receive an email back from Ema, reading: "YOU'RE NOT BREAKING UP WITH ME. I'M BREAKING UP WITH YOU. YOU'RE A FUCKING ASSH…" She's rambling on with obscenities, calling me every name in the book. But I *bounce* the email back to her because I don't want her to think that I actually read it. I simply must have the last word. Less than three minutes later, I get another vile email from her. And so I bounce *it* back, too. A few minutes later I get yet another one—but this time she crams as much of her "ALL IN CAPS" hate mail as she can into the subject line—obviously in an attempt to *force* me to read her words so that I'm subjected to the full brunt of her fury. The subject line starts with: "YOU ARE NOTHING BUT A COWARD YOU GOD DAMN MOTHER FU…." My hands shaking, I proceed to bounce this one back to her as well. And this dysfunctional ritual perpetuates where dozens of hate mails are written by Ema, sent to me, and, in turn, bounced back to her by me. After an hour of this insanity I realize that I am utterly exhausted, and so I shut my MacBook with disgust.

For the next couple of months, I continue to make appearances at Harry's Bar—mainly so Ema can see me ignoring her, giving her the "silent treatment," until one day I began to notice that she hadn't shown up for a while. When I inquire about her absence, I learn that she quit for no apparent reason. Saddened by this fact, I conclude that it's doubtful I'll ever see Ema again.

Fast forward six months…

I'm at the supermarket buying my weekly groceries and as I push my cart into the cereal section, I'm utterly horrified by the person I'm looking at standing at the far end of the aisle. It's Ema. And my god, she's looking *hot!* She's even wearing mascara, which she *never* did around me. And she's wearing high-heeled pumps. I *love* women in high-heeled pumps. She's also wearing skinny AG jeans that are accentuating every curvature of her perfectly formed ass. Ema notices me as well and the second she does, she seems positively *stunned*—like a deer in headlights. Lambasted by a shudder of sheer panic, I am now thinking: Should I just turn around and leave? Then there's a flash of memory where Ema's calling me a coward in the subject lines of her hate mails. So, in an attempt to prove her wrong, I choose to bravely face this unexpected encounter *head-on,* and in so doing I reluctantly begin pushing my cart down the very, *very* long aisle (it seems as if this is all happening in slow motion) that's occupied by only the two of us, and when I finally approach her, I stare fiercely and directly into her exotic blue eyes and the entire time it takes me to do this seems like an *eon.* Then Ema's gorgeous face contorts, and this is followed by the shaking of her head in a mock attempt to shame me. Ignoring this completely, I continue to walk on by without uttering a word. On the drive home from the store, the emotions I'm exploring are: highly charged sexual attraction, anger, frustration, hurt, sorrow, regret.

This is a perfect example of *like* attracting *like* if I've ever seen one. Without question, both Alex and Ema were a mirrored reflection from the get go. They even became attracted to each other by checking each other out *through* a mirror. Their pendants were nearly identical, they both adored art, they were both estranged from their mothers, and they were both romantic. The only problem was that they were both afraid of one another because of past relationships, specifically with their mothers. This caring, intimate, emotionally nurturing side, if not allowed to fully develop, can present serious problems in relationships in both genders during adulthood. Alex had never had a long-term relationship because his early trauma had not been addressed and subsequently allowed to heal. That's why women like Ema kept resurfacing into his life and why he rarely got past the second date. Alex's pain-body was very dense and was being repeatedly projected onto women by way of false expectations, deceit, anger, and revenge.

On the same token, Ema's early trauma with her mother had contributed to her pain-body that expressed itself as being overly cautious about giving of herself—physically and/or emotionally—to a *man*. Thus she was unknowingly blaming men for being too "needy," which was the way her mind rationalized not having to deal with her own fears of intimacy. She was projecting her repressed anger that she had toward her mother on every single man she dated. She even lumped Alex into the list of "a hundred men" that had apparently tried to kiss her but failed. Ema felt as if she didn't need to contribute much to the burgeoning relationship with Alex, and thus gave very little of herself. So essentially, she was taking advantage of him in a pathetic attempt to feel a little better about herself. Ema even prevented Alex from seeing her all dolled up, depriving him of her beauty (a subconscious form of punishment) so she could wield power *over* him.

Ema's contortions are typical of a very heavy pain-body, as are Alex's quick-to-anger responses to Ema's rejection of him. Also, Alex was not willing to accept the reality of the situation. He wanted things to happen *his* way and in *his* time, not in the universe's way and time. Instead of accepting Ema as she was, and subsequently leaving her as she was, he felt a deep-seated need to *make her pay* for disappointing him. Hence the email war. He internalized Ema's dysfunctional behavior as a personal attack on *him*. But it wasn't. It was simply Ema being Ema.

But the icing on the cake was when it was made quite clear to *both* of them that they were wasting a lot of time and energy pointing their fingers at one another for their own relationship problems. In the grocery store confrontation, it was as if the reflective universe was saying: "Here you are. This is your fear, hatred, and contempt for the opposite sex staring right back at you. Here is your *mirror self*."

Trevor and Rain.

Assumptions are the termites of relationships.

—Henry Winkler

When Trevor first laid eyes on Rain, he became intoxicated with euphoria. She was nothing like he had ever seen in a woman before. A mix of spunk, sexiness, and *sass*, Rain completely blew him away. At the party where they met, Trevor asked her out after a brief conversation, and Rain gladly wrote down her phone number on the palm of his hand. The following night, they went out.

Smart, irreverent, and cool, Rain was the kind of girl who could sport Ray-Ban Aviators in a dimly lit bar while wearing a skin-tight dress and gartered fishnets, holding a lit cigar in one hand and a dry martini in the other, and pull the whole thing off without a *hitch*. Her fiery red hair, curly and bobbed, accentuated her dolphin-like skin: tight, smooth, and *pore-less*. Trevor was not just infatuated by her, he was *mesmerized*. He also enjoyed being seen with her in public. Twenty-two and a generation younger, Rain had a movie star appeal that never failed to turn heads. It wasn't long before the thirty-five-year-old successful architect became lost in Rain's hooded, green eyes. In a New York minute, all of Trevor's caution and sensibilities were gone with the wind. He was utterly convinced that he'd finally met the woman of his dreams.

Trevor began to frequent the billiard bar where Rain worked as a server, playing pool and flirting with her on nights when she worked. He would always wait until her shift ended, and then afterward the two love birds would stroll up to the neighborhood coffee shop and sit on the patio where they would romantically flirt, chat, and laugh about everything and nothing for hours on end.

About a week later, on Rain's day off, Trevor took Rain to a Middle Eastern restaurant in the Upper West Side where they both lived. On a cool New York summer night they dined al fresco, drinking Greek wine while enjoying small plates of hummus, falafel, red lentil soup, baklava, and Armenian pizza. The evening was a glorious success, and it ended even better with Rain spending the night—in Trevor's bed. "It was the best night of my life," he revealed the following day to his buddy, Chase, adding, "We had such a great time together. We're a perfect match. I just know she's the *one*."

A few weeks later, Rain quit her job as a server since she was offered an office day job as a paralegal for a high profile law firm, and as a result, Trevor wasn't able to see her as often. But he took the news in stride, confident that the two would be together, for *life*. No one had ever made him feel the way he felt around Rain. He just needed to keep wining and dining her, he told himself. "If I can just keep giving to her selflessly, keep treating her right, and keep giving her all my time, all my love, and all my attention without expecting anything in return, then she'll be *mine*, forever," he reasoned. He further rationalized that the two of them always enjoyed each other's company, and they never fought about anything, ever. It was pure *bliss*.

A few months later, however, Trevor began noticing that Rain was promising a tad more than she was delivering…

TREVOR   "Hey Rain, what happened to you last night? You said you were going to come over, remember?" I ask, somewhat nervously.

"Oh, doll, I'm so, so sorry. I got busy doing stuff with my friends and time just *flew* by. Before I knew it, it was midnight and I figured you'd already gone to bed since you have to get up at six. So sorry about that, it won't happen again," Rain explains convincingly.

I believe what Rain is telling me in spite of the fact that she recently stood me up three times in the past four weeks (but hey, who's counting?)—every time having some lame excuse about having to "work late at the firm," or "forgetting a facial appointment at the spa." And every single time, she always says apologetically, "It won't happen again."

"Okay. No prob. So, are you available later on, I mean, when you get off work?" I ask eagerly.

"Yep, I'm all yours, sweetie. What shall we do?"

"Well, there's a great new restaurant called Half Moon Bay that just opened up here in on the West Side that I thought we could check out. Time Out gave it rave reviews, and the decor is supposed to be rather impressive."

"Sure. Sounds good, honey. What time?"

"Ummm, say six?"

"That's fine. I'll meet you there, okay?" There was something in her voice that didn't sound right. I'd prefer that she let me pick her up, and so I reply with, "Why don't you let me pick you up in a cab—your apartment is kinda on the way…"

"Oh, gosh, I'm not going to be home because I promised Rooney that I would meet her for a quick drink at the Mandarin after work. She wanted to share with me some fabulous news about her boyfriend, James. I think she's getting engaged. Isn't that just wonderful, honey?"

"Uhh, yesss…it *is*. Okay, well then, I'll meet you at Half Moon Bay at six, okay?"

"Okay sweetie. See you then. Bye."

My iPhone is showing me 4:27. After showering, shaving, and primping, I slip into a brand new Armani silk and linen seersucker suit and dress it down with a black Zegna tee. On the way out the door, I stop at the entryway closet to retrieve my new black leather sandals I just bought from Kenneth Cole, which will no doubt bloody my feet since they're not broken in yet, but I don't really care since they finish off this evening's attire quite nicely and make me look *sharp*. I take the elevator down from the 9th floor to the lobby, proceeding out of my building into a mild summer breeze, all the way down the street about six blocks to the critically acclaimed cafe. I'm excited to finally, after a whole week without seeing her, be reunited with my beloved *soul mate*. With my heart racing and perspiring in anticipation, I arrive at Half Moon Bay at 5:53, walk up to the brushed steel, halogen-lit bar, and order a much needed mojito.

After finishing off the last quaff of my second drink, I check my iPhone for messages (for the tenth time since I arrived) and there are none. It's 6:47 p.m. and I'm now beginning to wonder where Rain is, again. After texting her the query: "Where are you?" I set my phone down carefully on the shimmering steel bar and order another mojito. Minutes later, I get a text from Rain that reads: "Be there in 15."

Half Moon Bay specializes in Northern California cuisine and recently received a full page spread in Architecture Magazine for its cutting-edge, neoclassical decor, displaying dozens of ultra-sleek, narrow-beamed pin-lights that are strategically positioned downward from the 20-foot mahogany ceilings to the bar, dining room tables, and mirror-cut, black granite floors. After I've had my fill of inspecting the ambience, I strike up a light conversation with the bartender, explaining to him that I'm waiting for my girlfriend, and soon-to-be *wife*. He nods and smiles politely while wiping the bar with a towel, then takes an order from an attractive, chicly dressed couple standing to my right. I notice that the gentleman is the actor, Matthew McConaughey. I check the time and it's 7:27. I'm famished. I order a tuna tartare appetizer to keep from passing out, and another mojito, my *fourth*.

After 8:00, I decide to call Rain instead of text her, which I do, angrily. She doesn't answer. And so I text her again: "Are you coming or not?" I then order another mojito and three more appetizers: the carpaccio, shrimp cocktail, and a half-dozen blue point oysters on the half shell with horseradish and extra

Tabasco on the side. At 8:50, I pay my bill and leave. I don't hear from Rain. Hours pass. I can't sleep, at all. This is the fifth time in the last four weeks I was stood up. How could she? If she doesn't want to meet me, why doesn't she just say so? How could she stand me up five times in a month? I mean, who *does* this?

As it turned out, Trevor continued to ask Rain out for four more months after she had already successfully stood him up five times in a row. She would continue to see him on occasion and when she did, the romance would always recommence and it was just like it was in the beginning of their relationship. Trevor never had the courage to confront Rain and ask her why she kept standing him up because he was afraid that if he did, she would stop seeing him altogether. For Trevor, seeing Rain sporadically was better than not seeing her at all. No doubt, she was seeing several other men who, like Alex, were on the receiving end of her emotional torture. And when Rain did periodically see Trevor, her display of affection and charm was always *just enough* to convince him that she was still "the one"—his soul mate.

Because of his refusal to accept things *as they are*, rather than how he wished *they could be*, the cycle of deception was destined to repeat itself for poor Trevor. By concurrently accelerating and repeating the same scenarios, over and over, the communicative universe eventually made it clear to him that he was being played like a fiddle by Rain. By the tail end of their "relationship" over four months later, Rain would stand Trevor up on *seven dates in a row,* each time uttering her infamous phrase, "I'm so sorry, doll. It won't happen again." And by the time it all ended, Trevor was left a withering shadow of the man he was before he had met her. It was nothing less than excruciating torment for him and to vent his frustration he would talk about what Rain "was doing to him" to his friends and co-workers, frequently. His pain-body *feasted* on her psychological abuse and eventually, even his friends got tired of hearing about the madness of it all. Chase finally said to him, "No one is holding a gun to your head, Trevor. Why don't you just stop asking her out?"

Know that the pain-body is a complete and utter *addiction to pain* so until you become conscious of it, it will continue to drag you through the fires of Hades, all the while convincing you of the ecstasy of "what could be" if you only suffered *enough*. Trevor believed that if he just kept "giving of himself selflessly" to Rain, kept "treating her right," she would eventually come around, and be his, *forever*. He believed it *so blindly* that it didn't matter how horribly she treated him, he could always rationalize her abusive behavior.

What I also found interesting about Trevor was that he was married briefly when he was twenty-five. Not surprisingly, his wife acted out a similar pattern of deceptive behavior that drove him into depression for several years afterward. A decade later, Rain's abuse was significantly more severe and consequently, his pain became nearly unbearable. And that's what ultimately prompted him to seek spiritual guidance and begin working toward healing his passive pain-body.

Blair and Gavin.

> *The easiest kind of relationship for me is with ten
> thousand people. The hardest is with one.*
>
> —Joan Baez

Blair had just become a successful entrepreneur. After four years of highly focused hard work and diligence, her yoga studio was beginning to make a healthy profit, and she had just expanded it to accommodate a seventh instructor. As a result, she had classes available days, nights, and weekends. Being a brilliant marketer, the press, media, and the Internet helped put Blair and her business in the top echelon of yoga studios in New York. Gavin decided to take one of her classes because he was only interested in learning from "the best." He was five years older than Blair, who had just turned thirty. They were attracted to each other strongly from the very first class that Gavin attended. By the third class, Gavin asked Blair out to dinner which she excitedly accepted. After three months of dating, Gavin asked Blair to move in with him. Also a successful entrepreneur, Gavin had just secured an apartment on the 53rd floor on 42nd and 9th, in the Orion Building, overlooking the breathtaking midtown Manhattan skyline. Blair declined at first, but with a little coaxing, she finally relented, and leased her SoHo brownstone to a student of hers. Afterward, she would be shacking up with Gavin in the sky.

Within a few months after moving in with him, Blair began noticing a more "emotionally distant" Gavin. His lovemaking became more mechanical and less visceral. This "hot to cold" type of relationship was beginning to become all too familiar and reminded her of two former relationships. The most recent one was with a man named Bret with whom she lived with for ten months, three years prior. He seemed liked the "real deal" but shortly after she had moved in with him, like Gavin, he too became distant. Eventually, the fire between them dwindled and the two parted ways. Blair also recalled a relationship in college that was nearly identical to the one with Bret. His name was Derrick and he too was passionate about her until she moved in with him, only after a few weeks. Like with Bret, her relationship with her college sweetheart also fizzled out quickly, leaving her feeling dejected and unwanted. In all three relationships, things moved rather quickly and passionately at first, but when she moved in with them, things changed abruptly. At that point, Blair felt as if her partners were simply "not there."

On a snowy December day in Manhattan, Blair asked her friend Rooney to lunch at a popular Asian fusion restaurant to vent her frustrations…

BLAIR   "It's been almost a year now since I moved in with him and he's just been becoming more and more, well, you know, *distant*. I can't believe this is happening again. I can't believe this is happening *again*. How can this be happening again, Rooney? I'm thirty-one years old now and I want to get married and have children. Why does this same crappy relationship keep, like, repeating itself in my life?" I'm asking Rooney this as our server carefully sets down a bottle of ice cold Ozeki along with two porcelain sake cups onto a white marble two top.

"I don't know, Blair. Perhaps you should seek out a counselor for some guidance. I agree with you that Gavin's been a lot more reserved as of late. So why did he stop taking yoga classes again?" Rooney asks.

"He says that he just doesn't have the *time*. He says that he's simply too busy with his business right now and so he's, like, put the whole "yoga thing" on hold. He says that he's trying to negotiate some $50 million dollar merger between his company and some other company called, um, oh I forget the name right now but the result of this potential merger would provide him with uh, oh god, how did he put it? Oh yeah, a "golden parachute." I'm beginning to believe that the *real* reason though has much less to do with parachuting and a lot more to do with *me*. I just don't think he can stand to be around me. I mean, we no longer even *do* things together anymore. He's like always working in his office. The only time he comes out of there is to eat something I've prepared for him. We watch TV, have dinner, and then he goes straight back into his office to work. We don't even talk anymore, and, then, after that, I can't even remember the last time we had sex," I say, sighing, taking a much-needed sip of very fine sake.

"I'm so sorry, baby. You deserve so much better. You're stunning, successful, and men are always dropping at your feet. Why in the world would you want to stay with someone who's so, well, you know, *cold*? Don't you believe you deserve someone who's going to be there for you? You know, like, *present*?

"I…*guess*," I answer under my breath while drifting out the window, observing a sea of humans competing for the sidewalk in downtown SoHo, staring to no one. My mind reflects on my relationship in college.

"I mean, it was the same way with Derrick…and more recently with Bret. My god, I just realized throughout my whole life I've seemingly been attracted to carbon copies of the exact same man. *Clones*, I tell you. And even though it starts out great and it's all, like, passionate and wonderful at first, it seems like within a short time they barely have a pulse for me. Why do I keep attracting these cardboard cutouts as mates? Tell me, Roo. Tell me, please." I beg before taking another sip of dry Ozeki.

"I don't know what to say to you, love, except that I know you deserve better. But you have to *believe* that you do. Until you believe it with all your heart that you deserve to be truly and passionately loved, then you simply won't attract that kind of man into your life."

"Something in me? Maybe. I don't know. All I know is that if things continue to progress like this, I'm sure that Gavin will end up cheating on me just like Derrick and Bret did."

"They *cheated* on you?" Rooney asks, sincerely surprised.

"Yep, both of them. Derrick did with two different women that I know of and Bret did at least once for sure. Oh my god, maybe Gavin's *cheating* on me? That possibility just dawned on me." I stop and think about what I just said and mentally correlate his behavior to match. "*That's* why he stopped taking my yoga classes. He needs the extra free time to spend with the other woman!" My mind is now racing with very scary potential scenarios.

"No, Gavin wouldn't do that to you, Blair. He just doesn't seem like, well, you know, the cheating *type*. He's just too, uh, you know, like, conservative?" Rooney asks, unsure, and now *I'm* convinced that *she's* convinced that Gavin is, in fact, cheating on me.

"Yeah, you're probably right, Roo. I'm sure I'm just being paranoid."

As it turned out, Gavin was not only cheating on Blair, he ended up engaged to the other woman ten days after telling Blair to *get out*. Blair, in spite of her success in business as well as her extraordinary physical beauty could not attract to her the warm and caring man of her dreams. Why? One word: *trauma*.

Shortly after Blair was left hanging high and dry by Gavin, her mother summoned the courage to leave her father, after a marriage of thirty-three years. Apparently she finally had enough of his emotional unavailability, coldness, and detachment. She had also had enough of his cheating, which she later discovered he'd been doing since Blair was born. Thus, this became the "male imprint" that Blair had become exposed to as a little girl growing up into the world. Subsequently, she learned: *that's just the way men are*. She observed how miserable her mother was, and her psyche developed a similar deeply flawed and fear-based perception of the female role in a relationship. This contributed greatly to the formation of her passive pain-body which kept attracting the emotionally withdrawn, cheating men into her life.

I found it interesting that Blair never viewed the way in which her father treated her or her mother as "abusive." She even said, "My father never raised his voice to me or became angry with me, therefore I never saw myself as being abused." I then informed Blair that even though detachment and cheating are not the same as being beaten over the head with a club, it's still abuse. The pain-body cannot differentiate between someone who's screaming at you and someone who is emotionally *not there*. Both behaviors get registered in the subconscious mind as *abuse*.

A genetic mutation.

The reality of it all is, when you're on the threshold of a spiritual awakening, your life is going to remind you of the movie *Groundhog Day* when events and situations seem to ominously repeat themselves, until you begin to suspect that there must be a *pattern* forming in your life where you're constantly swearing that you've been there before, and even though the names and faces of the people around you may have changed, you will inevitably keeping waking up, day after day, month after month, year after year, finding yourself having the exact same argument—nearly word for word—exchanging the exact same abusive remarks, and enduring the exact same tumultuous breakups. The good news is that a déjà vu scenario is a powerful sign for a burgeoning Next Human who's on the verge of an evolutionary metamorphosis.

As I've said in prior chapters, neither the ego nor the pain-body is individualistic. Pain is pain and dysfunction is dysfunction, and this cloned energy field is of the exact same frequency in anyone and everyone in a relationship dynamic. The collective pain-body has been on this planet for hundreds of millennia, since the onset of the current human. But the human species is currently mutating: genetically, cognitively, sociologically, economically, ecologically, creatively, and spiritually.

In the genetic code of the Next Human, the pain-body will be in the "off mode" because she will have created healthy boundaries around the Self—a subtle, psychic shield of protection—preventing pain-body-possessed humans from abusing her. Thus, all relationships will be harmonious, loving, and joyous because before she enters into one, she will already have achieved *wholeness*. For the current human, on the other hand, what is initially perceived as true love often turns later into resentment, anxiety, and even hatred because she will always rebel against any relationship that she feels forced *into*. Codependency is by its very nature a *coercing* against the emotional freedom of the higher Self. When you feel as if you *have* to be with another because of a *lacking* to be complete, you can never be happy in that relationship. How could you be?

At the highest level, you are already a whole, nondual being. The greatest challenge to you on this plane of duality is to discover that truth. Until then, you'll be living a lie, your partner will be living a lie, and true intimacy will elude the both of you. You will only experience brief glimpses of it. After the egoic couple settle into a committed relationship, the little quirks that were initially accepted without judgment eventually become *fuel* for nonsensical conflicts and bitter discord that end in separation. In the United States, the divorce rate is a staggering 50 percent. But that doesn't mean that the half that remains married is living in perfect harmony. Not even close.

In Evolution 201 I introduced you to the phantom self and the energy exchange that takes place during a typical pain-body attack. In close relationships, the majority of attacks don't escalate past stage five. But just because most couples don't normally punch each other's lights out, emotional violence still prevails and can be just as harmful to the health of the body because of the inordinate amounts of *stress* it creates. Some relationships endure a pain-body attack on a daily or weekly basis for years on end, and when children are exposed to this, they are being subconsciously programmed to—upon adulthood—*re-enact* the same emotional violence with *their* partners, and hence the cycle of pain continues.

Because you live in a dimension of polarity, it's in your best interest to learn the rules of the game. Once understood, you won't have to become a victim of a broken heart ever again. You won't have to *fear* being hurt by another. Only the ego can become wounded, not your true Self. When the relationship stems from "ego-love," the heart is much like the bulb of a rose, closed and unable to express its full potential of beauty and fragrance. True love, on the other hand, stems from the Source. That's when you'll be looking into the mirror of your divine Self.

Healthy relationships begin with Self-mastery.

*Knowing others is intelligence; knowing yourself is true
wisdom. Mastering others is strength; mastering yourself
is true power.*

—Lao Tzu

You can never control or change the dysfunctional behavior in your
partner. You can, however, change it in yourself. When you start to work
on yourself and make improvements for the better, your partner will either grow with you or the pain of being around him or her will become
so unbearable that you'll simply see no other option other than to say
goodbye. It just happens that way, and it's a good thing when it does because it's always better for both partners. If you're not in sync spiritually
with your partner, then it doesn't serve either person. And if you ignore
the toxic situation, it will only repeat itself, either through the same
partner, or through the next, and the next, and the next.

When you finally learn to create a *space* in between your partner's
negative behavior and your peace of mind, you'll be practicing non-
reaction, non-resistance, non-violence, and peaceful acceptance to your
partner's behavior. When you do, you may find that your partner will
change his behavior for the better on his own, without having to be told
what he should or shouldn't do. If this doesn't happen and you still find
yourself living in misery for months on end, then it may be time for you
to take action and move on. If your partner is not ready to change, then
that's usually a sign that you've outgrown him or her on the level of emotional maturity and self-awareness. If you leave the relationship peacefully, you'll be able to attract a *new* partner with a higher frequency of
behavior that's more in tune with your own.

Most of us spend wasted time and energy searching for love from
somewhere other than our Selves. In reality, there's no such thing as
"finding love." There's only your ability to discover love from with*in*. If
you're searching for love "out there" because you feel unfulfilled in your

heart, then you're setting yourself up for a huge disappointment. Remember, there is no "out there." There is only the here and now. The now here. That person you are seeking is *you*. So look no further. We all come from love and it is the destiny of each and every soul to *return* to love. Find that love first within, and then allow the universe to bring you a reflection of that love in a partner.

Wholeness is akin to holiness.

Most current humans equate happiness with companionship because they've convinced themselves that they simply can't discover true joy without being with another. And *this* is why so many of their relationships are dysfunctional. When you are ready to *let go* of your fears of being alone, you'll quickly discover that your codependency for companionship will dissolve. You will find that you already *are* love. Then you'll no longer feel the need to justify your existence through another. Compulsions will always stem from feelings of incompleteness or loneliness. True love begins with *free will*.

Alcoholics, drug addicts, and food addicts are addicted to the biochemical rewards they receive from the intake of a specific *substance*. Gamblers are addicted to the thrill of the *risk*. But there is one dependency that afflicts more people than all of these combined. It's called *companionship*. Codependency can be defined as an obsessive need for a feeling—such as serenity, excitement, love, euphoria—in an *external* source. But all obsessive needs are *fear*-based. Furthermore, these deeply ingrained, suppressed, subconscious fears of not being complete all by your Self stem from a veiling of your inherent divinity. When you finally discover your magnificent Self and evolve into the Next Human, you'll be living every moment in the peaceful, loving bliss of the Now. As a result, you won't need to be searching for a feeling or stimulus anywhere outside of your Self.

Because most people have been emotionally *stomped on* their entire life and probably countless lives prior, it is difficult for them to accept at first that they are potentially divine. But since everything in the universe flows from the Source, then that must include every One in it, including you, does it not? Since the current human is so fast to point her finger at those she deems as inferior or "not worthy" of divinity, her egoic mind constructs a *false sense of separation* between herself and others. And because this finger-pointing is really a denial of those same feelings of *unworthiness* in herself—the same exact traits that she labels as flaws or "sins"—the projection is only reinforced. Know that there are no sins from the highest perspective of the Source. All mistakes are a necessary part of our evolutionary journey, onward and *up*ward. Nevertheless, because the current human feels unworthy of her natural birthright, she treks through life with her head drooped down, ashamed of her inner light, fearing the inescapable truth that she is already *whole*.

This feeling of incompleteness or separation from the Source bolsters our dependency on the other. And this is why the current human fails at intimate relationships. After all, how can you experience true love when the entire relationship is based on the *fallacy* that you need that person to complete you? This preconditioned neediness is rooted in the misconception that you are not already complete. Ergo, realizing your *wholeness* is akin to realizing your *holiness*.

To evolve into the Next Human, you must first learn to let go of attachment. Jealousy, possessiveness, and dependency are all shadows of *greed*. Every natal compulsion to *be* with another will be accompanied by an underlying suppressed *fear* of being connected with the Source. But the Source is also the Self. Many people falsely equate being *alone* with being *lonely*. The two, however, are not the same. In truth, you cannot reconnect your Self with the Source until you *are* alone. This is one reason why so many people rarely become One with their own divinity. They're afraid of being alone. They are afraid of meeting the Source face to face within them. Thus, their codependency continues from lifetime to lifetime.

When you finally allow your independent Self the time to awaken and discover your own divinity by going deeply within, you will discover a boundless treasure of love, compassion, and *joy* that you've been desperately seeking in the other. And when you're finally ready to surrender all of your anger, guilt, bitterness, and shame, you'll be making a *choice* to end the cycle of suffering for yourself, for good. All abusive relationships, no matter how fleeting, are nothing more than reflections of the lack of love from with*in*. Awaken to your inherent divinity, begin loving and nurturing your Self and you will be free. This is what the Buddha called *nirvana.*

True love and the spiritual relationship.

> *Spiritual relationship is far more precious than physical. Physical relationship divorced from spiritual is body without soul.*
>
> —Mahatma Gandhi

It sometimes happens that when two people meet, they instantly recognize their divine Selves behind the eyes of the other, also called the "windows of the soul." Even their voices awaken in them a deep familiarity, like a half-remembered song from long ago. Inexplicably, often without a word being spoken, they instinctively *know* that they are destined to walk down the road of life together as One. This describes the reunion of *twin souls.*

The term *soul mate* is frequently misused in today's vernacular. Before you can attract your soul mate to you, you must first become *whole.* People who are not spiritually awakened—and therefore identify themselves as an *ego*—are misled into believing that they are going to find their soul mate if they simply join an online dating service or follow the guidelines laid out in a particular book. But it doesn't work that way. It begins with first retrieving your *soul*, then attracting your *mate.*

For the current human, the soul mate relationship is very *rare*. Believe it or not, more than 90 percent of the current population is codependent (to varying degrees), and therefore *not* with a soul mate; they are with an *ego mate*. But even though most of the population is in a codependent relationship, that doesn't mean that they're not with the right person because you're always with the *right* person for you at any given time. This realm of duality guarantees it. The reflective universe is always matching everyone up with their perfect companion for *where they are* on the evolutionary ladder.

Non-judgment, non-conflict, and deep-seated presence are prerequisites for true intimacy in any relationship. If you are constantly judging your partner when he or she is around you, then some form of suffering within the relationship dynamic is inevitable because the ego will become inflamed and defensive. And defensiveness is always the first act to *war*. Relinquishing thoughts of judgment about your partner is necessary for peace and harmony in the relationship. This creates the necessary *space* for true intimacy to flourish.

Petty grievances strengthen and embolden the ego. Countless divorce lawyers have been consulted based on minor (and mostly ridiculous) grievances. To cement an intimate partnership, continual acceptance, forgiveness, and unconditional love toward the other is required. This is why it's necessary to become emotionally independent *first* before you can attract your soul mate. This process simply can't happen in the reverse.

The Next Human will naturally attract her soul mate without the need for searching because she will already be complete. He will intuitively know that companionship is not a compulsive need, or something to *long* for, but an honor and a blessing to be cherished. She will know that living in solitude is the universe's way of teaching us to be Self-reliant, and appreciative of what *is*. Because the Next Human will value the Self above all else, he will not allow a partner to abuse him. So before you can attract your *soul mate* to you, it is necessary to become emotionally independent first. You will then be with your partner because you *choose* to be, not because of an inner compulsion to be.

EVOLUTION
5 0 1

THE CREATIVE SELF
MANIFESTING FROM THE HEART

Morpheus: *When the matrix was first built there was a man*
born inside who had the ability to change what-
ever he wanted, to remake the matrix as he saw
fit. It was he who freed the first of us, taught us
the truth. As long as the matrix exists, the
human race will never be free.

—*The Matrix*

The universe cannot evolve until you do. A droplet in the cosmic sea of Source consciousness, you are a co-creator at your core. This is the ultimate destiny of every soul. Despite this esoteric truth, however, people tell me all the time: "I don't have a creative bone in my body." My retort: "You're creating your life right now, are you not?" Creativity comes in many ways. Take a glance at nature and take a leaf from her book. Observe the infinitude of forms she is endlessly creating, from subatomic quarks to galaxy superclusters.

Know that true creativity is never forced. It flows from the Source on its own volition as if it has a will of its own. True creativity is never planned, structured, organized, static, or systematic. Contrariwise, it's fluid, dynamic, sporadic, erratic, and unforeseen. When you are truly creative, you are honoring the living universe and its intention to channel its divine energy *through* you. Whether it be a painting, a song, a dance, a composition, a script, a design, a blueprint, a photograph, a sculpture, a performance, a book, a software program, a theoretical equation, or a business, we all create in accordance with our own specialized abilities. The Next Human will be completely familiar with her own unique creative talents and she'll implement them based on her acquired knowledge from countless past lives.

The development of the printing press by Johannes Gutenberg in 1440 paved the way for the rise of a cultural movement known as the Renaissance that began in Italy and eventually spread throughout Europe, culminating in a flowering of innovation in literature, music, architecture, politics, science, education, religion, philosophy, and yes, of course, *art*. The word renaissance stems from the Latin *rinascere:* "to be reborn." On a creative level, history is on the verge of repeating itself. But this time around, instead of being limited to a specific region of the globe, the New Renaissance will usher in a creative rebirth to the entire planet, a New Earth.

The art form of the 20th century has arguably been the motion picture. This wonderful new medium of creative expression has helped to bring the world together in many ways. In fact, movies top the list of America's biggest exports. Tied for a close second: TV programs, music, books, and computer software. But this is merely the beginning. In the coming years of the 21st century, Next Humans from a wide variety of nations will express more creativity than humanity has witnessed in the past five millennia.

Until you are heart-centered, all your emotions will come from the brain. And because the emotional body of the current human stems directly from the brain, mind-based love or "ego love" will always be polarized and therefore conditional. But all mothers—just after the birth of a baby—experience an unconditional love that is rooted in a second, untapped, and infinitely more powerful emotional body. The ancient Tibetan Buddhists were well aware of this secret source of love; they knew that it dwelled within the *heart*.[1]

The way in which the law of attraction is presented in the bestselling book *The Secret* is true, but comes with a heavy price. Because the brain is polarized (left and right hemispheres, eight lobes), it cannot create a harmonized reality. Ever. You can certainly attract to you what you want from the mind, but its polarization ensures a manifestation of what you *don't want* in return. And yes, this also includes **prayer**.

When you manifest your intention from the ego, then you will indeed get the mansion and Mercedes, but you'll also be laden with problems that will bring you a good dose of anxiety, stress, conflict, drama, and/or disease right along with it. So even though the brain is perfectly capable of delivering to you what you want, its polarity will eventually broadside you with the opposite of what you intended. The heart, on the other hand, transcends polarity, ensuring a creativity that is whole and unconditional: a mind*less* creativity. Zero stress. Zero drama. Imagine that. Moreover, when you learn how to manifest your reality directly from the heart, every soul around you benefits, not just *you*.

Because the ego dissolves in the wake of the heart, the mind will play a backseat role for the Next Human in his creative process. He will understand that it is the *heart* that holds the true power to creativity, not the brain. In the history of the *Homo sapiens* species, the ego has ruled the earth, allowing precious humans to be needlessly slaughtered, all in the name of separation. And it's for this reason alone why we have failed to protect, nurture, and *stand up* for our Selves, why creativity has been selective and reserved for those with means. For the Next Human, however, the heart will become the source of his strength. This is an evolutionary leap forward on a level that we have never witnessed before.

Ashamed of her inherent divinity, the current human is unaware of the polarized reality that she continually creates from her egoic mind. Because of this, she fails to realize her *heart*-based potential. Know that the heart is the true source of love, compassion, and creativity. When you prevent the heart from leading the mind, you remain nothing but an automaton clothed in flesh. Fortunately, the evolutionary journey of creativity that many current humans are now embarking on is rooted directly from the heart, not the mind. This is what I call *the creative Self*. From here, both the left brain *and* the right brain allow the heart to take the lead. And because of this, you're able to manifest a joyful reality from a place of unconditional love. And remember, only *love* is real. Everything else is false. Creativity from the heart exists only in the Now. Your egoic mind cannot exist in the Now.

This doesn't mean that the mind will no longer be accessed. But just like the physical body, the mental body will be viewed more as "software" rather than "hardware," i.e. a secondary tool that is tethered to the source of limitless power: the *heart*. Brain-based selfish creativity is exemplified in the imbalance of those who "have" and those who "have not" in our society. When the wealthiest 400 people in America own more wealth than the bottom half—about 150 million people—how can we be free to *create* what we want for our Selves?[2] How can we be free at *all*?

The right brain, left brain myth.

Psychologists are taught that the right hemisphere of your brain allows you to be more creative, visual, emotional, and imaginative, while the left hemisphere controls your logical and deductive reasoning, mathematical ability, intellect, and speech. This idea stems at least partly from the classic studies of split-brain patients performed by Sperry and Gazzaniga at the California Institute of Technology, beginning in the 1950s. Subsequently, it has since been academically accepted that if you are left-brain-dominant, you'll make a better engineer or scientist, and if you are right-brain-dominant, you'll be better at something more artistic. Well, as it turns out, the way in which the brain operates is not so cut-and-dry.

A 1996 study at the imaging laboratory of London's Institute of Neurology conducted by the esteemed neuroscientists Gereon R. Fink, M.D., Ph.D., and John C. Marshall, M.D., Ph.D., scanned the brains of people who were looking at a series of images called letter navons.[3] These are pictures in which a single large letter such as an S is made up of many smaller letters, such as a series of Fs. The researchers asked their subjects to report whether they saw the global image (the big S) or the local elements (the Fs) while a radioactive chemical injected into their bloodstream revealed which side of the brain was more active during each report.[4]

The results were as expected. When the subjects focused on the small (local) letters, areas on the left side of the brain lit up; when they viewed the large (global) letters, the right side lit up. But Marshall wasn't satisfied. He wanted replication and conclusion. The following year, he, Fink, and the entire team returned to the research lab and added a slight twist to the experiment. This time, instead of a letter navon, they would use an *object* navon—an image in which a large shape, such as an anchor, consists of smaller shapes, such as cups.[5] And, of course, the team expected to get the same exact results, but to their shock, the pattern of activity was completely *reversed*.[6] The scans clearly showed left-brain activation for processing the global picture and right-brain activation for the local elements. Fink concluded that in regard to our prior understanding of the roles of brain hemispheres, "simple dichotomies are out," and it's "how the two sides of the brain complement and combine that counts."[7] In other words, how these attention effects express themselves in terms of the activity of individual brain areas depends more specifically on the nature of the *task* being performed.

For visual creative tasks and musical abilities, it is the *left* hemisphere of your brain, not the *right*, which plays a key role, according to researchers at the University of Southern California (USC). "We need both hemispheres for creative processing," said Lisa Aziz-Zadeh, assistant professor of neuroscience.[8] Functional magnetic resonance imaging (fMRI) was used to scan the brains of architecture students who tended to be visually creative. Although it was mainly handled by the right hemisphere, the creative task actually lit up the *left* hemisphere more than the non-creative task.[9] The results suggested that the left brain is a crucial supporter of creativity in the brain. Aziz-Zadeh says she plans to explore more of how various types of creativity such as painting, acting, and singing are created by the brain, what they all have in common, and what makes them different.[10]

In a joint effort of psychologists at the U.S. Army Research Institute for the Behavioral and Social Sciences at Fort Benning, Ga., and the University of Melbourne, Australia, researchers found that mathematically gifted teens did better than average-ability teens and college students on tests that required the two halves of the brain to cooperate, as reported in the April issue of *Neuropsychology*, published by the American Psychological Association (APA).[11] The mathematically gifted boys showed no "hemispheric differences." Those who were precocious in math were equally good at processing global and local elements with either hemisphere, suggesting more interactive, balanced, and cooperative left and right brains.

The study supports the growing notion that the mathematically gifted are better at relaying and integrating information between the cerebral hemispheres, according to co-author Michael O'Boyle, Ph.D. "It's not that you have a special math module somewhere in your brain, but rather that the brain's particular functional organization—which allows right-hemisphere contributions to be better integrated into the overall cognitive/behavioral equation—predisposes it towards the use of high-level imagery and spatial skills, which in turn just happen to be very useful when it comes to doing math reasoning," O'Boyle said.[12]

Boyle believes that the research supports the notion that the organization of the brain may be an important contributor to individual differences in "cognitive abilities, talents, and information-processing styles."[13] In other words, the brain harmonizes both the right *and* left hemispheres in accordance with the demands of specific functions. Boyle added, "Various expressions of exceptionality, such as giftedness in math, music or art, may be the by-product of a brain that has functionally organized itself in a qualitatively different way than the usual left/right hemispheric asymmetry."[14]

In conclusion, the intelligent brain is a tad more complex and less simplistic than we once realized. We know now that there is no such thing as a permanent "right brain/left brain" dichotomy. There's obviously a great deal more interaction between the two hemispheres of the brain depending on the task performed, since they clearly appear to have much more beneficial results when both hemispheres are accessed, rather than one dominating the other.

The Next Human will not identify himself with the brain, either right or left. She will innately understand that, just like your computer and smartphone, it is only a *tool* designed to help facilitate specific tasks, and nothing more. The time has come to get out of your head and into your *heart.*

The law of heart-based manifestation.

Luke: *I don't believe it.*

Yoda: *That is why you fail.*

—*Star Wars Episode V: The Empire Strikes Back*

The *first* element in the law of heart-based manifestation is complete and total *presence.* In mind-based manifestation, which creates from the ego, presence does not enter into the equation because the Now always dissolves the ego, and therefore the ego will do everything it can to evade it by projecting your mind into the future or past. Mind-based creative goals can be achieved but always comes with a price. Enter the law of attraction: *like attracts like.* Subsequently, the ego can only attract to itself other *like* egos. I observe this all the time. For example, if your goal is to create a business for yourself and you manifest it from the egoic mind, you may find that your competitors in the marketplace will perceive you as a threat to their very survival. Why? Because when you assert your ego—especially in the business world—you will automatically *offend* other egos. This results in "competition wars" where underhanded and devious shenanigans, copyright infringements, libeling, slandering, and defamation incessantly repeat from one competitor to another, resulting in costly lawsuits, not to mention sleepless nights and tons of unnecessary, energy-depleting *stress*, which, over time, leads to disease and premature death. And all for what? Money? Status? The Next Human will always put *inner peace* before the desire for wealth or achievement.

To get to pure *presence* and begin the process of heart-based manifestation, you must learn to transcend your pseudo self (see Evolution 101) and the phantom self (see Evolution 201). Until you do, you won't be able to manifest a *bean* from the heart. You will only continue to create from the brain, and therefore the results will always bring you some form of suffering along with whatever you've created.

Imaging or *imagining* an idea is the *second* part of the equation. But this cannot be forced. It can only come spontaneously to you when you are calm, passive, and not lost in the mind. This is where meditation is key. Heart-based, creative ideas can only come to you when you are present and still. When you are able to achieve this peaceful place of non-thought, your heart will allow a creative idea to be received. After all, how can you be open to receiving subtle, creative messages from the universe when your mind is in static mode? This is where you'll not only *envision* your idea, but also where your idea *ferments*. Everything that has been created in this world of form began with a single idea, a creative thought. So from a place of deep-seated presence, imagine what you want, and in as much detail as you can. As the saying goes: "God is in the details." I recommend recording your creative thoughts in a journal with specific details of whatever it is you wish to achieve, and then *let it go*. Oprah wrote in her journal over twenty years ago that she would *own* a television network someday. And now she does: it's called OWN. But the universe cannot deliver *to* you until you place your order, and in *detail*.

The **third** element in the equation for heart-based manifestation is **belief**. You have to *believe* in your idea. Belief is the most powerful creative tool you have. Without it, no amount of thinking or feeling would be able to manifest as a single form of creation. When you fail to fully believe in what you're attempting to create, you fail to *create*. It's that simple. The law of heart-based manifestation does not work from positive thoughts or imaging alone. It can't. This is where faith, trust, and *surrender* are released from the heart, the source of unconditional love. This is exercising the true power of the heart. Without belief, nothing, no *thing* can be manifested.

High-frequency, heart-based emotions such as enthusiasm, excitement, and **passion** for your idea are the **fourth** aspect of the equation. Imaging combined with passion becomes very powerful indeed. When you are enthusiastic about your idea, the collective mirror will, in turn, be *just as enthusiastic*. This is because whatever the reflective universe presents to you is always a mirror of your inner emotional state. Positive or negative, the choice is yours. If you're tepid about your idea, then your chances of seeing it to fruition are *nil*.

Focused action is the **fifth** part of the equation. A laser-like *focus* on what you want is crucial for manifestation. Don't allow other people or situations to distract you, dissuade you, or weigh you down. Keep a narrow eye on your goals and pour all your energy into whatever it is you are doing in the present moment. It's also important to remember that you cannot manifest from *re*active energy. If you try, you will fail. For example, if you're desperately trying to create a new business because your current one is failing, or because you're afraid of being fired by your current employer, or because the bank has threatened to foreclose on your home, then you're only pushing back on the universe and saying *no* to what already is. This is *re*action, not action. Not only will you be attempting to create out of desperation, you'll be reacting out of fear, and fear can only manifest another like reality of fear. However, when you stop, collect yourself, become still for a while, and surrender to the universe, you will find that the so-called problems you were having will dissolve, allowing for your anxieties to subside. Then, when it comes to you spontaneously and intuitively to take action and manifest a new business for your Self, a whole new vibratory energy emerges. This is when the heart *syncs* with the universe and you'll be good to go.

Now, since most current humans are completely unaware of the law of attraction, they are manifesting their own reality with a mixed bag of positive and negative emotions combined with frequent mind changes, temper flare-ups, anxiety attacks, chats about their weekly dramas with everyone they know—thus empowering them and making them stronger—or, because they keep creating their own problems out of challenges, they simply throw their arms up in the air and *give up completely* on whatever it is they want to manifest. Once you decide on what you want, don't stop creating it just because you don't see it manifest overnight or within the timeframe that you've anticipated. This is another reason why the current human so frequently fails to reach his goals. He presumes that manifestation must occur according to *his* schedule. It's as if the ego says, "The universe must bring me what I want, how I want it, and *when* I want it." And so, because the universe takes its time—mostly so it can make your dreams as solid as possible—the current human runs out of patience, and consequently fails to reach his goals. He fails because he stops being present, and starts buying into the illusion of failure. Remember the age-old saying, "Where there is a *will*, there is a *way*." Next Humans have iron wills. They keep going, and are willing to do *whatever it takes* to manifest their creative ideas into reality. Remember, you only fail when you quit. As long as you keep getting up, in spite of apparent "setbacks," you'll find that those setbacks were, in fact, necessary for you. Therefore **persistence** is the **sixth** part of the equation and is critical for you to see your manifestation through *all the way* to its intended destination. If you give up on your heartfelt dreams, you may as well give up on life itself.

The **seventh** and final part of the equation for heart-based manifestation is **gratitude**. Being grateful for even the smallest things takes your consciousness away from your mind and straight into your heart. It is the creative Self's way of saying yes to what *is*. If you're not grateful for everything you have, no matter how inconsequential it may seem to you, you will never manifest anything long lasting. If you do manage to manifest something, it will most certainly be short-lived. Know that the universe *takes away* from those who are ungrateful and *gives* to those who are grateful. This is simply the law. When you learn to observe the law, you'll find that you'll end up with more abundance than you ever dreamed of. The reason for this is simple. The evolving universe is designed by the Source to grow in accordance with self*less*ness from the heart, not sel*fish*ness from the mind. In other words, it can only grow from *love*. And so when you are grateful for everything you have—even if you're living in a shack and riding a bicycle to work—the universe can only keep rewarding your heart's desires. On the other hand, if you become greedy, selfish, or ungrateful for what you have, the reflective universe is going to *mirror* those feelings and take away what you have.

And if you start playing the victim by complaining about it or becoming bitter or angry, then it will take away even *more* from you. And to the unbiased universe, it won't matter how important you think you are. It doesn't mind. It's just doing its job. So, you know, be *grateful.*

Okay, so here's the equation:

Presence + Imaging + Belief + Passion + Focus + Persistence + Gratitude = Heart-Based Manifestation

Note again that when you're able to begin the manifestation process from a place of pure presence, you'll find that your heart will open up and become a portal to the divine Source. This instantly puts the universe and all its angels on your side. But to get to presence, you have to let go of your ego and its shadow. Living in the Now is critical for heart-based manifestation. This is the ultimate surrender to the will of the living universe and trusting in it to manifest your dreams *for* you. When you learn to trust in your heart and connect it with the Source, you will inevitably reach a higher state of consciousness where serendipity and miracles come into your life, *in a big way.* Then, what you used to perceive as "miraculous" becomes an everyday occurrence.

Memoir 02.27.01.

Walking in the back door of my apartment after my weekly grocery shopping, my peripheral vision spots a red blinking light on my new Panasonic answering machine. I've sold nearly three times as many saunas so far this year (thirty-three) than I did in all of 2000 (twelve), thanks to my new website: www.sunlightsaunas.com. After setting two bags of groceries down on the kitchen counter I walk into the foyer and press *play* on my machine that sets atop a black and chrome Marcel Breur end table. It's yet another horrifying message from Mark Gericho (third this week), the vice president for HLP Products, the company that supplies the infrared saunas of which I've been a distributor for over a year.

"Okay, Jason, this is *it*. This is your final warning. Either you shut your website down or we're not going to send you any more saunas. I don't know how to make it any more *clear*. If your site is not down in 48 hours, our contract is terminated..." Gericho is informing me through this, uh, digital device. Ostensibly, some of the veteran sauna distributors have been complaining because my website sales are infringing on their assigned territories, and even after making several attempts to assuage their somewhat legitimate concerns—trying desperately to convince them that this wonderful new website can be a sales-generating tool for *all*, even going so far as to offer to sell them the leads (at a nominal fee) that my site receives from their territories (which would only increase their sales and profits)—they're *still* not budging. Apparently these "businessmen" can't seem to comprehend the fact that a competently designed and intelligently marketed website is a far more *innovative* approach to promoting and selling the infrared sauna product compared to the traditional decade-long strategy: setting up a booth at a home and garden show.

I play the message again, this time listening to the underlying tone, inflection, cadence, whatever I can use to ascertain just how *serious* Gericho is about this. Is he bluffing? Why on earth would he *fire me* when I just generated over $90,000 in sales for his company in two months? And, no doubt, because of the overnight success of the website, I'm just getting warmed up. Can he not see the potential for the infrared sauna industry here? I mean, really, is he out of his *mind*? What's wrong with this guy? I'm mulling it all over, rethinking my options, contemplating my next move.

Unpacking my groceries, I feel a rush of adrenalin coursing through my veins. To vent the anxiety, I begin pacing up and down the long hallway, walking barefoot over the freshly-sanded white oak floor that runs throughout my halogen-lit, newly renovated apartment. "Why this problem, and why *now?*" I'm asking myself out loud. I simply can't go back to working the dreaded home shows, sitting in a booth for countless hours on end, selling an average of three saunas a month. I simply refuse. I am thinking. The Internet is the only way this is going to work; it's the future of commerce, for Christ sakes. How can these Neanderthals be so damn short-sighted? I've worked *hard* to get where I am and now it looks as if I'm going to lose it all in *one fell swoop.*

Pangs of fear are now consuming me, enveloping every muscle, tendon, ligament in my neck, stomach, chest, back, and as each terrifying thought repeats itself over and over in my head, I'm finding myself struggling to keep my breath under control. Fearing that I may soon *faint*, I start searching the kitchen in a desperate frenzy, rummaging through each steel cabinet and drawer for a lunch-sized paper bag which after a very long time I eventually find, open, and place over my nose and mouth. "Breathe, Jason, just *breathe*," I'm listening to a beautiful female voice say to me audibly as if she's right here in the room with me. Following her instruction, I breathe into the brown lunch bag for about a minute, taking in my own carbon dioxide, effectively slowing down my breathing rate and preventing me from hyperventilating. This prevents me from passing out but now my chest is pounding and my pulse is racing and my thoughts return to Gericho's message. I recommence my pacing to quell my anxiety but after about ten minutes or so my heart is palpitating so hard and fast that I'm fairly sure I'm on the verge of having a heart attack. Minutes later I stop to catch my breath again and go back into the kitchen to retrieve my little brown bag but before I do I begin to tremble, uncontrollably *shake all over*, and instead of thinking about dialing 911, all I can think about is the message from Gericho and the disastrous implications it has for my new company, Sunlight Saunas. I'm now wondering: How am I supposed to get myself out of *this* mess?

After about an hour or so of thinking about all the misery that might, may, most likely at some future date *happen*, I then decide to give my buddy Drew a call to share the horrifying news with him, so I pick up my cordless phone from its base, press 3 on the speed dial, and after a few rings, I hear Drew's voice.

"Hello?"

"Heyyy…it'sss…mm mmmeeee," I choke out, my voice trembling with the rest of my body.

"Dude…you sound *tense*."

"Yeaaahh welll, I th think I may ay be havving a heaaart at tttack or something, I don't know what's wwrrrrong, I can't seeeemm to catch mmmy my breath cauzzz Gerrricho left yet another messssage that he wantsss me off the internet or heeezz not going to sennnd me anymorrre pa pra prr product."

"Dude, calm down. You're just having a panic attack because Gericho doesn't know how to properly run a business, that's all."

"Paniccckk attack?" I ask, unsure of what Drew's talking about. I've heard of them but am unfamiliar with its symptoms.

"Yeah, that's all it is. Your body's just reacting to your anxiety. Lana has them all the time. She should be home any minute and then we'll come to your apartment and bring you a Xanax. Within fifteen minutes, you'll be *chill*." Within half an hour, Drew and Lana arrive with the Xanax and after about fifteen minutes or so, my nerves begin to numb, the trembling stops, my breathing rate returns to normal, and I finally begin to calm down.

"I can't believe how powerful the mind is," I express to Drew and Lana in complete astonishment that this terrifying experience called a "panic attack" was the direct result of my fearful thoughts about what might happen in the future, and nothing more. I am genuinely shocked how the anxiety that brought on the attack was all created by my mind, and my mind alone.

As events played out in the spring months of 2001, instead of me losing my business, a much more beneficial opportunity arose. The "always-conspiring-in-my-favor" universe provided me with a different infrared sauna supplier that allowed my website free reign throughout the world—where it didn't intrude on anyone's protected territory. And in addition to this newfound marketing and distribution freedom, I was also given my own private label. As a result, my new company was about to *take off.*

Your life path and the true power of intention.

The Intention to live as long as possible isn't one of the mind's best intentions, because quantity isn't the same as quality.

—Deepak Chopra

Deep within your creative Self lies an *inner guide* or "divine spark" of creativity that originates not from your blaring mind, but from your *heart.* It is none other than the soft and subtle "little voice" that speaks to you every day, guiding you on your higher Self's chosen path. It is the *voice* of the heart communicating directly *to* you.

When you can learn to differentiate between the voice of the mind and the voice of the heart, you will have tapped into authentic, unlimited *power.* You will also be in perfect *sync* with universal intention. Situations will no longer happen *to* you. Instead, you'll be able to create whatever your heart can imagine, and then some. For the first time, you'll no longer be judging the universe when it brings you challenges. To the contrary, you'll be grateful for and lovingly accepting those challenges from it. Then from a place of unconditional love, you'll take action. You will no longer allow others to stomp on you or take advantage of you because you won't be ego-identified and therefore operating from an over-reactive mind. Suffering—in all its forms—will become a thing of a foggy, rarely thought about past. This is when you begin living in the eternal stream of the Now, and subsequently life itself transforms into a peaceful meditation.

Millions of current humans set creative goals for themselves with the intention of reaching them, but, unfortunately, a small percentage of them actually do. If you have set a particular goal for yourself and have not achieved it—for whatever reason—you've probably been wondering why you failed. Setting goals is indeed part of the creative process, but you're much more likely to attain a goal that's in perfect alignment with your *life path* compared to one that's not. In other words, if your creative Self's intention for you in this life is to be a social activist, i.e. someone who works with groups, social networks, and organizations toward a common goal of bringing an end to the horrific social and political injustices on this planet, but in spite of this "higher calling" you've decided on becoming an online stock broker, then you're seriously going against the grain of your soul's intention. Even if you eventually do manage to realize your career goal, you'll most likely find yourself miserable, and dealing with an uneasy truce.

Simply put, the power of intention becomes exponentially amplified when your goals are in perfect harmony with your unique and highly individualized life path, which also means that they'll be in alignment with the will of the living Source. This is when the universe truly "has your back." If you follow your bliss—which is the same as following your heart's desire—rather than the whims of your mind, you'll discover that doors will fly open for you, people will come out of nowhere to offer their assistance, opportunities for advancement will consistently present themselves to you, and serendipity will abound, all because the universal support system is designed to facilitate the realization of your *heart*-based, creative ideas.

If the process of achieving your goals is not fun, *stress-free*, and joyful, then even though you may indeed be going down the right path, you're most assuredly going down it the *wrong way*. Subsequently, you'll be creating a tremendous amount of unnecessary stress on your body, which results in physical disease. As I tell my clients all the time: being stressed out over your perceived problems doesn't help them go away.

And most of the time it'll just make the problems *worse* because not only are you not thinking clearly when you're stressed, you're also the furthest thing away from being heart-centered.

You may be wondering at this point: "How can it be a *choice* when the universe doesn't support my career goal to be a stock broker?" And here's your answer: You already made the choice. Your challenge right now is to understand *why* you made it. As an evolutionary astrologer, I counsel clients via Skype from all over the world on their specific life purpose that is revealed in the birth chart. I see each natal chart as a rough blueprint for the soul in its current life, and each chart is a very helpful tool in revealing the vocation that the higher Self has chosen so that it can acquire specific skills and talents, as well as learn certain lessons for the purpose of evolving. By the way: skills, talents, or abilities that are acquired by the soul, and subsequently perfected in lifetime after lifetime, are frequently and mistakenly referred to as "gifts," as if God granted some souls gifts and others he simply bypassed, leaving them "gift-less." And of course this is absurd because every single ability and ounce of knowledge we retain from our wide variety of lives are not simply handed over or "gifted" to us. They are *earned*. After all, that's the purpose of living all these lives in the first place. Ergo, the more abilities and wisdom an individual soul attains, the "older," wiser, and more *evolved* that soul becomes. That's not to say that an older soul is better or more special than a younger soul, just as a 12th grader is not any more special than a 1st grader. It can be viewed metaphorically as the floor where each soul accordingly *is* on the continuum of evolutionary awareness.

The astrological natal chart is also a helpful tool for discovering what the soul has chosen to leave behind or discard, i.e. remnants of negative patterns of behavior from numerous past lives that are currently causing the soul to suffer mentally, emotionally, and/or physically. In order for each soul to learn the lessons it has set out for its Self, fully realize its true potential in this life, and as a result, *evolve*, it's important that it becomes completely aware of what it's supposed to be doing—its "divine job," if you will.

Besides a life path astrology reading, you can also receive insight about your true vocation by meditating with heart-based intention. Do this every day for as long as it takes until you receive the answer. You'll know when you get it, too. The soul always re*members*. When an understanding of your true life path is at last gleaned, you can then set *realistic* goals for your creative Self. On the flip side, when you're not following your true calling, and when you're succumbing to the whims of the ego, you'll be traveling down a treacherous road that only ends with frustration, misery, and suffering.

Here is an excellent question that one of my clients asked me recently regarding goal setting and implementing the true power of intention: "Where do you draw the line between allowing and programming?" My reply: Always practice being still *before* you take any action. Presence should precede any decision making or planning of action. In other words, *be* before you *do*. It is pertinent for your personal evolution to become cognizant of your mental and physiological *reactions* to unwanted events or situations. On the other hand, when challenges arise and you're able to exercise your free will, you won't be creating any resistance or reaction *to* them. Instead you'll be *allowing* the universe to do its job (which is to ultimately help you reach your soul's intention) by saying *yes* to the situation at hand. Becoming aware of your brain's tendency to react in fear and anxiety toward life's little challenges will help you to learn the art of balancing doing with being.

The current human is all about controlling life. And it is this obsession with *control* that is the cause of his "one damn problem after another" stream of stress. When you learn to be still, on the other hand, the solutions to your problems will automatically present themselves *to* you. And when you enter a pure state of presence, your life's purpose will not only automatically surface, the perfect opportunities to pursue it will be presented to you *ready-made*. Unlike your egoic mind, the universe is not in any rush, and therefore it's not going to *push* you. Contrarily, it's gentle and *subtle*. When it comes to actualizing your true life path, establishing a solidity and firmness to its foundation is what the universe is designed to do. Trust in it. It's more intelligent than you are.

So by going into a place of stillness before you take action, you are allowing things to be as they *are*. This way, you don't go screwing it all up by getting in the way of what the helpful universe is trying to do for you. Many times, you'll find that what you initially perceived as problems end up taking care of themselves when you become present and appear to do nothing at all. I say *appear* to do nothing because even though you may seem to not be *actively* addressing the problem you're having, you are, on a higher level, dissolving it *passively* when you align your Self with the Now. As the wise old sage Lao Tzu wrote in the *Tào Té Chīng*, "The Tao does nothing, yet leaves nothing undone."

The brain-based innerverse.

> Cobb: *Well dreams, they feel real while we're in*
> *them, right? It's only when we wake up that*
> *we realize that something was actually*
> *strange. Let me ask you a question. You never*
> *really remember the beginning of a dream, do*
> *you? You always wind up right in the middle*
> *of what's going on.*
>
> Ariadne: *I guess, yeah.*
>
> Cobb: *So how did we end up here?*
>
> Ariadne: *Well we just came from the um…*
>
> Cobb: *Think about it Ariadne, how did you get here?*
> *Where are you right now?*
>
> Ariadne: {shocked} *We're dreaming?*
>
> —*Inception*

In ancient Sanskrit, the word *maya* simply means "not true." Since your brain is continually making up the world around you, the universe is, in actuality, an *illusion* that is more accurately defined as an *innerverse*. In other words, the entire universe exists only because your mind *makes it real*. This ancient esoteric truth has recently been corroborated by quantum physics which has shown us unequivocally that nothing is actually solid, and that everything we perceive as 3D is actually a 2D hologram. These recently established scientific principles substantiate the mystery of mysteries, the "game of life," of which the mystics, sages, shamans, and yogis were all well aware.

Physicists have never been able to prove that there is anything physically "out there"—*nothing*. And they never will because all forms that you identify as being part of the material world are only *perceptions* translated by your brain. Quantum physics posits that nothing really happens in the physical world unless a conscious mind observes it. In other words, consciousness must *perceive* whatever it creates in order for that creation to seem real. This is exemplified in the dream world. When you dream, you create and perceive your dream simultaneously. And you do it so seamlessly that you are oblivious that you are, in truth, the *dreamer*.

As it's clearly stated in the above quote from the blockbuster movie *Inception*, you never remember the beginning of a dream, do you? You simply take it for granted that "this is the way it is." Your mind automatically accepts the dream as reality, especially if it's a pleasant dream. Similarly, in the awakened state, most people can't remember any aspect of their lives before the age of two. One day you magically arrived into your "dream of life," not knowing exactly how you got here or even why you're here at all.

So what we call *life* can be perceived as nothing more than a dream. But for the Next Human, it's a *lucid* dream. The phenomenon known as *lucid dreaming* is when you "wake up" during the dream state and realize that you are actually dreaming. You become lucid to the fact that you are both the dreamer and the perceiver of the dream. And this can be quite empowering. Any fears or anxieties you were previously having in the dream tend to dissolve. Because you realize that it's just a dream, you further surmise that you cannot die, cannot be harmed, and cannot suffer—as long as you remain *lucid*. Many people will take off flying during a lucid dream. Some will move objects using nothing but the power of thought. Others will teleport themselves to exotic locations, instantly changing the scene of the dream. What we define as supernatural abilities are in truth, quite natural for your ethereal body.

When dreaming, the subconscious mind is motivated by emotion, not reason. When you dream, repressed emotions such as anger, guilt, or fear become powerful indeed. If your waking life is stressful or problematic, your dream life will reflect this by playing out all your anxiety on the dream stage. And it will be communicated to you metaphorically—the language of the subconscious mind—in a subtle attempt to help you become aware that you are the creator of your own problems, and to offer you viable solutions *to* them. If your waking life is *fear*-based, then your dream life will naturally reflect this same negative and dark emotional state by imaging stressful, nightmarish scenes that mirror your waking life.

The typical current human is so accustomed to living a nightmare in the waking state that he has, to a large degree, become *desensitized* to the truth that he is indeed suffering at all. His nightmare that he defines as "life" is interpreted by the brain as "reality," i.e. "the norm," and as a result of this blind acceptance, he continues to play out his "life dream" while it progressively escalates into more and more of a nightmare, until hopefully one day he becomes lucid to the truth that he is the dreamer of his own life, the *creator* of his own reality, and subsequently *wakes up*.

Lucid dreaming can also be a powerful tool for helping you become more conscious during your wakened state. You can have more frequent lucid dreams by programming your subconscious mind with a simple suggestion. You may say to yourself before falling asleep: "I will become aware that I'm dreaming during my dreams tonight." Practice doing this for as many nights in a row as it takes until you have a lucid dream. You can also learn how to begin lucid dreaming from Rebecca Turner, who has been successfully lucid dreaming for fourteen years and teaches a course on how to begin lucid dreaming within thirty days. Her site is: www.world-of-lucid-dreaming.com.

The film *Inception* is a wonderful depiction of the power of lucid dreaming. In it, dreams within dreams are intricately woven together to suggest that there may be no limit to how many planes of reality our consciousness can infiltrate. After all, planes are not actual "places," but rather *frequencies*, just like the channels on your television. There's a deep mystical truth in the ancient wisdom: You are not a being of mind or body but a being of *consciousness*, simultaneously living in a myriad of realities that embody varying vibrations of energy. In physics, this is referred to as the *multiverse*; however, physicists believe that they are *physical* manifestations. But when you fully understand that the entire universe is actually an *innerverse*, you quickly come to the realization that there's really no such thing as a "physical" reality. Everything, every *thing,* is playing itself out inside your head.

Physicist Fred Wolf believes that the holographic principle explains the phenomena of lucid dreaming. Wolf proposes that these dreams are visits to parallel realms. He also believes that the holographic principle will eventually lead to the breakthrough of a "physics of consciousness" that will pioneer the exploration of other dimensions.[15] I agree with Dr. Wolf that we will soon be giving birth to a physics of consciousness. Physics and metaphysics are simply two sides of the same coin.

On the quantum level, the intelligent universe creates subatomic particles to make forms appear solid to us here, the plane of the human, when in truth, they are not. Everything you touch, smell, hear, taste, and *see* are simple electrical signals interpreted by your brain. And each of these senses has its own unique range of detection that varies from species to species. For example, compared to us, a dog's ears can detect a higher octave of sound waves, and a snake's, owl's, or cat's eyes can view a much broader spectrum of light.

When your human brain perceives a vast sea of encoded information from the innerverse, its programming is automatically activated. As your brain filters the jumbled information it receives through the senses, it simultaneously images or *imagines* a sophisticated interpretation based on the raw data it collects through your fingers, nose, ears, tongue, and eyes. And this is what you end up experiencing firsthand—rather efficiently, I might add—as the *material world.*

All your sensual interpretations of your so-called reality are based solely on this internal mapping and nothing more. Your thoughts are directly intertwined with the innerverse as well. They literally *shift* the field of ethers on a particle-by-particle basis to create your physical life. The quantum world is very fluid, always in *flux,* and constantly being remolded by consciousness itself. For the Next Human, reality will be seen as her creative playground, a "blank canvas" if you will. And because the source of her creativity will be rooted in the heart, she will possess limitless power to remake the world as she sees *fit.*

The brain in your heart.

> Obi Wan: *Your eyes can deceive you. Don't trust*
> *them. Stretch out with your feelings.*
> —*Star Wars Episode IV: A New Hope*

In the embryonic stage, before your brain was created, you were nothing but a heart. The brain came out of the heart, not the reverse. In Chinese acupuncture, the heart is a bridge between mind and body. In all cultures of the ancient world, including Hindu, Sumerian, Egyptian, and Hebrew, it has always been the *heart* that is the source of creativity, not the mind. In fact, the heart has a brain all its own. There are at least 40,000 nerve cells in the heart—as many as are found in various subcortical centers of the brain.[16]

The heart communicates with the brain neurologically through transmissions of nerve impulses, biochemically through hormones and neurotransmitters, and biophysically through pressure waves. In addition, growing scientific evidence suggests that the heart may also communicate with the brain and body energetically through electromagnetic field interactions. Through these biological communication systems, the heart oversees the function of your brain and *all* your physiology.[17]

During twenty years of research throughout the 1960s and 1970s, psychophysiological researchers John and Beatrice Lacey discovered that there is indeed communication via the nervous system between the heart and the brain and that the heart affects how we all perceive and react to the world. A generation before the Laceys began their research, physiologist Walter Cannon, M.D., showed that changes in emotions are accompanied by predictable changes in heart rate, blood pressure, respiration and digestion.[18] According to Cannon, when we become aroused, the sympathetic nervous system energizes us for fight or flight, and in more passive moments, the parasympathetic nervous system cools us down. In his view, it was assumed that a stimulus activated the autonomic nervous system and all of the physiological responses were orchestrated directly from the brain.[19]

The Laceys, however, observed that this simple model theorized by Cannon only partially matched our actual physiological behavior. As their research evolved, they discovered that the heart had its own unique "mind" that frequently diverged from the direction of the autonomic nervous system.[20] The heart appeared to be transmitting meaningful messages to the brain that it not only understood, but *obeyed*. What was even more interesting was that it seemed as though these messages could affect a person's behavior. Soon after these findings, neurophysiologists discovered a neural pathway and mechanism where input from the heart to the brain could inhibit or facilitate the brain's electrical activity. Then in 1974, the French researchers Gahery and Vigier, working with cats, stimulated the vagus nerve which carries many of the signals from the heart to the brain.[21] As a result of this, the brain's electrical response dropped to about half its normal rate. This startling new evidence suggests that the heart does not take its commands from the brain, but conversely, the brain and nervous system receive their "orders" directly from the heart.

Later in 1991, Neurocardiologist J. Andrew Armour, M.D., introduced the "heart brain" concept. His work revealed that the heart's intricate circuitry allows to act independently of the cranial brain, i.e. to learn, remember, feel, even *sense*.[22] Dr. Armour found that the heart has a complex intrinsic nervous system that is more than sufficiently refined to qualify as a "little brain" in its own right. In fact, the heart's brain is a sophisticated network of various types of neurons, neurotransmitters, proteins and support cells *just like those found* in the brain proper.[23] Interestingly, in a heart transplant, the nerve connections that normally run through the vagus nerve and spinal column—connecting the heart with the brain—rarely, if ever, reconnect. Instead the newly transplanted heart is able to function perfectly in its new host through the capacity of its already intact, intrinsic nervous system.[24]

The heart's ability to alter DNA.

The way is not in the sky. The way is in the heart.
—The Buddha

We have been taught that the brain is the ultimate frontier of intelligence in the human body, but research at the Institute of HeartMath (IHM) has shown that this is simply not true. As it turns out, it is the *heart* that is the most powerful generator of electromagnetic rhythmic information patterns, and thus is the primary source of intelligence or starting point of consciousness. Not only is the heart's electrical field 60 times greater in amplitude than the electrical activity generated by the brain, the magnetic field produced by the heart, measured in the form of an electrocardiogram (ECG), is more than **5,000 times greater** in strength than the field generated by the brain, and can be detected up *to eight feet* in diameter around the body (see image below).[25,26]

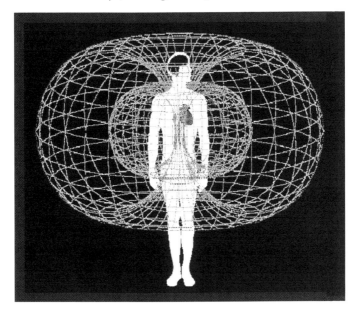

According to a study by quantum biologists Glen Rein and Rollin McCraty, one of the roles of DNA is to act as *antennae* for energy fields of the heart.[27] Drs. Rein and McCraty have conducted extensive research on the effect of conscious intention on DNA. Their results showed that it was possible to measure a direct energetic link between *heart-based intention* and the DNA molecule without intervening chemical signals from the nervous system within the body.

The results from the research of Rein and McCraty offer the first direct experimental evidence to support the hypothesis that the *loving state* can actually *alter* DNA, i.e. produce physiological effects at the level of DNA.[28] Control individuals who were not able to sustain their feelings of love showed low ratios of ECG coherence and were unable to intentionally alter their DNA.[29] This revolutionary research suggests that in the process of becoming heart-centered, you will automatically "switch off" the DNA programs that we call the *ego* and the *pain-body*.

It is clear now that the heart continually communicates with your brain through emotional and intuitive signals. Along with this new understanding that the heart works in concert with the brain, scientists are now discovering that the heart may even be *the force* behind intuitive feelings and psychic powers. This "heart intelligence" is a completely new paradigm for understanding our emotions. If you can *stretch out with your feelings* you will tap directly into the brain of the heart, subsequently bypassing the cranial brain altogether, which of course will take the ego out of the equation. The more you listen *to* and *follow* your heart intelligence, the more educated, balanced, authentic, coherent, and intuitive your emotions will become. And the more you will honor your creative *Self.*

The heart-based innerverse.

Just as the brain acts as a filter or lens of perception to what we call the universe, or what I call the *innerverse*, so does the heart. And *this* is the ultimate shift in consciousness that we, as a collective species, are moving toward. Six thousand years ago in ancient India, 108 spiritual masters shifted their consciousness from a brain-based innerverse to a heart-based innerverse, and then wrote about their experiences. These heart-based experiences are known today as the *Upanishads* and are considered by many poets, scholars, and writers—such as Seymour-Smith, Schopenhauer, Emerson, and Thoreau—to be among the most influential and significant words ever written. The following is an excerpt from the Chāndogya Upanishad:

> In the center of the castle of Brahman, our own body,
> there is a small shrine in the form of a lotus flower and
> within it can be found a small space. We should find the
> one who dwells there and we should want to know him.
> And if anyone asks, "Who is he who dwells in a small

shrine in the form of a lotus flower in the center of the castle of Brahman—whom should we want to find and to know?" We can answer, "The little space within the heart is as great as this vast universe, the heavens and the earth are there and the sun and the moon and the stars, fire and lightning and winds are there. And all that now is and all that is not for the whole universe is in Him and He dwells within our heart. Brahman is in all things and is the Atman of all living beings.

What is clearly being revealed here is that there is indeed a duplicate or alternate innerverse that exists in a "small shrine" and within this shrine there is a "small space" within your own body. And it is further revealed that this small, hidden space dwells within the human heart, hence the words, "The little space within the heart is as great as this vast universe," which is also a reference to another *reality* that is separate from the brain-based 3D reality that you are accustomed to experiencing. All the luminaries are in the same places, hence the words, "the heavens and the earth are there and the sun and the moon and the stars, fire and lightning and winds are there."

The Upanishads form the theoretical basis for the Hindu religion and are also known as Vedānta, the end of the Vedas. In Vedic literature, the Brahman is considered the universal Spirit or *Source* and the Atman is considered the *Self* or the individual Spirit. Both are divine and One.

The aboriginals of Australia as well as shamans from all over the world speak of an altered state of consciousness where everyone and everything is One and interconnected. It is in this higher frequency of consciousness, this higher dimension, that new worlds are literally *dreamed* into being. In simpler words, this higher realm is the *true source of creativity*. And just like the authors of the Upanishads, these shamans and indigenous peoples are accessing this "altered state of Oneness" through a small secret space deep within the human heart.

At the Institute of HeartMath, they are currently researching this secret space of the heart described by the ancients. But the actual experience of this hidden shrine in the heart may prove to be inaccessible from a scientific approach. I believe it can only be accessed by going deeply within, through an inner exploration and transformation of the Self. And *this* is what this book is all about. When you are finally ready to evolve, to get out of your head and into your heart, then the information given in this book will be beneficial. Until then, however, much of it simply won't make any sense to you. Evolution begins with *knowing* you are divine, not thinking you are. As a guide, I can only show you the door. But it is up to *you* to walk through it.

The resonance of the heart.

You don't see many caterpillars hanging out with butterflies, do you? Everything in the universe/innerverse has its own unique energetic vibration or *resonance*. Forms that share a common resonance will always be attracted to one another. Even though the male and female are opposite genders, it's really the *like*nesses that attracts the individual personalities to one another and sustains the relationship. Similar mental, physical, and spiritual vibrations in people also attract them to one another. As the saying goes, "Birds of a feather flock together." Similarly, there will always be an underlying strata of like frequency between individuals in a group as well as those sharing a particular ideology.

Just as in metaphysics, string theory in quantum physics predicts that everything in the universe consists of vibrational energy. Resonance, in fact, is what separates every object we can see, smell, taste, touch, or *hear* in physics. The frequency at which the quark, atom, cell, star, and galaxy *vibrates* is what determines its unique size, color, sound, content, density, function, and other characteristics.

Thinking thoughts and feeling emotions that contain higher vibratory speeds—such as love, gratitude, compassion, forgiveness, peace, and joy—stem from the *heart* rather than the brain. The Japanese biologist Masaru Emoto, M.D., has repeatedly demonstrated that words describing emotions have their own specific resonance, and that they have the ability to directly affect water molecules. After communicating to the water these heart-based emotional vibrations—such as "love," "compassion," "peace"—via written word and speech, Dr. Emoto discovered that the water consistently formed beautiful, symmetrical crystals. When negative, brain-based words such as "anxiety," "worry," and "anger," were communicated to the water molecules, no crystals formed whatsoever, only distorted, muddy, ugly shapes. When you consider the fact that you are 70 percent water, imagine what an impact it would have on your health, creativity, and success if you were completely rooted in your *heart.*

The key to the law of manifesting is to acclimate yourself to a specific vibration and allow the universe to orchestrate matching vibrations. This is how the reflective universe works. There's no more effort involved between manifesting an ocean-front condo and manifesting a pop tent in the woods. The resonance-based universe simply responds to the specific frequency of intention that you send to it. It resonates *to* you.

When you are constantly making excuses, complaining, criticizing, condemning, and blaming others and/or circumstances for your personal failures you have firmly established a beacon of resonance that emits from your core *outward* into the ethers. The ethers then collect that resonance and mirror it back to you in the form of what you call "reality." The dismal reality of one failure after another is manifested by individuals who are unknowingly sabotaging their success by their own thoughts, speech, and attitude.

On the other hand, when you accept things as they *are*, rather than resisting or reacting to them with judgment, you won't allow them to have a negative effect on future events. Remember that you're always projecting a specific frequency to the universe based on your own thoughts about a thing, subject, situation, person, or event in your daily life. Most current humans don't believe that you can easily attain your goals without stress, conflict, or drama. They say, "Life *is* stress." In truth, life is not stress, but it is the reaction or *resistance* that you give to it that manifests as stress in your body. Life simply *is*. People who go through life constantly stressed out about this drama or that problem are causing tremendous harm to their body's immune system, hormonal regulation, and ability to repair and rebuild tissue and cells. They are on their way to a chronic state of dis*ease*.

When you learn to stop reacting to every challenge that comes your way, you'll soon find that the problems you're accustomed to having will stop being created by you. All your problems are created by you, not the other, and certainly not by life. Life is not meant to be one long series of problem solving, combined with a toxic cocktail of stress, anxiety, and disappointment. Manifesting stems from either the creative self or the creative Self; the choice is yours.

One of the most common statements I hear from people who consistently attract failure to them is: "It's always *something*." This statement is frequently repeated by those who frequently fail at everything they set out to accomplish. But little do they realize that it is *they* who are ensuring their own failure because their resonance is completely aligned with the truth of their own divine power of manifestation. It's as if they're continually commanding to the intelligent universe: "It's always *something* that's causing me stress, worry, and disappointment." Then the universe, after receiving the command, reflects that same resonance of energy back *to* them by recreating that exact same reality *for* them.

Most current humans believe that the actions they take toward manifesting should be hard work and therefore they measure their chances for success based directly on how much "hard work" and its compliment, *stress,* is expended in the process of creating what they want. This certainly will be true if you're creating from the mind. But if you're completely aligned to a heart-based creative process, then the actions you'll take will be a delight and a *joy* and will feel much less like *work* and much more like *fun*. Heart-based manifesting is all about enjoying the journey, and in the process, you'll more readily attract to you what you want without a tether of stress, anxiety, and drama. Know that it's not what you *do* that determines your creative journey; it's about your vibrational alignment to what you want. The resonance of your thoughts will determine your journey, the length of it, and the quality of it. Instead of enduring your creative process, you'll be enjoying it. You won't think about how hard something is because you'll be loving it so much!

As with any personal creation, creating phenomenal success means offering little resistance and attention to what you *don't* want and giving all of your attention to what you *do* want. Remember, what resists persists, and what you focus on expands. As you focus more and more attention on what you want, you will naturally attract *to* you whatever it is you'll need to manifest what you want as your reality. This is how any process of personal creation occurs, whether it's for creating wealth, poverty, sickness, wellness, misery, or happiness. Setting the *tone* or vibrational frequency of your manifestation in the heart, and then keeping that tone consistently *in the heart* throughout the entire process—no matter how long it takes—is the key to realizing the true potential of your creative Self.

If you emanate a mixed vibration, to a lesser or greater degree, about the goal you're setting for yourself, then it will probably not manifest as your reality. In other words, you can't keep *changing your mind* about what you want because the universe will naturally reflect these changes. And if you really want to sabotage your creative success, then begin thinking or speaking negative phrases such as "I can't do this," or "I can't do that." As soon as you say, "I *can't*," you've affirmed to the universe that you cannot achieve. Period. Even if it's clear that you've failed over and over again at a particular goal, whenever you utter the two words, "I can't," it will only reassure you'll fail again. When you communicate these powerfully negative words to the universe, it can only return the same like frequency. It's as if it responds with: "I see that you *can't*, and therefore you're commanding me to continue to substantiate that you will continue to fail at whatever it is you set out to achieve." On the other hand, once you shift your thoughts and words to be in a positive, heart-based alignment with your goals, you'll see your momentum building in the direction you want within a short period of time.

Ending expectation.

Many motivational books will try and convince you that you always get what you *expect* in life, so therefore you should only "expect the best," otherwise your goals are doomed. But this is simply not true. Yes, of course you want to believe in your goals. But expectation and belief are not the same thing. Belief comes with surrender and being *open*. Whenever you *expect*, however, you are no longer open and therefore set yourself up for a disastrous fall every single time. Expectation is much like a fool's paradise. No, it's *exactly* like a fool's paradise. So stop *expecting* things to come to you. Instead, start *believing* in your creative Self. This begins by acting from a place of pure presence. Only those who are truly in the Now are living their lives to the fullest potential.

Expecting is the act of trusting in your egoic *mind* to bring you the future, which, of course, it can, but it always comes with a polarized price. If you want to transcend polarity, however, and you truly want to live out your dreams without a heavy dose of drama—and subsequent trauma—then expect *nothing*. Zero. Then you'll be *allowing* the loving universe to do its job and bring you everything your heart desires, and *more.* In truth, there's no end to the happiness and joy it can bring you. But you have to get out of its *way.* Expectations are like heavy weights, *burdens* to the Next Human, and are detrimental to his peace of mind and well-being.

The Next Human children.

Many children are already being born with natural metaphysical abilities and are incarnating on this planet to help humanity evolve into the Next Human. Many are already born *as* Next Humans, where others are awakening to their Next Human state later in life. They have been referred to as *star children, indigo children, crystal children, rainbow children,* and *dolphin children.* They are not of one specific race or gender so you may not immediately notice a Next Human child by merely looking at him or her although some have distinguishing features such as very deep, liquid, or mystical *eyes.* They also have a magnetic presence, are very creative, charismatic, live in the Now, and, if they were born after 1996, will be naturally heart-centered. Next Humans have been coming to Earth for over fifty years—more so in the last thirty years—and have a critical role to play in the evolutionary process.

Next Human children often find it difficult to *fit in* to any specific category of society because they have a difficult time relating to the herd mentality that our mainstream media imposes on its viewers. At birth they appear to be the same as any other infant, but within the first few years of life they will begin exhibiting traits of their abilities such as having conversations with invisible friends, reading the minds of people around them, or having out-of-body experiences. Next Human children will also show signs of premature levels of intelligence and creativity in areas such as painting, singing, designing, writing, acting, movie directing or producing, or technological innovation. Some may develop their own business before they graduate from high school that becomes highly successful. Because they allow the heart to lead the mind they are able to completely trust in their heart-based intuition which results in the success of all their endeavors.

Next Human children will have a difficult time understanding the conforming ways of religion and will question why so many people allow religion to control their lives. They will feel a divine purpose in life, a mission to help humanity at large rather than limit their assistance to only a few. If a Next Human is raised to be religious, it will result in a cognitive dissonance between what he or she was taught in that religion and what they feel inside their heart. They are the "spiritual rebels" and will not tolerate conformity, control, or oppression in anyone. Being natural pariahs, they will follow the beat of their own drummer.

Many Next Human children are currently labeled with attention deficit disorder (ADD or ADHD) and may be placed on medication to help maintain focus in school. But they don't have a disease; they simply have a plethora of energy and need to find creative ways to *expend* this energy. They typically have a difficult time focusing on anything they find mundane such as school, rules, authority figures, or anyone in general who cannot relate to or understand them. Next Human children have volunteered to come to Earth to help with the evolution of our species, and therefore have little or no karmic debt.

Education can be an incredible experience for the Next Human children once they find their true life paths. And the mislabeled ADD Next Human children will demonstrate the focus of a brain surgeon when they're doing something creative that they actually *enjoy* doing. Once they find their niche in life they'll move forward toward their goals with much more intensity, enthusiasm, and optimism than the current human adult. And they'll be highly successful at it.

Some Next Human children are described as scattered, loners, or wanderers who are trying to find others who are like them or people who can accept them for who they are without conforming to societal standards. Many feel they don't belong here and have a sense of where home is but just know that it's not Planet Earth. Always thinking out of the box, anything they focus their attention on they're able to *innovate*.

Next Human children born after 1985 have abilities that are more accepted and cultured within their family unit. They are also more likely than prior Next Humans to form social groups of peers with similar esoteric principles and are less likely to be afraid of public ridicule when talking about their abilities. As our senior citizen population returns to the ethereal plane, our planet is being infused (in very high numbers) with high-frequency energy from Next Human children who will become government leaders, technology innovators, and spiritual teachers as we head into the New Age of Enlightenment. Some are being born with advanced DNA structure and therefore will display supernatural abilities, such as accelerated healing, telekinesis, acute reflexes, or hypnotic abilities. All Next Human children have exceptional psychic powers and will learn to trust in their own high-powered perception more and more as they mature.

Next Human children despise any toxic environment such as living near or around polluted cities or being around negative or abusive people. They also feel the need to represent those who are unable to speak for themselves, such as abused children and animals. They know instinctively what needs to be reformed in our society. Naturally possessing a sense of justice and harmony, they are here to restore balance to the Earth: sociologically, politically, economically, and ecologically. Next Human children are truth seekers who initiate awareness and inadvertently start others on their own spiritual paths. They feel a connection between themselves and their fellow human beings, the Earth, the solar system, and far away galaxies. Many Next Human children are awakening every day to their true divine purpose for being here and joining forces with the others who were already born awoken in order to lead humanity toward the purification of Gaia Sophia, Mother Earth.

The following are some of the main characteristics of Next Human children (these will vary depending on the individual, type, and age):

- Are highly intelligent, although may not have had top grades, especially in high school.

- Are highly psychic, and can readily intuit what others are feeling or thinking.

- Are highly creative, especially in art, design, music,

business, or computer fields.

- Loathed much of the required, mundane, and redundant work in school.

- Had experienced early depression, feelings of despair, or suicidal feelings while in high school.

- Have difficulty in service-oriented jobs because they are far more productive and creative when working alone without pressure from others.

- Have deep empathy and compassion for others, yet are intolerant of stupidity and incompetence.

- Trouble controlling anger or rage.

- Despise political, educational, medical, and legal systems that are broken or ineffective.

- Alienation from, anger with, or repulsion toward politics because of a feeling that their voices won't count and/or that the outcome doesn't matter.

- Anger at rights being taken away, and the "Nanny State."

- Have a burning desire to do something significant that will help to change and improve the world. May be confused about or have trouble identifying their life path.

- Erratic behavior patterns and show symptoms of attention deficit disorder (ADD) such as trouble focusing on assigned tasks or paying attention in class.

- May have repeatedly demonstrated clairaudience,

clairvoyance, clairsentience, or other psychic experiences, such as premonitions, seeing angels or
ghosts, or have had an out-of-body experience
(OBE), near-death experience (NDE), or kundalini
awakening.

⦿   Possess a keen awareness of parallel realities and
other dimensions, and don't feel at home here on
Earth because of a longing to return to home
somewhere in the stars.

⦿   When their true life path is at last learned, and inner peace and harmony is finally achieved, they
become very strong, healthy, happy individuals.

Allowing the heart to lead the mind.

The coming shift in consciousness that all the spiritual teachers are talking about these days is indeed articulating this transition from mind-
based intention to *heart*-based intention. Mind-based intention has a
very low resonance. Heart-based intention, on the other hand, has a
much higher vibration of emotion altogether. It is pure love expressed
unconditionally. When you learn to tap into this new emotional body,
you will be accessing *limitless* power.

The ego has a hard time surrendering to the heart. So much so that
it will fight with all its might to prevent it. This is what I call "sabotaging
your happiness." I see this all the time among people who seem to do
everything in their power—once their dreams are just within their
reach—to completely sabotage whatever it is they are attempting to
manifest. They may do this physically (through addiction) or emotionally (through pain-body attacks) or mentally (through egoic displays of
melodrama). Know that the brain doesn't want to *let go* of its command
over your life because, well, that means the end of the ego's reign, and the

beginning of the heart's reign. When you allow the heart to lead the mind, a new world, indeed an entirely *new reality,* emerges before your very eyes. It will mark the birth of a new innerverse created *for* you, *by* you. You become god-like or goddess-like, and will have all the tools you'll need to create anything your heart desires. Literally.

The key word here in transitioning from mind-based intention to heart-based intention is *allow.* In Evolution 101, I explained how the ego is neither your friend nor your enemy. So, again, ego transcendence cannot be forced. The ego will resist you only if you suppress it. Therefore, an allowance, a complete surrender, is necessary to make the shift out of your head and into your heart.

Love is the creative *force* of the universe. It always has been. The mind will always limit you. And it knows this. This is why it fights its demotion with every ounce of energy it has. Codependency is the most powerful armament in its arsenal because it keeps you *weak.* It instinctively knows that as long as it can continue to keep you *wanting* someone, some*thing*, some concept, it will perpetuate the delusion that this slightly out-of-reach desire will somehow, in some way, bring you the happiness for which you are longing. And this is not living from the heart. The ego *knows* that the heart is the source of wholeness, completeness, and unconditional love. The ego *knows* that when you become heart-centered, that will mean the end of *it.* And as long as you allow your ego to confine you in codependent stage, you will never be free. How can you be? True love comes only from free will. And free will only comes from ego transcendence. This is when all inhibitions, guilt, anxieties, and fears are *released.*

The mind will continue to repeat situations that keep creating fear so it can keep those situations afloat. This is how the ego sustains itself. This is how it perpetuates fearful situations that, in the end, were nothing but mirages created by the mind itself. It's a repeating cycle of psychological madness. So in a sense, the mind confines you to your own psychic imprisonment, a hellish cell that you've defined as your reality.

But from the perspective of the Next Human, those who are lost in their minds and who have totally identified themselves with the material world of form have a mental disease. Taken to its extreme this is what psychologists refer to as *schizophrenia*.

Heart-based emotions, on the other hand, invoke an infinitely higher resonance of love that is given without expectations or preconditions. It is the same kind of love that's given from a mother to her newborn baby. No matter what the baby does, the love from the mother remains unconditional. When we as a species begin to love one another with this same vibratory field, we will be witnessing a *shift* on this planet unlike anything we've seen before. This is when our sense of family will no longer be confined to our individual bloodlines, but will be expanded outwardly to include every One of our seven billion brothers and sisters. This is the New Earth.

EVOLUTION

601

THE ETHEREAL SELF
RAISING THE SERPENT OF LIGHT

Morpheus: *Let me tell you why you're here. You're here*
because you know something. What you
know you can't explain but you feel it.
You've felt it your entire life, that there's
something wrong with the world. You don't
know what it is, but it's there, like a splinter
in the back of your mind, driving you mad.
It is this feeling that has brought you to me.
Do you know what I'm talking about?

Neo: *The Matrix?*

Morpheus: *Do you want to know...what...it...is?*

—The Matrix

Our soul collective is currently at a crossroads on the path toward enlightenment. Planet Earth and the human race that inhabits her are in dire need of *balance*. We are living in a time when it's needed to become conscious of our Selves more than ever in history. Evolution is now no longer a luxury but a matter of survival for our species. A return of the Goddess or God *S* will reinstate the delicate balance of the yin and yang, the synthesizing harmony of diametrical opposites. Before we can evolve, balance *must* be restored.

The word *goddess* contains the syllables expressing both the masculine, *god*, and the feminine, *ess,* sound tones. The suffix *ess* and the letter *S* sounds represent the sound tone of the sacred feminine energy vibration and is used in words that are distinctly feminine such as count*ess*, duch*ess*, and lion*ess*. This self*less*, nurturing, protective, and creative energy of the God *S* has been suppressed from our planetary culture for too long. Few realize that the worship of the sacred feminine was prevalent among all ancient civilizations. Interestingly enough, remnants of this worship can be found in many of the modern, patriarchal religions. For example, in Christianity, the goddess is exemplified by the third aspect of the Holy Trinity, known as the Holy Spirit, which is not a personality but rather an energy field representing the feminine divine. An embodiment of the sacred masculine, Jesus, was complemented by his mirror Self, Mary Magdalene, who was an embodiment of the Holy Spirit or sacred feminine.

In Hinduism, the sacred feminine is personified in the goddess *Shakti,* also called "The Great Divine Mother," who represents the primordial creative power in the universe. Her consort is *Shiva,* the god of transformation. Together they symbolize a divine balance of the sacred feminine/masculine, the yin/yang. In ancient Egyptian mythology, Isis was the "Mother Nature" goddess and was an embodiment of the feminine divine. Her consort was Osiris, the god of the ethereal plane. Together they personified the *union* of the divine feminine and masculine energies. The ancient Hebrew name for God, Yahweh, contains within it syllables expressing both the divine masculine, *yah*, and divine feminine, *weh*. The origin of the worship of the sacred feminine actually dates back to pre-recorded history. One of the oldest goddess artifacts found to date is the Venus of Willendorf figurine from 24,000 BP.

The ancients were well aware that you cannot actualize your higher Self without first becoming whole. Most people believe that matriarchy is the opposite of patriarchy. Not true. Matriarchy is about achieving divine *balance* and its symbolism can be found throughout the art of the ancient world, especially Egypt. For example, in the art of Tutankhamun's throne, the boy king wears the right sandal while Queen Ankhesenamun wears the left, indicating that they will walk down the road of life together as One with the sacred masculine and feminine perfectly *intact*. In *ess*ence, they were the personification of both wholeness and *holiness*.

In ancient Egyptian art, gods and goddesses are always depicted holding the crook, flail, and/or scepter in various combinations. The flail signifies the *mental* body, the crook is the *emotional* body, and the scepter symbolizes the *physical* body. To the ancient Egyptians, it was critical to purify, heal, and balance these three bodies before one could achieve higher states of consciousness. Once this was achieved, a fourth and more *ether-real, ethereal Self* awakens through a small vortex at the base of the spine. It is through this portal that the Holy Spirit—known to the ancient Egyptians as *ka*—is able to access the material plane from the ethereal plane, and open the final door to enlightenment. In addition, the gods and godd*esses* of Egyptian art always hold the scepter (staff, wand, or rod) *in the air*, never allowing it to touch the ground. This symbolizes the ancient esoteric truth that we are divine beings having an earth-bound experience.

Today, if you asked the average person on the street: "What is the nature of God to you?" The answer may begin with, "He is…" But if you happened to come across a Next Human and asked the same question, the answer would not begin with a gender reference point. This is because, to the Next Human, the divine not only transcends gender, but is a state of being that harmonizes a perfect balance of both the sacred masculine *and* sacred feminine.

In the 6th century BP, Pope Gregory incorrectly and inhumanely connected the unnamed prostitute in the Gospel of Luke with Mary Magdalene. This heralded the beginning of Christianity's oppression of the feminine divine. If women spoke their minds, they were considered a threat to the Church. Many were feared, controlled, murdered in droves, proclaimed to be witches, and considered downright *evil*. As I write these words in May, 2012, Pope Benedict XVI continues to reaffirm a ban on women to be priests in the Catholic Church. This ongoing pathological state of paranoia against an entire gender is rooted within the male *ego*.

Much of the female oppression that's been occurring for the last two millennia was partially lifted when women in 1920 were granted the legal right to vote in the United States. However, even today in the U.S. women do not receive equal pay for equal work and in most other parts of the world, women are still not viewed as equal citizens. Not even close. Out of 192 seats in the Chinese government, only 22 women are currently serving as legislators. In the U.S. Congress, only 90 out of 535 seats are being held by women. This simply has to change if we're going to make it as a species.

The chalice of the Holy Grail is a representation of the ancient "V" symbol and is a metaphor for the sacred feminine. It is the shape of a woman's womb and represents the life that comes forth from it. In the ancient Chinese book of poetry, the *Tào Té Chīng*, Lao Tzu associates the sacred feminine with the "V" shape of a mountain *valley* in chapter six:

> *The Valley Spirit never dies.*
> *It is named the Mysterious Female.*
> *And the doorway of the Mysterious Female*
> *Is the base from which Heaven and Earth sprang.*
> *It is there within us all the while;*
> *Draw upon it as you will, it never runs dry.*

In direct contrast to the sacred "V" described by Lao Tzu as the "Valley Spirit" is the shape of the blade or mountain which symbolizes the male. Now, let me clarify something here. There are two aspects to the masculine energy. The lower aspect—just as it is with the feminine—is always personified by the *ego*. The higher aspects are represented by the sacred masculine and sacred feminine where the ego is transcended. But again, since the ego is typically more dominant in the male, the female gender, as a whole, is awakening first.

So the mountain can also be viewed as a symbol for the lower aspect of the masculine or male ego that has—in very few numbers I might add—ruled, controlled, dominated, manipulated, and oppressed the masses of our entire species for the last 5,000 years. This is because the ego *craves* to be the mountain; it craves it so badly that it will do everything it can to acquire power, to be righted, to be superior, to be special, and, yes, of course, to be *separate*. The mere thought of unity or Oneness to the ego is nothing less than toxic and threatening to its very existence. And it knows very well how to keep us all separate. If you're halfway awake you can observe this in the media when you see right-wing political leaders speaking intolerantly to their audiences. They speak these divisive words because the ego knows that ultimately, this can lead to conflict and *war*, which, of course, bestows the leaders with more power and control over the masses. Death to other human beings? Yes. This is the madness that continues to play out through the pseudo self of the male in key positions of power on our planet.

No movie in recent years captures the **ess**ence of the divine feminine more than James Cameron's *Avatar*. In it, the sacred "Tree of Souls"— representing the Tree of Life—was home to the ancestors of the Pandoran Na'vi, a humanoid tribal culture depicted by a powerful yet nurturing and communal species with a great passion for *life*. They also lived in perfect harmony with their Mother Pandora Goddess, *Eywa*. It's not surprising that many people became depressed—due to withdrawals, no doubt—shortly after watching the movie in the theater for the first time.

Perhaps they intimately identified with the story because they experienced a number of lifetimes when they themselves embraced the unconditional love and feelings of community, togetherness, and Oneness that exemplifies the balancing nature of the sacred feminine. On a subconscious level, they may have had brief glimpses into a time in the ancient collective past where we all lived as One with Gaia Sophia, *our* Mother Earth Goddess. In the last decade, there have been an increasing number of people who are re*member*ing their peaceful, serene, and spiritual lives on the ancient continents of Atlantis and Lemuria.

Embracing the sacred feminine is about honoring equality in *all* humans, no matter the gender, race, ethnicity, culture, sexual orientation, or class. In many countries such as North Korea and Iran, we still see the oppression of both genders, male and female, where they express cruelty, inhumane and degrading punishment, public executions, absence of due process, and an excessive number of prison camps and forced labor. In Iran, stoning people to death remains a form of punishment for infidelity. It's not surprising that these two nations have allied themselves with one another. Undoubtedly, this is a pathetic attempt of evil to sustain itself on this planet. You may find it interesting that the word *evil* is *live* spelled backwards. It is also an anagram for the word *veil*. Evil is nothing less than the *veiling* of *light* and can further be defined as an unknowingness of truth combined with repressed self-hatred. It is a fall, descent, or *devolution* of the soul. But evil is not to be feared, unforgiven, resisted, or hated. And evil should not be retaliated by the vengeful. If so, then be warned: you will suffer the same consequences of evil itself.

The narcissistic men in the governments of these two defiant nations, North Korea and Iran, are no more than infants on the evolutionary ladder of souls and know not what they do. Therefore, it is up to *us*, the Next Humans, to lead by example, to show them the way. And leading by example does not include bombing them to kingdom come just because we can. What kind of example is *that?* We would be killing a lot of innocent people in the process—as we did in Iraq. It means exercising acceptance and understanding for what is: childish and ignorant behavior. Remember, this is their *purpose*. The darkness must play a role with the light, otherwise there would be no way to evolve; the "game of life" would be over. It means protecting our Selves by keeping these evil governments at bay, but doing it peacefully through unified diplomacy. After all, isn't that what the United Nations was founded for in the first place? So let's stop *killing* one another, and start coming together as One people of One planet. The young people of this planet want peace, especially the women. Until the delicate balance of the sacred feminine is fully restored, "We the People of Planet Earth" will continue to be stalled by the aggressive, egoic male power players, preventing us from *peacefully* extinguishing the nuclear threats that exist in the world today. We can begin by electing *all new* government leaders who reflect what the spiritual core of the human population *wants*. To do this, a much larger percentage of the younger generations, especially women, need to *vote*. Be grateful that you have this right!

Because the Next Human male will have transcended his ego, he will honor the sacred feminine virtues of cooperation, compassion, and unconditional love. A return of the Goddess means a shift *away* from the collective intolerance, inequality, social injustice, violence, and wars on this planet, and a shift *toward* the selfless, protective, nurturing, creative, and *peaceful* frequencies of the heart.

Memoir 05.11.01.

> Caterpillar: *Who...are...you?*
> Alice: *Why, I hardly know, sir. I've changed so much since this morning, you see...*
> Caterpillar: *No, I do not C, explain yourself.*
> Alice: *I'm afraid I can't explain myself, you see, because I'm not myself, you know.*
> Caterpillar: *I do not know.*
> Alice: *I can't put it any more clearly, sir, because it isn't clear to me.*
>
> —*Alice in Wonderland*

In the past three days, I've been noticing a slow but steady increase in heaviness that doesn't feel like the chronic fatigue I've been accustomed to for the last decade but is somehow different, foreign, *enigmatic*, and by noon it has escalated to the point where I decide to give my assistant the rest of the day off. The second she's out the front door, I'm feeling a strange rhythmic pulsation, dense and hot, stirring somewhere deep inside the base of my spine, and within minutes I find myself frantically pacing up and down the hallway in nothing but my underwear after cranking up the air conditioning since I feel as if I'm literally *on fire*. Stunned and feverish, electrical tingling sensations are now shooting sporadically from the base of my spine *upwards* and within minutes my entire upper body suddenly feels like stone-hard granite. Responding to this sudden increase in heaviness—my knees weaken, buckle, then eventually *give way*, and when they do, gravity captures me and pulls me toward the center of the Earth, and then—*as if in slow motion*—my 160-pound body *slams* knees first into the hard oak floor with a thundering *boom!* After realizing that I've landed in a kneeling position, I feel as if someone has their hand firmly placed on top of my head and is pushing it slowly yet steadily *downward*, and all the while this is happening I'm resisting with all my might. In a desperate attempt to halt this descent, I brace my hands on the floor to counter the mysterious force that is pushing my head further and further downward, but my arms are spaghetti-limp, and so the effort to bolster myself is futile and my forehead meets the floor with a sound-echoing *thud!*

Genuflecting to the gods and statue frozen, I'm feeling the strange tingling expanding outward from my lower back, engulfing my pelvic region, buttocks, groin, lower torso, and while this is happening I'm feeling blissful sensations emanating from my chest and forehead. My unexpected guest then proceeds to climb, slowly and deliberately, slithering in a snake-like spiraling motion up my spine, one vertebra at a time. The blissful energy seems to be dancing, swirling about, and as it continues to expand itself upwards to the top of my skull and outwards—enveloping my ribcage, chest, stomach, arms, legs, and feet—it's creating intensely *erotic* feelings that are emanating from my groin that make me feel as if, well, as if my entire body has somehow become a sexual organ. Without warning, I am being fiercely *aroused*.

I feel as if I am light-years away from anyone on Earth. Everything that I identified with as "my life" now seems trivial, banal, insignificant. Somehow this all seems so familiar to me, as if I've somehow come *home*. I shut my eyes tightly and when I do I feel a strong focus of energy on the center of my forehead, and soon after this I'm seeing what appears to be a slideshow in high definition as if someone has downloaded images into my brain from an "astral computer." As the stream commences I'm being shown ancient symbols and sacred geometry. The images from the cosmic slideshow include dodecahedrons, the caduceus, the yin yang symbol, the Kabbalah tree of life, fractals, a double torus, the flower of life, and strange glyphs that appear to be from the Hebrew alphabet.

After what seems like a very long time, the slideshow ends and after I open my eyes I'm feeling much lighter, the heaviness seems to be subsiding, but the muscles in my arms and legs are cramping, causing major discomfort. In an effort to get some relief, I pry myself up off the floor—using the narrow hallway walls as a buttress—then recommence pacing, allowing my limbs a sufficient stretch so that the cramps can be alleviated, which they are. As I pace, the euphoric energy permeates my lower back, spine, neck, and now my head is feeling weightless—it actually begins to bob, practically *float,* on its own volition from left to right, right to left, like a king cobra rising, posturing a strike. There's only one word that remotely describes what I'm feeling right now: *godlike.*

Subtle popping sensations resembling the effect of tiny bursting air bubbles are felt in my upper back and neck and this is followed by what feels like a thousand mosquitoes biting me on my arms, legs, and feet, followed by more muscle twitches and slight electrical "shocks" that seem to come randomly, in both frequency and location. Time has stopped. Power is swelling. Memory of who I am is returning. Wherever this mystical force has come from and why it's here eludes me yet I sense it to be sacred and one thing is for sure: it's certainly not of *this* world.

The sun—whose name I inexplicably know to be *Ra*—is now peeking through my windows through the brushed aluminum blinds and as the limbs of the trees sway in sync with the wind outside, the sunlight floods the floor, walls, furniture with abstract shapes, and upon seeing the beauty of it all I come to a stop, shut my eyes, and as I do the exhilarating energy accelerates its journey upward from my neck to my head and this is followed by a culmination and concentration of tingling at the roof of my skull, as if someone is trying to pry, actually *crack it* open. As this is happening, the sensations morph into fiery hot pulsations originating from the center of my chest where I'm now feeling what seems like a small motor or fan-like *whirling* sensation. Instinctively, I touch the "fan" in my chest gently which reveals to me that there is indeed something *in* there—an *actual foreign device* located inside the middle of my chest—and it is, in fact, *spinning.* It spins for a while one way, then slows down quickly to a sudden stop but immediately picks up again and starts spinning in the opposite direction. And it proceeds to do this like a high precision instrument, spinning one way, then the other, back and forth, at the same exact intervals.

I feel like a newborn baby being held, caressed, *nurtured* in his mother's arms. I am in no pain, just bliss. No, it's more than bliss now. Ecstasy? More. Rapture? More. I would say that if you could combine the intoxicating joy received from being madly in love, then add the pleasure you might receive from having a dozen orgasms at once, then top it off with being enveloped in a cocoon of caressing, unconditional love, the result still wouldn't come close to what I'm experiencing right now. It is unfathomable, immeasurable, indescribable. I am truly *blessed*.

When I finally open my eyes I'm amazed to be observing a fireworks show going on inside my apartment which is now filled with tiny white fireflies the size of gnats, and they're all swirling, swimming, *sparkling* about. They leave a trail of their luminous white fire behind them as they fly in darting, spiraling motions. Seconds inflate into minutes and minutes seem like hours.

I am now sensing deeper, underlying truths about events in my life that I failed to recognize before, and have become acutely aware that I've been afraid of living life as it was *meant* to be lived. Pictures of my stepfather spanking me with a two-by-four when I was six after failing to rake up every single leaf in the yard appear on the screen inside my forehead, followed by images from every subsequent beating, bullying, and abusive relationship that brought me pain and sorrow. I suddenly realize that my fears have been controlling my actions and because of this I had subconsciously created a reality that was restricting, stifling, prison-like. I understand now that I've been staving off, actually *thwarting*, my own peace, happiness, and health just because I didn't find myself to be worthy of these wonderful things. I can now see clearly that the diseases I've been chronically suffering from for so long have been created by a very fearful and shameful *me*.

After receiving these profound realizations, I find myself asking out loud: "Why have I been so hard on myself? Why have I felt so inadequate, like such a failure at life? Why have I always judged myself so harshly? What have I been so *afraid* of? And *why,* for Christ sakes, have I allowed so many people to abuse me, deceive me, and take advantage of me?" It seems that throughout my entire life I've been nothing but a dupe, a *pawn.* I've never truly *loved* myself before. To the contrary, I've mainly hated myself. No wonder I've been so sick and miserable. How can my body be healthy and vital when it's constantly being bombarded with hatred by its Commander in Chief? I always felt as if I had to "do something" to be appreciated, respected, and loved. Being loved just because I *exist* never even entered into my mind.

I have also become keenly aware that I've actually been hiding my intelligence, spiritual wisdom, insight, intuition, and creative abilities from the world. I've been hiding my true *Self* from the world! I was always ashamed of the fact that I was so different from others, that I didn't belong here. I've always felt that I needed to somehow *disguise* myself. Ergo I had, over time, deeply suppressed the sensitive, spiritual boy so that I could simply *fit in.* But fit in to *what*—the *insanity* of society? As a result of these newfound epiphanies, I am now feeling the need to *stand up* for my Self and stop giving my power away to those who not only use it to their advantage, but use it to walk all over me. I unequivocally understand now that I am a *divine being* and deserve to be treated with *respect.*

The blissful energy is now converging and intensifying in my throat area and it feels as if someone is physically *choking* me, and while this is happening, a hot wave of energy engulfs my tongue, larynx, esophagus, and neck. As I lose my breath and begin to panic, my fears are quelled when I hear the familiar female voice say, "Be still and surrender, Jason." After a long while, the energy retreats from my throat and continues its trek upwards.

I feel as if I've been experiencing this soul-healing energy now for days even though the sun seems as if he hasn't moved and he continues showing off his artwork to me in the same location over the surfaces throughout my apartment. All my senses have greatly amplified: sight, hearing, touch, sound, and curiously, I'm identifying distinct geometric shapes everywhere around me. Even my abstract paintings are unveiling a beautiful hidden imagery that I never noticed before. On my books I'm recognizing anagrams, encoded hidden messages, within the titles and subtitles. How could I have been so blind? There is an entirely new, larger, and far more interesting world being revealed here before me and I'm elated to be watching the show. It's suddenly become obvious to me that I've never used my eyes before. Everything now seems wondrous and *alive!* It's as if the universe is communicating directly *to* me, and in a not-so-subtle way. I begin exploring everything in my apartment, staring intensely into the hidden imagery in my art, furniture, books, and as I'm doing this the little fireflies continue to swim through the air, and I'm feeling lighter and lighter, borderline weightless, nearly *airborne;* the perception is akin to being submerged underwater. While I struggle to keep my feet on the floor, I'm finding it more difficult to breathe in air because each breath I'm taking is becoming shorter and shorter and the fears of my recent panic attack are returning to my mind and body. After recommencing with my pacing in an attempt to catch my breath, I hear the voice of my father speak to me audibly, "Remember to breathe from your *diaphragm,* Jason." Following his reminder, I move my breathing from my chest down to my stomach and promptly retrieve sufficient air, or at least I *think* it's air, and the mere breathing of it causes an intense surge of bliss from my tailbone to the top of my head as if I've inhaled a drug reserved for the *gods.* Afterward the same little motor that I felt in the center of my chest I can now feel in my stomach and it seems to be spinning, too. Tempering it with my left hand, I walk to the bathroom where I run some cool water from the tap, splash some on my face, hair, neck, then as I'm patting myself dry, I meet a strange reflection in the mirror: there's something very *different* about me.

Looking into the mirror I can see that my eyes have mysteriously changed, so much so that I no longer recognize them as *me.* They've become wider, larger, more almond-shaped, and when I look deeper into them I can clearly see that they're made of *light*—what used to be brown irises are now made of liquid gold. They also appear to be wiser and "older" than my human eyes. One word comes to mind: *majestic*. Now a mask made of butterfly wings in metallic rose gold is appearing around my eyes as if someone is painting my face. After the wings appear, the butterfly's head makes itself seen but only briefly because it quickly transforms into a *third eye* which is vertically shaped and in the exact center of my brow, precisely where the energy has converged. "You have your wings now," is then spoken to me audibly by the soothing female voice.

Feeling a strong pressure in the center of my forehead I instinctually move my left index finger to temper it and when I do, my left thumb lands on my left nostril, closing it. I then take my next breath deeply and deliberately through my right nostril and my entire body is engulfed with a fiery sensation of exhilarating, hot, unbridled *power*. I then repeat the same procedure and breath, but through the *left* nostril. The result is another "hit" of this intoxicating energy but this time it's followed by a calming, *cooling* wave of pure serenity.

Suddenly I feel the need to leave my apartment and get some fresh air so I quickly dress and I'm out the door on my way up the street to Borders, the bookstore about four blocks away from where I live. Coldplay's *Don't Panic* plays through the earphones of a Sony MiniDisc player as I walk. After about half a block, another revelation is revealed: every part of my life that I've been "living" up to this point was nothing but a dream—a nightmare mostly—but a dream, nevertheless. And now, for a reason unknown to me, I have awakened *inside that dream*. What I thought was real has now become *sur*real, and my purpose for being here at this particular time on this particular planet seems so, oh, I dunno, *clear*.

Ra is shining brightly in a cloudless sky and finding myself instinctually drawn to him, I place my gaze directly into his light and when I do, my eyes well up, but instead of blinking the tears away, I allow them to trickle down my cheeks in awe of his glory. This feeling is so overwhelming that I don't want to move my gaze to the traffic signals so I continue to walk through each of the three crosswalks, intensely alert (even though I'm not actually *looking*) to where I am in relation to the traffic (my peripheral vision is apparently pegging 360), knowing intuitively that I am in no danger, and the entire time it takes me (about seven minutes or so), I'm staring directly into the blazing fire of Ra. When I finally arrive at Borders, I stop and stand in the middle of the sidewalk, bow my head, and thank Ra for his warmth and light, then shut my eyes tightly. After a few moments, I reopen them and enter Borders Bookstore.

After purchasing an Evian water at the cafe, I take a seat at a table in the middle of the room. I'm now feeling the tangible energy focusing at the top of my skull again, succeeded by yet another feeling that something is trying to *open*. The heaviness returns, and within minutes it feels as though I've gained a thousand pounds. So I just sit here, rock still, until I eventually realize that I've been sitting here motionless for a half hour? An hour? During this time, the foreign yet familiar energy has continued to caress me, shooting waves of bliss throughout my body— back, groin, diaphragm, chest, throat—while my head continues to bob freely. I am now faintly aware of something immensely powerful looming *behind the scenes* and the inevitability of it consuming my entire being. Looking around the room at the college students in the café, I observe them chatting, laughing, drinking lattes, perusing magazines, studying, and the weightiness seems to be lifting now and suddenly I'm feeling light as air, as if I'm going to levitate, literally *rise* right out of my chair. Time has, again, come to a standstill. Since the others in the café seem oblivious to my presence, no one pays attention, they don't even pretend *not* to pay attention, so I decide to meditate and even when I close my eyes I can still see everyone around me on the little screen inside my forehead. Panning around the room with my eyes closed, I can clearly see people enter the café, approach the counter, get in line, place their orders, and I can hear them speak as if I'm standing right next them, even though I'm at least twenty feet or so away. That's when I realize that I can also hear the thoughts in their heads which, within seconds, expands to me hearing the thoughts of everyone in the room and when this happens I'm finding it increasingly more difficult to differentiate between them since the sound of it all is mumbled and jumbled like an audio of thirty different voices simultaneously playing on top of each other, and eventually this hive mind chatter becomes just too much for my brain to process and so I say out loud to myself, "I need peace." Then, as if the universe instantly received my command, all the mind chatter abruptly *mutes* but these same words are then eerily echoed by a person sitting at a table in front of me, a young woman, obviously a college student, who informs her friend across from her, "I need peace." This is followed by the same words being repeated by yet another woman at a table behind me. When I hear my words repeated twice by two other people in the room, it freaks me out, so much so that I become positively *scared*. I now fear that I'm utterly *losing my mind*. And this fear is so intense, so piercing, so amplified, that I feel as if I'm going to faint from the severity of pain I'm enduring because of it. It's as if I'm being electrocuted and now not only do I fear that I'm going crazy, I'm also fearing that my body is not going to be able to bear it. I then whisper out loud to myself: "What the hell is *happening* to me?" And like clockwork, a young man at the table to my left echoes the very same question to himself in a hushed whisper, saying, "What the hell is *happening* to me?" Following him, a woman at a table to my right asks herself the very same question. My words continue to echo throughout the room, one person at a time, no matter what I think or say. It's apparent to me that there is some sort of interactive field of reverberation going on in here. The reality that I've stumbled into appears to be reflecting all my thoughts through the minds of each person in the room. But how can any of this be *real*? I'm thinking that I may have yet another panic attack. The roof of my skull feels as if it's cracking open now and the blissful energy is now flowing, pouring, *gushing* out of it and this progresses to some sort of flowering sensation, a blossoming of something infinitely *more* real, to something higher...

Then the curtain is drawn...

And as if in *slow motion* my head is thrust backward by a tangibly-felt flash of blinding white light along with an ear-splitting ***POP!!*** And I'm suddenly made aware that I've somehow *merged* with every human being in the room. My consciousness is now *in* every single person around me. I have become *them*, and them, *me*.

I am he. I am she. I am everyone and I am no one.

The sense of self that I've come to know as "me" during "my life" has now dissolved and an infinitely more powerful and exalted *Self* has emerged. I feel as if I've been illuminated to a "behind-the-scenes" computer program, a virtual reality *construct*, and it's all been specifically designed for *me*. Yet I am also everyone else. And everyone else is me. So how can this entire universe be designed specifically for me, unless it's also designed for everyone else at the same time? It seems obvious to me now that there is only *one of us here.* Just **one**. Not just here at Borders but everywhere throughout the universe, encompassing an infinitude of life forms, not just humans, but *all sentient beings.* They were right, I am thinking. The ancients were right! I now realize that it has only been a game. Just a *game*.

After this newfound Self-realization sinks in—I can feel my body beginning to panic at the sheer shock of this and as soon as I feel fear, the illusion of separation returns, and I'm back to seeing myself as a separate entity from the others in the room. After catching my breath I wonder if the other patrons have shared with me this immeasurably enlightening experience of "oneness" but I'm about to discover that nothing could be further from the truth. Upon returning to the plane of duality, I find myself *freezing;* my entire body literally feels like *ice*. I look down to find a table covered in sweat. Shivering and shaking, I slowly peel myself up from the wooden chair and proceed to wobble my way to the men's room to splash some water on my face. Once there, I look into the mirror and notice the radiant, mystifying "butterfly eyes" staring straight back into me. I conclude that I couldn't have been dreaming—this simply *must be real.*

Standing in front of the mirror, my eyes now become fixated on their exotic new reflection, and that's when the energy recommences her manipulation of my head, but this time, instead of pushing it vertically downward, she's pushing it horizontally closer and closer to my reflection in the mirror until I have the strange urge to meld *into* it—to literally become *one with* my own reflection. This frightens me so I resist, but the magnetic pull is simply *too strong* and my face is reeled closer and closer to the mirror until my eyes become *locked* onto their opposite image in the glass. Now it feels as if she has her fingers on my eyelids and she's forcing them wider and wider apart and because of this I have no choice but to look deeply into the dark vacuum of my pupils, and I'm sensing an omniscience, an endless sea of sentience, and I don't know why she's doing this but there's nothing I can do about it, and then my breath escapes me and just when I'm about to have another panic attack I'm shockingly blinded by yet another immensely bright flash of white light accompanied by another ear-piercing ***POP!!***

Trying to catch my breath from my diaphragm—I realize that my mouth is dry, parched, and it feels as if I've just swallowed a handful of sand despite the fact that I've already drunk the entire bottle of Evian I purchased earlier, so I decide to buy another one. Leaving the restroom like a toddler taking his first steps, I somehow manage to make it on my own all the way to the counter and get in line. While I'm waiting, I am observing beads of sweat dripping off of me on to the countertop, splashing as they land (yes, I can actually *hear* them splash) and as I'm wiping the countertop with my left hand and my brow with my right—hoping no one will notice—my body jerks and shakes uncontrollably. I am *freezing.* After the people in front of me pay for their drinks, the barista asks what I would like but when I open my mouth to speak my order nothing comes out due to the fact that the tip of my tongue is stuck, seemingly *glued,* to the roof of my mouth just behind my front teeth and when I finally manage to murmur, "Ann Eeevvviiaaann wa wa wader pleeeazzzze…," I stutter, twitch, shake, and my body jerks uncontrollably as I fail to articulate the words distinctly. In response to this display of "craziness" the girl behind the counter, smirking and fighting a burst of laughter, gives the other patrons in line a look like I've just escaped from the insane asylum. As my body continues to uncontrollably tremor, she finally loses it and laughs out loud, ridiculing me openly. My sensitivity to this is so raw, I can't help but take in the full brunt of the humiliation, and as a result my body feels as if someone has just doused it with battery acid. I'm *burning up.*

After downing the entire bottle of water I exit Borders Bookstore and I'm feeling that I just need to walk, to be freed from the confines of the building, the people, and to be closer to nature. After a block or two I learn that the movement of my walk is quelling the jerks and shakes. I also want to be left alone so that I can observe this wonderful new world I've just discovered. A fire engine approaches and the wall-of-sound siren is so blaring, so uncomfortably *loud,* my entire body reacts with debilitating pain, and as I double over, I reactively plug my ear drums with the tips of my fingers. After the fire engine passes, I continue down the hill where I spot a dense grove of trees in a distant park and begin walking toward it. I seem to be looking at the world with high-definition vision lenses since everything appears to be radiating with such clarity, pulsating and vibrating with an intensity and beauty that I've never witnessed before. The colors are more vivid, the sounds more clear, the aromas more pungent.

I eventually come to the end of my town's business district where the park begins and I see a milkman walking to the rear of his truck where he opens the door and retrieves a case of milk, but I'm noticing that his movements are robotic, autonomic, and his limbs appear *geometric*. Something about him seems blatantly proportionate, the ratio of his fingers to hands, hands to forearm, forearm to shoulder, head to waist, waist to knees, knees to feet, upper body to lower body—all of this seems precisely *patterned*. I'm shivering uncontrollably.

I then make my way into the park where the trees seem to greet me, their branches bowing down to me with the wind. I can hear a variety of birds singing loudly and they seem to be rejoicing that I've finally arrived on the scene. Even the squirrels and rabbits don't appear to be startled by my presence. Eventually I arrive at a large maple tree and take a seat at its trunk, resting my back against its bark. When I look up into the limbs of the tree, I see the same geometry I observed on the milkman, except I'm now identifying it in the branches, the leaves, the veins of the leaves. As I sit here in bliss I take in the wonder of it all, marveling at the precision, the perfection, the *divine order*, savoring every awe-inspiring moment as if I were observing the world from the eyes of an infant.

After what seems like several hours in the park I find my way back to my apartment where reset the air conditioning to 63 degrees. I'm on fire again. After removing all my clothes, I hear the words from the soothing female voice, "Get a paper and pen, Jason. Do it now." Following her instructions, I get up and walk into my office, retrieve a pen and notepad, and retreat to the living room sofa. As soon as I can put pen to paper, the words begin to flow effortlessly and before I know it I'm taking automatic dictation as fast as I can write in shorthand. The first words that I write are:

> Go/Stop
> Inhale/Exhale
> Expand/Contract
> Get Up/Sit Down
> To Be/Not to Be

After nearly five hours of channeling, I'm feeling the need to rest, and so I lie back on the soft leather sofa, close my eyes, and within seconds, the slideshow returns to my mind's eye and the scene I'm being shown now is nothing less than *other-worldly*. I'm looking at a glimmering crystal pyramid in the middle of an ocean somewhere and I can clearly see a giant "all-seeing eye" in its apex. There's a sky of densely grouped multi-colored stars in the background. It's obviously nighttime there (but where?) and the entire pyramid is not only transparent but illuminated by a shimmering fire located in its center. It's also enveloped in a dome of translucent white light—like a force field of some sort. Because it resides in a sea of crystal clear blue water and I can clearly see its reflection coming from the water below, it appears to me as an octahedron inside of a sphere. I then hear the words audibly in the sound of the female voice, "This is the shape of your universe." There are also many pods of jumping dolphins in the water surrounding this awe-inspiring, magnificent structure. Based on the size of the dolphins, I surmise that this giant crystal pyramid must be larger than the Great Pyramid. It's the most beautiful vision I've ever seen and so I just lie here on my back with my eyes closed, taking in the awe-inspiring beauty of this divine tableau.

May the Force be with you.

Obi Wan: *Remember a Jedi can feel the Force flowing through him.*

Luke: *You mean it controls your actions?*

Obi Wan: *Partially. But it also obeys your commands.*

—Star Wars Episode IV: A New Hope

In the Star Wars movies, George Lucas introduces us to the Force, which is explained as an energy field created by all living things that surrounds us, penetrates us, and *binds* the universe together. The Force has two movements: it speaks to us but it also obeys our commands. In other words, it is simultaneously a transmitter *and* a receiver. Because the Next Human will have already transcended her egoic mind and will be living purely from her heart, she will possess "Jedi powers," which she will use for the good of all. But we have to be careful. As the saying goes, "With great power comes great responsibility." If we had developed these advanced paranormal abilities before now, I think it would have probably gone straight to our heads. The ego would have most likely used them for its own gratification, i.e. evil, rather than for serving humanity.

You may find it interesting to learn that there was actually a time in the Earth's distant past where the "Jedis" did indeed exist. In ancient Persia they were known as the Narts from the Scythian tribes who were the protectors of enlightened Sufi philosopher kings and guardians of a Holy Grail called the Nartmongue. Upon returning from the Middle East in the 13th and 14th centuries CE, these guardian knights were introduced to the West as the Knights Templar (founded in 1118 CE), who distilled their Sufi history into what we know today as the Holy Grail legends.[1] The Knights Templar possessed the ancient wisdom of a mystical energy field called "life force" or *the Force* that was passed down to them by their antecedent Narts who learned of the Force from Sufi masters in the 9th century CE.

But the Knights Templar made it clear that they were not just historians but a real-life, latter-day version of "Jedi" Knights whose ancient wisdom stems back over a thousand years before them to ancient Egypt where the Masters of the Force were known as Djedi (actually pronounced *jedi*)—powerful guardians and protectors of the Egyptian Pharaohs.[2] Interestingly, the Djedi Knights of ancient Egypt most likely received their knowledge of the Force from a much earlier prehistorical Djedi Order on Atlantis. One Djedi priest mentioned in the Egyptian's Westcar Papyrus is said to have possessed the *key* that opened the "secret chambers of the sanctuary of Thoth."[3] Many esoteric historians believe that Thoth was a Djedi Master from Atlantis.[4] The Greeks related Thoth to their god Hermes due to the fact that they shared his similar attributes and responsibilities. Thoth was also one of the most important gods in the Egyptian pantheon and was almost always depicted holding a scepter (symbolizing power) in one hand and an ankh (a symbolic *key* to the *breath of life*) in the other. Some believe that Merlin the Magician from the Arthurian Legend was the same soul as Thoth. The Gnostic texts "The Emerald Tablets of Thoth" and "The Divine Pymander" reveal that Thoth was also the architect of the Great Pyramid. Through Thoth's alchemy, the esoteric symbol of the *caduceus* (a winged sphere with two serpents entwined around a scepter) could awaken the dormant Serpent of Light, the fiery Force located at the base of the spine, and then raise it upwards, where it would ultimately express itself through spiritual enlightenment, psychic powers, supernatural abilities, and gnostic wisdom. This marked the Djedi's *initiation* into the Djedi order.

The name "Djedi" comes from the hieroglyph depicting the Djed pillar or column meaning "stability" and is the symbolic *spine* of the god Osiris. The root word or sound *Dj* or *J* was depicted as the hieroglyph of a snake or serpent. Ergo, a Djedi was one who had awakened the *Dj* or sacred Serpent of Light at its seat and then raised it up his or her Djed pillar or *spine* to the crown of the head, resulting in en*light*enment.

The God *S* in you.

> *The serpent was the most subtle of all the wild beasts that God had made.*
>
> —Genesis: 3:1, *The Jerusalem Bible*

The experience I've described in this chapter's memoir is my personal Self-realization or what the ancient Vedas of Hinduism referred to as a *kundalini awakening*. The Sanskrit word *kundalini* is "she who is coiled," and is derived from the root words *kund*, "to burn" or *kunda*, "to coil as in a spiral." *Shakti* translates as "life force," "the cosmic force," or simply *the Force*. The root word of Shakti is *shak*, "the enabler." In Hinduism,

Shakti is the personification of the sacred feminine, the goddess of creativity. In the body when she unites with Shiva, the sacred masculine energy, the yin binds with yang, and the initiate receives the *divine bliss.*

The kundalini Shakti is always coiled in a spiral, like a serpent at rest, precisely three and one-half times at the base of the spine. Here she remains dormant in every human on Earth until she is awakened at the appropriate time—dictated by the free will of the higher Self. I see the Shakti as the divine **S**-ence, or Holy Spirit, which translates from the Hebrew *ruach*, meaning "vital breath" or "active force" of creation that "moves over the surface of the waters," mentioned in Genesis 1:2.

Just like the Hebrew word *ruach*, the Sanskrit word *prana* translates as "first breath of the life force," "life force," or "vital breath." In China, prana is known as *qi* or *chi*, in Japan, *ki*, in the Pacific Islands, *mana*, and in ancient Greece, *pneuma*. This vital breath or life force is not air but rather a quantum energy (only visible through the third eye) that all forms in the universe ultimately consist of below the currently known quantum level. What physicists are currently calling *dark matter* is actually *this exact same life force* which makes up all the so-called "empty space" and binds the universe together into One.

Kundalini Shakti is a highly intelligent aspect of the life force energy that cannot be directly controlled. She can be transferred, unblocked, and assisted temporarily by a master—known as a *Shaktipat* guru—to an initiate but after that, the Shakti energy will be, like any intelligent life form, moving on her own volition. Prana (chi, ki, mana), on the other hand, can be manipulated fairly easily. Rather than the independent and active Shakti, prana is more passive and therefore "obeys your commands." Yoga, tai chi, chigong, and all of the martial arts such as kung fu, karate, and aikido are physical disciplines where this more malleable life force energy is directed throughout the body. A master martial artist can easily move his *chi* energy anywhere he wants, empowering both his defenses and his attacks. Similarly, in the Japanese healing art of Rei*ki,* this same *ki* energy is directed by the practitioner for the purpose of clearing and balancing the energy centers of the ethereal Self, which, in turn, facilitates healing in the physical Self.

This same pranic energy (chi, ki, mana) is also the vibration of sunlight and can be seen—if you have an opened third eye—around trees, plants, flowers, animals, and around flowing water such as springs, streams, rivers, lakes, seas, and oceans. This is why we always feel renewed and recharged with "electricity" when we commune with nature. If you've ever been caught in a thunderstorm where there's lots of lightning in the sky, you'll have a rough idea of what it's like to experience firsthand what pranic energy feels like. It's intensely *electrical* in sensation. In the memoir, the "spiraling fireflies" leaving a stream of white light behind them is a description of what prana looks like to someone with an opened third-eye. Even if you've never experienced a kundalini awakening, you still can become aware of the pranic life force that's already very present in your body through disciplines that I will mention later in the chapter.

During the last 13,000 years, a very small percentage of the human population has experienced a kundalini awakening. The few that did were called mystics, sages, shamans, yogis, or enlightened masters. In the last fifty years, however, and much more so in the last decade, there has been a much broader demographic of individuals from around the world who have awakened the Serpent of Light from within.

You may have noticed by now the repeating pattern of the *S* and *K* sounds and their derivatives *Sh* and *Ch* in words related to the God *S* energy, the sacred feminine *Shakti.* Words such as goddess, shaman, sage, kundalini, force, initiation, transformation, transcendence, etheric, essence, spiritual, source, sanskrit, chakra, chi, ki, ka, ruach, creation, ankh, snake, serpent, sacred, sacrum, sanctity, and sacrament, just to name a few. Egypt, which was originally a colony from Atlantis, was initially called "the land of Khem" and many pharaohs such as Rameses, Ankhenaten, Tutankhamun, Hatshepsut, and Cleopatra have the *K*, *S*, *Sh*, or *Ch* sounds in the pronunciation of the words. In our modern English alphabet, the shape of the letter *S* resembles the shape of the serpent. In hieroglyphics, the *basket*, which is how coiled snakes were transported, was symbolic of the dormant kundalini serpent and also illustrated the *K* sound. And just like the *K*-sounding root word *kunda* from Sanskrit, the Egyptian root-word *kebb* translates "to coil as in a serpent."[5] The reason for all of this has nothing to do with coincidence but is because every life form, object, symbol, and *sound* in the universe retains its own unique resonance, and the creative and transformational energy of the kundalini *Shakti* vibrates specifically with these *tone* frequencies.

You'll find that the word "subtle" is used to describe the serpent in Genesis 3:1 (see the quote at beginning of this section). The word *subtle* is also a synonym for *ethereal, etheric* or *astral* and these four terms are used interchangeably to describe the spiritual body that exists deeper within you that you cannot become fully aware of until you: *A.* Transcend into the ethereal plane by shedding your physical sheath, i.e. "dying." *B.* Have an *out-of-body experience* (OBE). *C.* Have a *near-death experience* (NDE). Or *D.* Awaken the Shakti through an *inner-body experience* (IBE), also known as a kundalini awakening.

You may also find it interesting to know that the original meaning of the three holy sacraments of initiation in Christianity—baptism, confirmation, and the Eucharist—are misguided, diluted, and ritualistic interpretations of the *awakening, rising,* and *flowering* of the kundalini Shakti. In fact, the Greek *khristós*, or Latin *christus*—derived from the Hebrew *māŝîah*—simply means "the anointed." It was never a person's name but rather a *title* indicating that Jesus—who was the same spiritual teacher known as the Master of Justice and Teacher of Righteousness referred to in the Dead Sea Scrolls—was indeed initiated, anointed, and *sanctified* by the Serpent of Light from within his own *body* for the purpose of ego liberation, and achieving Self-realization. Furthermore, the ancient Hebrew name for Jesus was *Yahoshua*—note that the "o" was added for phonetics and therefore it was pronounced "yah-**hosh**-u-a" to annunciate the vital *breath* or life force.

The serpent mentioned in the book of Genesis is referring to none other than the sacred Serpent of Light, the kundalini *Shakti*. In Genesis, the serpent tempts Adam and Eve with "forbidden fruit" because the Serpent of Light's very purpose is to en*light*en the initiate to the "fruit" or hidden *knowledge* from the tree of the knowledge of good and evil. As it is written in Genesis 3:3 (The Jerusalem Bible):

> *...But of the fruit of the tree in the middle of the garden God said, 'You must not eat it, nor touch it, under pain of death.'*

The "death" that this verse refers to is not a *physical* death but rather a metaphorical "death and rebirth" of the soul that is attained after the knowledge—fruit from the tree—of the ethereal/immortal Self is "eaten" or digested. Remember, the serpent has always been an ancient symbol for death *and* rebirth, for *transformation*. When you actualize and fulfill the potential of the Serpent of Light, you will be like a god or goddess and will have experienced a knowing of both good *and* evil, light *and* darkness. Through enlightenment, your eyes will indeed be *opened* to the higher truth that both the light/good and the dark/evil are *necessary* to experience duality and the world of form, as well as for your personal and collective evolution. After all, without the veil of darkness, how can you know the *light?* How can you recognize your true majesty, your inherent divinity? When you finally realize your own godliness, you will no longer curse the darkness since you will understand that without it, you cannot truly know your true Self. Moreover, you will also realize that evil or the *veil* has its own vital part to play in the broader "game of life." As it is written in Genesis 3:4:

> *Then the serpent said to the woman, 'No! You will not die! God knows in fact that on the day you eat it your eyes will be opened and you will be like gods, knowing good and evil.'*

The serpent here—symbolizing ancient, esoteric *wisdom*—says, "You will not die!" implying that if Adam and Eve did indeed eat or consume the sacred wisdom of the primordial Serpent and subsequently awakened her from within their own bodies, they would not die but rather become "like gods." Note that the serpent says, "Your eyes will be opened," meaning they will become enlightened, and thus will *know* that they are, in truth, divine beings. And, of course, "God"—or whatever earth-bound, physical deity this verse is actually referring to—did not want this to happen because if Adam and Eve became *aware* that they were of the same genetic material as their Lord, then they would no longer serve *him*.

Furthermore, not only was the sacred Serpent of Light symbolic of esoteric wisdom, it was also considered the key to *eternal life* according to mystical texts from all four corners of the globe. For example, in ancient Egypt it was believed that the Djedi who succeeded in the raising of the fiery Serpent up the spine to the top of the head, allowing it to bloom, could potentially become *immortal*, which is yet another meaning of the word *Djedi*. The Egyptian priests and priestesses associated the vertical spine with immortality because they were well aware of the primordial Serpent and her secrets. Thus, the Djed pillar—representing the spinal column—became their symbol for immortality, hence the reason why they covered their mummies and sarcophagi with hieroglyphs of the Djed: so the deceased would receive immortal life on the ethereal plane.

Now, let me be clear here. All souls are immortal. All souls have eternal life. But until you become aware of the truth that you *are* immortal, you will continue to fear death. And *fear* is the only thing preventing you from evolving into the Next Human. As long as you hold on to the fear that you are mortal, you will share the same fate of mortals, which is *suffering*. And then you will have to continue to come back to the physical realm and live another mortal life over and over and over again until you wake up to the truth that you are creating your own "mortality." Know that you've already *made it*. Your very birthright is that you are already divine and therefore immortal so you have nothing to fear, *ever*. The ancient knowledge I'm revealing here and now in this chapter was once understood by only the few. But in the decades ahead, *millions* of people around the world will be experiencing a kundalini awakening, and therefore this knowledge will no longer be esoteric. For the Next Human it will be basic knowledge because she will intuitively understand the importance of raising the frequency of her physical Self so that it can become intimately connected with her ethereal Self. She will *know* that she's immortal as opposed to believing she is. There is a difference.

Balancing the Serpent of Light within.

> *A hundred and one are the arteries of the heart, one of them leads up to the crown of the head. Going upward through that, one becomes immortal.*
>
> —*Chandogya Upanishad*

It's important for you to understand that your ethereal Self is simply an *inner* body that exists on a higher frequency, and as long as you are here on this material plane, this ethereal body will be in the same exact "location" or space as your physical body and thus it fits perfectly, *like a glove*, underneath it. I like to think of it as the *K*ryptonian suit that *S*uperman wears underneath his human-made suit. In this metaphorical sense, it is your supernatural body that you've only temporarily forgotten.

Nādi translates as "stream" or "channel" and there are a total of 72,000 of these energy channels within the ethereal body but the three most important are the *sushumna*, *ida*, and *pingala*. The purpose of the *nādi* is to transport the life force energy (prana, chi, ki, mana), through the subtle body for the purpose of healing, empowering creativity, acquiring spiritual wisdom, and evolving into the Next Human. You could say that the veins and arteries of your physical body are much like the *nādis* of your ethereal body. Just as blood and oxygen of the physical body sustains its health and life, *life force energy* sustains the health and life of the subtle body.

Serpentine *ida* nādi represents the sacred feminine *yin*, which are aspects associated with the parasympathetic nervous system, negative polarity, lunar energy. It corresponds to the left nostril and transports prana that has a cooling, soothing, calming effect. Serpentine *pingala* nādi transports prana that corresponds to the sacred masculine *yang*, sympathetic nervous system, which are aspects associated with positive polarity, solar energy. It's connected to the right nostril and has a warming, energetic, exhilarating effect.

To experience your ethereal Self first hand, you must awaken the kundalini and enable her ascent up the *sushumna* nādi, which is the central canal that connects the root chakra—located in the coccyx or tailbone—all the way to the crown chakra—located at the exact center and top of the skull. You will recognize when the sushumna is active and transporting lots of life force when your body is tingling, twitching, jerking, or having involuntary muscle cramps or spasms. These are signs that the life force energy is alive and kicking within you and that your body is responding to the movement and flow of it through the channel of sushumna and in the process, being prepared for the ascent of the fiery Force, the Serpent of Light.

The vortices of the ethereal body.

Just as your physical body consists of organs such as the heart, brain, lungs, liver, kidneys, etc., your ethereal body also contains organs. The word "chakra" (pronounced *cha*-kra or *sha*-kra) from the Sanskrit *cakra* means "vortex" or "spinning wheel." The human chakra system consists of eight chakras that are the energy centers of your ethereal Self or *lightbody* and instead of being made of physical matter (cells, blood, tissue), chakras are made of ethereal light or life force energy.

In a musical octave, there are eight sound tones: do, re, mi, fa, so, la, ti, do. Similarly, there are eight chakras spanning eight *tones* or frequencies in your ethereal body. Once she becomes aroused, the Serpent of Light rises to the top of the head via the spinal cord, opening, spinning, balancing, and purifying each chakra along the way. These eight chakras are as follows:

The Root Chakra is the first chakra and is located about nine inches above the anus near the perineum between the rectum and testicles in males and between the vagina and clitoris in females. In Sanskrit it is called *mūlādhāra*, meaning "root support," and is the portal to Gaia Sophia, our Mother Earth. What lies within the root chakra is dormant, unrealized, raw, creative potential. This vortex is represented by a lotus flower with four petals.

The mandala or symbol is a V-shaped triangle (*yoni* in Sanskrit) representing the sacred feminine Shakti and *womb* of Mother Earth. It is surrounded by a square, symbolizing foundation, as well as the four cardinal directions of north, south, east, and west. Within the yoni, the kundalini lies dormant, coiled up as a sleeping snake until she awakens from a hunger. This hunger arises as a consequence of spiritual practice, moral discipline, and a deep, inner exploration of the psyche. The kundalini is wrapped around the lingam—a "pillar of light" representing the phallus of the sacred masculine—which points upward, away from the earth and toward the higher frequencies of the ethereal plane. The color of this vortex of light is a vibrant red, the longest wavelength and lowest frequency in the electromagnetic spectrum.

The densest of all the chakras, the root chakra governs the ego's primal survival instincts. When the root chakra is closed, blocked, or out of balance, we are without grounding or stability, and thus will be greedy, stingy, overbearing, aggressive, and unsympathetic toward others. This is due to an underlying fear of safety and of security.

Primal and instinctual, the root chakra connects us to what Jung termed the collective unconscious, which are memories from our ancestral past, our evolutionary heritage. When this etheric organ is activated and cleared, we are firmly rooted on Earth. Our true life path is realized and we are empowered with a comforting and divine sense of security, an inner knowing that no matter what, we will be protected from want and harm. Like a baby being held in its mother's loving arms, we feel nurtured and protected. Subsequently, prior anxieties and fears for the basic survival needs such as food, clothing, and shelter completely dissolve. Material wants and obsessions are replaced with authentic financial independence.

The **Sacral Chakra** is the second chakra center known as *svādhisthāna,* meaning "one's own abode" in Sanskrit and its element is water. Its symbol is the half-moon and its god is Vishnu, the sustainer of the universe. The animal symbol is a sea monster representing dominion over the waters which are symbolic of the subconscious mind and its emotional body. It is located four fingers below the navel in the small pelvis near the genital region, and governs the union of opposites, sexual desires, psychic feelings, the pain-body, and the nervous system. It influences our ability to cooperate, compromise, be open-minded, and be amicable when we disagree with others. When this vortex is clogged, we attract stressful situations and events into our lives, our fight or flight response is heightened, and we tend to see life as hostile.

The sacral chakra governs the ego's shadow, the phantom self, so when it's blocked, we'll be in deep denial of this hidden, repressed aspect of the psyche. Secret addictions, substance abuse, dependencies, obsessions, and fantasies need to be addressed and brought out into the open. We will be unaware of projections of judgment, criticism, blame, and condemnation onto others. These negative emotions are expressed either aggressively through sadism or passively through masochism.

The Sanskrit word *tantra* means "to stretch into a weave" and from this medieval Indian philosophy arose an understanding of the sacredness and divinity of the human body. The frequency of the sacral center is attuned with the physical union of diametrical opposites, the joining and balancing of yin with yang. During sexual intercourse, a couple will not only experience an exchange between the genitals but the two partners will also have their chakras synchronized. For the Next Human, as each chakra begins to spin, a higher union between the lovers is achieved. The sacral center governs the sexual aspect of the kundalini Shakti and through it, the entire body becomes a "sexual organ," not only the genital regions. This is what I call "spiritual sex" and is a much higher frequency of sex since it involves a reunion and divine *balancing* of the sacred masculine with the sacred feminine polarities in *both* partners.

When the sacral chakra is cleared, the pain-body—and the anxiety and depression that comes with it—completely dissolves, the phantom is transcended, and we begin to see life as supportive and cooperative. We develop a sense of true Self-respect. Healthy boundaries are drawn in relationships as our emotional baggage is discarded. Freed from incessant misery and suffering, we can evolve to experience all the pleasures that the physical realm has to offer us. Instead of enduring life, we can now *enjoy* it.

The **Solar Plexus Chakra,** or *manipūra,* meaning "lustrous gem," is the third chakra and is the center of dynamic and exuberant energy, passion, ambition, action, autonomy, self-esteem, willpower, and achievement. Hence the name, the solar plexus chakra shines like the sun with the colors of yellow and gold, and thus its element is fire.

The root chakra relates to the material realm (earth), the sacral chakra relates to our emotional realm (water), and the solar plexus chakra relates to the energetic realm (fire). It is the "divine spark" of enthusiasm that ignites our willpower to achieve in life, to *make things happen* in the world. As the saying goes, "Where there is a will, there is a way." Associated with our vitality and metabolism, as we activate this center our power is directed outward onto the world. Our egoic sense of self is refined through this center and expressed *outwardly* as we expend our energy toward specific goals and achievements. Because our egoic identity is derived through a sense of separation from the world, i.e. feeling inferior or superior to others, here we feel the full brunt of this separation.

When the third center is blocked, the ego overcompensates for fears of "not fitting in" or not being seen as a success in society. It can also result in excessive pride or arrogance, recklessness, and aggressiveness where we tend to run roughshod over others in an effort to ambitiously get what we want no matter what it takes. Consequently, we become our own worst enemies due to our excessive pride, self-centeredness, and great rises end up as great falls. The worst aspects of the ego surface and material successes are unconsciously sabotaged. Drama is perpetuated over and over in an effort to bring more attention to the pseudo self.

Purification of the solar plexus chakra transforms false self-esteem into authentic Self-esteem. Haughtiness, attachment, and egocentricity are supplanted by humility, gratitude, magnanimity, and generosity. We are motivated to achieve because of the enrichment and enjoyment it brings when we help others and contribute to the advancement of society, rather than an obsession to do so out of a repressed fear of inferiority.

The Heart Chakra, or *anāhata,* meaning "invulnerable," is the fourth chakra and the *bridge* between the higher four chakras and the lower three, a mediator between the physical and spiritual realms. It is associated with the element of air, the sense of touch, and with the actions of the hands. The heart chakra is located in the exact center of the chest or ribcage just above the sternum, and its colors are green, pink, and rose gold.

The symbol of the heart chakra is the superposition of two triangles, one pointing upwards and the other downwards, forming a star with six points (*shatkona*), also known as the Star of David or Seal of Solomon. This form symbolically represents the union of Shiva/Shakti, a divine balance between the sacred masculine and feminine energies. When the heart chakra is blocked, true love is always confused with ego love, and therefore we are always dependent on another to compensate for a sense of incompleteness and lacking in the self. We are with another because of an inner compulsion to be, rather than a choice to be. As a consequence, true intimacy cannot be attained because the love given is always conditional. Feelings of possessiveness, jealousy, obsession, and selfishness end up ruining our relationships because we are loving from the brain, not the heart.

When the heart chakra is opened, cleared, and balanced, we learn to love our Selves and others unconditionally—without judgment, condemnation, or expectation. Compassion, acceptance, and intimacy flow freely from the heart. This chakra is also associated with charity, philanthropy, altruistic endeavors, and all forms of psychic healing. When the heart chakra is in balance we feel uninhibited yet grounded. We accept and love our Selves unconditionally. We are trusting and have opened our hearts to receive love, compassion, and generosity from others.

There is also a secret chamber to the heart chakra that is called *ananda-kanda* or "seat of bliss" in Sanskrit. It is located inside the human heart, which is about an inch lower and to the left of the main heart chakra. Its mandala contains eight lotus petals and consists of a "three-fold flame" that is the source of (from left to right) authentic *power*, authentic *wisdom*, and authentic *love*.[6] The colors of the three flames are sky blue, light yellow, and soft pink, respectively.

The **Throat Chakra,** or *viśuddha*, meaning "pure place," is the fifth chakra and is the purification center. It governs higher discrimination, creativity, manifestation, inspiration, and self-expression. This is the power center and its mandala contains sixteen lotus petals and is the center of the blue flame. It is located in the larynx and is associated with the sense of hearing, as well as the action of speaking. Its influences include communication, artistic expression, Self-belief, knowledge, discernment, truth, justice, and clairaudience.

This is the place where Shiva and Shakti begin to celebrate their mystical union. It is a portal to freedom from the confines of the realm of polarity and the material plane, and its element is *akāsha* (white ether), which sits upon a white elephant. If this energy is blocked, our ability to communicate our ideas and/or feelings will be inhibited or distorted. People will misunderstand us or we will make fools out of ourselves by speaking too much about things we know very little about. We tend to have "foot-in-mouth disease," and may also be seen as crass, undiplomatic, and rude. People may find us to be overcritical, blunt, and offensive.

When the throat chakra is open, clear, and balanced, negative experiences are transmuted into wisdom and learning. Subtle imagery, symbols, and ancient archetypes are perceived with keen insight. Communication skills such as writing and speaking are greatly refined. One is viewed as erudite, knowledgeable, and an authority on many subjects. We have an ability to listen and empathize with others; being able to communicate clearly results in Self-empowerment and Self-esteem. We know intuitively when silence is beneficial and when our motivational words can empower others.

The throat chakra is also our creativity center. If it is blocked, we will struggle to manifest our ideas into reality. When it is clear and balanced, the creative process is heart-based rather than mind-based, and therefore we don't attract to us "what we don't want" such as stress, conflict, and drama, but rather we selflessly manifest abundance so that everyone around us benefits, not just us. Our creative powers and self-expression become highly focused, and our beliefs, creativity, and emotional needs are expressed clearly without fear of what others will think, thus we are able to articulate our message cogently to the world.

The **Third Eye Chakra,** or *ājñā,* meaning "command," is the sixth chakra and is the center for the sacred geometry of creation and our psychic abilities. When an image is seen in the mind's eye, or in a dream, it is being viewed by the third eye chakra. It is our intuition or "inner knowing" of things. It is located in between the brow and its flame is the color of indigo. The mandala consists of the yoni flanked by two white lotus petals symbolizing the merger of the ida and pingala nādis with the central channel sushumna, resulting in the *divine bliss* and the dissolution of duality. The mantra associated with this chakra is the sacred Aum (or Om), so this is an excellent mantra to use if your desire is to open your third eye.

When this chakra is blocked, it will affect the physical body by causing a lack of concentration, headaches, confusion, psychological disorders, anxiety, and panic attacks. Also if you are frequently taken advantage of, gullible, or easily deceived, then it's most likely due to a closed ājñā chakra.

The sixth chakra's inner aspect relates to the access of intuition. Mentally, it governs visual consciousness, and emotionally, it governs clarity on an intuitive level. When the third eye chakra is open and cleared, we are bestowed with enhanced psychic powers including clairvoyance, clairaudience, and mental telepathy. We have foresight, insight, hindsight, and keen, high-powered perception into people, situations, and events. We are also able to learn from our past experiences and make solid plans for the future. This chakra is the home of our rationality, emotional intellect, and wisdom. From here we begin to connect to our higher Selves and move beyond the physical plane.

The Crown Chakra or *sahasrāra,* meaning "thousand-petaled lotus," is the seventh chakra located at the roof of the skull—in the same area as the soft spot on a baby's head. Its mandala is the "thousand-petaled, multi-colored lotus," and symbolizes detachment from the realm of maya or *illusion.* The crowns worn by the ancient gods and goddesses were later emulated by the pharaohs, and later kings and queens from a wide variety of nations. This headdress crown was symbolic of the crown chakra flowering. The colors of light of the crown chakra vortex are violet and white.

When the crown chakra is opened by the kundalini Shakti, the ego dissolves, and a realization of the higher Self is attained. When it reaches the crown chakra, the blissful union between Shiva and Shakti occurs,

324

which results in an acute awareness of the true *nonduality* of the Source. When the crown is blocked, we are frequently confused, misinformed, and unaware of spiritual truths. Our vision becomes limited to our material existence. It may be difficult for us to connect with the world around us and to find the true joy in life. Our sense of wonder, spirituality, and creativity will be seriously lacking. The world can be a dense physical place without energy. We may become materialistic, stuck in the past, and worried about the future.

When it is opened, balanced, and cleared, it functions as the *brain* center for the ethereal body. It is the portal to the infinite intelligence and spiritual wisdom of the Source. We simply *know* what is divine truth and what is not. We are able to see far beyond the material world and into our true nature. The more balanced the crown chakra is, the more we will receive guidance and be drawn to esoteric, mystical, metaphysical, and spiritual teachings. And not only will we easily understand these teachings, we will incorporate them into our daily lives. We will also pay attention to our inner guidance and divine spark.

When cleared, the crown chakra allows for inner communications with our higher Selves to take place, and could also be considered the bottomless well from which intuitive knowledge is drawn. When the flowering of the crown chakra is achieved, we become Self-realized, enlightened, and One with the Source.

The Soul Chakra is the eighth chakra, and is the Godhead associated with ascension to the higher realms of consciousness. When you shed your physical sheath, the soul chakra expands into a luminous globe that envelopes the remaining seven chakras and transports the soul to the appropriate frequency plane of the ethereal realm. In spiritual art, it is depicted as a halo or band of light that hovers about six inches to a foot above the head. The soul chakra is the second root chakra, and the "first note" of a higher octave of chakras located above the head.[7]

Dissolving the fear of death.

> Yoda: *Death is a natural part of life. Rejoice for those*
> *around you who transform into the Force. Mourn*
> *them do not. Miss them do not.*
> — *Star Wars Episode III: Revenge of the Sith*

We only live one life. But during this one eternal life we will change forms countless times. As the frequency of Earth continues to rise, more and more souls are remembering their past forms that we call "lifetimes." Nearly all trauma is rooted in past incarnations, not the current lifetime. This is the value of knowing your past lives and in recent years, there have been a growing number of past-life regression hypnotherapists such as Dolores Cannon and Dr. Brian Weiss, who understand the therapeutic benefits that past-life regression can give. They have regressed thousands of individuals from all over the world, and have written some wonderful books about these remarkable cases where primal traumas from past lives are recalled and subsequently *healed*. If you are interested in undergoing a past-life regression, then I suggest contacting the International Association of Regression Research and Therapies (IARRT) for a practitioner near you. Their site: www.iarrt.org.

From the perception of the Next Human, death is always followed with *rebirth* because this is how the evolving universe *grows*. We simply morph from one form to another. The newborn baby form that you were when you were being held in your mother's arms eventually had to "die" before you could become a toddler. And you couldn't become an adolescent until you shed your toddler form, which of course, had to "die" before you could become a teenager. And as your body continues to mature, you will need to shed your current form yet again. So death is, from this higher perspective, much like the serpent shedding its own skin. It is only a death and rebirth of *form*, a trans*form*ation.

In spite of this truth, however, thanatophobia, or "fear of death," is a disease of the mind that plagues a very large majority of our current human population. It is the number one fear that people have. And for *what?* This fear is completely unnecessary and only serves to create stress and disease in the physical body. It is true that the more you fear your own death the more likely you'll attract to you the circumstances to accelerate it. This is simply the law of attraction at work. Remember, thoughts plus emotion constantly create your reality and the universe will send to you whatever you fear because *fear* is the most powerful of all the dark emotions. Anger, hatred, regret, guilt, shame, bitterness, rage, frustration, sorrow, animosity, and hopelessness are all shadows of fear. So once you free yourself completely from the fear of death, which is really a subconscious fear of *transformation*, you will be freed from these other dark emotions as well.

Contrary to popular belief, *birth* is the opposite of death, not life. Because life is eternal for all of us, it has no opposite. Many psychologists and neuroscientists theorize that the reason the fear of death is so prevalent among our species is because it's a survival instinct, a "defense mechanism" that helps to keep us alive. But this is not true. All animals have an innate instinct to protect themselves from becoming prey when they sense danger, i.e. the reactive dinosaur brain which prompts the fight or flight response, but they certainly don't possess a fear of death any more than they have a fear of life.

Children have no fear of death unless we teach them to fear it. Elders and those with terminal illnesses eventually come to know an inexplicable peace at the end of their lives. The current human always fears what he doesn't understand, and to fear death is to face the unknown. But every time you go to sleep at night, you *are* facing the unknown, are you not? Can you guarantee that you'll wake up from your sleep? No, of course not. You are innately trusting in something greater than yourself that you will eventually awaken, and you've been doing this since you were born. So think of dying as the way your soul simply goes to sleep. The only difference is that when you wake up, you're in heaven—the *ethereal plane.*

As the frequency of Planet Earth continues to rise, more and more people will be having IBEs, OBEs, and NDEs. If you visit the website for the Near Death Experience Research Foundation at www.nderf.org, you'll find thousands of NDE testimonials from around the world that have been posted since 1999. The most remarkable account of an NDE that I've ever read about or even *heard of* comes from a truly amazing woman by the name of Anita Moorjani, who—before her NDE—believed from childhood that she needed to somehow prove herself to others and to the world that she deserved to be loved. She was afraid that if she didn't do something, act a certain way, or meet certain expectations, she wouldn't be accepted or appreciated—not just from others, but more importantly, from herself. Because of this, Anita never really learned how to stand up for herself, or love herself unconditionally. Eventually she was diagnosed with Hodgkin's Lymphoma, a cancer that infects the lymph nodes which, in less than four years, progressed to an advanced stage four.

During her NDE, Anita became astutely aware that she is a divine, magnificent, eternal being that is intricately connected to the Source. She also realized that *we are all One*. Because she experienced the truth of her divine *ess*ence, her soul remembered that she exists now and forever beyond the realm of form, that her true Self is nothing less than *pure consciousness*. Before her NDE, no amount of positive thinking, praying, meditating, yoga, chanting, or holistic healing modalities could overpower her ingrained *fear of death* as well as her inability to love herself unconditionally. Even though she forgave everyone in her life who ever caused her pain, she still couldn't forgive herself. And this, she believes, is what brought about the cancer in her body.

So because of Anita's fear, no matter what she did, the universe was unable to reverse the progression of the cancer that was eating her body alive. It wasn't until she finally stopped *fighting* her cancer and *surrendered* completely to her disease that she was freed from the shackles of her deeply entrenched fears.

In her 2012 book, *Dying to be Me: My Journey from Cancer, to Near Death, to True Healing,* Anita reveals the reason for her miraculous recovery back to perfect health:

> *While I was in that state of clarity in the other realm, I instinctively understood that I was dying because of all my fears. I wasn't expressing my true self because my worries were preventing me from doing so. I understood that the cancer wasn't a punishment...It was just my own energy, manifesting as cancer because my fears weren't allowing me to express myself as the magnificent force I was meant to be...I saw that I never loved myself, valued myself, or had seen the beauty of my own soul... This understanding made me realize that I no longer had anything to fear...And so I made one powerful choice: to come back. Once I woke up again in my body, I knew that every single cell would respond to the decision to come back, so I knew I was going to be fine.*[8]

Now, what I found truly incredible about Anita's story is that after she woke up from her coma and returned from the ethereal plane, not only did her cancer go into complete remission from stage four lymphoma, the lemon-sized tumors on her lymph nodes completely disappeared in a matter of *days.* And the multiple lesions on her skin that a reconstructive surgeon had assessed as being too gaping and severe to heal on their own *did just that.* Anita emphasizes in her book that it certainly was not her beliefs that caused her to heal but instead a "complete suspension of all previously held doctrine and dogma" that allowed her body to *reset* itself.[9]

Honoring the intelligent body requires an acceptance and a listening to what the physical Self is trying to communicate *to* you. Know that you're always the creator of your own reality, so that includes any and all disease that forms in your body, no matter how small or severe. Needless to say, I cannot recommend Anita's wonderful book enough to you. It is, without a doubt, one of the most inspirational, spiritually healing, and transformational books you'll ever read.

Another one of my favorite metaphysical books is *Only Love is Real* by Brian Weiss. In it, he documents two cases of past-life regression, a man and a woman who, even though they didn't know each other in the current life, appear from the information revealed during their sessions to have shared similar incarnations in the same places at the same times. I'm not going to tell you anymore because I don't want to spoil it for you but I will say that it's one of the most romantic stories I've ever read. And it's true!

Reincarnation is a natural, normal, necessary part of your evolution. Without it, you simply wouldn't learn, wouldn't *grow*. Mistakes, trauma, and suffering are all part of the process. And forgetting your wounds has also been necessary. After all, when you're ego-identified and you're able to remember a past life where someone "did you in," maimed you, or perhaps even *killed* you, then you're probably not going to think twice about seeking revenge on that soul in the next life. But this, of course, would only perpetuate the karmic cycle and thus no growth would be achieved. Moreover, if you remembered past lives where you hurt other people then, of course, you would have to deal with an incredible amount of regret and guilt in your current incarnation, which would, again, only impede your growth. So, to facilitate your soul's evolution, when you reincarnate, you will naturally have amnesia of prior lives which bestows you with an opportunity to start with a "clean slate" so you can learn how to exercise your free will without harvesting feelings of regret or revenge. Again, free will comes only with *non-reaction* to what happens to you in your life. If you continue to react to situations with fear-based drama, then the karmic wheel will continue to spin.

Today, because so many souls are finally transcending their egos, they're being allowed to remember past lives. Revenge doesn't enter into their minds because they are living purely from the heart. These are the souls on this planet who have grown past this vindictive and unforgiving stage of personal evolution. And not only have they completely forgiven the other for all past harms inflicted, they have also forgiven their Selves. These are the souls who are now ready to take an evolutionary leap forward—to become like *gods* and *goddesses*—and to realize that together, we are One. This is what this book is all about, and if you are one of these souls who is ready to evolve, then this book is meant for you. Congratulations. You *are* the Next Human.

Connecting with your life force.

I would now like to give you some tools that will help you to connect with your own life force, your prana, chi, ki, or mana within your ethereal Self, so that you can bring it into your physical Self. This will allow you to feel the divine electrical energy firsthand. You can use it for the empowering and healing of your physical, mental, and ethereal bodies. You can also use it to empower and heal others. This will also help you to facilitate your own kundalini awakening, if it is your desire to do so.

The *first* step is to begin living every moment in the eternal Now. This is the most important part of the process. If you are lost in your egoic mind and are constantly reacting to people and situations, then you are not aligning your frequency with the life force within.

The *second* step is to read and study as many metaphysical books and literature, watch as many videos and programs, and listen to as many radio shows on spiritual and New Age topics as you can. You may also want to hire a spiritual teacher or coach who can help guide you on your transformational path toward enlightenment. It is true that the more high-frequency information you feed your mind, the more your body's resonance will become in *tune* with the frequency of the life force within.

The *third* step is to transcend your ego, the pseudo self (see Evolution 101). The *fourth* step is to transcend your ego's shadow, the phantom self (see Evolution 201). The *fifth* step is to honor your intelligent body by feeding it a balanced, sugar-free, nutrient-dense, ketogenic diet (see Evolution 301).

The *sixth* step to help you connect with your life force is through physical practices. There are a number of them but my top four recommendations are *yoga, chigong, tai chi,* and *pranic breathing.*

The word *yoga* is derived from the Sanskrit root *yuj,* meaning "union," and its ultimate purpose is to unite or *bind* the sacred feminine and masculine energies (yin/yang) into One for the purpose of attaining enlightenment. This is fulfilled by the raising of the Serpent of Light, the kundalini Shakti, from the base of the spine to the top of the skull.

Yoga originated from the lost continent of Lemuria during a long peaceful age of abundance in which humans had plenty of time to search within. It blossomed organically, out of the intuition and spontaneity of the practitioner. The goal of the yogi/yogini was to ascend into the immortal realms of pure spirit, to imbibe the omniscience of the divine, heal any and all dis*ease* within the physical and ethereal sheaths, liberate the ego, and end all suffering. At some time around 200 BCE these practices were written down by Patañjali in India and thus gained a structure of training and discipline that evolved into various systems given out by contemporary gurus. This structure was called the *Eight Limbs of Patañjali's Yoga* which are as follows:

1. Five *yamas* or *social disciplines*:
   a. Respect, reverence, and compassion for all living things.
   b. Right communication.
   c. Non-attachment.
   d. Moderation in all actions.
   e. Non-greediness.
2. Five *niyamas* or *personal disciplines*:
   a. Cleanliness.
   b. Contentment.
   c. Balance and harmony.

   d. Introspection.

   e. An acute awareness of the life force that dwells within every atom of the universe.

3. *Asāna* or "correct postures for a healthy and vital body."
4. *Prānāyāma* or "breath control" of pranic life force.
5. *Pratyāhāra* or "mastery over the senses."
6. *Dhāranā* or "focused presence."
7. *Dhyāna* or "meditative stillness."
8. *Samādhi* or "becoming One with the Source, i.e. the whole, non-dual, singular consciousness."

Chigong is a practice of aligning breath, movement, and awareness for exercise, healing, and meditation. With roots in Chinese medicine, martial arts, and philosophy, chigong is traditionally viewed as a practice to cultivate and balance your chi life force within the body. During a typical session, rhythmic breathing is coordinated with slow, stylized repetition of fluid movement, and a calm, highly present state of mind helps the practitioner to visualize and direct the chi throughout the body. Chigong is practiced throughout China and the world, and is not only a wonderful meditation and a healthy exercise but a wellness modality recommended by alternative medicine practitioners for a number of physical ailments.

Tai chi is also a wonderful way to help you connect with the life force within. It is a combination of both hard and soft Chinese martial art techniques that help to increase blood circulation and physical longevity. Not only is it an excellent physical exercise, it is calming, balancing, and increases circulation. Tai chi focuses on allowing the life force energy to flow freely through you, thus clearing out any lingering energy blockages in your chakras. It also helps you to become centered in the Now, and raises the frequency of your physical Self. Like yoga, it has become extremely popular in America recent years.

The fourth physical modality I recommend to help you connect with your life force energy is ***pranic breathing***. This is simply the closing of one nostril at a time, breathing through it and exhaling through your mouth. Do this seven times on the right side (pingala) and seven times on the left side (ida) once a day—alternating between left and right with each breath. And when you breathe, know that you're breathing in *prana*, not air. I also suggest that you place the tip of your tongue on the roof of your mouth (just behind your front teeth) when you do. This allows for an easier flow of life force energy through the nādis, which will help it to penetrate every cell in your body.

Weeks, months, even years before a full-blown kundalini awakening, you may become aware of brief glimpses into altered states of consciousness. You may begin to notice "echoes" of specific words from your thoughts or speech mirrored by someone speaking on the television, radio, or from others around you at work or in a public place. You may begin to see repeating patterns on a clock. For example, the minutes will—in abnormal frequency—reflect the number 11 such as 11:11 or 7:11 or 1:11. You may also notice repeating numbers on the clock such as 12:12 or 3:33, or if your birthday is, say, May 24, you may repeatedly wake up at 5:24 a.m. and look at your bedroom clock. You may also observe an increase in peculiar synchronicities occurring in your daily or weekly life, or you could suddenly start to dream more lucidly and vividly. A dramatic increase in extra sensory powers such as claircognizance (knowing things before they happen) or clairaudience (hearing words being spoken audibly) are also signs that an IBE may be on the horizon.

Another sign is to become aware of subtle and sporadic feelings of euphoria after a session of pranic breathing, meditation, yoga, tai chi, or even following a glass of wine. These blissful feelings are due to the brain's release of a chemical from the pineal gland known as Dimethyltryptamine (DMT)—also called "the spirit molecule"—which is a naturally occurring neurotransmitter (similar in structure to serotonin) found in the human brain that is also ubiquitous throughout the plant kingdom. For centuries, shamans of the Amazon rainforest have used Ayahuasca brew as a medicine and "plant teacher" that has greatly facilitated their exploration into altered states of consciousness that are very similar to those experienced during a kundalini awakening.

The **seventh** and final recommendation I have for you on connecting with your life force and awakening the Serpent of Light is to *know* that the kundalini resides within you, and also know that she is coiled right now inside your tailbone even though she may be dormant, at rest. Further know that the kundalini of your body connects you directly to the kundalini of Gaia Sophia, Mother Earth. In the ancient Hindu spiritual practice of tantra, the kundalini gland is called the "coccygeal body" which is an irregular, oval-shaped gland between the rectal wall and the tip of the coccyx. When you begin to feel tingling, pulsations, or rhythmic movement in this area, then this will be a sign that the Shakti is becoming active. By acknowledging her presence there it's as if you're sending her an "invitation" to awaken and *rise*.

If you believe that you've had, are having, or are about to have a personal kundalini awakening and would like to connect with others with whom you may be sharing the same symptoms, I suggest contacting the Kundalini Research Foundation (KRN) at www.kundalininet.org. It is founded by an international group of researchers, health care professionals, and scholars who are educated on the wide variety of kundalini symptoms, and its transformational powers of unity consciousness.

In summary.

The kundalini experience I have described in this chapter reflects my personal awakening, and the range and intensity of the symptoms experienced will vary from one initiate to the next. The initial awakening may be more subtle in some, and more violent in others. As you can probably tell from reading this chapter's memoir, I had no clue as to what a kundalini awakening was when it occurred eleven years ago. Even though I had read a little about her, I didn't really understand what was happening to me until years later when I began my extensive research. After all, the difference between merely *reading* about a kundalini awakening and actually *experiencing* one firsthand is incomparable. You could probably read and study what the astronauts wrote about on their journey to the moon to the point of earning a "Ph.D. in astronaut research" but until you actually become an astronaut and travel into the heavens yourself, you'll never fully appreciate what it's like.

For about two weeks following May 11, 2001, the altered states of consciousness continued in the same intensity then very gradually waned over a period of four months until September 11, 2001. On that day, the Shakti subsided and became relatively quiet until January 11, 2005, when she began to rise again. Since that time, I have experienced—over a period of seven years—well over a hundred subsequent kundalini "risings"—some of them violent but most of them very pleasant—where she focused more on the clearing, balancing, and spinning of my chakras, especially the heart chakra. During these transformational *risings*, I received a renewed and more detailed understanding of what I refer to as the *construct* or innerverse—what we define as the physical realm of duality. Also during the subsequent risings, I frequently heard the sound of children (no doubt angels) chanting, the sound of thunder clapping (during clear skies), and beautiful mantric sounds that some refer to as the "music of the spheres." Much of the automatic writing received since May 11, 2011 has been shared with you in this book. And gratefully, the sacred Shakti is still "alive and kicking" in my body as I write these words.

Even though it appeared to occur spontaneously, the kundalini did not ascend in my body until I had gone deeply *within* and explored my inner Self for over a decade. And even though I transcended my pseudo self and became Self-realized during the initial awakening, my ego eventually returned and reclaimed a firm hold over my mind (except briefly during subsequent risings) until September 11, 2007, the day that my nephew Hudson was born. The months and years following that time have permitted me to become more and more conscious of the ego, to the point where I am now able to successfully transcend it, thus exercising my previously untouched *free will*.

As I reflect on those prior years of immense suffering, the chronic fatigue syndrome and other diseases I endured turned out to be tremendous blessings in disguise. Since I had very little energy to do much of anything, I escaped my debilitating disease and depression by immersing my mind in the studies of metaphysics, philosophy, comparative religion, alternative medicine, holistic wellness, transpersonal psychology, and theoretical physics. I received spiritual counseling, past life regressions, practiced tai chi and yoga, meditated, and did everything else I could to *heal*: spiritually, mentally, and physically. I somehow knew that if I practiced right action, spiritual discipline, and just kept *searching* for *why* I was suffering, I would someday eventually discover the truth, find the answers. So I didn't give up. Then one day, the sacred Serpent of Light simply awakened in me—like a bolt of lightning out of the blue.

EVOLUTION
701

THE ZERO-POINT SELF
BECOMING ONE WITH THE SOURCE

Neo: *Tell me how I separated my mind from my body without jacking in. Tell me how I stopped four sentinels by thinking it. Tell me just what the hell is happening to me.*

Oracle: *The power of the One extends beyond this world. It reaches from here all the way back to where it came from.*

Neo: *Where?*

Oracle: **The Source.**

—*The Matrix Revolutions*

My ally is the Source. And a powerful ally it is. When you are finally ready to become One *with* it, your entire being resonates with the timeless eternity of the Now. The time has finally come for humanity to recognize and realize its true potential, its *divinity*. This is known as Self-realization, a coming to consciousness that you are the epicenter of all creation, a goddess or god clothed in flesh. As you awaken to this esoteric truth, you will further awaken to the truth that every One else on this planet is potentially divine. Therefore, this is not an ego*centric* perspective, but one that is ego*less*. It is the difference between knowing the path and walking the path to spiritual enlightenment. A passion for helping others becomes your new focus in life. Anxiety, depression, and physical disease are replaced with inner peace, compassion, and unconditional love for all of humanity, not just a select few. As you change your "little me who means nothing to the universe" perspective to an "I am the center of all creation" perspective, your whole existence and reason for living transforms. You become a living and breathing example of the eternal light that was always there but never allowed yourself or others to see. You start to awaken to your relevance, your significance, your duty to life, and you realize that the universe cannot evolve until *you* do.

Unfortunately, the current human does not yet see herself as being needed by the universe, nor does she see herself as divine. Instead, she sees herself as a mental concept in her head. This is what we call the *ego*. The Next Human, on the other hand, will have transcended this very limiting and dangerous perception of the self. In so doing, he will be aware of a gap or *rift* in between what was originally perceived as "I" and that of Source consciousness. This awareness reunites the Self to the spiritual dimension, and can also be described as a space *in between* your thoughts. As you gradually invite more and more of this space into your life, you will naturally widen the rift. This is what I call *zero-point* consciousness. This transformation is the next stage of human evolution.

Modern astronomers claim to have proven that our universe contains a multitude of black holes, which are giant stars that have collapsed into infinitesimal size. This happens when a massive star reaches a point where it's only able to hold its shape because the outward force of its radiation balances the attractive force of its gravity. When the star stops burning, the force of gravity becomes so immense that not even the densely-packed mass can support itself, and consequently, the star quickly shrinks in size until it's compressed to the size of a pinhead, then to the size of a microbe, then to the size of an atom, and then it just keeps going until its size equals **zero** in all spatial dimensions: infinite density, infinite temperature, and infinite space-time curvature. The star has now become a black hole. This "zero-point" size is called a *singularity*. When you finally *know* (not merely believe) that you are part of a *singular*, infinite, all-pervading consciousness, you have evolved into what I call the *zero-point Self.*

Know this: you are not and never have been separate from the divine. When you become aware of this esoteric truth, you must also accept that no One else can be separate from the divine. The cosmic Force that binds the universe together is within all of us. A more common term used today to describe this unity/zero-point consciousness is *nonduality,* which is nothing new but a very ancient concept stemming back to Advaita Vedānta, the philosophical branch of Hinduism. The Sanskrit word *advaita* translates "not two."

As mentioned in Evolution 501, every particle or object, from the tiniest quark to the largest quasar, and every single form of creation in between, is *in* you and not physically "out there." This is what I call the *innerverse* or what quantum physicists call "nonlocality." This current theory in physics of nonlocality poses that by your very nature, you are seamlessly connected to everything in the universe; the planets, stars, galaxies, and to every soul in existence.

The ultimate truth behind the mystery of mysteries is that you are *beyond* the ephemeral entropy of things; beyond form, beyond objects, beyond particles, beyond gases, and even beyond energy itself. This is the pure, unmanifested vacuum of no-*thing*-ness. And it is at this zero-point core where there is only *One*. All of our differences, both large and small, between people and nations dissolve in this zero-point state. Conflicts, arguments, violence, and wars seem absurd, *ludicrous*. Forgiveness doesn't even enter into the equation because from here, no matter what that person, tribe, faction, party, or nation did, there was never anything to forgive. Everything that we perceived to be negative was purposeful and engineered for our growth, our evolution.

We have always been now here and always will be *nowhere*. There is only us. From here, there is no beginning and there is no end. There is no "was" and there is no "will be." There is only the Now. This subtle *undercurrent* in between your thoughts is indeed a void, a vacuum, a singular and formless consciousness. It is the zero-point Source from whence everything in the universe simply *is*.

A God of war.

The adherence to and belief in an ideology or religion can never reveal to you your own divinity because in religion, egoic doctrine tends to smother out the divine fire that can only be found from with*in*. The once pure spirituality that all religions have been initially founded on, has—primarily due to the power-hungry male ego—been replaced with dogmatism for the purpose of *control* over its followers. If you want to study the enlightening material of the ancients without the influence of dogma, then I suggest looking into the philosophies of Kabbalah, Sufism, Zen Buddhism, Advaita Vedānta, the Upanishads, the *Tào Té Chīng*, and Gnosticism, and leave the dogma well enough alone.

We are now in the nascent stages of a New Age of Enlightenment, and if we continue to allow dogma to be forced down our throats, it's only going to result in a serious regurgitation. When humans finally recognize the divinity in their Selves, there will no longer be a need to look for God in a temple, church, mosque, synagogue, tent, or any other confined, limited, or designated "outer" space.

Throughout my life I believed that if I obeyed the doctrines set forth by a particular creator or "God" and did his will, then I would, in turn, be loved, rewarded, blessed, and protected for my practices and *faith*. But I never stopped to think that if this were true, then the God that I believed in only bestowed his love to me on the precondition that I accepted *him*, prayed to *him* and placed my faith in *him*. Eventually I began to realize that my mind had fashioned a God who was just like *me*. After all, I never really loved anyone who didn't love me back. My love, like my God's love, was conditional and selective. I was also critical, harsh, and judgmental toward myself and others, and I if I didn't measure up to my inordinately high standards, then I would give myself a "mental whipping." I hated my constant and never-ending illnesses and I hated my body for coming down with them. I hated my art. I hated my writing. I hated my looks. I also believed very strongly that I had to *do* something to be worthy of love. Whenever a family member would say, "I'm so proud of you," my response would be, "But I haven't *done* anything yet." And since I never felt worthy of receiving love, whenever someone would compliment me, it just made me feel, well, uncomfortable. So, I loved my Self very little and whenever I did, it was highly conditional. Looking back, it was no wonder that I perceived God in the exact same way.

If you are a Christian, then you must accept Jesus Christ as Lord and Savior because, well, if you don't then you don't get to reap the rewards of a heavenly afterlife. If one is a devout or orthodox member of any particular religion, then his or her behavior will be extremely restricted by a *system of control* masqueraded by its clergy under the guise of "moral values." Of course, teaching moral values is important, but being commanded to adhere to them "or else" is not only psychologically abusive, it's not unconditional love. Moreover, you cannot instill moral values into anyone who is not ready to become spiritual, and so when you are forced to obey the commandments and doctrine of a particular religion it will inevitably result in a cognitive dissonance. This subtle coercion that is intrinsic to dogmatic religions only serves to stunt your spiritual growth, and to seriously delay your Self-realization.

Beginning with the Council of Nicea in 325 CE, and the Roman government embracing Christianity as its official religion, the male ego took *charge* of the moral discourse of the Western world and has *been* in charge ever since. On January 29, 2002, and repeatedly throughout his presidency, President George W. Bush labeled Iran, Iraq, and North Korea the "axis of evil" as well all other governments accused of assisting terrorism and seeking weapons of mass destruction. Subsequently, the War of Iraq that caused the deaths of nearly 5,000 troops and over 100,000 innocent civilians, in the eyes of President Bush, was seen as a Christian moral crusade against the tyranny of evil. Wars continue to be fought, lives continue to be lost, and blood continues to be spilled around the globe, and for whom? No one else but the ***God of war***.

As I write these words there are currently eight U.S. Republican Party candidates running for the presidency. Some of the candidates have publicly admitted to being on a "mission" or "battle" to become President all in the name of their Christian God. They frequently use divisive phrases such as "take the country back" and "continue the fight." Many are staunch, right-wing conservatives who oppose a "woman's right to choose" and oppose equal rights for gay people. They recklessly impose their Christian morals onto the "infidels," because, well, they just see themselves as morally superior. Some of them have even referenced our founding fathers to substantiate their Christian ideology, but they are obviously unaware of the fact that our founding fathers were *deists*, not *theists*, meaning that they believed in a divine consciousness that created the universe, but that this consciousness was indifferent to creation and not an egoic personality who limited his favor, love, and protection to only those who worshiped *him*. This patriarchal, insane "my God is the true God and your God is the false God" mentality has to ***stop*** if we're going to survive as a species. There simply is no other way.

In the early history of our patriarchal society, war was simply the way of life. If deemed worthy, boys were raised and trained to become warriors in ancient Greece and Rome. If a particular nation state viewed another as having a different opinion about the world (religiously, politically, economically), they were declared the enemy. Generally, foreign nations were seen as the enemy just because they *were* foreign. What the male ego didn't understand, it feared, and therefore perceived as a threat to its very survival. "Divide and conquer" became its mantra. Eventually, war became so prevalent among ancient Rome that toward the end of its reign as the world's most powerful nation, the Roman people didn't even know what they were fighting over. Consequently, all the money the Roman government spent on war ended up bankrupting its treasury and causing its demise. Sound familiar? It seems that history may be repeating itself right before our very eyes. As I write this, the United States of America spends $600 billion on defense annually and has over 300,000 troops deployed far and wide in over 150 countries for reasons unclear, which has, in effect, nearly bankrupted the U.S. treasury.[1,2] And all for *what?* Domestic security? Come on. Wake up America! Just as it was in ancient Rome, ***you are funding a patriarchal empire.***

Many popular religious texts and books have been written and edited by egoic men in search of power and control over the masses. Jesus loved every One unconditionally and if he were on earth in the physical form today, he most certainly would *not* be a Christian. Not only does Christian doctrine foster delusions of superiority over those who are not Christian, it also bolsters the dangerous fallacy that humans need to be separated according to their beliefs. So where's the unconditional love, the Holy Spirit, in *this belief?*

Many current humans think that just because a particular soul has special talents, they must be, in turn, worshipped. We observe this all the time with public performers such as musicians and actors. But this idolization of souls is nothing but an inflation of the ego, making the idolized appear to be more special, i.e. "very important people." Ergo, the idolizer's ego extracts power vicariously from the idolized. It's as if the ego says, "Because I'm smart enough to identify someone who is incredibly talented and therefore special, I, too, must be special." Take Jesus for example. In the last two millennia, the egoic human has exalted him to the status of God, and therefore those who worshipped him were elevated to be special and separate from the infidels who did not accept him as God. But Jesus, like you and me, was also human, and before he could be come a wise, compassionate, and sympathetic counselor, he had to first confront the demons that every human does. How else could he understand first-hand why humans suffer? How else could he know that the Kingdom of God was within each and every One of us? His divinity exemplified what we can all become when we transcend the ego, become heart-centered, and merge with our higher Selves. Because he was far more evolved than every other human on Earth during his time, Jesus became a highly revered spiritual teacher. In spite of this simple truth, however, an entire religion was founded around his status as God himself in the flesh, indoctrinating that those who worship him are saved and those who don't, are, well, condemned to an eternal burning damnation in *hell*.

Throughout the thousands of edited revisions of the Bible, man has perceived God in his own *egoic* image. Because the current human is living his life from the level of his pseudo self, he concocts a God that must meet that same level of narcissism. So, naturally, the God of Abraham, Isaac, and Jacob is seen through similar lenses by the Jew, Muslim, and Christian as a vengeful, judgmental, controlling, dictatorial, punishing, *male* deity.

The Next Human will understand that a priest, rabbi, monk, imam, or minister is not a necessary "middle man" to the divine. He will know that the material forms of doctrine or a "brick and mortar" temple of worship is, well, unnecessary to communicate directly with God. He will instinctively know that he is already divine, already "saved." He will realize that the Source of All resides within each and every One, and therefore the search for God begins and ends with the Self. He will know that God is not "out there" somewhere waiting to be discovered, accepted, or worshipped, and is certainly not limited to a singular personality because the divine is both singular *and* plural, dual *and* nondual. When you finally evolve into the zero-point Self, the notion that God must be separate from you will seem, well, a little *silly*.

The Next Human will intuitively know that her soul does not need to worship a particular spiritual teacher or accept him as her "messiah" in order to get into heaven, because she will understand this to be a patriarchal tenet based on conditional love that was concocted for one specific purpose: *control*. She will know that every soul is on its own righteous path back to the zero-point Source, in its own way, in its own time, and does not need to be *codependent* upon another soul for its own personal "salvation." She will realize that we all create our own reality through our actions and reactions, and are therefore individually and solely responsible for our personal evolution. The time has come for us to *grow up* and become spiritually independent, Self-reliant "soul adults" on the ladder of evolutionary consciousness. The time has come, dear reader, for a spiritual *revolution*.

Mind before matter.

Einstein once said, "The most incomprehensible thing about the world is that it is comprehensible." What if physics and metaphysics have been on tangential paths in their pursuit of the truth about creation, each one stemming from distinct perceptions of reality but ultimately converging at a singular point of divine truth?

I believe that a unified field theory or "one theory of everything" will be proved to be true very soon. There is indeed a divine order to the cosmos, an underlying intelligence. Some define this intelligence as "physics" and leave it at that. But is it so hard to comprehend that physics and metaphysics are simply two different ways of explaining what is ultimately the same thing?

In quantum mechanics there's a principle known as *entanglement* or nonlocal connection. This is no longer a theory but a real phenomenon. The physicists John Bell and Alain Aspect established that the universe at its most basic level is nonlocal. It proves that—once particles physically interact at the quantum level—information between them no longer needs to travel from point A to point B because it doesn't need to travel at all. This interpretation presents us with the vision of a participatory universe in which everything is unified and interdependent: a seamless *whole.*

Einstein called entanglement "spooky action at a distance," which has been demonstrated repeatedly through experimentation. It's the way in which two or more particles of energy sharing common origins become correlated to predictably interact with each other, even if these particles are separated over large distances. In other words, they remain intertwined, interconnected, *one* with each other, even though they appear to be separated. Ostensibly, on the quantum level, appearances are deceiving.

What is truly amazing about their entanglement is that their communication is infinitely faster than the speed of light. It is operating instantaneously, at the speed of, well, *thought.* It's as if the spacetime between the two particles being measured never even existed. Perhaps this is because these interacting particles are connected somewhere beyond the realm of spacetime, as in a *zero-point field?*

In a sense, the human body is quantum entangled with the Earth because the body responds to the Earth's natural biorhythms and circadian cycles. No doubt, the female's menstrual cycle is entangled with the cycles of the moon. The ancient art of astrology is an excellent example of quantum entanglement with the planets, stars, and constellations of the heavens.

In his September 19, 2009, Sirius XM radio show, spiritual teacher, Deepak Chopra interviewed theoretical physicist Michio Kaku, and commented on this nonlocal phenomenon of entanglement, saying, "You know, the more I hear about quantum entanglement, it sounds like a mathematical description of omniscience, omnipresence, omnipotence." To which Dr. Kaku responded, "That's what it leads to. Their theory says that I exist because you look at me, somebody looks at you so you exist, so who looks at her? Who looks at us? Well, God."[3]

Quantum physics was discovered through the study of the motion of elementary particles at the subatomic level, so it's assumed by many materialists that entanglement must be restricted to the quantum world. But I believe this to be an extremely limiting view of what entanglement is really revealing to us. Unexplained supernatural phenomena such as synchronicity, telepathy, telekinesis, remote viewing, clairaudience, clairsentience, clairvoyance, and other psychic powers are clear examples of quantum entanglement. Moreover, mystics, oracles, artists, poets, musicians, yogis, sages, and shamans have been transcending the local mind and accessing nonlocal consciousness since the advent of our species.

I believe that the property of quantum entanglement is evidence in support of a zero-point, singular consciousness. It clearly demonstrates that the world of physical matter is preceded by a "behind the scenes" spaceless and timeless Source, and because of this, no spacetime is required in between two objects at the quantum level. In truth, there is no separation at all. Spacetime itself becomes an illusion. How else can these particles interact simultaneously? As Sir Arthur Conan Doyle so eloquently communicated through his character, Sherlock Holmes: "When you eliminate the *impossible*, whatever remains, however *improbable*, must be the truth." Well then, we know it's impossible for these particles to interact seamlessly unless they were never separated to begin with. Therefore, *mind before matter* is the correct order of the equation for creation, not matter manifesting itself randomly or "spontaneously" so that consciousness can "sprout from nothingness." That's utterly ridiculous. A unified zero-point consciousness simply *is*.

The hive mind.

So what is consciousness anyway? Conventional scientists tell us that it's nothing more than electrical signals bouncing around in our brains. But new evidence suggests that there exists a *hive mind.* In the Princeton University's Global Consciousness Project, random number generators (RNGs)—also called "eggs"—have been placed in 70 host sites around the world beginning in the late 1990s and have tracked the minds of millions of people for the purpose of detecting anomalous *spikes* in what would normally be randomized data.

This is how it works: Quantum event based RNGs produce completely unpredictable sequences of zeroes and ones. When human consciousness becomes synchronized, the behavior of these random, unpredictable sequences are altered to non-random, predictable, cohesive behavior. This consistently happens when a great event—such as a tsunami, an Olympics, or Academy Awards broadcast—synchronizes the feelings of millions of people into a feeling of One. That's when the RNGs become structured. The probability of this is less than one in a billion that this is due to chance. This evidence suggests an emerging noosphere or *hive mind.*

"We may be able to predict that a major world event is going to happen," says Roger Nelson, the GCP leader, then added, "But we won't know exactly what will happen or where it's going to happen."[4] In response to critics' accusations of the Princeton team looking too hard at raw data to find patterns, Nelson disagrees, saying, "We're perfectly willing to discover that we've made mistakes, but we haven't been able to find any, and neither has anyone else."[5]

For example, the 1997 funeral ceremonies for Princess Diana and the 1998 international Winter Olympics in Nagano, Japan, generated shared emotions and a consciousness coherence that resulted in an anomaly in what would otherwise be random data. On 9/11, the RNG eggs began recording non-random, ordered numbers beginning at 5:00 a.m. EST that eventually led to some the most significant anomalies ever received by the GCP. But what was truly interesting about this event was that the anomalies began occurring nearly *four hours prior* to the first airplane collision (see graph[6] below). It was as if the hive mind somehow *pre-sensed* that something very terrible was looming on the horizon. It's also evident from this project that the hive mind doesn't just *react* to major events but it is inextricably connected *to* them. This proves incontrovertibly that we are all part of a unified global consciousness.

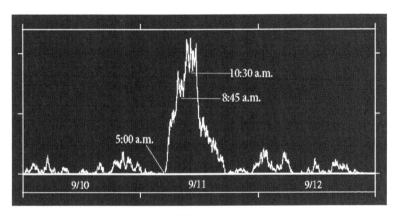

Courtesy of the Global Consciousness Project

A holographic universe.

If you take a holographic portrait of your mother (from head to foot) and produce the photo onto holographic film, then with a pair of scissors cut out just her face and then enlarge that portion to the photo's original size, the result will not be an enlarged version of your mom's face, but rather a restored portrait of the original whole-body version. In other words, in each tiny, little *pixel* of the picture will be stored all the information of the source imprint or *whole* picture in condensed form. Similarly, if you were able to convert your favorite movie into a holographic film, and you cut out one single "frame" of that film, then that would mean that one single frame must retain *all* the information of every other frame in the entire movie. And so now I ask you: what if life itself was being projected to us by a sort of virtually interactive "holographic projector," but instead of a movie or TV screen receiving the imagery, it's being converted from a 2D source imprint to 3D reality solely by an organic "holographic computer" that you call your *brain?* Well, according to the *holographic principle* in quantum physics, it *is.*

In 1981, renowned physicist Stephen Hawking argued that black holes destroy everything they swallow without a trace. However, a principal author of string theory, Leonard Susskind, passionately disagreed, and began working on formulating a theory that would prove Hawking wrong. This was known as the "Black Hole War." Twenty-eight years later, Susskind finally solved the problem. Susskind's new principle says that the event horizon of a black hole is a 2D representation of a 3D object at its center. Ergo, no energy or "information" is lost. In 2004 at a scientific conference in Dublin, Hawking conceded defeat to Susskind and a new understanding of physics was discovered. This exciting new principle not only reveals how black holes store information, but how our entire 3D universe stores information as well. Because of Susskind's work, "holographic theory" is no longer a theory but now a fundamental principle of physics.

I believe that the source of supernatural powers could be explained under the holographic principle as described by David Bohm, a former protégé of Einstein and one of the world's most respected quantum physicists. Bohm proposed that there are two orders of reality: the implicate order and the explicative order. The *explicative* order is our interpretive or perceived 3D universe that *unfolds* from the *implicative* order, which is a deeper, unseen 2D informational source imprint or "frequency realm" where the laws of spacetime don't apply. This process can be compared to the same way in which a piece of holographic film gives birth to a hologram. Bohm uses these terms because he sees the manifestation of all forms in the universe as the result of countless enfoldings and unfoldings between these two orders.[7] In other words, Bohm characterizes consciousness as a process in which at each moment, content that was previously a 2D source or "film imprint" becomes presently our perceived 3D reality, and content which was previously a 3D effect reality gets stored as a 2D film imprint. So in a sense, the universe is always just "one step ahead of us." Bohm theorized this many decades before Susskind established it as a principle for the way black holes store information.

In addition, one of the founders of transpersonal psychology, Stanislov Grof, reasoned that if the implicative and explicative orders are accurate descriptions of our true reality, then "it would be possible to modify phenomena in the phenomenal world by influencing their generative matrix."[8] In other words, if we could somehow access the source imprint—the 2D holographic film—then we could alter the current 3D reality.

A collaborator with David Bohm, the esteemed psychologist Karl Pribram, also concluded that the brain operates like a hologram. He discovered that the neurons in the brain acted much like a laser does when bounced off an object to be photographed. A hologram is only visible because of a similar "interference pattern" created by the laser. Although to the naked eye the holographic film appears as nothing more than concentric rings, when a laser beam is shined through the film, the original object materializes.[9] According to Pribram, in the explicate or manifest realm of space and time, things and events are indeed separate and discrete. However, *behind the scenes*, in the implicate or frequency realm, "all things and events are spacelessly, timelessly, intrinsically, one and undivided."[10] In simpler terms: *a seamless whole*.

So, for every scene that you view as a 3D reality, there is concurrently a 2D holographic film version of it that's completely scrambled yet contains the same exact information. In other words, it is the human brain that unscrambles the holographic version of what we perceive as reality or what Plato referred to as the "world of forms." What you are constantly interpreting as reality in this universe/innerverse is nothing less than a single unified frequency manifesting itself into a holographic

3D, interactive, virtual movie. In the underlying frequency realm, everything is timeless, spaceless, nondual, and One. A *Source* consciousness.

The zero-point singularity.

1. *There exists movement in the world.*
2. *Things that move were set into motion by something else.*
3. *If everything that moves were caused to move by something else, there would be an infinite chain of causes. This cannot happen.*
4. *Thus, there must have been something that caused the first movement.*
5. *From 3, this first cause cannot itself have been moved.*
6. *From 4, there must be an unmoved mover.*

—Aristotle, *Metaphysics Book XII*

In 1915, Albert Einstein published his General Theory of Relativity and today it remains the geometric theory of gravitation. It generalizes special relativity and Newton's law of universal gravitation, providing a unified description of gravity as a geometric property of space and time, or spacetime.

In the center of a black hole, the singularity causes the physics as we know them to break down completely. In a 2011 episode of the Science Channel's *How the Universe Works*, professor Michio Kaku had this to say about a zero-point, black hole singularity: "A singularity is a point of infinite gravity where space and time become meaningless. Now that is ridiculous. A singularity is basically a word for saying, 'I don't know.' It's a word for saying, 'I'm clueless.'"[11]

A physicist will be happy to teach you how you came to be, how you got here. But it's left to the *meta*physicist to offer insight as to *why* you are here. The term metaphysics, dating back to the works of Aristotle, simply means "beyond physics." And as it turns out, Aristotle was right. Physicists can aptly explain how matter forms from energy, how atoms form from electrons, protons, and neutrons, and how people form from stars. But in spite of all the explaining of how things happen, we are still left with the age-old, unanswered question of *how and why did space and time **begin?***

The solution to the problem lies in the truth that everything that has a beginning must also have an end. Like a 0 or the number 8, the zero-point Source has no beginning, and therefore has no end. It was never the Source of the past and it will never be the Source of the future. It is only the Source of the eternal Now, in the ever-existing sea of cosmic consciousness.

To propose that the Big Bang was the advent of form which eventually evolved into us, i.e. the human brain and subsequently consciousness is *false*. The only thing that the Big Bang did was mark the beginning of a universe of form. As the ancient Greek philosopher Plato concluded from the observation of the world, concepts cannot be derived from experience, but can only *precede* it. In other words, mind always comes before matter. For example, the idea of an airplane had to be envisioned by the Wright Brothers *before* they could design and fly it. Idea plus visualization plus intention plus action is the simple equation for every material form created since the beginning of the human race.

Every form we as sentient beings have fashioned, from the book in front of you to the civilization that surrounds you, was originally just a thought, a mere idea in someone's head. So why should it be any different when we wind the clocks back 13.7 billion years to the explosion of the Big Bang? The *micro* world is always a reflection of the *macro* world, and vice versa. As above, so below. Ergo, human consciousness is no different from Source consciousness. Thus, Source consciousness has always *preceded* all universes of form. It is the impulse, the divine spark, the inspiration, and the idea preceding creation itself. Indeed, it is the *unmoved mover.* Because Source consciousness was needed before the universe of form could exist, the Big Bang cannot be the "first cause" or spontaneously create itself from nothingness as Stephen Hawking theorizes.

The best way to comprehend Source consciousness is to meditate in the Now. In reality, the past and future are only conceptual reference points. They don't intrinsically exist. The eternal Now, on the other hand, does, always. No matter what time it is on the clock, or where you are in the world at any given moment, it will always be the Now. Even if you had access to a time machine and were able to travel backwards or forwards in time a million years, it will still be the Now. Ruminate on *that.*

The One.

> *You, you may say I'm a dreamer,*
> *but I'm not the only one*
> *I hope some day you'll join us*
> *And the world will be as one*
> —John Lennon, *Imagine*

The One is not limited to an identity; it is egoless and genderless. The One is not limited by space; it is everywhere and nowhere. The One is not limited by time; it is eternal. The One is not limited by knowledge; it is omniscient. The One is not limited by power; it is omnipotent. There is no boundary between you and the One.

The following are a few of the spiritual teachers, as well as philosophical, metaphysical, and mystical schools of thought in history expressing the ancient truth that humanity and the Source are One:

The Buddha. Siddhārtha Gautama, also known as the Buddha, translates from the ancient Sanskrit as "the awakened one." He lived and taught in the northeastern Indian subcontinent some time between the 6th and 5th centuries BCE. He was an enlightened spiritual teacher who shared his insights to help sentient beings end their suffering or *dukkha,* achieve nirvana, and evolve past the cycle of death and rebirth, known as reincarnation. The Buddha taught that in *essence*, we are all One.

Jesus the Christ. Christ or *khristós* translates from the ancient Greek as "the anointed." Jesus, or the name he was called at the time, Yahoshua, was an enlightened spiritual teacher who shared his insights to help humanity end their suffering by finding the Kingdom of Yahweh from with*in*. In the book of John 10:30, Jesus said, "I and my father are one." He later said in John 14:12, "What I have done you can do also and more," communicating clearly to his disciples that divinity was not limited to *him*, but that it extended outward to include all of humanity, thus we are all One.

Kabbalah. In the 13th century CE, the Kabbalah originated as a mystical movement among Jews in Provence, France. The word Kabbalah means "tradition," and as the Jewish mystics assert, its doctrine has been passed on orally from one generation to the next, going all the way back to the time of Adam. Kabbalah teaches how to listen to our spiritual Self and that the only time we have free will is when we *transcend the ego*. At its most fundamental level, Kabbalah teaches that we are all One.

Buddhism. In the Kegon School of Japanese Buddhism, the Jijimuge doctrine says: "All things are One and have no life apart from it; the One is all things and is incomplete without the least of them. Yet the parts are parts within the whole, not merged in it; they are interfused with reality while retaining the full identity of the part, and the One is no less One for the fact that it is a million-million parts."

Gnosticism. Gnosticism consisted of a broad number of branches in a variety of countries that included pre-Christian religious beliefs and spiritual practices common to early Christianity: Hellenestic Judiasm, Greco-Roman mystical religions, Zoroastrianism, and Neoplatonism. In many schools of Gnosticism, God is called the One, the Source, and Aeon. Aeon is also alternatively spelled "eon" which is an anagram for "one." Aeon translates as "eternal" or "everlasting."

Nondualism. Nondualism simply means "not two." Today it is a rapidly expanding paradigm in Western scholarship that pervades a diversity of academic disciplines such as philosophy, transpersonal psychology, mysticism, spirituality, metaphysics, and mainstream religion. It implies that the universe is a *single entity* and therefore we are all One.

> *Never have I not existed,*
> *nor you, nor these kings;*
> *and never in the future*
> *shall we cease to exist.*
> —Krishna, *The Bhagavad-Gītā*

The Vedas. The word *véda* translates from ancient Sanskrit as "knowledge," and the Vedas are a large body of philosophical texts dating back to the onset of Indian civilization. They constitute the oldest layer of Sanskrit literature and are the oldest scriptures of Hinduism. There is no caste-system in the Vedas. It teaches us that no one is superior, no one is inferior, that we are all One through the knowledge of the Atman which is revealed as being One with Brahman—with only one distinct difference. The Atman is the *individual* Spirit and the Brahman is the *universal* Spirit. The word Brahman translates from Sanskrit "to grow" and is believed to transcend time, space, and reality. It is the eternal Source from whence everything in the universe sprang forth. The Atman, on the other hand, is a singular "drop of water" in the endless ocean of Brahman. It is the *Self.*

Hermeticism. Hermeticism is a set of philosophical and religious beliefs based on the Hellenistic Egyptian writings by Hermes Trismegistus, known by the Greeks as Hermes and the Egyptians as Thoth. In the Emerald Tablet of Hermes Trismegistus is a short work which coins the maxim, "As above so below; as below so above; as within so without; as without so within." The text defines that this relationship of duality manifests the miracle of the One Thing. In Hermeticism, the supreme deity or principle is referred to variously as the All, or the One.

Monad. Monad translates from the Greek *monos*, meaning "alone," and *monas*, meaning "single unit." It was used by the Pythagorean mathematicians as a term for God, the first being, the Source, or the One. Its symbol is a circle with a dot in the middle. Interestingly, this is also an illustration for what modern physicists call a *singularity*.

Taoism. A combination of theological and philosophical doctrine, Taoism posits that we gain knowledge of the universe by understanding the Self. It teaches that the microcosm is One with the macrocosm, and that the Self is One with the All. Tao literally means "the way" and it is defined as infinite, unlimited, transcendent, indistinct, and formless.

Evolving into the zero-point Self.

> *You are not just the drop in the ocean. You are the mighty ocean in the drop.*
>
> —Rumi

Evolving into the zero-point Self is not part of your awakening, dear reader. It *is* your awakening. Actualizing your divinity from both a scientific and spiritual perspective is indeed the next quantum leap in the evolution of the human race. When you evolve into the zero-point Self, you are no longer bound to suffering because you have reunited your Self consciousness with Source consciousness. Simply put: You have become *One with the Source.*

By relinquishing your lower, egoic, pseudo self you become an integral part of the intelligent universe. In so doing, you are allowing life to support you, nurture you and *take care of you.* The fleeting sense of separation and superiority that the ego offers in its pathetic display of power over the other will always diminish your divine power and end with more suffering for yourself and others. Bombing each other to kingdom come is no longer going to work anymore if we are going to *evolve* as a species. I believe that there are countless highly advanced extraterrestrial civilizations in the cosmos, but I don't think they've evolved to where they are by blowing up their own people. And I also don't believe they're going to formally introduce themselves to us until we stop behaving like iPod-toting cavemen, disarm our nuclear weapons and begin living with each other in peace and harmony.

One with her higher Self, the Next Human will be imbued with the sacred feminine energies and will be focused on restoring a heavenly balance to Gaia Sophia, Mother Earth, this beautiful and beloved planet that we all call *home*. She will intuitively know the importance of loving one another, taking *care* of one another, and respecting one another. Because of the Internet, we are now communicating with our fellow humans around the globe much faster and more efficiently than we could have imagined just a decade ago. And this is just the beginning. Facebook membership expanded from zero to 901 million members in just *eight years*.[12] That's nearly a seventh of the planet's population! It would seem that our longing to be reunited with one another—with the One— is increasing exponentially. The younger generations of today are entering into a society that's perplexing to them. They simply cannot relate to the madness of violence, conflict, polarity, social injustice, intolerance, and war that pervades our world. So what are they doing to counterbalance this? They are "hugging" one another through social networks. Many of these Next Human children are being born into this world already evolved as zero-point Selves, hence their third-eyes are already *opened*. Because of their higher frequencies, they are helping to raise our collective state of consciousness on subtle yet *powerful* levels.

Discovering the zero-point Self requires awakening to the timeless dimension of formlessness within, that which is eternal. This is the Source that exists within you. When you do, you will realize that you are already worthy of unconditional love. You don't have to *do* anything. You will know that you're already pure, already perfect. Most current humans believe that something needs to happen *to* them before they can be happy, be at peace, and feel fulfilled in their lives. And when these things don't happen, a feeling of resentment arises. They also dwell in the past and cling to events that have brought them suffering, and this *clinging* causes toxins in the body that leads to disease. The Next Human, on the other hand, will not dwell in the past because he will already know that there is no such thing as "the past," and therefore anything that has happened there can no longer have any more power over him in the present. And because his zero-point Self will be realized, he will *be* peace, *be* happiness, *be* fulfillment, *be* completion, rather than waiting on the universe to bring these things to him.

One of the most amazing demonstrations of directing life force energy I've ever seen, read, or even *heard* of was shown in a 2010 episode of Stan Lee's Superhumans.[13] In the show, I watched a real-life modern Samurai by the name of Isao Machii actually slice through the precise center of a BB pellet with his sword. But here's the amazing part: he sliced though it while the BB was moving toward him at a speed over 200 mph after a being fired from a gun. A normal person would take three tenths of a second just to register the sound of the gun being fired before they could even *begin* to think about reacting. From a thought-processed reactive response, by the time he moved into position the BB would have already whizzed by. This action happens at such an incredible speed that it's impossible for the human eye to see it. So in order to visually capture this astounding feat, a state-of-the-art high-speed camera was used for slow-motion analysis.

Ramani Durvasula, Ph.D., a clinical psychologist at California State University, had this to say about Isao Machii's supernatural feat: "This is about processing on an entirely different sensory level because he's not visually processing it. This is a different level of anticipatory processing …something so procedural, something so fluid for him. He's working as a perfectly calibrated machine."[14]

Swordmaster Machii doesn't appear to be reacting because he's not *reacting* at all. Through intense stillness and presence, he has learned to *transcend* his reactive mind and align his awareness with the singularity of the Now. This zero-point Self-actualization enables him to become *one with* the BB—since at the quantum level of nonlocality, there is no separation between the form that is his sword and the form that is the BB. No doubt—through heart-based intention—Machii directs his *life force* to guide his movement of the sword so that it meets the BB at the appropriate place in spacetime, thus slicing it in two without having to visually process it. This is a clear example of *heart-based intuition*. I wouldn't be surprised at all if Machii could perform the entire action again blindfolded. Many Next Humans will possess powerful "Jedi" abilities such as this. In Sanskrit these superhuman powers were called *siddhis*, meaning "attainments," and include: past life recall, telekinesis, telepathy, enhanced speed and reflexes, precognition, bilocation, hypnotic abilities (the "Jedi mind trick"), materialization, teleportation, and the ability to alter the body's size, density, and appearance.

The secret of the sphere.

Physicists tell us that the universe is based on mathematics. But this is not entirely true. It's actually based on *proportion*. More specifically, the

proportion of a sphere. The math is secondary to the primary sacred geometry of proportion. Everything in this existence and indeed *every law of physics* in the universe stems from the sacred geometry of a *sphere*. The image of the flower of life (see image left) is found in nearly every ancient civilization dating back over

10,000 years, spanning over *twenty countries and*—to date—*five continents.*

In 1486, Leonardo da Vinci completed The Vitruvian Man, his most famous sketch in which he incorporated sacred geometry. This sacred or golden geometry is based on the golden ratio (1.618...) also known as *phi* (pronounced "fee"). Phi is an ubiquitous ratio found in nature that expands according to the Fibonacci sequence (0, 1, 1, 2, 3, 5, 8, 13, 21...), where each subsequent number must equal the sum of the prior two. This is the "law of spirals and fractals," and is the fundamental pattern in which a Nautilus, a pine cone, a sunflower, a tornado, a hurricane, Saturn's rings, the solar system, and a galaxy *form.* (Side note: perhaps this ancient knowledge will be someday taught to every first grader on the planet.) Phi is also the divine ratio in which all plants, trees, lightning, and rivers branch *out*ward. This divine proportion further governs the way in which your body forms. There's a phi ratio between the tip of your finger or distal phalange to the intermediate phalange, and from it to the proximal phalange, and from it to the metacarpal. There is a golden phi ratio between your hand to your forearm, and your forearm to your upper arm. This golden ratio of divine proportion consistently *repeats* itself through *all* forms of creation.

Leonardo, who incorporated the golden ratio of phi into all of his paintings, drew the Flower of Life numerous times as well as its various components such as the Seed of Life, Vesica Piscis, the sphere, a torus, and all the platonic solids. So, now I ask you: why do you think Leonardo was so fascinated with sacred geometry? Well, probably because he knew what the ancients were aware of: The Flower of Life is indeed the *key code* that unlocks all the secrets of the universe, merging physics with metaphysics, science with spirituality, and I believe its secrets someday soon unveil a "unified theory of everything." This ancient sphere is nothing less than the *container,* the source of all other forms of sacred geometry, and is therefore a rendering of the multi-dimensional zero-point singularity from whence the *world of form* has sprung forth,

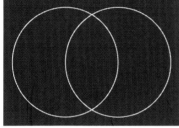

from where creation itself has manifested.

To create the Flower of Life, you must first create the Seed of Life, which is formed from seven circles being placed in sixfold symmetry, forming a pattern of circles and lenses (see image upper left). The first step in forming the Seed of Life and its larger scale version, the Flower of Life, is to begin with a 3D sphere (or 2D circle). The second step is when the Vesica Piscis (see image lower left) is formed when a second sphere of the same diameter intersects with the radius of first sphere. This design is one of the simplest forms of sacred geometry and has also been depicted around the world at wide variety of sacred sites.

The word "universe" translates from the Latin *ūniversus*, meaning "turned into one." The root word "verse" stems from the Latin verb *versus*, which is the past participle of *vertere*, meaning "to turn." A synonym for *turn* is "spin." Einstein believed that gravity is the result of spacetime curving like the surface of a trampoline. The avant-garde scientist Nassim Haramein believes that spacetime not only curves, it also *curls*—just like water going down the drain.[15] This *curling* process generates *spin*, or angular momentum, and is "the source of the spin of all things."[16]

When you observe the universe, you can clearly see these dynamics of spin in action. Spin is a fundamental characteristic property of protons, neutrons, and electrons in the nuclei of atoms. Hurricanes, tornadoes, dust devils, even waves in the ocean all *spin*. In the cosmos, we can observe spin dynamics in the creation of solar systems, nebulae, galaxies, and pulsars. In fact, every luminary in the universe seems to be spinning around a larger object. The moon *spins* around the earth, the earth *spins* around the sun, the sun *spins* around the galaxy, and the galaxy *spins* around a super cluster of galaxies.

The first sphere in the Seed of Life represents the beginning of the universe of form, and according to Drunvalo Melchizedek, an esteemed authority on sacred geometry, the *spinning octahedron* is the very first stage of the Seed of Life. The octahedron, made up of strictly straight

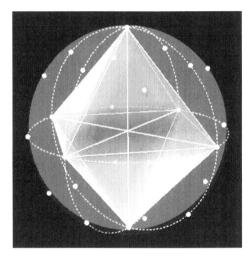

lines, exemplifies the sacred masculine. When you *spin* the octahedron on its axis, it becomes a *sphere,* exemplifying the *sacred feminine* (see image left).[17]

After studying the rotation of over 15,000 galaxies, astrophysicist Michael Longo and his team from the University of Michigan have boldly concluded that the entire universe was actually *born out of spin.* In a recent article by the Institute of Physics, he explained, "If galaxies tend to spin in a certain direction, it means that the overall universe should have a rather large net angular momentum. Since angular momentum is conserved, it seems it [the universe] must have been 'born' spinning...I picture the Big Bang as being born with spin, just like a proton or electron has spin."[18]

In addition, the secret of the *yin yang* symbol also lies in the "spinning sphere." When you view the spinning double torus (each torus spinning in the opposite direction of the other) from either the top down or bottom up directly onto its axis pole in the exact center (where the singularity is in the center of a black hole), you'll find the origin of the *yin yang* symbol (see images[19] below), an ancient symbol for the *fusion* of the masculine and feminine aspects of the divine—a union of the polarity of opposites.

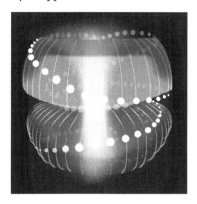 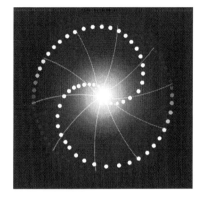

A theory of everything.

The term "unified field theory" was coined by Albert Einstein, who—up until his death—attempted to unify the general theory of relativity with quantum theory. A "theory of everything" is a term closely related to unified field theory, but requires a fundamental pattern in every constant of the universe, including psychology (mind), biology (body), and the mystical (spirit).

Flying in the face of conventional physics is the iconoclastic, self-taught theoretical physicist, Nassim Haramein, who believes that instead of a fundamental particle, we should be looking for a fundamental *principle of division* if indeed we want to find a unified field theory and the key to all of creation. This *key*, according to Haramein, can be found in the expressions of *sacred geometry*.

According to Haramein, if our universe is expanding then there must, simultaneously, be something *contracting*, a compression, or a feedback between the complimentary opposites.[20] He suggests that we're only observing the universe from a one-sided perspective. For example, if you blow up a balloon, the balloon expands but, at the same time, your lungs are contracting. When you breathe in air, your lungs are expanding but the air in the room is contracting. And when your heart beats, it expands, while your arteries contract. Thus, a Big Bang explosion creating one universe could simultaneously be marking the *implosion* of yet another universe. Just like the expansion and contraction of your heart and lungs, universes could also be constantly expanding and contracting. From this perspective, it would be more accurate to say that the Big Bang marked the ending of something that we cannot yet see or determine, and that this ending of one universe is what allowed our universe to be born. After all, everything in nature can be exemplified by the ongoing cycle of death and rebirth, from the tiniest cell to the largest star. This "banging in" and "banging out" of universes may indeed have been going on forever. Like with the circumference of a sphere, there is no beginning and no end to creation. It simply *is*.

Haramein believes that fractal geometry clearly demonstrates that within a finite boundary lies an infinite potential for information, structures, and possibilities. He illustrates this using a simple tetrahedron and inserting it into a spherical boundary, then adding a second tetrahedron to it, then taking the double tetrahedron times six, then times 36, and on and on times infinity all within the same spherical boundary (see images below).[21]

When we found the cell, we thought that it was the smallest object in the universe. Then we discovered the atom, and we thought that *it* was the smallest object in the universe. Billions of atoms in every cell we exclaimed! Then we discovered protons and neutrons in the nuclei of the atom, and then the quark, and so every time we discover a new boundary to the universe, we keep saying, "This is it." We did the same thing with the stellar objects. First it was the earth, then the solar system, then the Milky Way galaxy, and then billions of other galaxies. But now many physicists are already theorizing that there are a multitude of universes!

Haramein believes that fractal geometry is the fundamental *pattern* to a universe that continues to divide itself all the way to infinity. He has hypothesized that everything we can observe would have infinite density or a *singularity* at its center, including our entire universe.[22] To test his hypothesis, Haramein, along with his colleagues Michael Hyson, Ph.D. and Elizabeth A. Rauscher, Ph.D., measured various objects in the universe to determine whether or not there was an organizational structure or direct relationship in which the universe divides itself from the macro large to the micro small.[23] They measured the frequency of quasars, galaxies, stars, the cell, the atom, and the planck length (Big Bang) to determine its energy level against the radius of the object.[24] What is truly fascinating about this new scaling law is that not only is there a linear progression between data points, but that progression between them is in alignment with the divine proportion, golden ratio or *phi*.[25]

Now, quantum theory and Einstein's relativistic theory currently don't reconcile. Their laws are interdependent of one another. However, this new scaling law bridges the gap between the subatomic micro world and the cosmological macro world with the measurements of the biological *cell*. When measuring the frequency of the surface boundary of the cell, Haramein discovered that the lipoprotein oscillates at 10^{11} hertz (cycles per second), a rather intense oscillation for something previously thought to be nothing but a "slow-moving gooey blob."[26] He says that if you combine that 10^{11} hertz energy with the radius of a cell and then apply Einstein's relativity physics, you'll find that the biological cell obeys the same fundamental dynamics of a *black hole*.[27] Neither quantum theory nor Einstein's general relativity theory account for the biological cell. But the Haramein-Rauscher Holofractographic Universe Theory *does* (see Scaling Law chart below).[28]

In his DVD workshop *Crossing the Event Horizon*, Haramein describes the ramifications of this new unified theory:

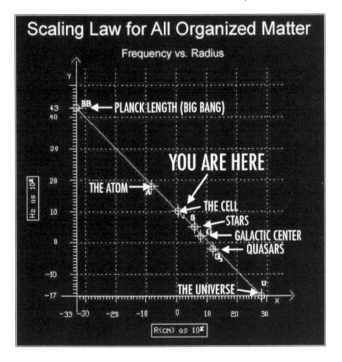

The biological resolution is the link in between the large and the small. You are the event horizon loosely termed and you are the data transfer boundary from the extremely large to the extremely small...You gather information and transfer it to your internal self, which in this view has infinite boundary potential, thus you're transferring that information through your boundary to the

> *infinity of the universe within yourself…Instead of see-*
> *ing yourself as an insignificant little dot that means*
> *nothing to the universe, you start to see yourself as the*
> *center of creation.*[29]

Zero-point energy can take us to the stars.

Nassim Haramein has concluded from his research that the vacuum between atoms is not empty space, but contrarily, completely *full* of fluctuating energy that is the underlying *Source* of the universe. Convinced
since the age of ten that the macro-large is simply a reflection of the
micro-small (and vice-versa), his research has recently revealed that this
fluctuating Source energy can be thought of as quantum-sized pixels, or
what he calls "planck micro pixels" (PMPs) that are all around us, per-
meating us, and organizing every form in the universe into fractal
vortices.[30] As previously mentioned, fractals form in accordance to the
golden ratio, *phi.*

In a radio interview on July 21, 2012, Haramein announced that he
is currently working on a new paper where his calculations will prove
from a scientific perspective that the universe is indeed a singular entity,
thus ***we are all One***.[31] He said that his research demonstrates that every
atom is a mini-black hole that contains within it all the information of
every other atom in the universe, just as a pixel of holographic film contains within it the complete hologram.[32] After studying the fundamental
aspects of these micro pixels, Haramein found them to be part of a holographic universe, in which each point represents the entire system. Furthermore, by calculating the mass of the micro pixels inside the proton,
he has been able to deduce the exact mass of the entire universe.

Haramein took the holographic principle a step further when he
measured the planck micro pixels *inside* of a proton as well its *outside*
surface, and then after studying the relationship between the two, discovered an "exact solution to gravity," which can be applied to an object

of any size.[33] He declared that these are none other than the "baby steps of quantum gravity" that will eventually provide us with "very advanced drive proportion systems" that could open the door to wormhole travel and the universe as a whole.[34] These planck micro pixels could also be considered little capsules of information, and you could think of *time* "as the memory of the structure of the vacuum," as form moves through it, Haramein said, adding that "this model may actually predict that memory is not a function of the brain directly but is a function of the brain accessing the information in the vacuum—so the brain acts much like a radio."[35] He believes that this model "opens doors that we can't even fathom today," and that it may eventually allow us to transport ourselves anywhere in the universe, or access any time period.[36]

I believe that this revolutionary understanding of quantum gravity will lead to a complete transformation in how we access electricity and power transportation. The use of fossil fuels as an energy source—and the toxic pollution that comes with them—will become a thing of the past. Like Nassim Haramein, I also believe that this clean, unlimited, perpetual, zero-point energy will literally *take us to the stars.*

The New Age begins on 02.19.13.

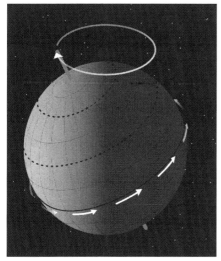

Like the roots of every tree in the forest, the roots of the kundalini energy is firmly planted in the Earth. And like your ethereal body, Earth also has an ethereal body with vortices: her very own chakra system. The kundalini Shakti energy in your human body is actually rooted to the epicenter of the Earth's core, in between the north and south poles which change from time to time depending on the rotational tilt of the Earth's axis. This "axial precession" traces out a circle (see image above) and is known as the *precession of the equinoxes*. Earth goes through one such complete precessional cycle roughly every 26,000 years or one degree every 72 years, during which the positions of stars will slowly change in both ecliptic longitude and equatorial coordinates.

In his book *The Serpent of Light*, spiritual teacher Drunvalo Melchizedek reveals that the Mayans were aware that every 13,000 years, or one-half of an axial precession, the location of Mother Earth's kundalini and root chakra changes location on her surface.[37] This circular area of highly concentrated life force energy encompasses about 700 miles in diameter. For the last 13,000 years, the kundalini of the Earth has been located in the western mountains of Tibet, and the precessional cycle of 13,000 years before that, on Atlantis, which is the location where the Atlantean inner priesthood dwelled, the Nakkal Brotherhood.[38] In the nascence of this last precessional cycle and the ending of the cycle prior, the Nakkal Brotherhood had to abandon their beloved home of Atlantis to follow Mother Earth's Serpent of Light and after they did they ended up high in the Himalayan mountains of Tibet where they built a magnificent *white pyramid*—larger than the Great Pyramid of Giza—in a valley there.[39] This pyramid would be the new location for the Earth's root chakra—the electromagnetic vortex for the Earth's kundalini energy—for the subsequent 13,000 years.[40] ***Until now.***

Because it was buried underneath the Tibetan snow fifty weeks out of the year, the exploration team was left with only a two-week window to observe the ancient pyramid. During those two weeks the snow melted to reveal a flawless structure that looked as if it had just been built yesterday. After many attempts over a period of several years in the mid-1980s, they were finally able to make their way inside it.[41] Unlike the Great Pyramid of Giza, the Tibetan pyramid's glimmering white alabaster casing stones remained perfectly intact and its entrance was not sealed.[42] After entering the pyramid, the team eventually came upon an inner chamber.[43] Just as in the Great Pyramid, there are no carvings of text, pictures, or hieroglyphics. What they did find, however, high on the chamber wall was none other than the *flower of life.*[44]

Forced to evacuate Atlantis due to an ever increasing number of natural disasters such as tsunamis, earthquakes, and volcanoes, the outer priesthood (not the *inner* priesthood Nakkals) relocated to the shores of what is now the Yucatan peninsula in Mexico.[45] This former priesthood of Atlantis is known today as the Maya, who are well aware of their origins. This was also verified by the historian Augustus Le Plongeon from his translation of a Mayan Codex known as the Troano document.[46]

For 6,000 years after the waters rose over the land of Atlantis, the Nakkals remained with the Great White Pyramid and thrived on its kundalini life force energy.[47] Eventually they seeded the Tibetan race who influenced many of the great spiritual teachers in history, such as Siddhārtha Gautama (the Buddha) and Lao Tzu—the author of one of the most spiritually enlightening books of all time, the *Tào Té Chīng.*[48] From these two teachers sprang the spirituality-based religions, Buddhism and Taoism, respectively.

Whenever the location of the Earth's kundalini energy moves from one location to another, our collective consciousness expands and attunes itself with the higher frequency of the new 13,000 year cycle. This is where we are *now*, and the Mayans, whose calendar ends on December 21, 2012, were well aware of this new cycle of precession, marking a giant *leap forward* in the evolution of our species: physically, mentally, and spiritually. So they recently held a grand meeting that included all the Mayan tribes—the first time in history that such a meeting has taken place.[49]

When the Dalai Lama fled Tibet for India in 1959—due to the suppression of the Tibetans by the Chinese—Mother Earth's kundalini went with him, and after remaining in India for many years she left to roam the planet for several decades. Eventually the Serpent of Light settled in her new location for the next cycle of precession: a valley in the high mountains of Peru and Chile. And according to the Mayan elders, this new 13,000-year cycle—the New Age of Enlightenment—begins on February 19, 2013.[50]

A new heaven and a new Earth.

Then I saw a new heaven and a new earth; the first heaven and the first earth had disappeared now...Then I heard a loud voice call from the throne, 'You see this city? Here God lives among men. He will make his home among them...his name is God-with-them. He will wipe away all tears from their eyes; there will be no more death, and no more mourning or sadness. The world of the past has gone.'

—The Book of Revelation 21:1-4 (The Jerusalem Bible)

The Source of One has two movements: expansion and contraction. It has been doing this—not since the beginning (because there was no beginning)—forever and ever. It simply *is*. As it expands *outward* from its zero-point vacuum of no*thing*ness, it creates what we see as a universe of form. The longer it does this, the more complex and detailed the form becomes, thus the more intricately the One is able to experience its Self *through* form. This is the act of consciousness becoming conscious of its Self, through you and me. So this is its *outer* purpose. As the universe contracts, the One begins its journey home and returns *inward* to the unified, singular, inconceivable, unmanifested Source. This is its *inner* purpose.

So because the Source has two purposes, you have two purposes. Your *outer* purpose is to gain knowledge, skills, talents, and wisdom through experience, thus becoming a co-creator with the Source. Your *inner* purpose is to discover your true *essence*, your divinity, your zero-point Self.

As our species evolves into the Next Human, the frequency of the Earth will elevate from a three-dimensional frequency to a higher *fourth*-dimensional frequency. This is achieved by becoming heart-centered. This "higher frequency" Earth is indeed the "new Earth" spoken of in Revelation 21:1-4. And in this paragraph, the phrase "his name is God-with-them" is nearly identical to when Jesus said, "the Kingdom of God is within you" in Luke 17:21. This is the "new heaven." It refers to the return movement of the One. This is the discovery of your *inner* Self, your true Self that you have only forgotten. This has been mistranslated by biblical scholars to imply that God is an egoic personality and therefore must be worshipped as a governor or "Lord" that is separate from you. And this is why so many people continue to suffer—because they are constantly searching for the divine *outside* of the Self.

The phrase "He will wipe away all tears from their eyes; there will be no more death, and no more mourning or sadness" clearly describes the end of the karmic cycle of human suffering, of reincarnation. No doubt, we will learn how to extend our life spans in the physical body indefinitely. As a result, this new cycle will mark the final stage of the soul for many in this material, 3D plane. This is what I call the "butterfly stage."

When you reach this level of evolution, you realize that life is always a *reflection* of your inner state. You relinquish your servitude to the ego and its shadow. The madness and collective dysfunction that exists in this world becomes transparent because you are able to readily identify the egoic mind, the insanity in others. In this final stage for the soul in the dense, corporeal realm, the perception of the Self is now inseparable from the Source and subsequently your concept of God extends beyond the world of form to the timeless state of now here, no where. It is finally realized that God—the sum total of everything in existence—can never be *separate* from any of its parts. This higher understanding of God reflects an unconditional love for the Self and therefore all of humanity. Evolving into this *zero*-point Self means living a life of *zero* resistance, *zero* reaction, *zero* violence, and therefore *zero* suffering. This butterfly stage is the evolutionary stage of the Next Human. It is nothing less than the metamorphosis from Homo sapiens to ***Homo luminous***.

NOTES

INTRODUCTION

1. Bill Smirnow, "Global Nuclear Weapons Count, *Rense.com*, accessed June 2012, http://www.rense.com/general47/global.htm.
2. *Pakistan's Nuclear Weapons: Proliferation and Security Issues,* CRS Report for Congress, Paul K. Kerr, Mary Beth Nikitin, June 26, 2012, http://www.fas.org/sgp/crs/nuke/RL34248.pdf

EVOLUTION 101: THE PSEUDO SELF

1. "Your Genetic History," *The Genographic Project,* NationalGeographic.com, http://www.nationalgeographic.com/xpeditions/lessons/09/g912/h aplogroupA.pdf.
2. Ann Gibbons, "Ancient Skeleton May Rewrite Earliest Chapter of Human Evolution," *Science Now,* October 1, 2009, http://news.sciencemag.org/sciencenow/2009/10/01-01.html.
3. Jesse Emspak, "World's Smallest Hard Drive Built of Atoms," *Discovery News,* January 12, 2012, http://news.discovery.com/tech/worlds-smallest-hard-drive-12011 2.html.
4. Luke 17:21 (King James Bible).
5. *Dictionary.com,* s.v. "Evil," http://www.dictionary.reference.com/browse/evil (accessed 2012).
6. Sandra Blakeslee, Dr. Joseph LeDoux, "Using Rats to Trace Routes of Fear," *The New York Times,* http://www.cns.nyu.edu/ledoux/the_emotional_brain/book_time_ reviw.htm.
7. Ibid.
8. M.K. Gandhi, *Excerpts from The Law of Love (edited by Anand T. Hingorani)* http://sfr-21.org/sources/lawoflove.html.
9. Luke 14:10 (King James Bible).

EVOLUTION 201: THE PHANTOM SELF

1. George Santayana, (1905) Reason in Common Sense, volume 1 of *The Life of Reason*
2. Matthew White, *Source List and Detailed Death Tolls for the Pri-*

mary Megadeaths of the Twentieth Century, http://necrometrics.com/20c5m.htm (accessed February 2012).

3. Ibid.
4. Bootie Cosgrove-Mather, "Poll: Talk First, Fight Later," *CBS News,* February 11, 2009, http://www.cbsnews.com/stories/2003/01/23/opinion/polls /main537739.shtml (accessed February 2012).
5. "Iraq War Illegal, Says Annan," *BBC News,* September 16, 2004, http://news.bbc.co.uk/go/pr/fr/-/2/hi/middle_east/3661134.stm (accessed February 2012).
6. Jan Frel, "Could Bush Be Prosecuted for War Crimes?" July 10, 2006, http://alternet.org/waroniraq/38604/ (accessed February 2012).
7. Ibid.
8. *Wikipedia,* s.v. "Iraq War," http://en.wikipedia.org/wiki/Iraq_war (accessed February 2012).
9. *Wars Since1900,* The Polynational War Memorial, http://www.war-memorial.net/wars_all.asp
10. Piero Scaruffi, *Wars and Genocides of the 20th Century,* http://www.scaruffi.com/politics/massacre.html
11. "State of the Union with Cindy Crowley," *CNN,* January 29, 2012, http://transcripts.cnn.com/TRANSCRIPTS/1201/29/sotu.01.html.
12. Chris Keane, "Ron Paul fights indefinite detention of Americans," *RT.com,* January 19, 2012, http://rt.com/usa/news/ron-paul-ndaa-detention-209/.
13. Declaration of Independence, 1776, http://www.earlyamerica.com/earlyamerica/freedom/doi/text.html.
14. Tara Parker Pope, "Narcissism No Longer a Psychiatric Disorder," November 29, 2010, http://well.blogs.nytimes.com/2010/11/29/narcissism-no-longer-a -psychiatric-disorder/
15. Andy and Larry Wachowski. *The Matrix.* DVD. Warner Bros. Entertainment Inc., 1999.
16. Anup Shah, "Poverty Facts and Stats," *Global Issues,* September 20, 2010, http://www.globalissues.org/article/26/poverty-facts-and-stats (accessed February 2012).
17. C. G. Jung, *Aion: Researches into the Phenomenology of the Self,* (London: Princeton University Press, 1996).

18. Eckhart Tolle, *The Power of Now* (Novato, New World Library, 1999), 31.

19. Ibid., 29.

20. Ibid.

21. Ibid., 30.

22. David Postill, "Wilhelm Reich - Only you yourself can be your liberator!" Dance Your Life, (2008-2012) 2012http://www.danceyourlife.eu/sourcesofbiodanza/WilhelmReich.html (accessed February 2012).

23. "Larry King Live," *CNN*, September 8, 2010, http://transcripts.cnn.com/ TRANSCRIPTS/1009/08/lkl.01.html.

24. William Dalrymple, *The Muslims in the Middle*, New York Times, August 16, 2010, http://www.nytimes.com/2010/08/17/opinion/17dalrymple.html?_r=2&pagewanted=all (accessed February 2012).

25. Cordoba Initiative, "Cordoba Initiative: About Us," Cordoba Initiative, http://www.cordobainitiative.org/about/ (accessed February 2012).

26. "Norwegian Mass Murderer Breivik Comments on Croat-Serb Relations in his Manifesto," *Croatian Times*, July 27, 2011, http://www.croatiantimes.com/news/ General_News/2011-07-27/20837/Norwegian_mass_murderer_Breivik_comments_on_Croat-Serb_relations_in_his_manifesto (accessed February 2012).

27. Ben Hartman, "Norway Attack Suspect had Anti-Muslim, Pro-Israel Views," *The Jerusalem Post*, July 24, 2011, http://www.jpost.com/International/ Article.aspx?id=230762 (accessed February 2012).

28. M. Scott Peck, *People of the Lie*, (Touchstone, 1998), 76.

29. Bullying Statistics, "Bullying and Suicide," Bullying Statistics, http://www.bullyingstatistics.org/content/bullying-and-suicide.html (accessed February 2012).

30. Ibid.

31. Ibid.

EVOLUTION 301: THE PHYSICAL SELF

1. Grete Hausler, An Introduction to the Teachings of Bruno Groening (2008).

2. "Current methods can prevent more than half of all cancers," The

Hudson Valley Press, May 9, 2012,
http://www.hvpress.net/news/123/ARTICLE/11100/2012-05-09.ht
ml.

3. "How much money is spent on cancer research," National Cancer Institute, February 2, 2010,
http://www.cancer.gov/cancertopics/factsheet/NCI/research-fundi
ng.

4. GB Challis, HJ Stam (1990), "The spontaneous regression of cancer. A review of cases from 1900 to 1987," Acta Oncol 29 (1990): 545–50. http://www.ncbi.nlm.nih.gov/pubmed/2206563.

5. "U.S. Death every 19 minutes from overdose," UPI, January 13, 2012,
http://www.upi.com/Health_News/2012/01/13/US-death-every-1
9-minutes-from-overdose/UPI-28581326514265/.

6. Katherine Harmon, "Prescription Drug Deaths Increase Dramatically," Scientific American, April 6, 2010,
http://www.scientificamerican.com/author.cfm?id=1822.

7. Ibid.

8. Liz Szabo, Prescriptions now biggest cause of fatal drug overdoses, USA Today, August 20, 2010,
http://www.usatoday.com/news/health/2009-09-30-drug-overdos
e_N.htm.

9. Gary Null and others, eds., "Death by Medicine,"
http://www.webdc.com/pdfs/deathbymedicine.pdf, accessed June 2012.

10. Bill Berkrot, "Global drug sales to top $1 trillion in 2014," Reuters, April 20, 2010,
http://www.reuters.com/article/2010/04/20/pharmaceuticals-fore
cast-idUSN1921921520100420.

11. Eric J. McNulty, "It's Time for a Public Health President," Renegotiating Health Care, February 1, 2012,
http://renegotiatinghealthcare.com/2012/02/its-time-for-a-public-
health-president/.

12. Karen Davis, Ph.D., Cathy Schoen, M.S., and Kristof Stremikis, M.P.P., Mirror, "Mirror on the Wall: How the Performance of the U.S. Health Care System Compares Internationally, 2010 Update," The Commonwealth Fund, June 23, 2010,
http://www.commonwealthfund.org/Publications/Fund-Reports/
2010/Jun/Mirror-Mirror-Update.aspx.

13. Ibid.

14. Maggie Fox, "U.S. scores dead last again in healthcare study," Reuters, June 23, 2010, http://www.reuters.com/article/2010/06/23/us-usa-healthcare-last-idUSTRE65M0SU20100623.
15. The World Factbook, Central Intelligence Agency, Country Comparison: Life Expectancy at Birth, https://www.cia.gov/library/publications/the-world-factbook/rankorder/2102rank.html.
16. "Cancer Surpasses Heart Disease as Number One Cause of Death in Americans Under Age 85," Cancer Prevention, http://www.nypcancerprevention.com/issue/5/con/features/cancer-surpasses-heart-di.shtml, accessed June 2012.
17. Otto H. Warburg, "The Prime Cause and Prevention of Cancer," http://healingtools.tripod.com/primecause1.html/, accessed October 30, 2007.
18. Alastair Jamieson, msnbc.com, Report: World's population is 17 million tons overweight, (June 18, 2012), http://vitals.msnbc.msn.com/_news/2012/06/18/12278587-report-worlds-population-is-17-million-tons-overweight.
19. Ibid.
20. Bill Hendrick, "Percentage of Overweight, Obese Americans Swells," WebMD Health News, February 10, 2010, http://www.webmd.com/diet/news/20100210/percentage-of-overweight-obese-americans-swells.
21. Jeff Toney, "The Two Ton Sugar Burden," Dean's Corner, April 18, 2011. http://scienceblogs.com/deanscorner/2011/04/the_two_ton_sugar_burden._php, accessed June 2012.
22. "2011 National Diabetes Fact Sheet," American Diabetes Association, January 26, 2011, http://www.diabetes.org/diabetes-basics/diabetes-statistics/, accessed June 2012.
23. "One million people in UK unaware they have Type 2 Diabetes," Diabetes UK, June 30, 2010, http://www.diabetes.org.uk/About_us/News_Landing_Page/One-million-people-in-UK-unaware-they-have-Type-2-diabetes/.
24. "2011 National Diabetes Fact Sheet," American Diabetes Association, January 26, 2011, http://www.diabetes.org/diabetes-basics/diabetes-statistics/, accessed June 2012.

25. William Davis, M.D., Wheat Belly - Loose the Wheat, Lose the Weight, and Find Your Path Back to Health, (New York, Rodale, 2011), back cover.
26. Alice Park. "All Sugars Aren't the Same: Glucose is Better, Study Says," Time Magazine, April 21, 2009, http://www.time.com/time/health/article/0,8599,1892841,00.html
27. R.J. Johnson and T. Gower, "The Sugar Fix: The High-Fructose Fallout That is Making You Sick and Fat," Harvard Health Publications (2009): 416.
28. D. Schwarzbein and N. Deville, The Schwarzbein Principle (Deerfield Beach: Health Communications, Inc., 2009).
29. Manabu Nakamura, "U of I Study: Fructose Metabolism More Complicated than Was Thought," ACES News, December, 9, 2008, http://www.aces.uiuc.edu/news/stories/news4597.html.
30. Crina Frincu-Mallos, "ENDO 2009: Use of Artificial Sweeteners Linked to 2-Fold Increase in Diabetes," Medscape Medical News, June 15, 2009.
31. Rebecca Coffey, "20 Things You Didn't Know About…Sugar," Discover Magazine, October 30, 2009, http://discovermagazine.com/2009/oct/30-20-things-you-didnt-know-about-sugar.
32. S.B. Eaton and others, eds., "Paleolithic Nutrition Revisited: A Twelve-Year Retrospective on Its Nature and Implications." European Journal of Clinical Nutrition 51, no. 4 (1997): 207-16.
33. W.H. Calvin, A Brain for All Seasons (London: University of Chicago Press, 2002).
34. V.M. Bryant, Jr. and G. Williams-Dean, "The Coprolites of Man." Scientific American (1975), 100-109.
35. Patricia Gadsby, "The Inuit Paradox," Discover Magazine, October 1, 2004, http://discovermagazine.com/2004/oct/inuit-paradox.
36. Lieb and others, eds., "The Effects of an Exclusive Long-Continued Meat Diet." Journal of the American Medical Association, July 3, 1926.
37. "Jeffrey Friedman, Discoverer of Leptin, Receives Gairdner, Passano Awards," Medical News Today, April 14, 2005, http://www.medicalnewstoday.com/releases/22784.php.
38. Nora T. Gedgaudas, Primal Body, Primal Mind (Rochester: Healing Arts Press, 2009, 2011).
39. Raja Mishra, "Hormone therapy still a hope for the obese," The New York Times, July, 14, 2005,

http://www.medicalnewstoday.com/releases/22784.php.

40. "Fructose Sets Table For Weight Gain Without Warning," Science Daily, October 16, 2008.

41. M. Wabitsch and others, eds., "Insulin and cortisol promote leptin production in cultured human fat cells," Diabetes 45 10 (1996): 1435–1438.

42. Stephen C. Benoit and others, eds., "Insulin and Leptin as Adiposity Signals," Recent Prog Horm Res 59 (2004): 267-285.

43. The New England Journal of Medicine 340 (1999): 169-176, 223-224.

44. "Food for thought—3 million years ago," BBC News, February 16, 2012, http://www.bbc.co.uk/sn/prehistoric_life/human/human_evolutio n/food_for_thought1.shtml.

45. Mary Newport, "What if There was a Cure for Alzheimer's Disease and No One Knew?" Coconut Keytones, July 22, 2008, http://www.coconutketones.com/WhatIfCure.pdf.

46. Ibid.

47. E.G. Neal and others, eds., "The ketogenic diet for the treatment of childhood epilepsy: a randomized controlled trial." Lancet Neurol 6 (2008): 500-506.

48. Maciej Gasior and others, eds., "Neuroprotective and disease-modifying effects of the ketogenic diet," Behav Pharmacol 17(5-6) (2006): 431-439, http://www.ncbi.nlm.nih.gov/pmc/articles/PMC2367001/.

49. Berit Brogaard, "The Pros of the Ketogenic Diet for Anxiety," LiveStrong.com, July 24, 2011, http://www.livestrong.com/article/499778-the-pros-of-the-ketoge nic-diet-for-anxiety/.

50. "Ketogenic diet for bipolar," Active Low-Carber Forums, September 14, 2008, http://forum.lowcarber.org/showthread.php?t=382164&page=1& pp=15.

51. "Advanced cancer and the ketogenic diet," Ketogenic Nutrition, August 11, 2011.

52. "Facts & Statistics," Anxiety and Depression Association of America, Retrieved August 8, 2012, http://www.adaa.org/about-adaa/press-room/facts-statistics.

53. Ibid.

54. P.E. Greenberg and others, eds., "The Economic Burden of Anxi-

ety Disorders," J Clin Psychiatry 60(7) (1999): 427-435,
http://www.ncbi.nlm.nih.gov/pubmed/10453795.

55. D. L. Musselman and others, eds., "Relationship of depression to
diabetes types 1 and 2: epidemiology, biology, and treatment," Biol
Psychiatry 54(3) (2003): 317-329,
http://www.ncbi.nlm.nih.gov/pubmed/12893107.

56. Chris Kresser, "Treating depression without drugs – Part III,"
Chris Kresser, L.Ac, August 19, 2008,
http://chriskresser.com/treating-depression-without-drugs-part-ii
i.

57. Hussein M. Dashti and others, eds., "Ketogenic Diet Modifies the
Risk Factors of Heart Disease in Obese Patients," Nutrition 19
(2003): 901-902.
http://www.dashticlinic.com/articles/KetogenicWeightLossKuwait
.pdf

58. Frans Pouwer, "Does Emotional Stress Cause Type 2 Diabetes
Mellitus? A Review from the European Depression in Diabetes
(EDID) Research Consortium," Discovery Medicine, February 17,
2012,
http://www.discoverymedicine.com/Frans-Pouwer/2010/02/11/do
es-emotional-stress-cause-type-2-diabetes-mellitus-a-review-fro
m-the-european-depression-in-diabetes-edid-research-consortiu
m/.

59. NAL USDA National Nutrient Database, accessed June 2012,
http://ndb.nal.usda.gov/.

60. B. Ludvik and others, eds., "Mode of action of ipomoea batatas
(Caiapo) in type 2 diabetic patients," Metabolism 52 (2003):875–
880.

61. NAL USDA National Nutrient Database, accessed June 2012,
http://ndb.nal.usda.gov/.

62. D. Grotto, 101 Foods That Could Save Your Life (New York: Ban-
tam Bell, 2008).

63. "The Health Properties of Sweet Potatoes," Reader's Digest,
http://www.rd.com/health/the-health-properties-of-sweet-potatoe
s/.

64. Ibid.

65. Ibid.

66. M. Leonardi, "Treatment of fibrocystic disease of the breast with
myrtillus anthocyanins. Our experience." Minerva ginecologica
45(12) (1993): 617–621.

67. "Potential mechanisms of cancer chemoprevention by antho-cyanins," Curr Mol Med 3(2) (2003): 149-159, http://www.ncbi.nlm.nih.gov/pubmed/12630561?ordinalpos=3&i tool=EntrezSystem2.PEntrez.Pubmed.Pubmed_ResultsPanel.Pub med_RVDocSum.

68. J. Cho, "Antioxidant and memory enhancing effects of purple sweet potato anthocyanin and cordyceps mushroom extract," Arch Pharm Res 26(10) (2003): 821-825, http://www.ncbi.nlm.nih.gov/pubmed/14609130.

69. M.D. Willcox and others, eds., The Okinawan Program (New York: Three Rivers Press, 2001).

70. "EGCG - potent extract of green tea," Dr. Ronald Hoffman, ac-cessed June 2012, http://www.drhoffman.com/page.cfm/118.

71. J. Teas, "Dietary seaweed (Laminaria) and mammary carcino-genesis rates," Cancer Res 44 (1984): 2758-61.

72. Duangrat Inthorn, "Sorption of mercury, cadmium and lead by microalgae," Science Asia 28 (2002): 253-261, http://www.scienceasia.org/2002.28.n3/v28_253_261.pdf.

73. R.E. Merchant and C.A. Andre, "A review of recent clinical trials of the nutritional supplement Chlorella pyrenoidosa in the treat-ment of fibromyalgia, hypertension, and ulcerative colitis," Altern Ther Health Med. 7(3) (2001): 79–91, http://www.ncbi.nlm.nih.gov/pubmed/11347287.

74. Shiro Nakano and others, eds., "Plant Foods for Human Consump-tion – Chlorella pyrenoidosa – Supplementation Reduces the Risk of Anemia, Proteinuria and Edema in Pregnant Women," Plant Foods for Human Nutrition 65(1) (2010): 25-30, http://www.springerlink.com/content/671736k33wj23008/?MUD =MP.

75. T.K. Mao and others, eds., "Effects of a Spirulina-based dietary supplement on cytokine production from allergic rhinitis pa-tients," Journal of Medicinal Food 8 (1) (2005): 27–30, http://online.liebertpub.com/doi/abs/10.1089/jmf.2005.8.27.

76. H. Park and others, eds., "A randomized double-blind, placebo-controlled study to establish the effects of spirulina in elderly Koreans," Annals of Nutrition & Metabolism 52 (4) (2008): 322–328, http://www.ncbi.nlm.nih.gov/pubmed/18714150.

77. T. Sato and G. Miyata, 2000. "The nutraceutical benefit, part 4: Garlic," Nutr 16 (2000): 787-88.

78. Rob Poulos, "Hot Pepper Nutrition Facts – Health & Fat Burning

Benefits of Hot Peppers," Fast Fit Tips, accessed June 2012, http://www.fatburningfurnace.com/blog/.

79. Ibid.

80. D. Kumar and others, eds., "Free Radical Scavenging and Analgesic Activities of Cucumis sativus L. Fruit Extract," J Young Pharm 2(4) (2010):365-368.

81. "Cucumbers," The George Mateljan Foundation, accessed June 2012, http://whfoods.org/genpage.php?tname=foodspice&dbid=42.

82. D.H. Lee, "Cucurbitacin: ancient compound shedding new light on cancer treatment," Scientific World Journal 10 (2010):413-418.

83. "Cinnamon may help to alleviate diabetes says UCSB researcher," University of California - Santa Barbara, April 13, 2004, http://www.eurekalert.org/pub_releases/2004-04/uoc--cmh041304.php.

84. K. Sakano and others, eds., "Suppression of azoxymethane-induced colonic premalignant lesion formation by coenzyme Q10 in rats," Asian Pacific Journal of Cancer Prevention 7(4) (2006): 599-603.

85. F.L. Rosenfeldt and others, eds., "Coenzyme Q10 in the treatment of hypertension: a meta-analysis of the clinical trials," Journal of Human Hypertension 21(4) (2007): 297–306.

86. T. Hanioka and others, eds., "Effect of topical application of coenzyme Q10 on adult periodontitis," Mol. Aspects Med. 15(Suppl) (1994): S241-248.

87. J. Quiles and others, eds., "Coenzyme Q supplementation protects from age-related DNA double-strand breaks and increases lifespan in rats fed on a PUFA-rich diet," Experimental Gerontology 39(2) (2004): 189-194.

88. P.S. Sándor and others, eds., "Efficacy of coenzyme Q10 in migraine prophylaxis: a randomized controlled trial," Neurology 64(4) (2005): 713-715.

89. "Turmeric," The George Mateljan Foundation, accessed June 2012, http://www.whfoods.com/genpage.php?tname=foodspice&dbid=78.

90. Ibid.

91. Ibid.

92. Ibid.

93. Alison Motluk, "Curry spice could alleviate cystic fibrosis," New Scientist, April 22 2004,

http://www.newscientist.com/article/dn4912-curry-spice-could-a
lleviate-cystic-fibrosis.html.

94. Ibid.
95. Ibid.
96. "Curry spice 'kills cancer cells,'" BBC News, October 28, 2009,
   http://news.bbc.co.uk/2/hi/health/8328377.stm.
97. Tina Clancy, "Cancer: Are there alternative health solutions," He-
   lium, March 02, 2008,
   http://www.helium.com/items/900886-cancer-are-there-alternativ
   e-health-solutions.
98. W. Gao and others, eds., "Luffin-S—a small novel ribosome inac-
   tivating protein from Luffa cylindriea; Characterization and
   mechanism studies," FEBS Lett 347 (1994): 257-60.
99. Michael N.D. Murray, The Encyclopedia Of Healing Foods (New
   York: Atria Books, 2005).
100. "Broccoli beats most other veggies in health benefits," CNN
   Health, April 17, 2000,
   http://articles.cnn.com/2000-04-13/health/broccoli.benefits.wm
   d_1_brassica-chemoprotection-laboratory-broccoli-isothiocyan
   ates?_s=PM:FOOD.
101. Robert Heaney, Calcium in Human Health (Humana Press:
   2005).
102. "Broccoli beats most other veggies in health benefits," CNN
   Health, April 17, 2000,
   http://articles.cnn.com/2000-04-13/health/broccoli.benefits.wm
   d_1_brassica-chemoprotection-laboratory-broccoli-isothiocyan
   ates?_s=PM:FOOD.
103. Andrew Hickman, "How much doesn't your doctor know about
   nutrition?" Omaha Vegan Examiner, July 5, 2009,
   http://www.examiner.com/article/how-much-doesn-t-your-doct
   or-know-about-nutrition.
104. D.C. Willcox, "The Okinawan Diet: Health Implications of a Low-
   Calorie, Nutrient-Dense, Antioxidant-Rich Dietary Pattern Low
   in Glycemic Load," J Am Coll Nutr Suppl. 28(2009): 500S-516S.
105. "Are Phytates Bad or Good?" Drweil.com, July 19, 2010,
   http://www.drweil.com/drw/u/QAA400758/Are-Phytates-Bad-or
   -Good.html.
106. Ibid.
107. M. Enig, Know Your Fats: The Complete Primer for Understanding the Nutrition of Fats, Oils, and Cholesterol (Bethesda: Be-

thesda Press, 2001).

108. "New findings on cholesterol metabolism in the brain and Alzheimer's disease," News Medical, October 4, 2007, http://www.news-medical.net/news/2007/10/04/30820.aspx.

109. D. Schwarzbein and N. Deville, The Schwarzbein Principle (Deerfield Beach: Health Communications, Inc., 1999).

110. "Interview with Dr. Schwarzbein on the Crook & Chase Show," 1999, http://www.schwarzbeinprinciple.com/pgs/dr_schw/dls_2.html.

111. D. Schwarzbein and N. Deville, The Schwarzbein Principle (Deerfield Beach: Health Communications, Inc., 1999).

112. Ibid.

113. Ibid.

114. Nora T. Gedgaudas, Primal Body, Primal Mind (Rochester: Healing Arts Press, 2009, 2011), 77.

115. "Statins for High Cholesterol, Heart Disease: Drug Comparison," Consumer Reports, 2006-2011, http://www.consumerreports.org/health/best-buy-drugs/statins.htm.

116. Melissa Healy, "Effectiveness of statins is called into question," The Los Angeles Times, August 9, 2010, http://articles.latimes.com/2010/aug/09/health/la-he-statins-20100809.

117. Mark Hyman, "Why Women Should Stop Their Cholesterol Lowering Medication," Huffington Post, January 21, 2012, http://www.huffingtonpost.com/dr-mark-hyman/women-cholesterol-medication_b_1219496.html.

118. National Cholesterol Education Program, accessed June 2012, http://www.nhlbi.nih.gov/about/ncep/index.htm.

119. Robert Crayhon, "An Interview with John Abramson, M.D.: The Overselling of Statin," Townsend Letter, June 2008, http://www.townsendletter.com/June2008/nutmed0608.htm.

120. Melissa Healy, "Effectiveness of statins is called into question," The Los Angeles Times, August 9, 2010, http://articles.latimes.com/2010/aug/09/health/la-he-statins-20100809.

121. Mark Hyman, "Why Women Should Stop Their Cholesterol Lowering Medication," Huffington Post, January 21, 2012, http://www.huffingtonpost.com/dr-mark-hyman/women-cholesterol-medication_b_1219496.html.

122. G.K. Hansson, "Inflammation, Atherosclerosis, and Coronary Artery Disease," N Engl J Med 352 (2005): 1685.
123. I.J. Schatz and others, eds., "Cholesterol and all-cause mortality in elderly people from the Honolulu Heart Program: a cohort study," Lancet 358(9279) (2001): 351-355.
124. A.J. Taylor, "Does ENHANCE Diminish Confidence in Lowering LDL or in Ezetimibe?" Engl J Med 358 (2008):1504.
125. Mary Enig, "Health and Nutritional Benefits from Coconut Oil: An Important Functional Food for the 21st Century," AVOC Lauric Oils Symposium, April 25, 1996, http://www.westonaprice.org/know-your-fats/new-look-at-coconut-oil.
126. B.M. Hedge "View Point: Coconut Oil – Ideal Fat next only to Mother's Milk (Scanning Coconut's Horoscope)," JIACM 7 (2006): 16–19.
127. M.T. Tarrago-Trani and others, eds., "New and existing oils and fats used in products with reduced trans-fatty acid content" Journal of the American Dietetic Association 106(6) (2006): 867–880. http://www.ars.usda.gov/SP2UserFiles/Place/12354500/Articles/JADA106_867-880.pdf.
128. Ibid.
129. Mary Enig and others, eds., Fed Proc, 37(9) (1978):2215-2220.
130. S. Malhotra, Indian Journal of Industrial Medicine 14 (1968): 219.
131. Kang-Jey Ho and others, eds., Archeological Pathology 91 (1971): 387; G.V. Mann and others, eds., Am J Epidemiol 95 (1972): 26-37.
132. N.A. Fernandez, Cancer Res, 1975, 35: 3272; I. Martines and others, eds., Cancer Res, 1975, 35: 3265.
133. M. DeBakey and others, eds., JAMA, 189 (1964): 655-59.
134. D.T. Lackland and others, eds., J Nutr, 120:11S (1990):1433-1436.
135. Nutr Week 21 (1991): 12:2-3.
136. Junshi Chen, Diet, Life-Style and Mortality in China: A Study of the Characteristics of 65 Chinese Counties (Ithaca: Cornell University Press, 1990).
137. Y. Koga and others, eds., Recent Trends in Cardiovascular Disease and Risk Factors in the Seven Countries Study: Japan, and H. Toshima and others, eds., Lessons for Science from the Seven Countries Study (New York: Springer, 1994).

138. M.D. Willcox and others, eds., The Okinawan Program (New York: Three Rivers Press, 2001).

139. Molly O'Neill, "Can Foie Gras Aid the Heart? A French Scientist Says Yes," The New York Times, November 17, 1991, http://www.nytimes.com/1991/11/17/world/can-foie-gras-aid-th e-heart-a-french-scientist-says-yes.html.

140. Frank A. Cooper, Cholesterol and The French Paradox (Lulu.com Publishing: 2009).

141. A. Keys, Coronary heart disease in seven countries, Nutrition (1997) 13(3): 250-252.

142. A.P. Simopoulos, "The Mediterranean diets: What is so special about the diet of Greece? The scientific evidence." J Nutr (2001); 131(11 Suppl): 3065S-3073S.

143. M. Enig, Know Your Fats: The Complete Primer for Understanding the Nutrition of Fats, Oils, and Cholesterol (Bethesda: Bethesda Press, 2001).

144. A.P. Simopoulos, "Importance of the ratio of omega-6/omega-3 essential fatty acids: evolutionary aspects," World Review of Nutrition and Dietetics 92 (2003): 1–174.

145. William S. Harris, "N−3 fatty acids and serum lipoproteins: human studies," Am J Clin Nutr 65 (5 Sup.) (1997): 1645S–1654S.

146. H.C. Bucher and others, eds., "N−3 polyunsaturated fatty acids in coronary heart disease: a meta-analysis of randomized controlled trials," Am J Med 112(4) (2002): 298–304.

147. Jeppe H. Christensen and others, eds., "N−3 fatty acids and ventricular extrasystoles in patients with ventricular tachyarrhythmias," Nutrition Research 15(1) (1995): 1–8, http://www.sciencedirect.com/science/article/pii/027153179591 647U.

148. Kuan-Pin Su and others, eds., "Omega-3 fatty acids in major depressive disorder: A preliminary double-blind, placebo-controlled trial," Eur Neuropsychopharmacol 13(4) (2003): 267–271, http://www.europeanneuropsychopharmacology.com/article/S09 24-977X(03)00032-4/abstract.

149. Pnina Green and others, eds., "Red cell membrane omega-3 fatty acids are decreased in nondepressed patients with social anxiety disorder," Eur Neuropsychopharmacol 16(2) (2003): 107–113, http://www.europeanneuropsychopharmacology.com/article/S09

24-977X(05)00111-2/abstract.

150. Katarina Augustsson and others, eds., "A prospective study of intake of fish and marine fatty acids and prostate cancer," Cancer Epidemiology, Biomarkers & Prevention 12(1) (2003): 64–67, http://www.ncbi.nlm.nih.gov/pubmed/12540506.

151. V. Pala V and others, eds., "Erythrocyte Membrane Fatty Acids and Subsequent Breast Cancer: a Prospective Italian Study," JNCL 93(14) (2001): 1088–95, http://jnci.oxfordjournals.org/content/93/14/1088.full.

152. Camilla T. Damsgaard and others, eds., "Fish oil supplementation modulates immune function in healthy infants," J Nutr1 37(4) (2007): 1031-1036, http://jn.nutrition.org/content/137/4/1031.full.pdf+html.

153. C. Ruggiero and others, eds., "Fatty acids from fish: the anti-inflammatory potential of long-chain omega-3 fatty acids," Curr Pharm Des 15(36) (2009): 4135–48, http://www.ncbi.nlm.nih.gov/pubmed/20041815.

154. E. Ernst and others, eds., "Acupuncture: Does it alleviate pain and are there serious risks? A review of reviews," Pain 152(4) (2011): 755–764, http://www.dieutridau.com/thongtin/detai/acupuncture-does-it.pdf.

155. "Drinking Water Contaminants," U.S. Environmental Protection Agency, http://water.epa.gov/drink/contaminants/index.cfm#List.

156. "FDA Approves Fluoride In Bottled Water," Food Chemical News, November 28, 2006, http://www.rense.com/general74/fda.htm.

157. Brian Howard, "Despite the Hype, Bottled Water is Neither Cleaner nor Greener than Tap Water," E/The Environmental Magazine, December 9, 2003, http://www.commondreams.org/headlines03/1209-10.htm.

158. Ibid.

159. Ibid.

160. "10 Facts about Fluoride," Fluoride Action Network, http://www.fluoridealert.org/fluoride-facts.htm, accessed June 2012.

161. Ibid.

162. Karen Esienbraun, "Side Effects of Fluoride," Livestrong.com, March 7, 2011, http://www.livestrong.com/article/133760-side-effects-fluoride/.

163. 10 Facts about Fluoride, Fluoride Action Network, http://www.fluoridealert.org/fluoride-facts.htm, accessed June 2012.

164. Susan Hooper and Allison Manis, "Upper Cervical Care in a Nine-Year-Old Female With Occipital Lobe Epilepsy: A Case Study," Journal of Upper Cervical Chiropractic Research (2011): 10-17, http://uppercervicalsubluxation.health.officclive.com/2011_1053_occipital_lobe_epilepsy.aspx.

165. E.L. Elster, "Upper Cervical Chiropractic Care For A Nine-Year-Old Male With Tourette Syndrome, Attention Deficit Hyperactivity Disorder, Depression, Asthma, Insomnia, and Headaches: A Case Report" Vertebral Subluxation Research (2003): 1-11, http://www.cedarparkchiro.com/wp-content/themes/cedarpark/asthma.doc.pdf.

166. Michael T. Burcon, Journal Of Vertebral Subluxation Research (2001), http://www.burconchiropractic.com/g5-bin/client.cgi?G5button=626&articleID=940.

167. E. L. Elster, "Chiropractic And Multiple Sclerosis Case Study," Journal Of Vertebral Subluxation Research, http://www.sitochiropractic.com/ms.html.

168. Crystal D. Brown, "Improved Hearing and Resolution of Otitis Media with Effusion Following Chiropractic Care to Reduce Vertebral Subluxation," J. Pediatric, Maternal & Family Health, March 25, 2009, http://www.chiropractic-germany.de/fileadmin/user_upload/Pediatric_Case_Study__Otitis_Media_.pdf.

169. Erin L. Elster, "Female, Age 2 years, Chronic Sinus / Ear Infections. Case Studies - Chronic Ear and Sinus Infections," accessed June 2012, http://www.erinelster.com/CaseStudies.aspx?ConditionID=6.

170. Erin L. Elster, "Upper Cervical Chiropractic Care for a Patient with Chronic Migraine Headaches with an Appendix Summarizing an Additional 100 Headache Cases," accessed June 2012, http://www.erinelster.com/pdfs/headache%20paper.pdf.

171. Nimira Alibhoy, "Resolution of Fibromyalgia Following Upper Cervical Chiropractic Care: A Case Study." Journal of Upper Cervical Chiropractic Research (2011): 39-44, http://www.vahlchiropractic.com/blog/2011/06/21/chiropractic-

case-study-resolution-of-fibromyalgia-following-upper-cervical-chiropractic-care/.

172. Fredrikus G. J. Oosterveld and others, eds., "Infrared sauna in patients with rheumatoid arthritis and ankylosing spondylitis, a pilot study showing good tolerance, short-term improvement of pain and stiffness, and a trend towards long-term beneficial effects," Clinical Rheumatology 28(1) (2009): 29-34, http://www.springerlink.com/content/l811255n25841811/.

173. Margaret T.T.Wong-Riley and others, eds., "Photobiomodulation Directly Benefits Primary Neurons Functionally Inactivated by Toxins: Role of Cytochrome C Oxidase," JBC Papers in Press. November 22, 2004.

174. Ibid.

175. Richard Beever, "Do Far-Infrared Saunas have Measurable Health Benefits? A Sequential Longitudinal Interrupted Time Series Design Study," (2009). Richard Beever, "Do Far-Infrared Saunas have Cardiovascular Benefits in People with Type 2 Diabetes?" Canadian Journal of Diabetes 34(2) (2010): 113-118.

176. Masakazu Imamura and others, eds., "Repeated Thermal Therapy Improves Impaired Vascular Endothelial Function in Patients With Coronary Risk Factors," Journal of American College of Cardiology 38(4) (2001): 1083-1088.

177. Harry T. Whelan and others, eds., "Effect of NASA Light Emitting Diode Irradiation and Wound Healing," Journal of Clinical Laser Medicine & Surgery 19(6) (2001): 305-314.

178. B.A. Russell and others, eds., "Study to Determine the Efficacy of Combination LED Light Therapy (633nm and 830 nm) in Facial Skin Rejuvenation," Journal of Cosmetic and Laser Therapy 7 (2005): 196-200.

179. K. Matsushita and others, eds., "Internal Medicine (Tokyo)" The First Department of Internal Medicine, Kagoshima University Hospital, Kagoshima, Japan August 15, 2008.

180. Lidija Kandolf-Sekulovic and others, eds., "Immunomodulatory Effects of Low-Intensity Near-Infrared Laser Irradiation on Contact Hypersensitivity Reaction," Photodermatol Photoimmunol Photomed 19 (2003): 203–212.

181. "Core Temperature Study. Solo Test Results - Reference to Protocol," Golden Telecommunications Co., Ltd., May 18, 2001.

182. "Vitamin D proving to be the 'it' nutrient - Loyola nursing researchers report on the benefits of vitamin D in diabetes, cancer,

osteoporosis, heart disease and now diabetes," Loyola University Health System, http://loyolahealth.org/about-us/newswire/vitamin-d-proving-be-it-nutrient.

183. Dr. Mercola, The Surprising Cause of Melanoma (And No, It's Not Too Much Sun), Mercola.com, November 20, 2011, http://articles.mercola.com/sites/articles/archive/2011/11/20/deadly-melanoma-not-due-vitamin-d deficiency.aspx.

184. Nora T. Gedgaudas, Primal Body, Primal Mind (Rochester: Healing Arts Press, 2009, 2011), 95.

185. Ibid.

EVOLUTION 501: THE CREATIVE SELF

1. Drunvalo Melchizedek, 2012 The Prophecies from The Heart, YouTube.com, uploaded December 18, 2011, http://www.youtube.com/watch?v=53G690K5Dak&feature=related

2. Madelyn Hoffman, "Bloomfield opinion: Richest 400 have more wealth than U.S. bottom half," July 12, 2012, NorthJersey.com, http://www.northjersey.com/news/opinions/162168235_Richest_400_have_more_wealth_than_country_s_bottom_half.html?c=y&page=2.

3. John McCrone, "Right Brain' or 'Left Brain' - Myth or Reality?" The New Scientist, July 21, 2000, http://www.rense.com/general2/rb.htm.

4. Ibid.

5. Ibid.

6. Ibid.

7. Ibid.

8. Amara D. Angelica, "'Creative right brain' myth debunked," March 7, 2012, http://www.kurzweilai.net/creative-right-brain-myth-debunked.

9. Ibid.

10. Ibid.

11. Harnam Singh and Michael W. O'Boyle, "Interhemispheric interaction during global-local processing in mathematically gifted adolescents, average-ability youth, and college students," Neuropsychology 18, no. 2 (2004).

12. Ibid.

13. Ibid.

14. Ibid.

15. Christopher A. Tucker, "The Holographic Paradigm and Its Adaptation to Psychological Anthropology," paper presented at Southwest Anthropological Association's Conference, April 12, 1996.
16. "Role of Heart in Human performance," An Institute of HeartMath Publication, https://sites.google.com/a/madure.org/www/roleofheart, accessed June 2012.
17. Ibid.
18. Ibid.
19. Ibid.
20. Ibid.
21. Ibid.
22. Ibid.
23. Ibid.
24. Ibid.
25. Glen Rein, Ph.D., Rollin McCraty, M.A., "Modulation of DNA by Coherent Heart Frequencies," Proceedings of the Third Annual Conference of the International Society for the Study of Subtle Energy and Energy Medicine, 1993, http://206.192.23.201/dan/connectivity/phibiz/rein/.
26. Ibid.
27. Ibid.
28. Ibid.
29. Ibid.

EVOLUTION 601: THE ETHEREAL SELF

1. Mark Amaru Pinkham, "The Return of the Djedi: The Knights of Star Wars Were Preceded Long Ago by Egyptian and Persian Orders," *Atlantis Rising*, (March/April 2009).
2. Ibid.
3. Ibid.
4. Ibid.
5. Charles William Johnson, *The Sound of Meaning* (Wichita: Gyldan Edge Publishing, 2004), 15.
6. Drunvalo Melchizedek, *The Ancient Secret of the Flower of Life, Volume 2* (Clear Light Trust, 2000), 314.
7. Anita Moorjani, *Dying to be Me: My journey from Cancer, to Near Death, to True Healing* (Hay House, Inc., 2012), 135-136.
8. Ibid., 137.

EVOLUTION 701: THE ZERO-POINT SELF

1. "Federal Government Outlays by Function and Subfunction: 1962–2015 Fiscal Year 2011 (Table 3.2)". United States Government Printing Office. Retrieved 21 December 2010.
   http://www.gpoaccess.gov/usbudget/fy12/pdf/BUDGET-2012-BUD-7.pdf

2. "Active duty military personnel strengths by regional area and by country" U.S. Department of Defense. 2010. Retrieved 31 December 2010.
   http://siadapp.dmdc.osd.mil/personnel/MILITARY/history/hst1012.pdf.

3. Michio Kaku interview by Deepak Chopra. Sirius XM radio show, September 19, 2009,
   http://www.sdparanormal.com/articles/article/1961531/143524.htm.

4. Daniel Lew, "Random Event Generators Predict the Future," *Damn Interesting*, December 10, 2005,
   http://www.damninteresting.com/random-event-generators-predict-the-future/.

5. Ibid.

6. "Variance Deviations on September 11," accessed August 2012,
   http://noosphere.princeton.edu/911variance.html

7. Chistopher A. Tucker, *The Holographic Paradigm and Its Adaptation to Psychological Anthropology*, p. 2. Paradox Technologies, Modesto, California. A paper presented at the Southwest Anthropological Association's Conference, Pasadena, CA, April 12 1996.
   http://www.scribd.com/doc/75918454/Holographic-paradigm.

8. Ibid.

9. Ibid.

10. Ibid.

11. "How the Universe Works: Black Holes (Episode 2)," *The Science Channel*, 2011.

12. Somini Sengupta, "Facebook's Prospects May Rest on Trove of Data," *The New York Times*, May 14, 2012.

13. "Stan Lee's Superhumans 'Super Samurai,'" *The History Channel*, 2010.

14. Ibid.

15. Nassim Haramein, *Crossing the Event Horizon*, Nassim Haramein, DVD workshop symposium, Disk 2 of 4, Scene 8: Accounting for Spin. Rogue Valley Metaphysical Library and Event Center (2006).

16. Ibid.

17. Drunvalo Melchizedek, *The Ancient Secret of the Flower of Life, Volume 1* (Flagstaff: Light Technology Publishing, 1999), 150.

18. "Was the universe born spinning?" *Physicsworld.com*, July 25, 2011,

http://physicsworld.com/cws/article/news/2011/jul/25/was-the-universe
-born-spinning.

19. Nassim Haramein, *Crossing the Event Horizon*, DVD workshop sympo-
    sium, (Rogue Valley Metaphysical Library and Event Center, 2006), Disk
    2 of 4, Scene 9: At the Center.
20. Ibid., Disk 1 of 4, Scene 11: A Scaling Law.
21. Ibid., Disk 1 of 4, Scene 5: In Simple Terms.
22. Ibid., Disk 1 of 4, Scene 11: A Scaling Law.
23. Ibid.
24. Ibid.
25. Ibid.
26. Ibid., Disk 1 of 4, Scene 12: Biological Resolution.
27. Ibid.
28. Ibid.
29. Ibid.
30. *Redefining Space & Time*, Coast to Coast A.M. with George Noory, Hour
    2 (July 21, 2012) http://www.coasttocoastam.com/show/2012/07/24.
31. Ibid.
32. Ibid.
33. Ibid.
34. Ibid.
35. Ibid.
36. Ibid.
37. Drunvalo Melchizedek, *Serpent of Light - Beyond 2012*. (San Francisco:
    Weiser, 2007), 11.
38. Ibid., 18.
39. Ibid.
40. Ibid.
41. Ibid., 31.
42. Ibid.
43. Ibid., 32.
44. Ibid.
45. Ibid., 17.
46. Ibid.
47. Ibid., 18.
48. Ibid.
49. Ibid., 20.
50. Ibid., 21.